MASASHI KISHIMOTO

I got the hint to create this manga from the scene in the animated movie *Akira* where the two heroes are talking in a jail cell.

AKIRA OKUBO

This is the final volume. I hope you can see Hashimaru's story through to its finish.

SAMURAI 8
THE TALE OF HACHIMARU
05

SHONEN JUMP Manga Edition

Story MASASHI KISHIMOTO
Art AKIRA OKUBO

Translation/STEPHEN PAUL
Touch-Up Art & Lettering/SNIR AHARON
Design/JULIAN [JR] ROBINSON
Editor/ALEXIS KIRSCH

First published in Japan in 2019 by SHUEISHA Inc., Tokyo.
English translation rights arranged by SHUEISHA Inc.

Printed in the U.S.A.

Published by VIZ Media, LLC
P.O. Box 77010
San Francisco, CA 94107

10 9 8 7 6 5 4 3 2 1
First printing, February 2021

VIZ MEDIA
viz.com

SHONEN JUMP

ratings.viz.com RATED T TEEN

PARENTAL ADVISORY
SAMURAI 8 is rated T for Teen and is recommended for ages 13 and up. This volume contains fantasy violence.

SAMURAI 8

THE TALE OF HACHIMARU

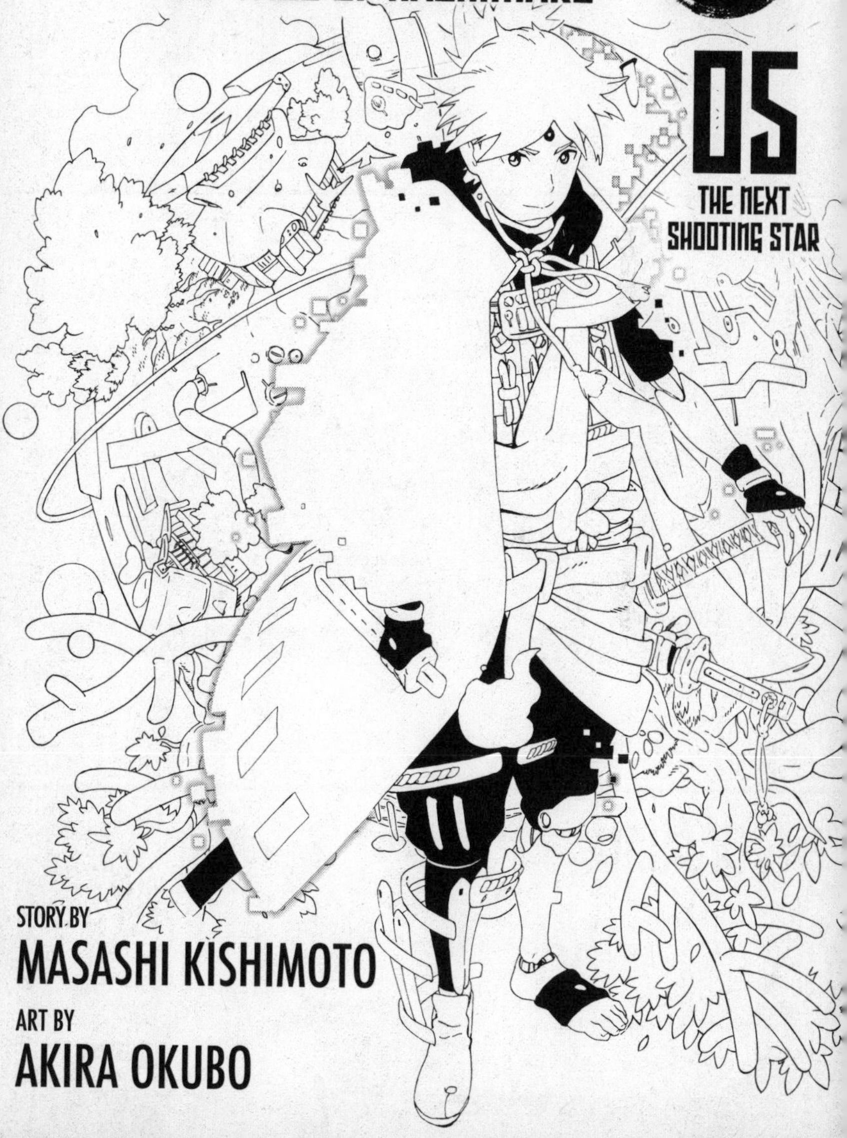

05

THE NEXT SHOOTING STAR

STORY BY

MASASHI KISHIMOTO

ART BY

AKIRA OKUBO

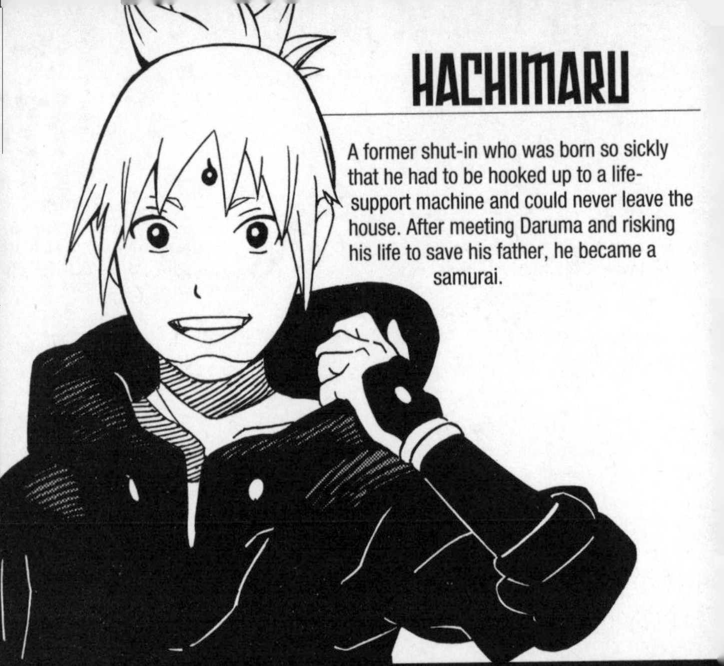

HACHIMARU

A former shut-in who was born so sickly that he had to be hooked up to a life-support machine and could never leave the house. After meeting Daruma and risking his life to save his father, he became a samurai.

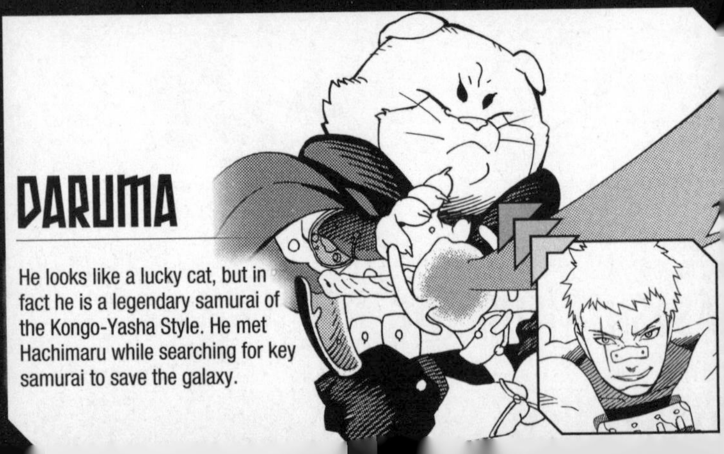

DARUMA

He looks like a lucky cat, but in fact he is a legendary samurai of the Kongo-Yasha Style. He met Hachimaru while searching for key samurai to save the galaxy.

SAMURAI 8

ANN

A young princess in training. She lost her Locker Ball, which is necessary to complete the samurai ritual.

HAYATARO

Hachimaru's Pet Holder, who is now his Key Holder. Says "meow" despite being a dog type.

WHAT IS A HOLDER?
A lifeform(?) that inhabits this galaxy. Their name changes based on their role: Pet Holder, Guard Holder, etc. Ones who serve a samurai master are called special Key Holders.

RYU

SANDA (KOTSUGA)

ATA

STORY

Hachimaru is a boy with a weak body. He can't survive without being hooked up to a life-support device, and he believes his dream of becoming a samurai will never come true. But one day, he meets Daruma, a samurai in the form of a large, round cat. With the approval of the warrior god Fudo Myo-o, Hachimaru gains the life of a samurai! While training under Daruma, Hachimaru gets attacked by the menacing Ata. Hachimaru's father sacrifices his own life to drive him off, but the effect is only temporary. Hachimaru decides to make his samurai calling to fulfill his promise to his father and protect the planet! The group heads out to space to look for companions, where they meet an eccentric pair named Kotsuga and Ryu, who invite them to take part in a battle royale. But the event is a trap set up by the wicked Benkei! Through great struggle, Hachimaru and his companions defeat Benkei and head back into space, where many plots are afoot...

05

THE NEXT SHOOTING STAR

CONTENTS

34	LICENSE DOWNLOAD	007
35	WABI-SABI	027
36	HANAICHI AND GOKU	047
37	RIVALS	067
38	ANN AND HACHIMARU AND GOKU	087
39	SNEAK ATTACK	107
40	LOSS OF SUPPORT	127
41	NANASHI THE SAMURAI	147
42	THE NEXT SHOOTING STAR	167
FINAL CHAPTER	PANDORA'S BOX	187

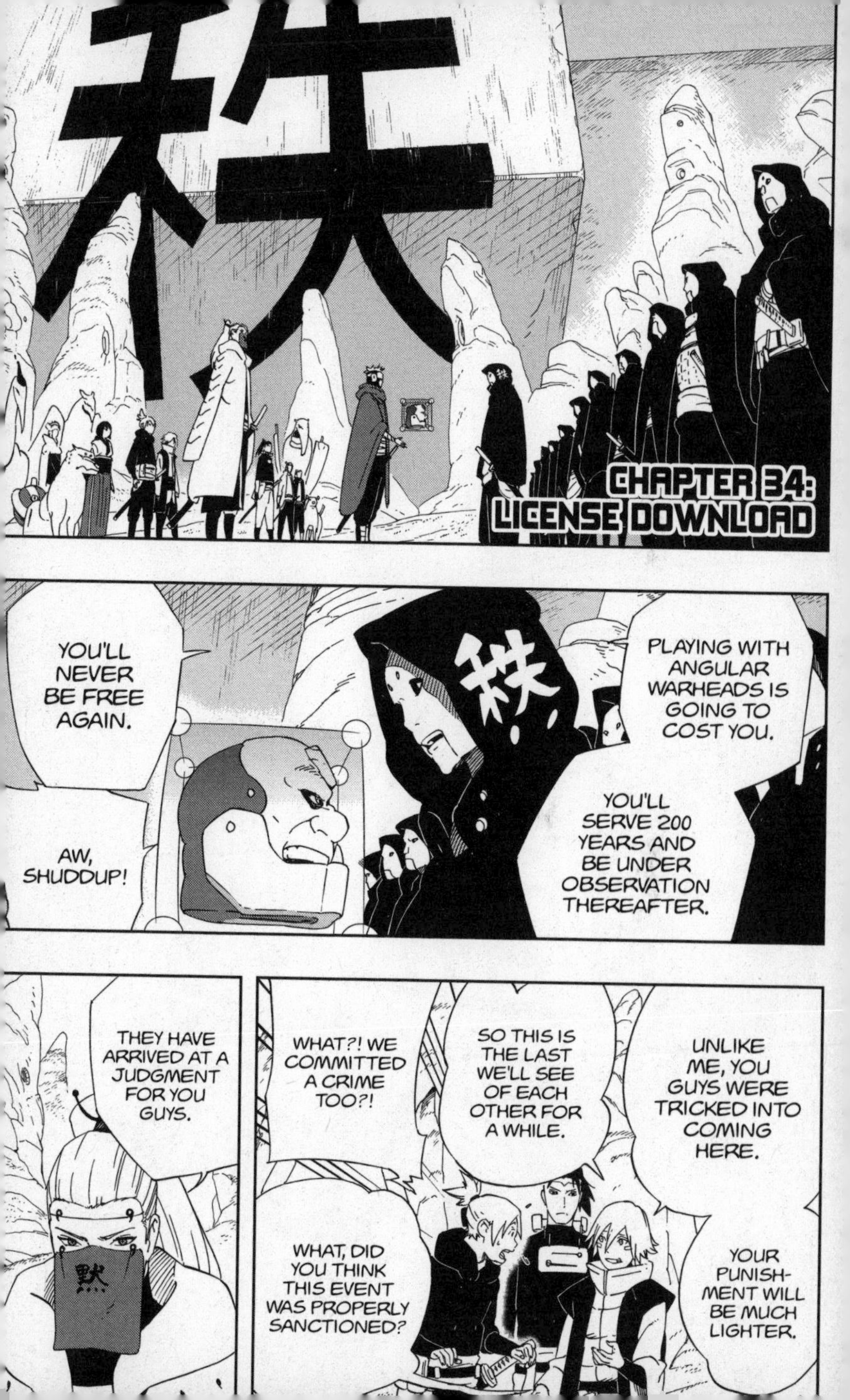
CHAPTER 34:
LICENSE DOWNLOAD
PLAYING WITH ANGULAR WARHEADS IS GOING TO COST YOU.
YOU'LL SERVE 200 YEARS AND BE UNDER OBSERVATION THEREAFTER.
YOU'LL NEVER BE FREE AGAIN.
AW, SHUDDUP!
UNLIKE ME, YOU GUYS WERE TRICKED INTO COMING HERE.
SO THIS IS THE LAST WE'LL SEE OF EACH OTHER FOR A WHILE.
WHAT?! WE COMMITTED A CRIME TOO?!
YOUR PUNISH-MENT WILL BE MUCH LIGHTER.
WHAT, DID YOU THINK THIS EVENT WAS PROPERLY SANCTIONED?
THEY HAVE ARRIVED AT A JUDGMENT FOR YOU GUYS.

CHAPTER 34: LICENSE DOWNLOAD

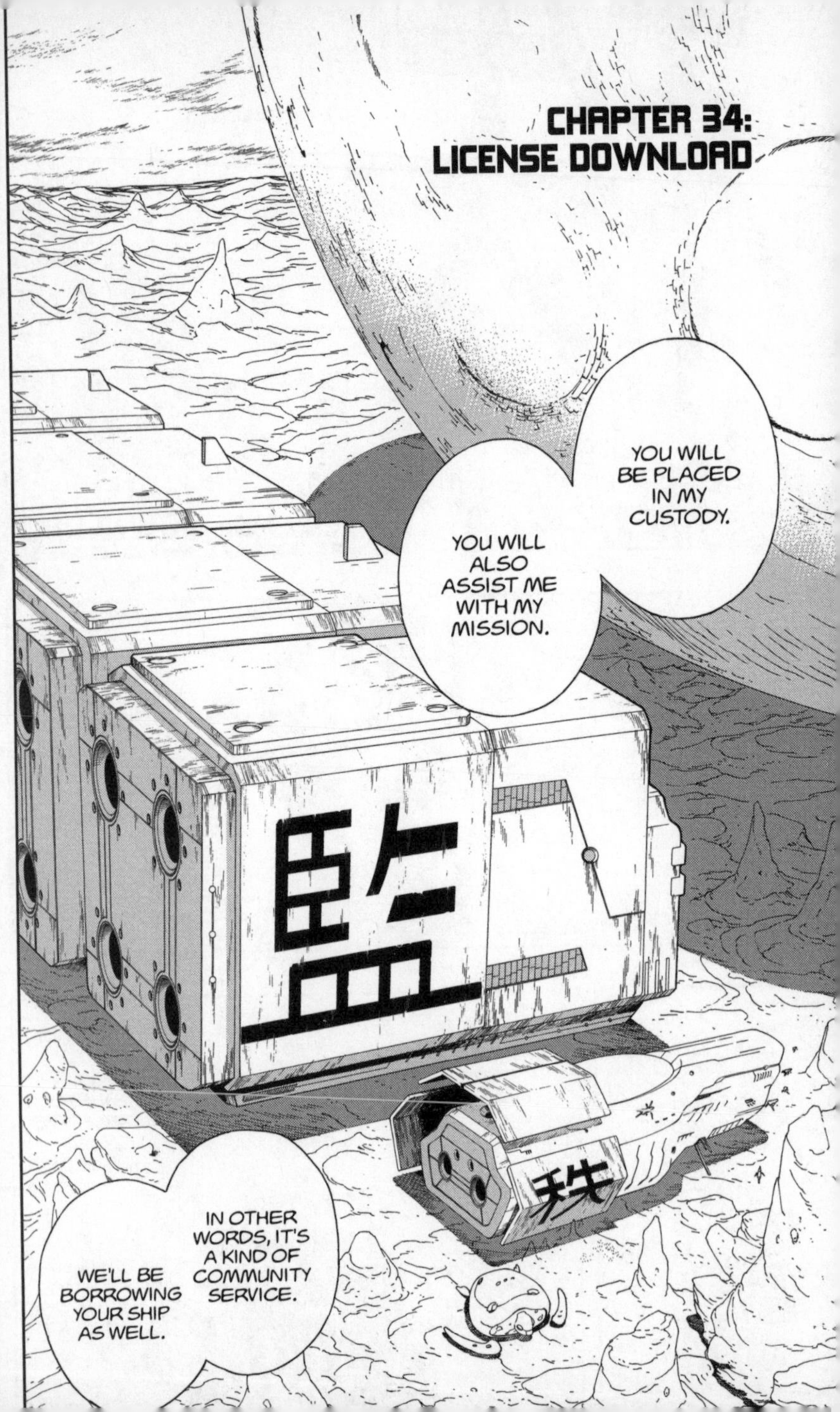
YOU WILL BE PLACED IN MY CUSTODY.
YOU WILL ALSO ASSIST ME WITH MY MISSION.
監
秩
IN OTHER WORDS, IT'S A KIND OF COMMUNITY SERVICE.
WE'LL BE BORROWING YOUR SHIP AS WELL.

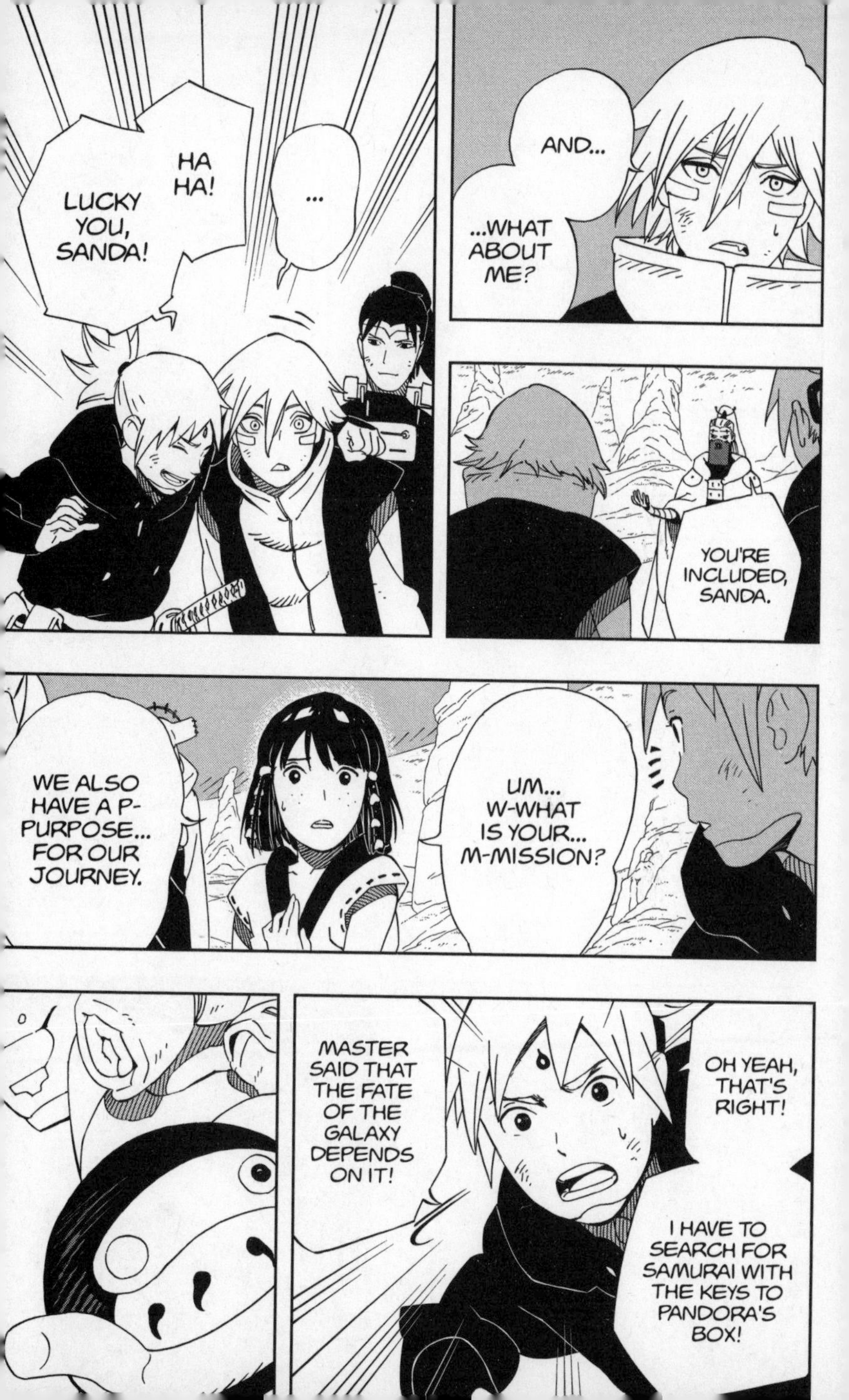
AND...
...WHAT ABOUT ME?
YOU'RE INCLUDED, SANDA.
...
HA HA!
LUCKY YOU, SANDA!
UM... W-WHAT IS YOUR... M-MISSION?
WE ALSO HAVE A P-PURPOSE... FOR OUR JOURNEY.
OH YEAH, THAT'S RIGHT!
I HAVE TO SEARCH FOR SAMURAI WITH THE KEYS TO PANDORA'S BOX!
MASTER SAID THAT THE FATE OF THE GALAXY DEPENDS ON IT!

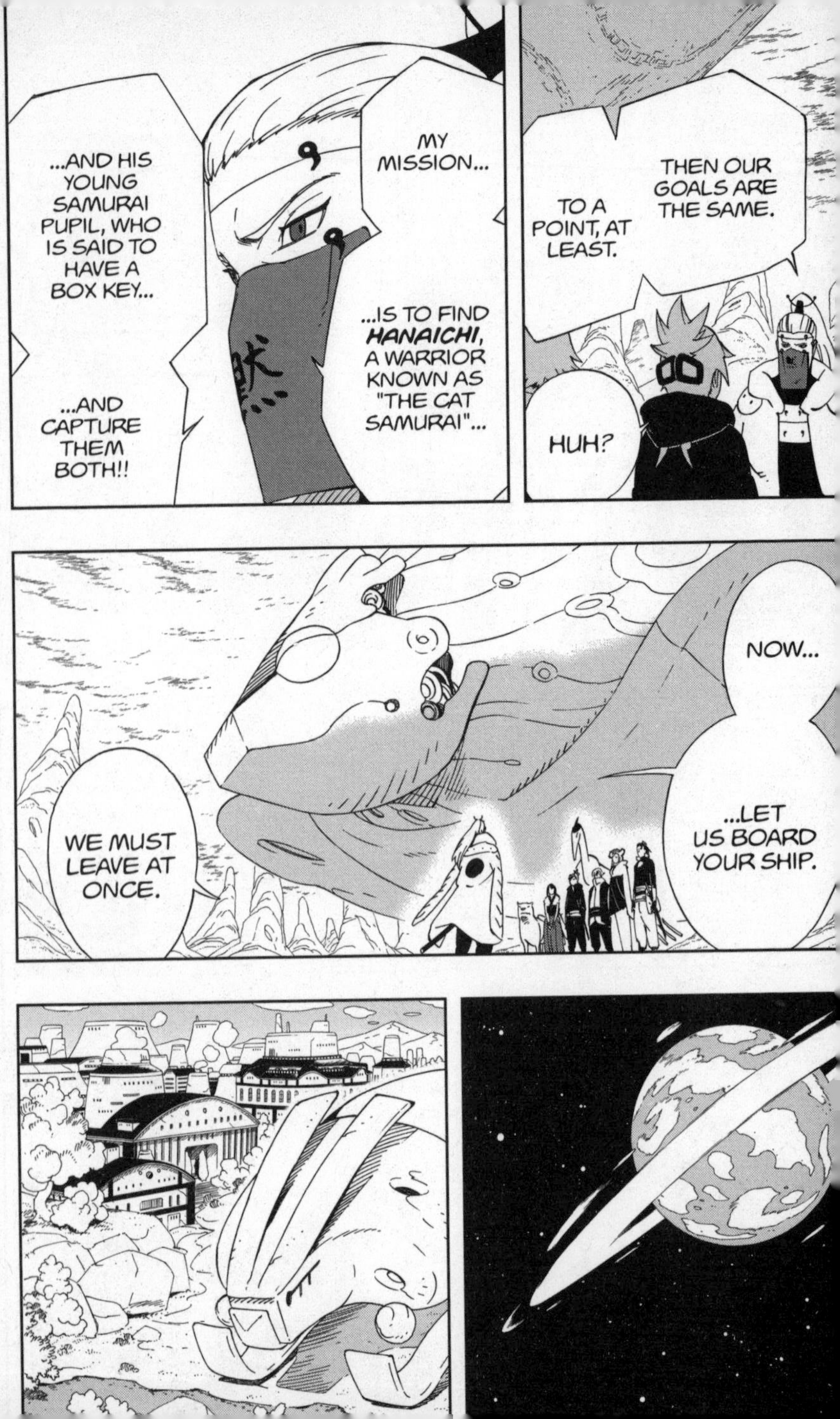
THEN OUR GOALS ARE THE SAME.
TO A POINT, AT LEAST.
HUH?
MY MISSION...
...IS TO FIND **HANAICHI**, A WARRIOR KNOWN AS "THE CAT SAMURAI"...
...AND HIS YOUNG SAMURAI PUPIL, WHO IS SAID TO HAVE A BOX KEY...
...AND CAPTURE THEM BOTH!!
NOW...
...LET US BOARD YOUR SHIP.
WE MUST LEAVE AT ONCE.

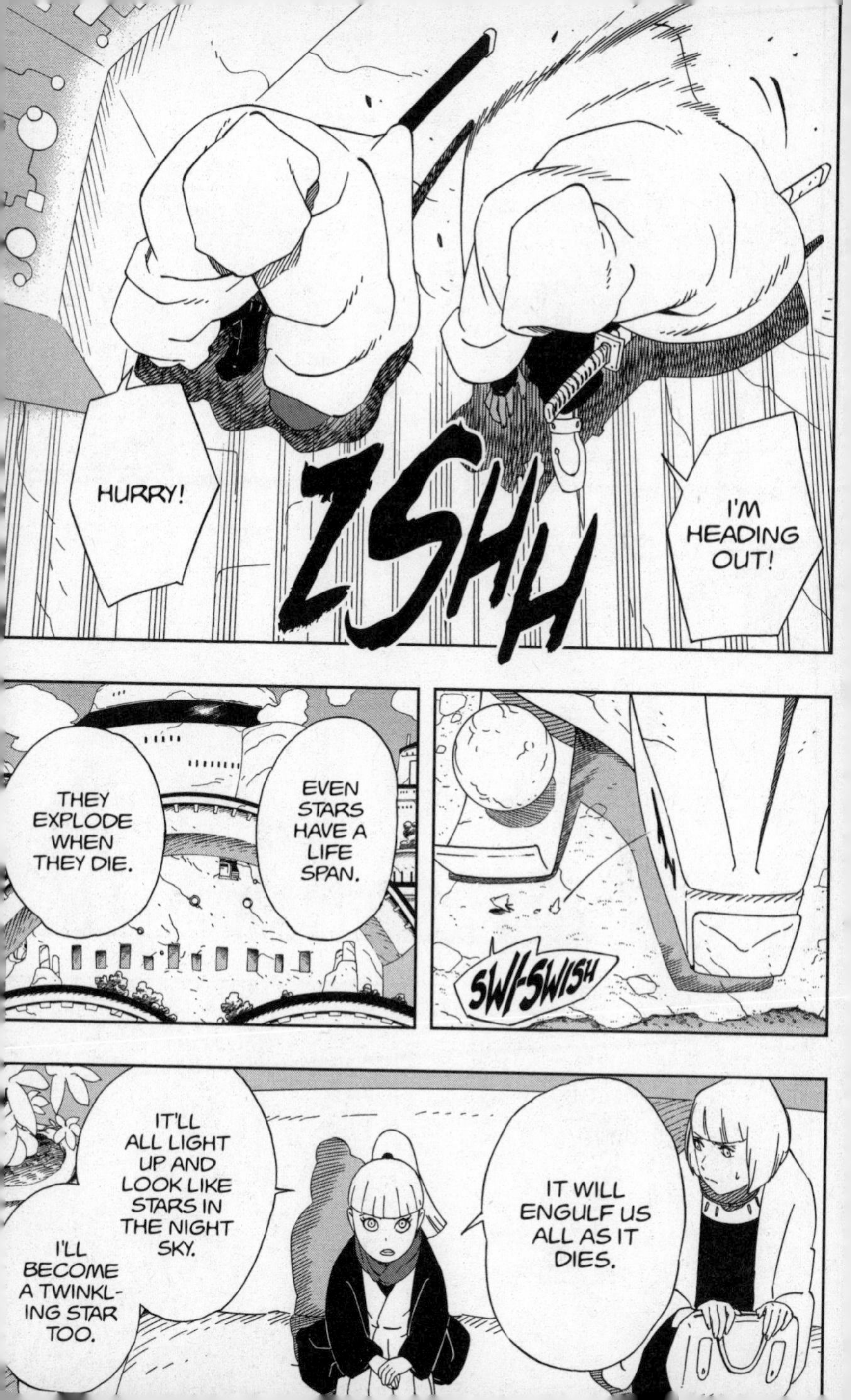
I'M HEADING OUT!
ZSHH
HURRY!
SWI-SWISH
EVEN STARS HAVE A LIFE SPAN.
THEY EXPLODE WHEN THEY DIE.
IT WILL ENGULF US ALL AS IT DIES.
IT'LL ALL LIGHT UP AND LOOK LIKE STARS IN THE NIGHT SKY.
I'LL BECOME A TWINKL-ING STAR TOO.

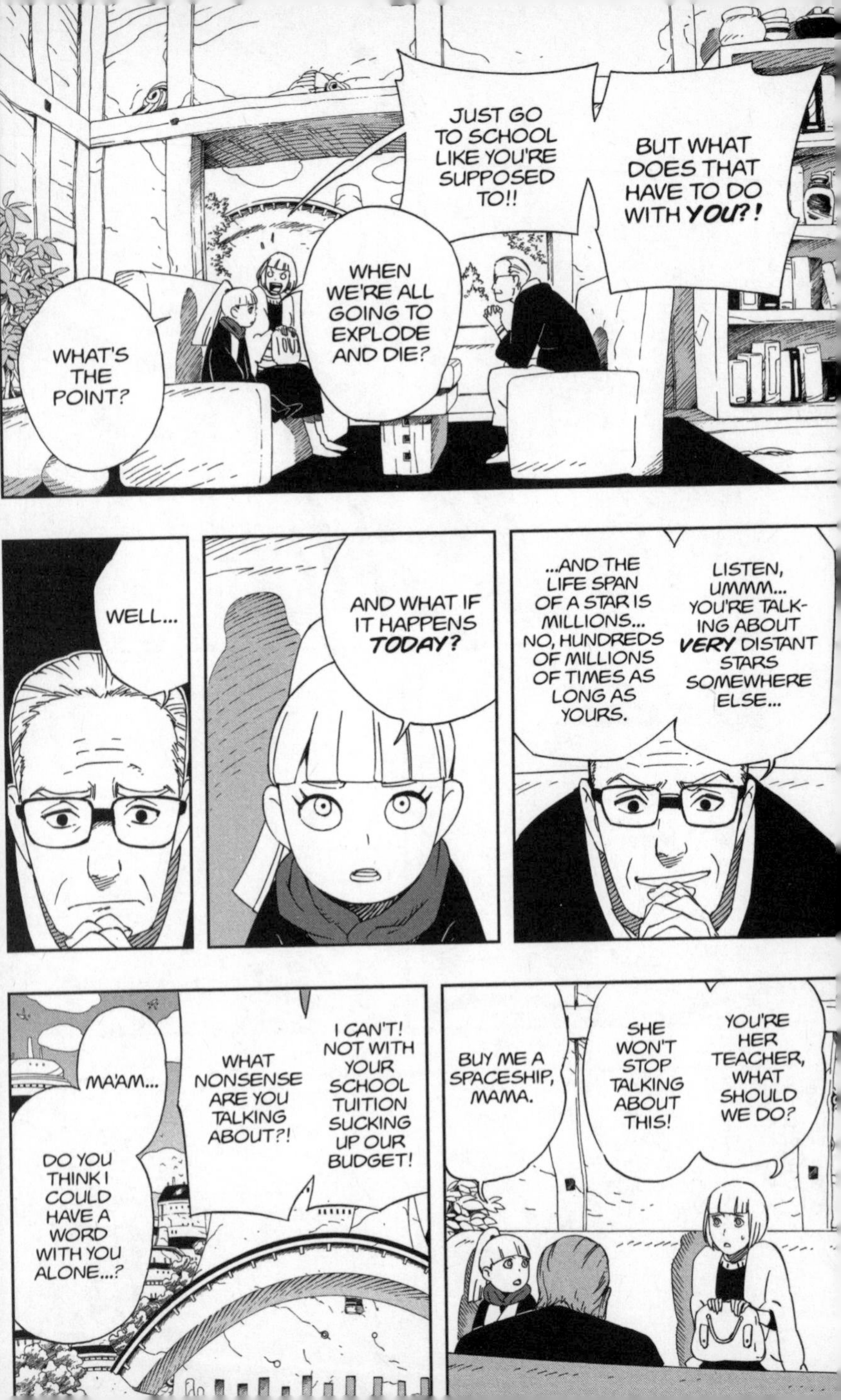
BUT WHAT DOES THAT HAVE TO DO WITH *YOU?!*
JUST GO TO SCHOOL LIKE YOU'RE SUPPOSED TO!!
WHEN WE'RE ALL GOING TO EXPLODE AND DIE?
WHAT'S THE POINT?
LISTEN, UMMM... YOU'RE TALK-ING ABOUT *VERY* DISTANT STARS SOMEWHERE ELSE...
...AND THE LIFE SPAN OF A STAR IS MILLIONS... NO, HUNDREDS OF MILLIONS OF TIMES AS LONG AS YOURS.
AND WHAT IF IT HAPPENS *TODAY?*
WELL...
YOU'RE HER TEACHER, WHAT SHOULD WE DO?
SHE WON'T STOP TALKING ABOUT THIS!
BUY ME A SPACESHIP, MAMA.
I CAN'T! NOT WITH YOUR SCHOOL TUITION SUCKING UP OUR BUDGET!
WHAT NONSENSE ARE YOU TALKING ABOUT?!
MA'AM...
DO YOU THINK I COULD HAVE A WORD WITH YOU ALONE...?

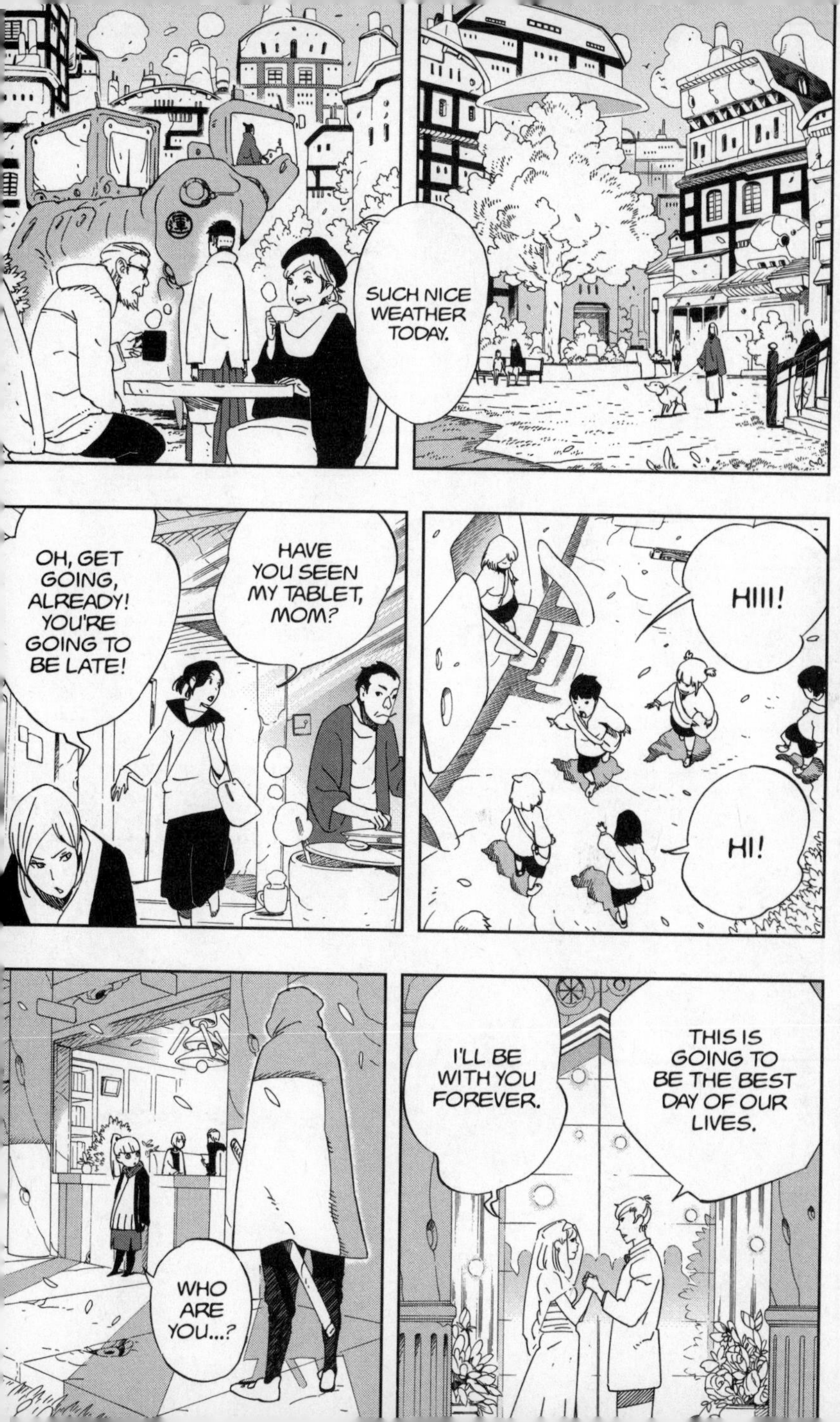
SUCH NICE WEATHER TODAY.
HIII!
HI!
HAVE YOU SEEN MY TABLET, MOM?
OH, GET GOING, ALREADY! YOU'RE GOING TO BE LATE!
THIS IS GOING TO BE THE BEST DAY OF OUR LIVES.
I'LL BE WITH YOU FOREVER.
WHO ARE YOU...?

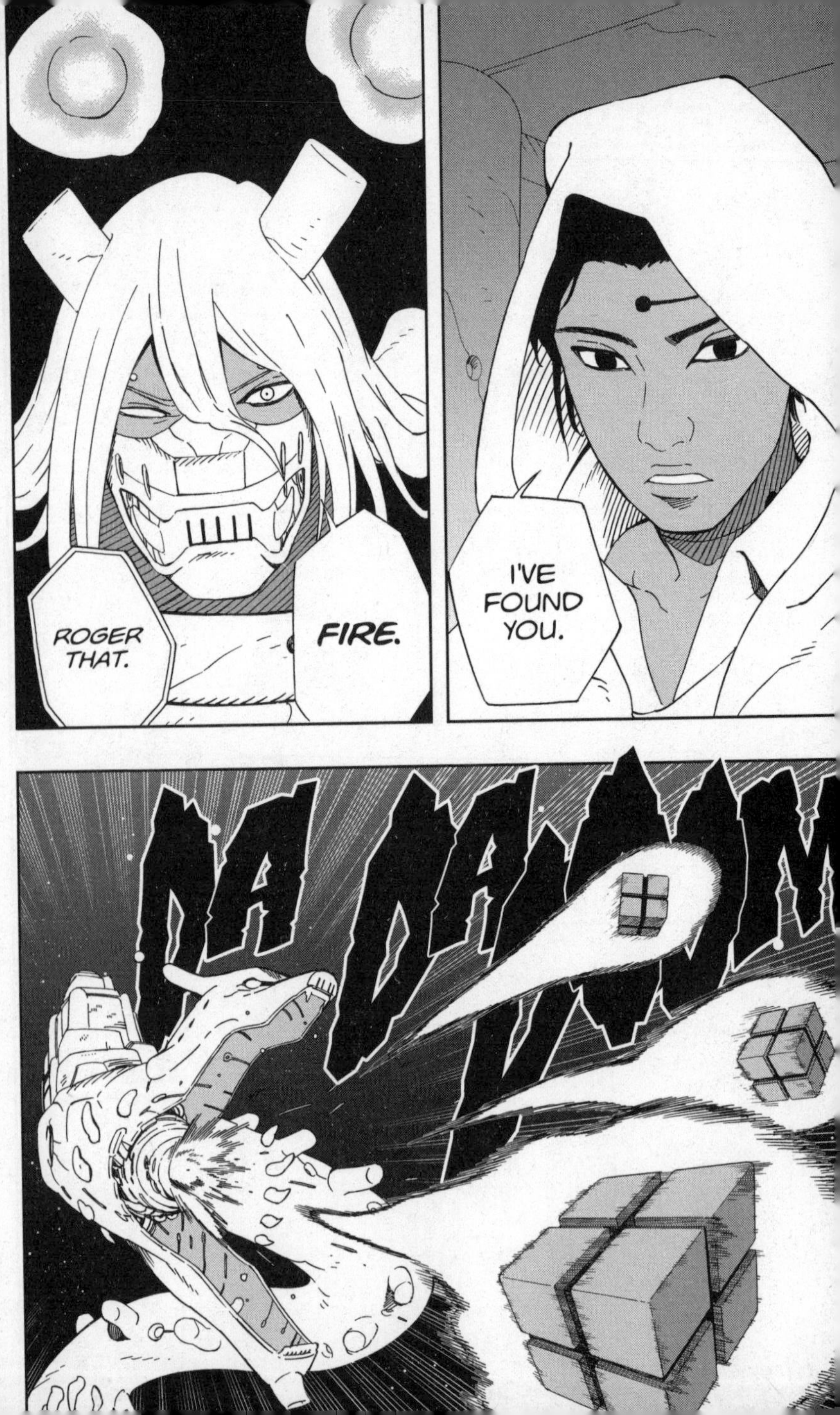
I'VE FOUND YOU.
FIRE.
ROGER THAT.

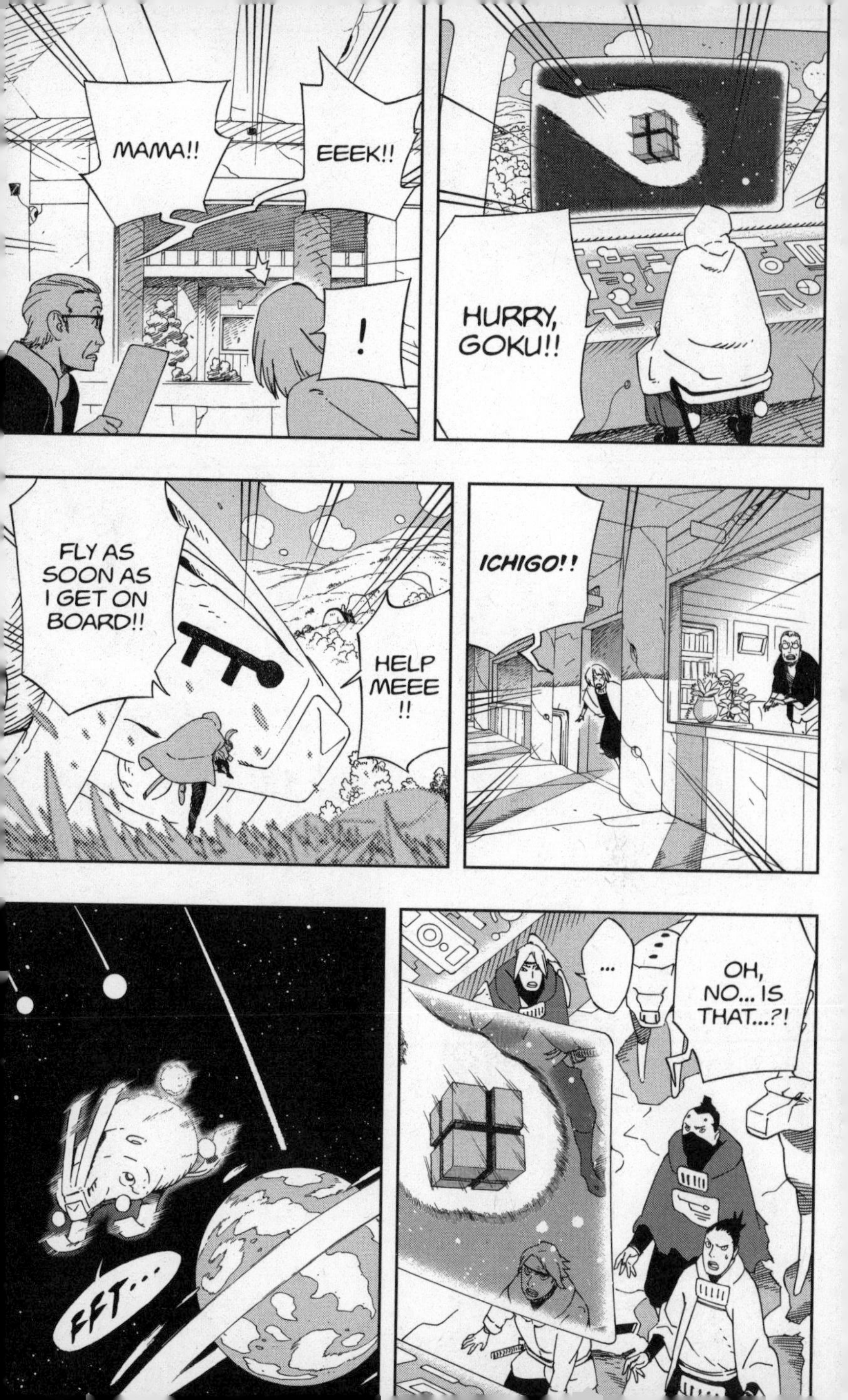
HURRY, GOKU!!
EEEK!!
MAMA!!
!
ICHIGO!!
FLY AS SOON AS I GET ON BOARD!!
HELP MEEE !!
OH, NO... IS THAT...?!
...
FFT...

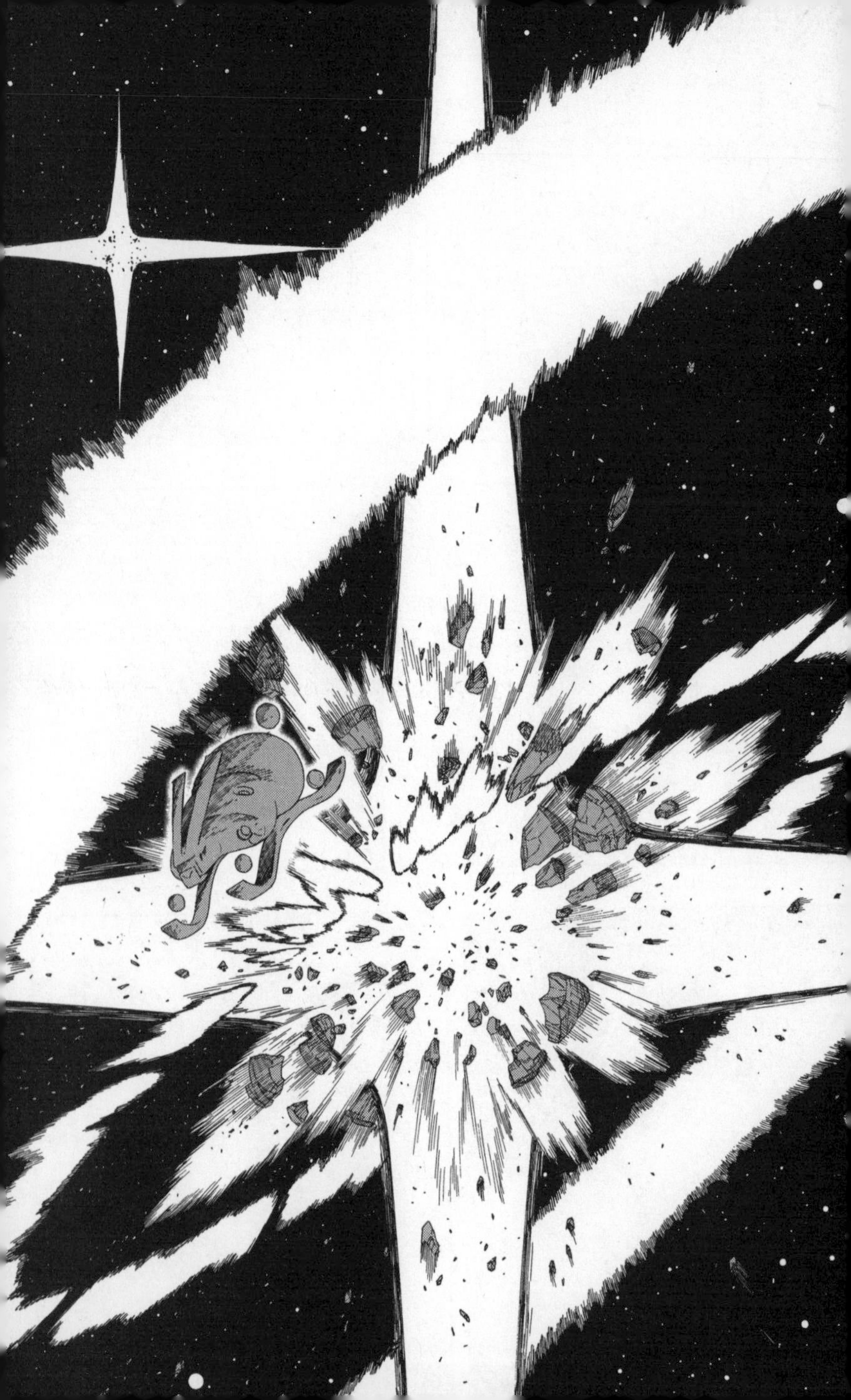

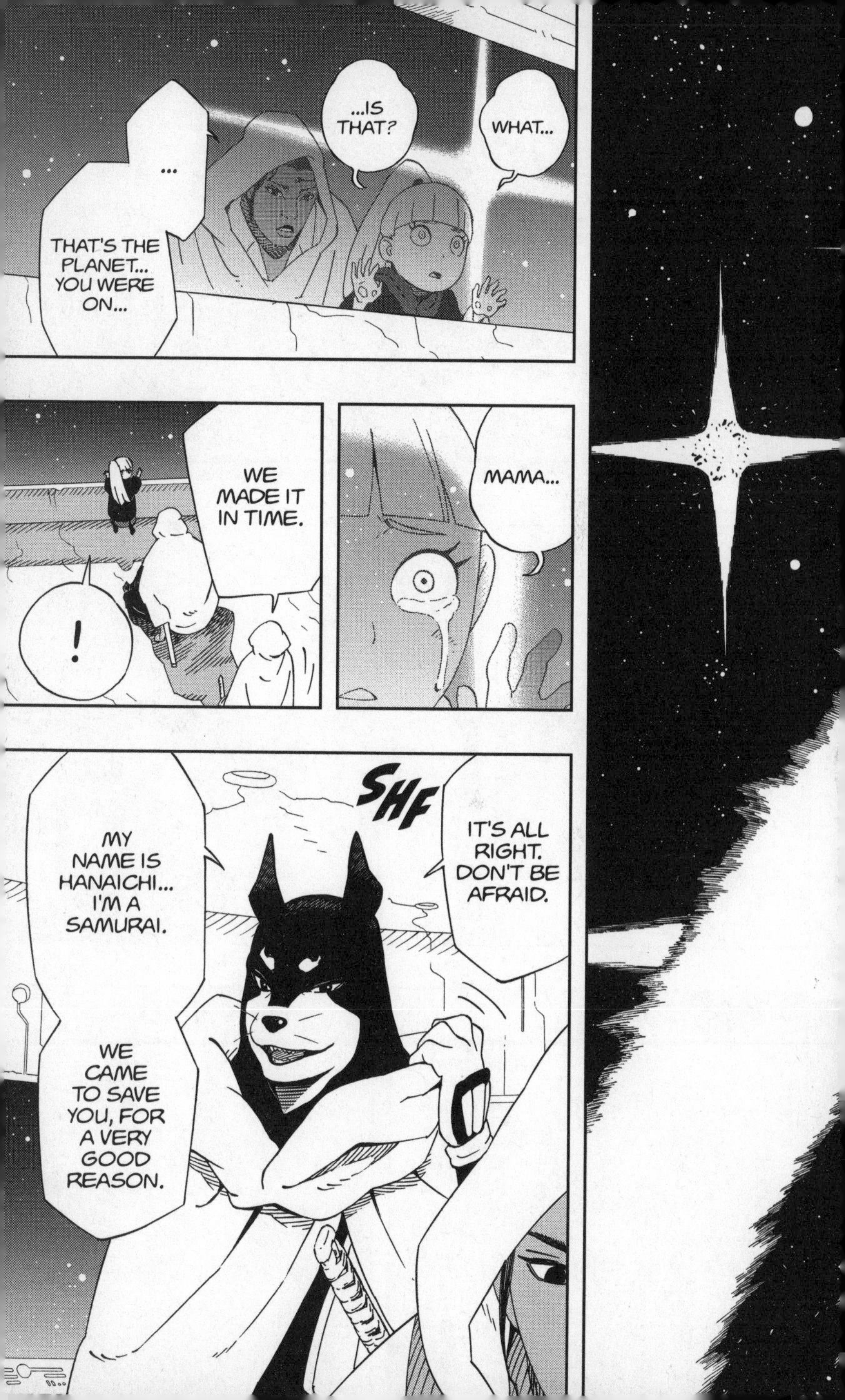
WHAT...
...IS THAT?
... THAT'S THE PLANET... YOU WERE ON...
MAMA...
WE MADE IT IN TIME.
!
SHF
IT'S ALL RIGHT. DON'T BE AFRAID.
MY NAME IS HANAICHI... I'M A SAMURAI.
WE CAME TO SAVE YOU, FOR A VERY GOOD REASON.

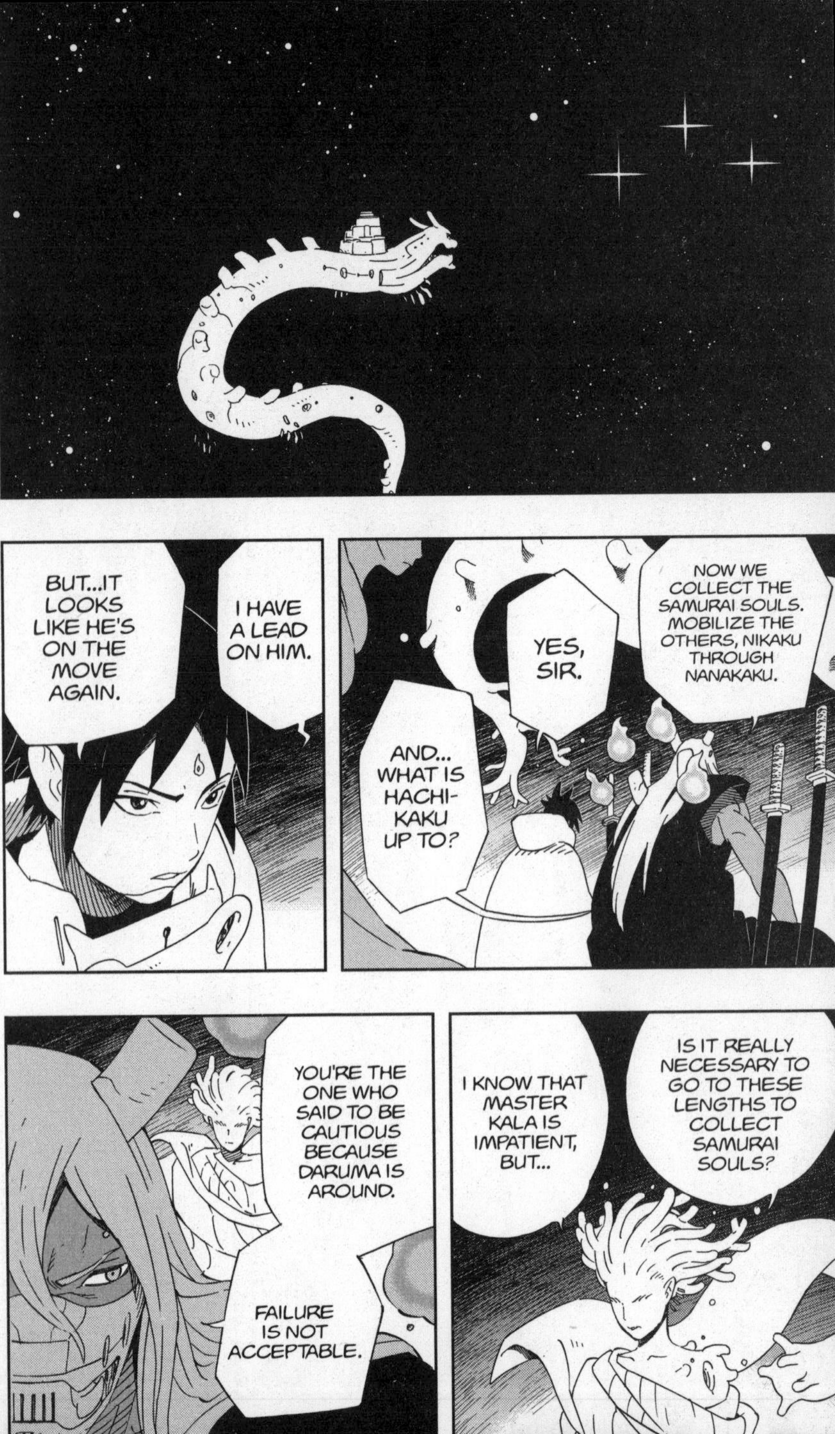
NOW WE COLLECT THE SAMURAI SOULS. MOBILIZE THE OTHERS, NIKAKU THROUGH NANAKAKU.
YES, SIR.
AND... WHAT IS HACHI-KAKU UP TO?
I HAVE A LEAD ON HIM.
BUT...IT LOOKS LIKE HE'S ON THE MOVE AGAIN.
IS IT REALLY NECESSARY TO GO TO THESE LENGTHS TO COLLECT SAMURAI SOULS?
I KNOW THAT MASTER KALA IS IMPATIENT, BUT...
YOU'RE THE ONE WHO SAID TO BE CAUTIOUS BECAUSE DARUMA IS AROUND.
FAILURE IS NOT ACCEPTABLE.

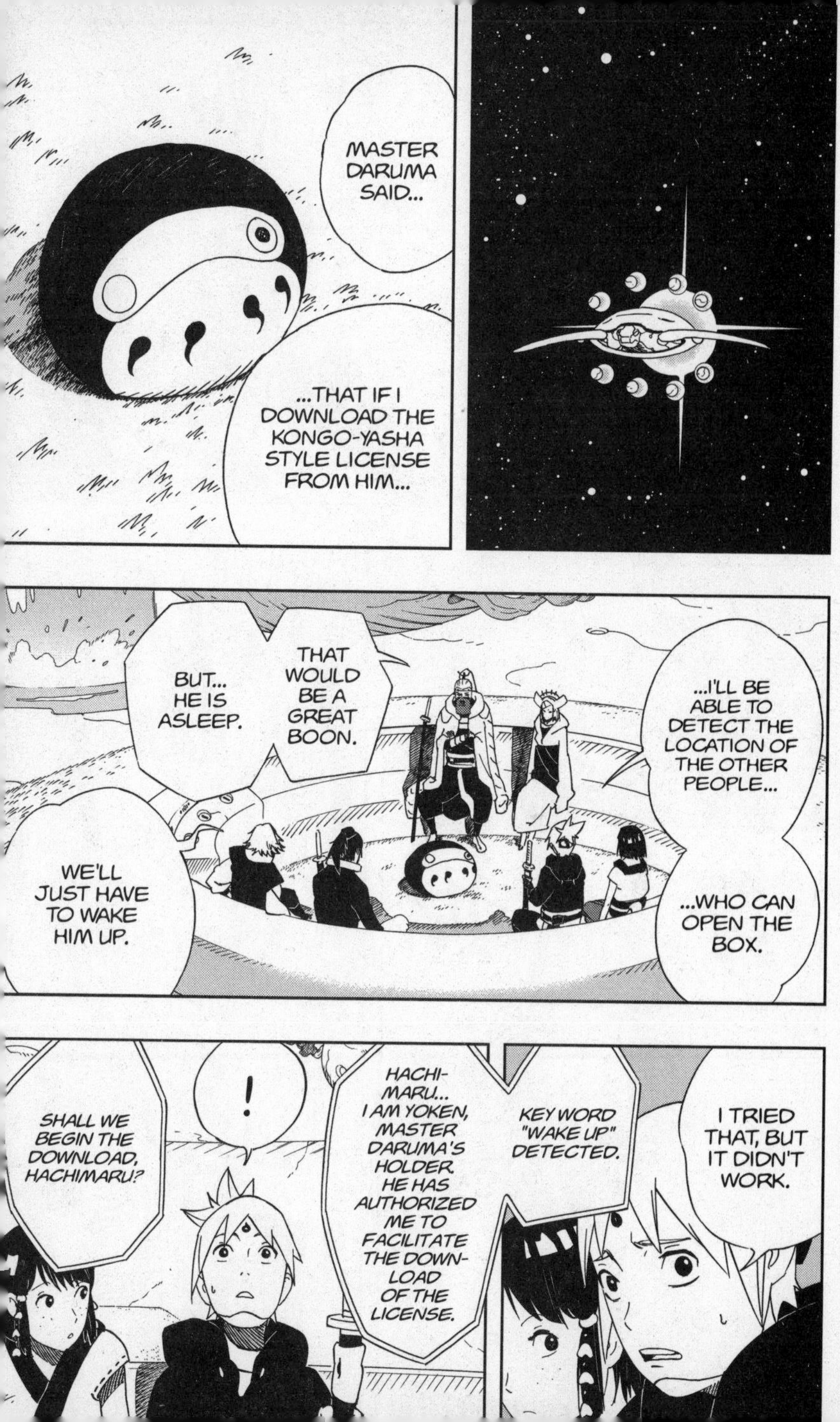
MASTER DARUMA SAID...
...THAT IF I DOWNLOAD THE KONGO-YASHA STYLE LICENSE FROM HIM...
...I'LL BE ABLE TO DETECT THE LOCATION OF THE OTHER PEOPLE...
...WHO CAN OPEN THE BOX.
THAT WOULD BE A GREAT BOON.
BUT... HE IS ASLEEP.
WE'LL JUST HAVE TO WAKE HIM UP.
I TRIED THAT, BUT IT DIDN'T WORK.
KEY WORD "WAKE UP" DETECTED.
HACHIMARU... I AM YOKEN, MASTER DARUMA'S HOLDER. HE HAS AUTHORIZED ME TO FACILITATE THE DOWNLOAD OF THE LICENSE.
!
SHALL WE BEGIN THE DOWNLOAD, HACHIMARU?

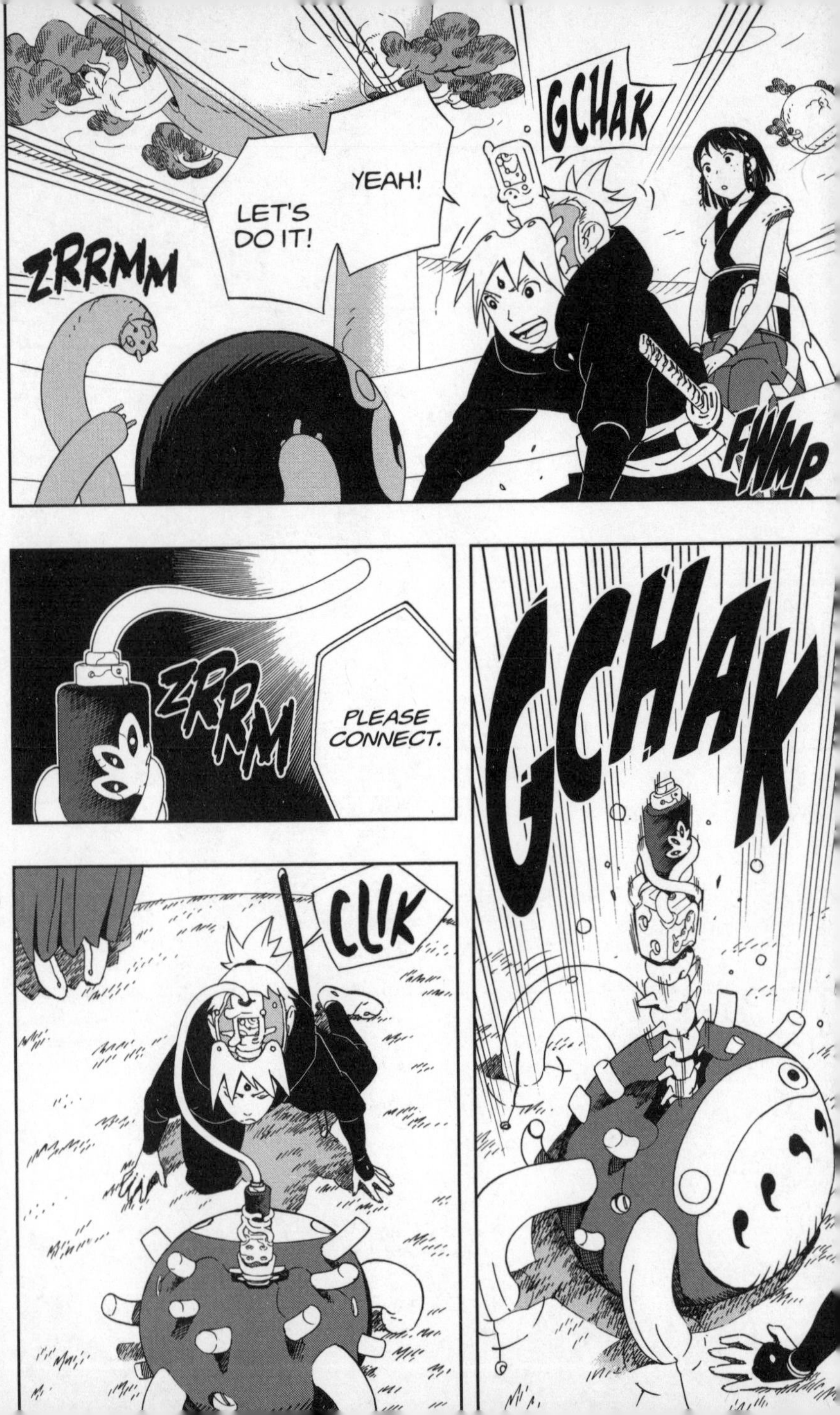
GCHAK
YEAH!
LET'S DO IT!
ZRRMM
FWMP
GCHAK
PLEASE CONNECT.
ZRRM
CLIK

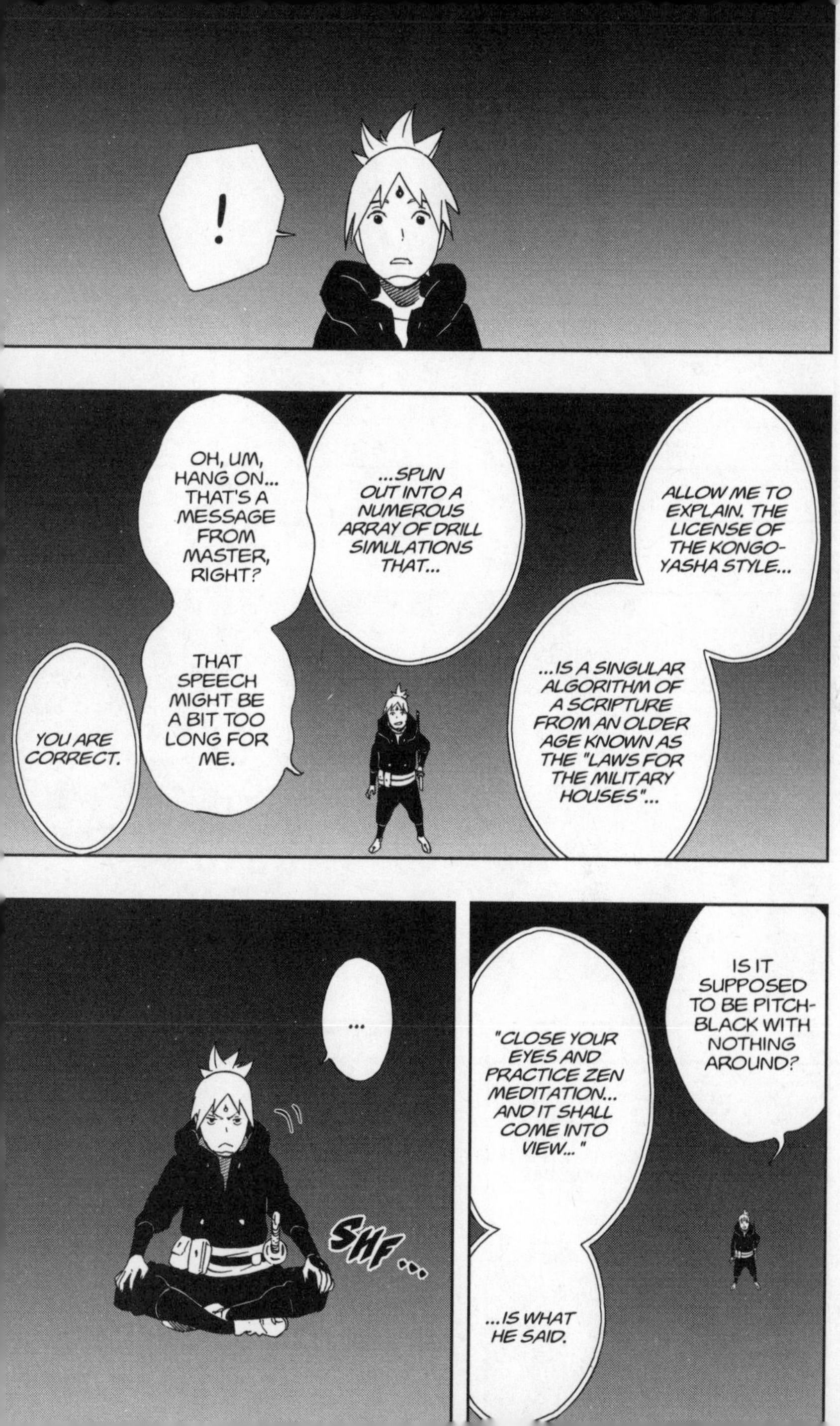
!
ALLOW ME TO EXPLAIN. THE LICENSE OF THE KONGO-YASHA STYLE...
...IS A SINGULAR ALGORITHM OF A SCRIPTURE FROM AN OLDER AGE KNOWN AS THE "LAWS FOR THE MILITARY HOUSES"...
...SPUN OUT INTO A NUMEROUS ARRAY OF DRILL SIMULATIONS THAT...
OH, UM, HANG ON... THAT'S A MESSAGE FROM MASTER, RIGHT?
THAT SPEECH MIGHT BE A BIT TOO LONG FOR ME.
YOU ARE CORRECT.
IS IT SUPPOSED TO BE PITCH-BLACK WITH NOTHING AROUND?
"CLOSE YOUR EYES AND PRACTICE ZEN MEDITATION... AND IT SHALL COME INTO VIEW..."
...IS WHAT HE SAID.
...
SHF...

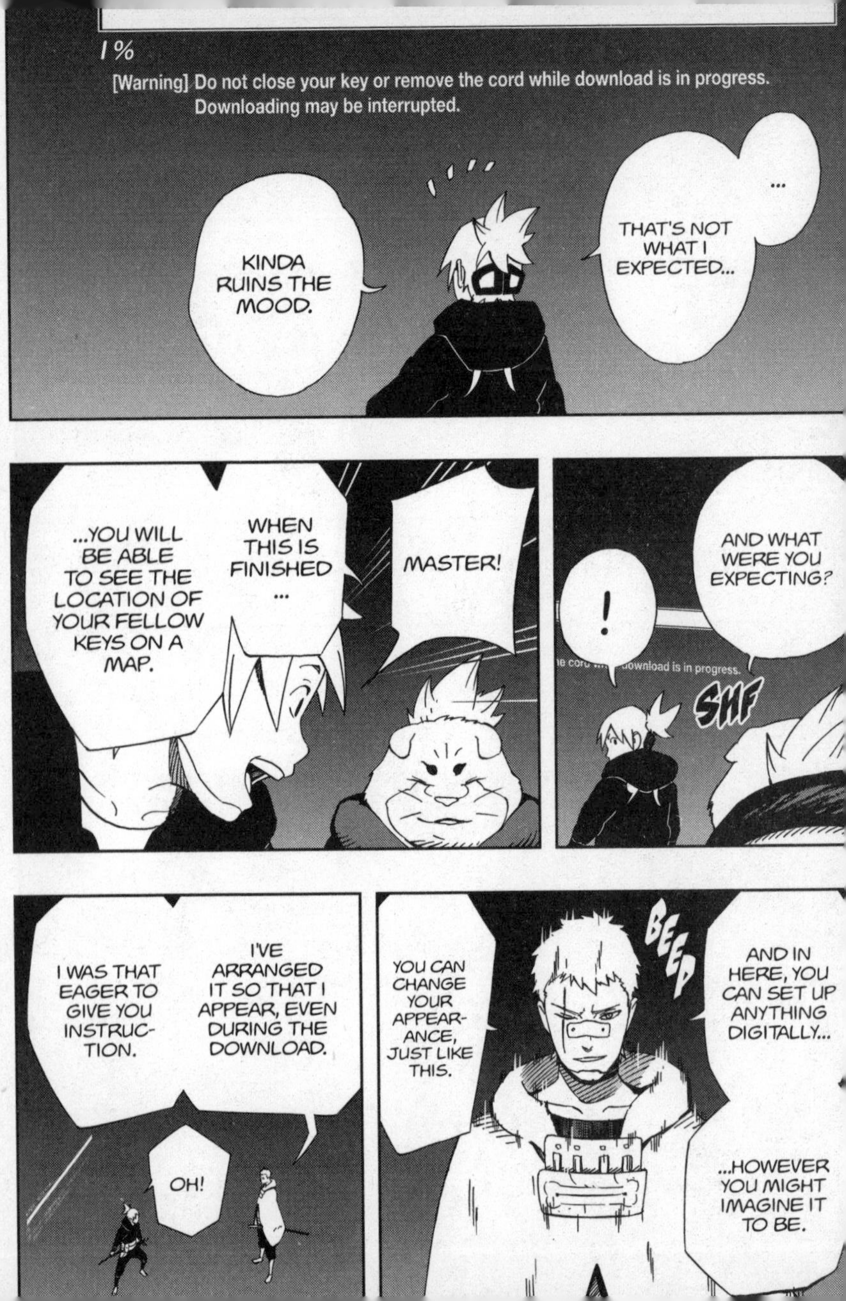
1%
[Warning] Do not close your key or remove the cord while download is in progress.
Downloading may be interrupted.
...
THAT'S NOT WHAT I EXPECTED...
KINDA RUINS THE MOOD.
AND WHAT WERE YOU EXPECTING?
!
download is in progress.
SHF
MASTER!
WHEN THIS IS FINISHED ...
...YOU WILL BE ABLE TO SEE THE LOCATION OF YOUR FELLOW KEYS ON A MAP.
AND IN HERE, YOU CAN SET UP ANYTHING DIGITALLY...
BEEP
...HOWEVER YOU MIGHT IMAGINE IT TO BE.
YOU CAN CHANGE YOUR APPEAR-ANCE, JUST LIKE THIS.
I'VE ARRANGED IT SO THAT I APPEAR, EVEN DURING THE DOWNLOAD.
I WAS THAT EAGER TO GIVE YOU INSTRUC-TION.
OH!

B-BMP
B-BMP

THIS LICENSE IS REALLY AMAZING!

IT CAN DO ALL THESE THINGS ON TOP OF SHOWING THE OTHER GUYS ON A MAP?

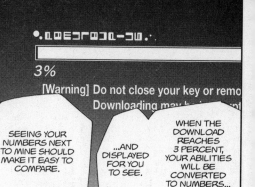

SEEING YOUR NUMBERS NEXT TO MINE SHOULD MAKE IT EASY TO COMPARE.

...AND DISPLAYED FOR YOU TO SEE.

WHEN THE DOWNLOAD REACHES 3 PERCENT, YOUR ABILITIES WILL BE CONVERTED TO NUMBERS...

3%

[Warning] Do not close your key or remo

Downloading may b

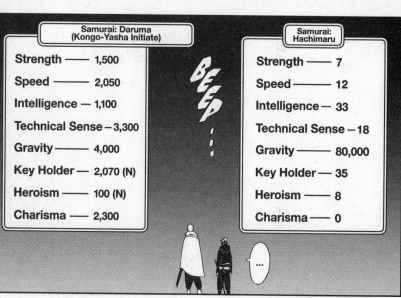

Samurai: Daruma (Kongo-Yasha Initiate)		Samurai: Hachimaru	
Strength	1,500	Strength	7
Speed	2,050	Speed	12
Intelligence	1,100	Intelligence	33
Technical Sense	3,300	Technical Sense	18
Gravity	4,000	Gravity	80,000
Key Holder	2,070 (N)	Key Holder	35
Heroism	100 (N)	Heroism	8
Charisma	2,300	Charisma	0

BEEP!

...

HEY! MY CHARISMA IS ZERO?!

EXCEPT FOR CHARISMA...

BECAUSE OF THE *HEROISM* YOU SHARE WITH ANN, ALL OF YOUR NUMBERS CAN BE BOOSTED AS MUCH AS EIGHTFOLD.

DON'T BE DOWN ABOUT IT.

MY NUMBERS SUCK!

YOUR NUMBERS ARE OFF THE CHART!

Holder — 35

Heroism — 8

Charisma — 0

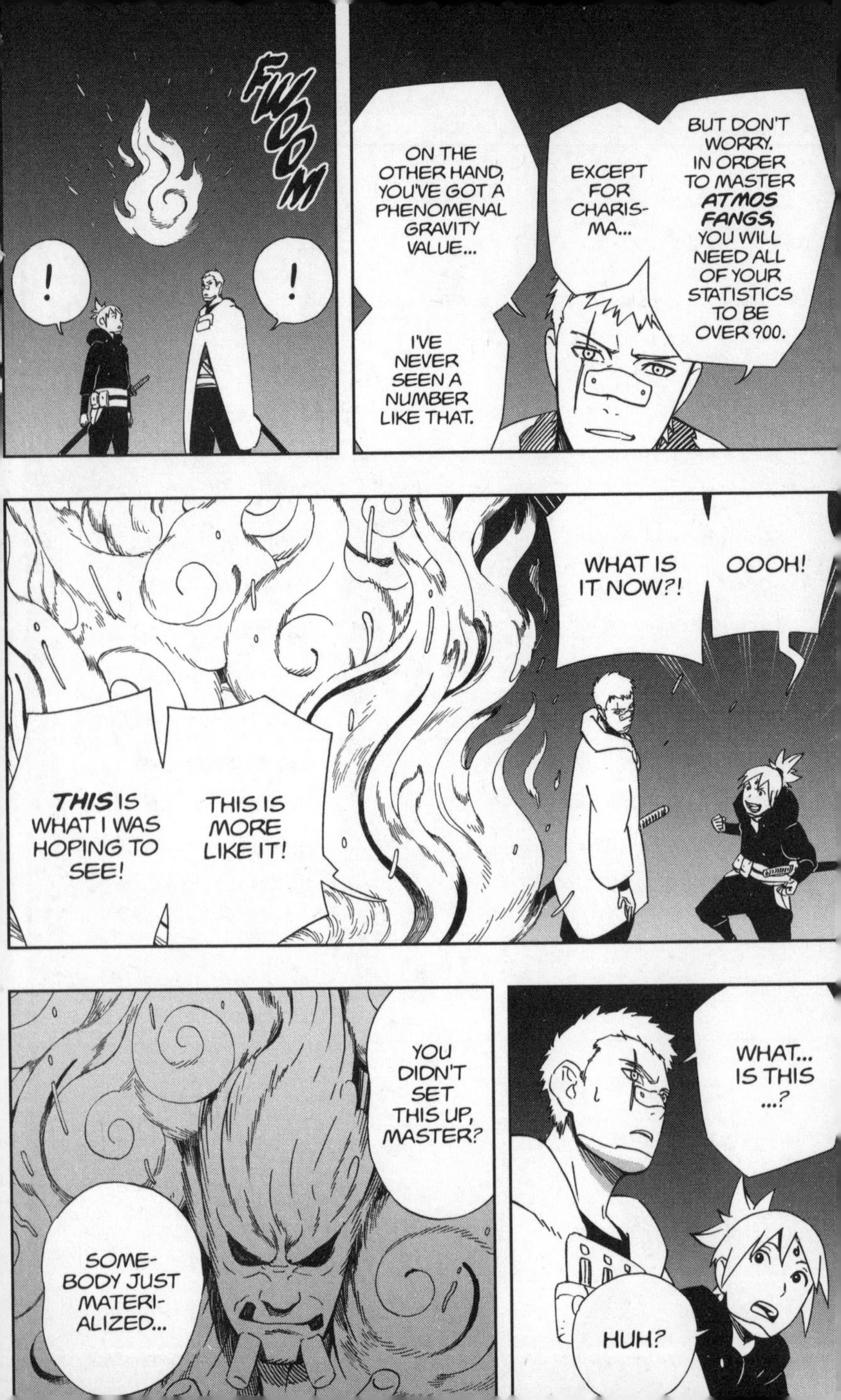
BUT DON'T WORRY. IN ORDER TO MASTER ATMOS FANGS, YOU WILL NEED ALL OF YOUR STATISTICS TO BE OVER 900.
EXCEPT FOR CHARIS-MA...
ON THE OTHER HAND, YOU'VE GOT A PHENOMENAL GRAVITY VALUE...
I'VE NEVER SEEN A NUMBER LIKE THAT.
FWOOM
!
!
OOOH!
WHAT IS IT NOW?!
THIS IS MORE LIKE IT!
THIS IS WHAT I WAS HOPING TO SEE!
WHAT... IS THIS ...?
HUH?
YOU DIDN'T SET THIS UP, MASTER?
SOME-BODY JUST MATERI-ALIZED...

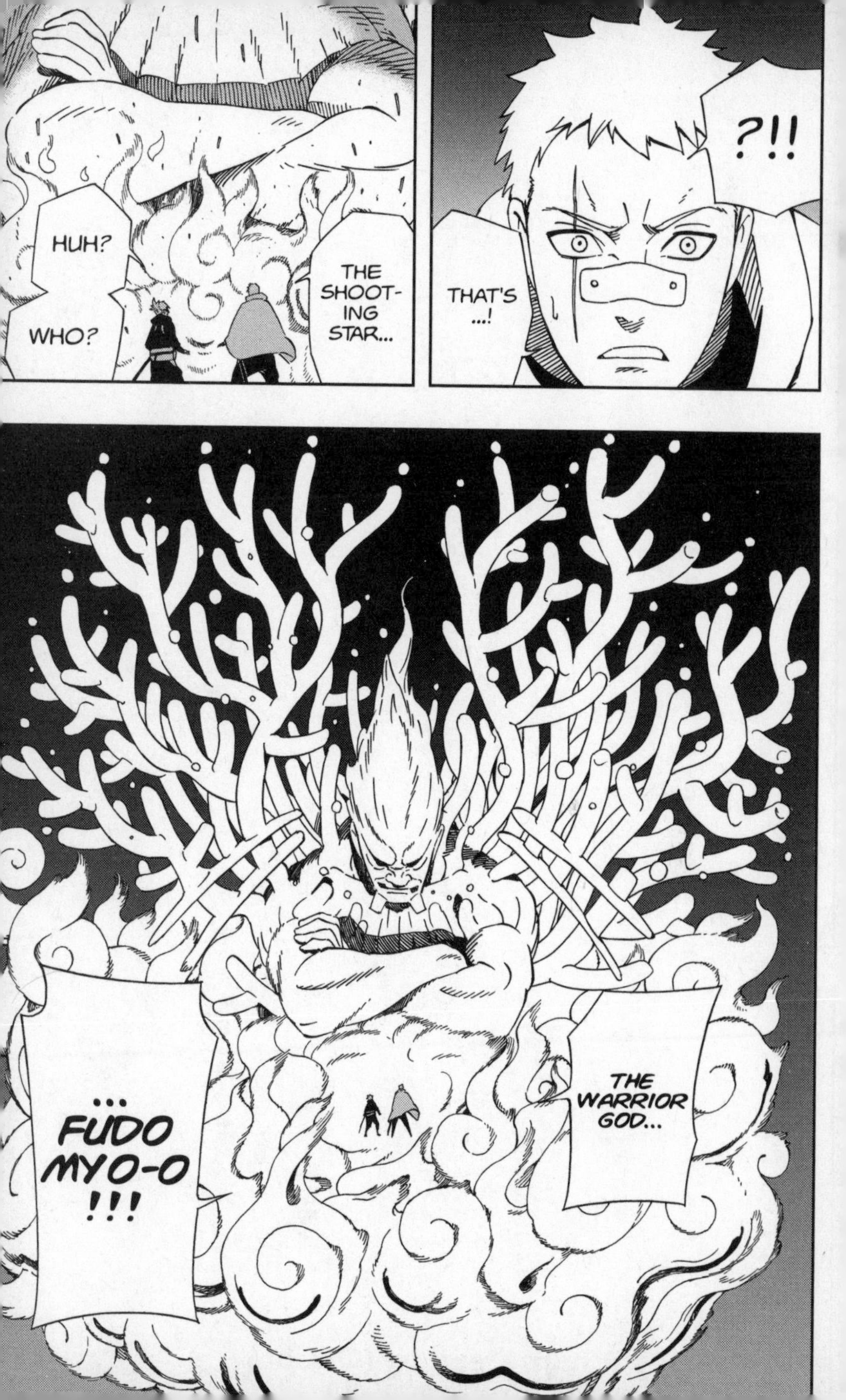
?!!
THAT'S ...!
THE SHOOTING STAR...
HUH? WHO?
THE WARRIOR GOD...
... FŪDO MYO-O !!!

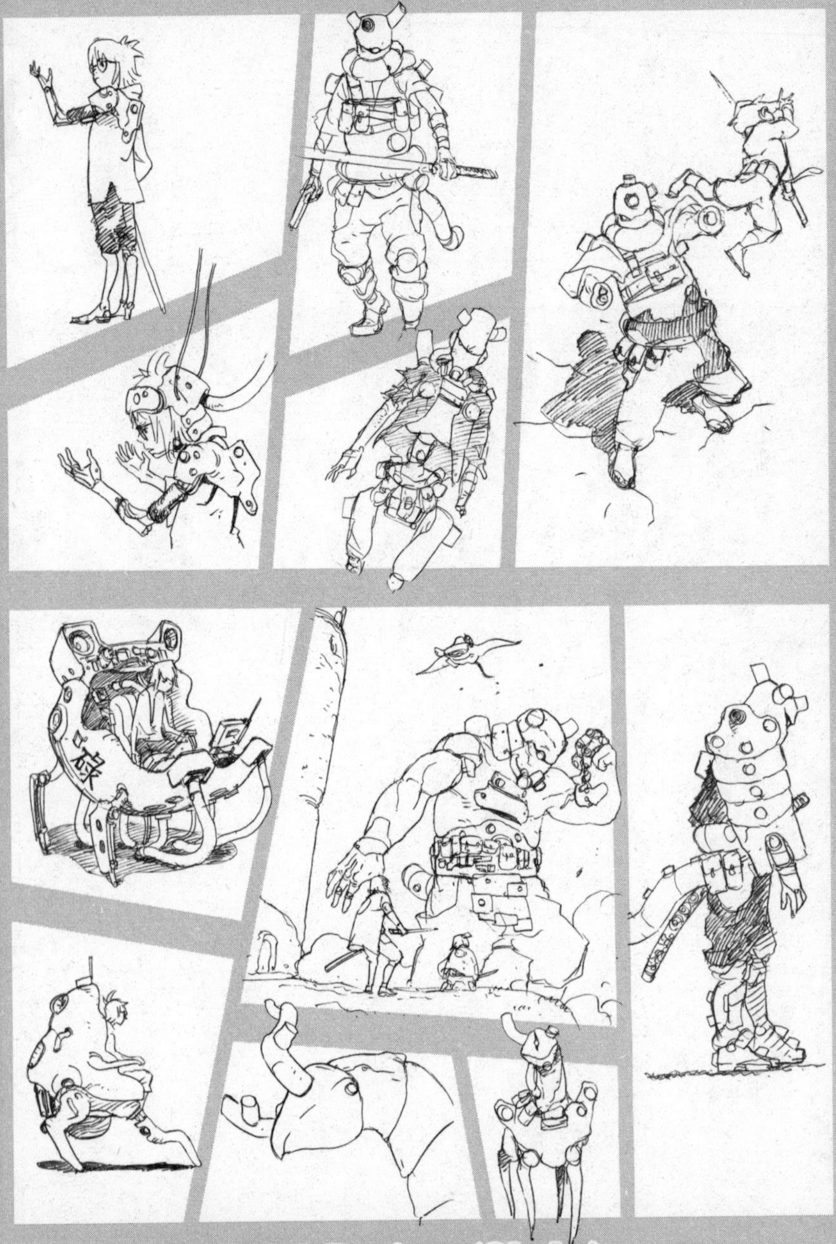

Pre-Series Rough Designs (Okubo)

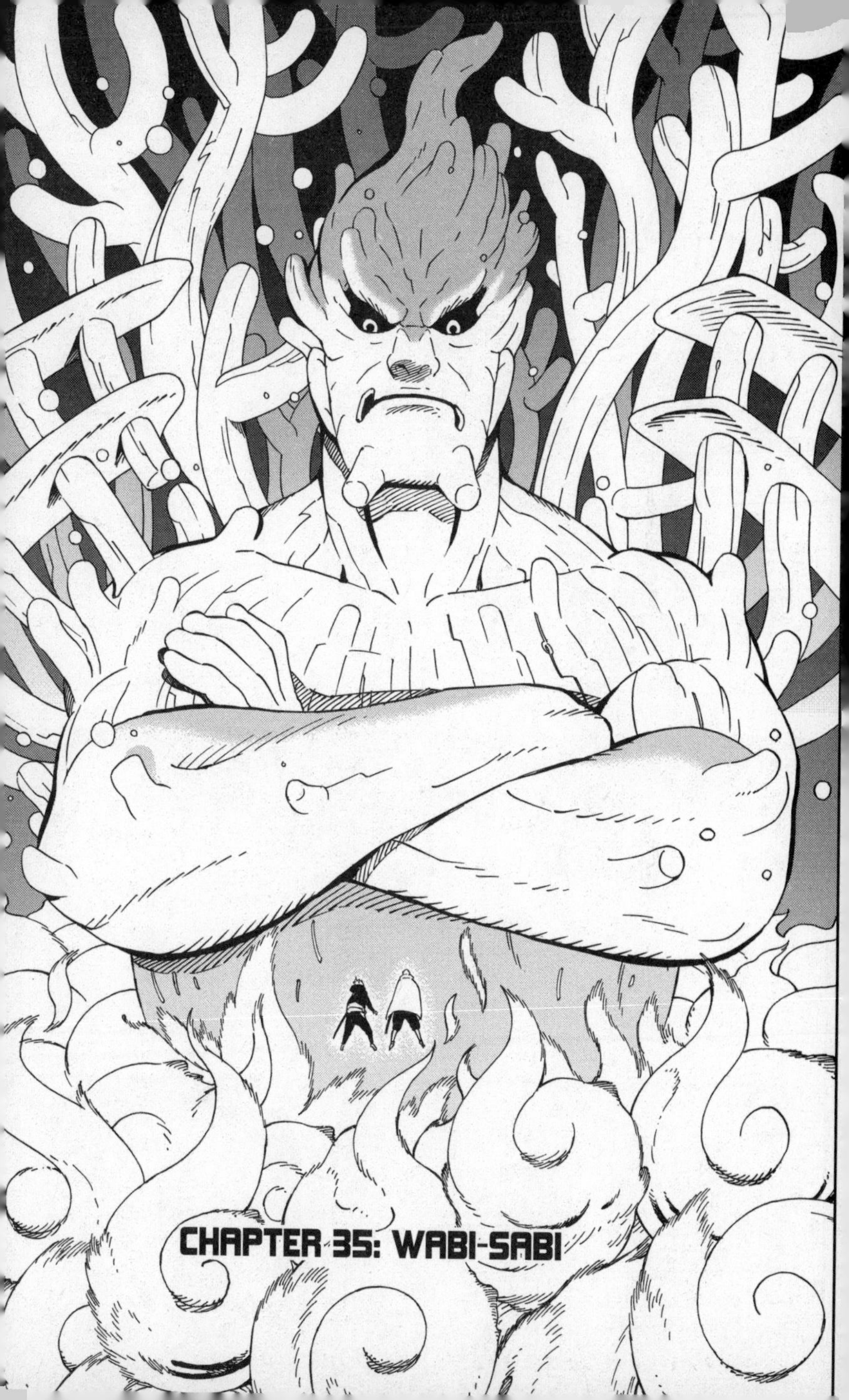
CHAPTER 35: WABI-SABI

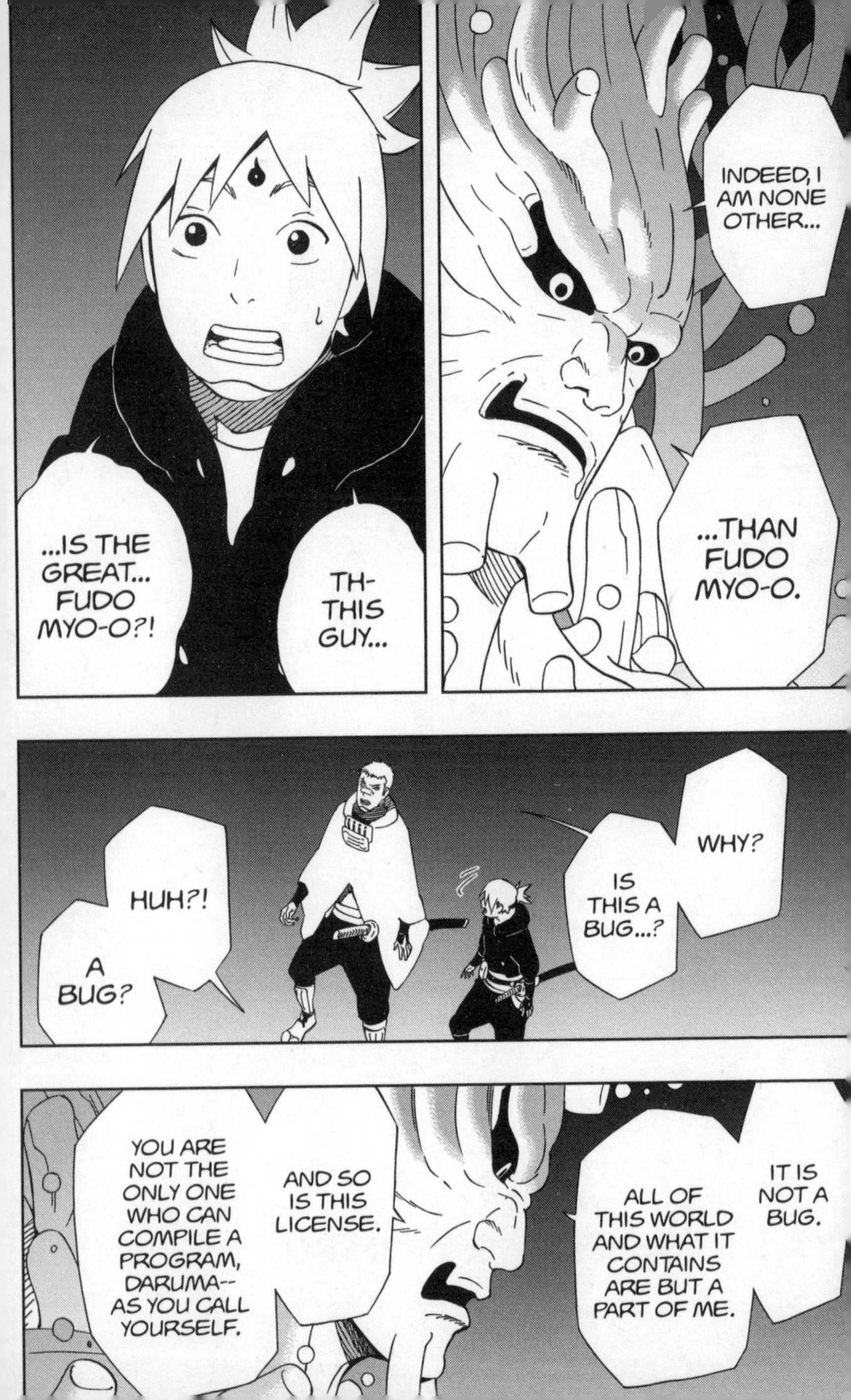
INDEED, I AM NONE OTHER...
...THAN FUDO MYO-O.
TH-THIS GUY...
...IS THE GREAT... FUDO MYO-O?!
WHY?
IS THIS A BUG...?
HUH?! A BUG?
IT IS NOT A BUG.
ALL OF THIS WORLD AND WHAT IT CONTAINS ARE BUT A PART OF ME.
AND SO IS THIS LICENSE.
YOU ARE NOT THE ONLY ONE WHO CAN COMPILE A PROGRAM, DARUMA--AS YOU CALL YOURSELF.

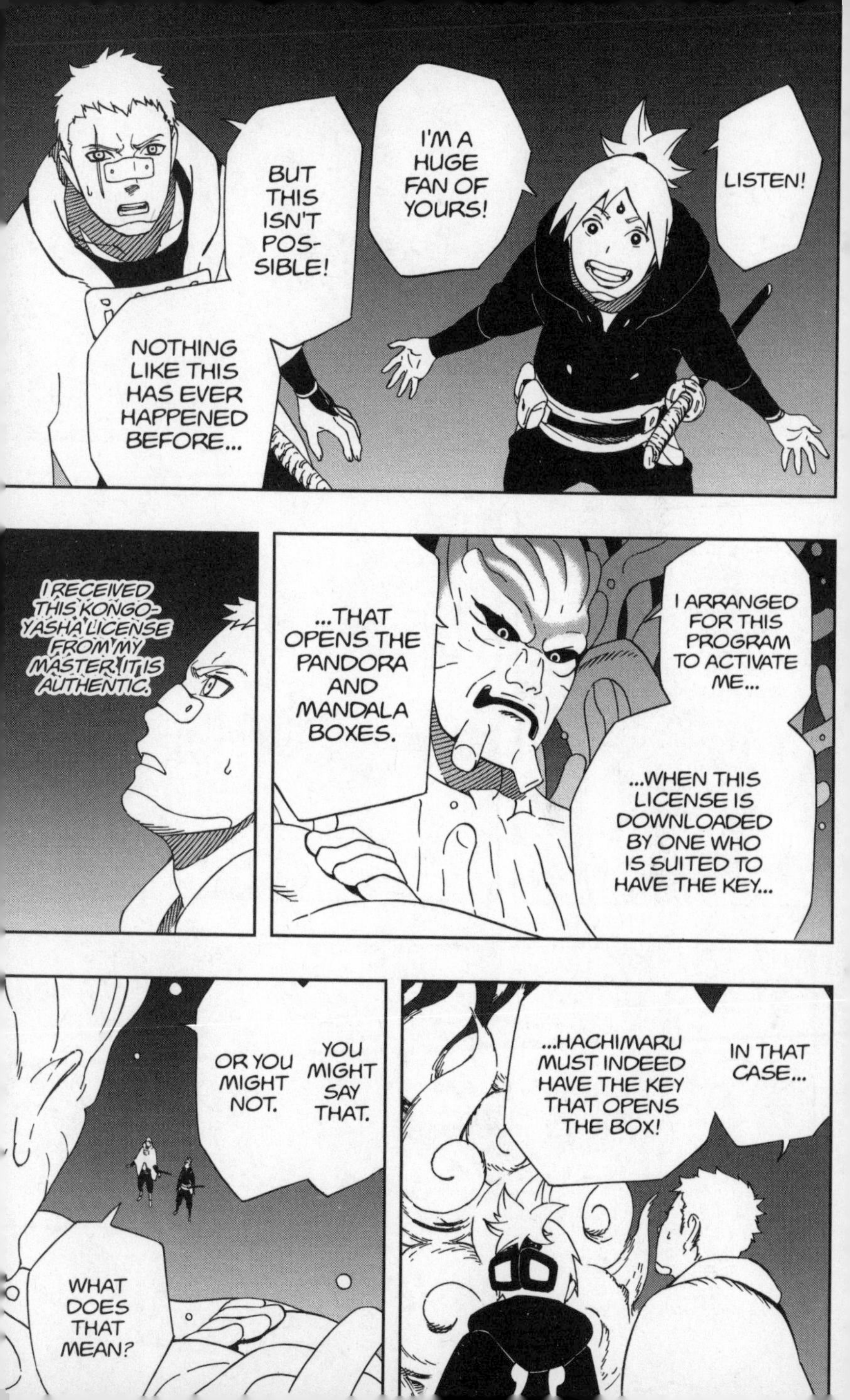
LISTEN!
I'M A HUGE FAN OF YOURS!
BUT THIS ISN'T POS-SIBLE!
NOTHING LIKE THIS HAS EVER HAPPENED BEFORE...
I ARRANGED FOR THIS PROGRAM TO ACTIVATE ME...
...WHEN THIS LICENSE IS DOWNLOADED BY ONE WHO IS SUITED TO HAVE THE KEY...
...THAT OPENS THE PANDORA AND MANDALA BOXES.
I RECEIVED THIS KONGO-YASHA LICENSE FROM MY MASTER. IT IS AUTHENTIC.
IN THAT CASE...
...HACHIMARU MUST INDEED HAVE THE KEY THAT OPENS THE BOX!
YOU MIGHT SAY THAT.
OR YOU MIGHT NOT.
WHAT DOES THAT MEAN?

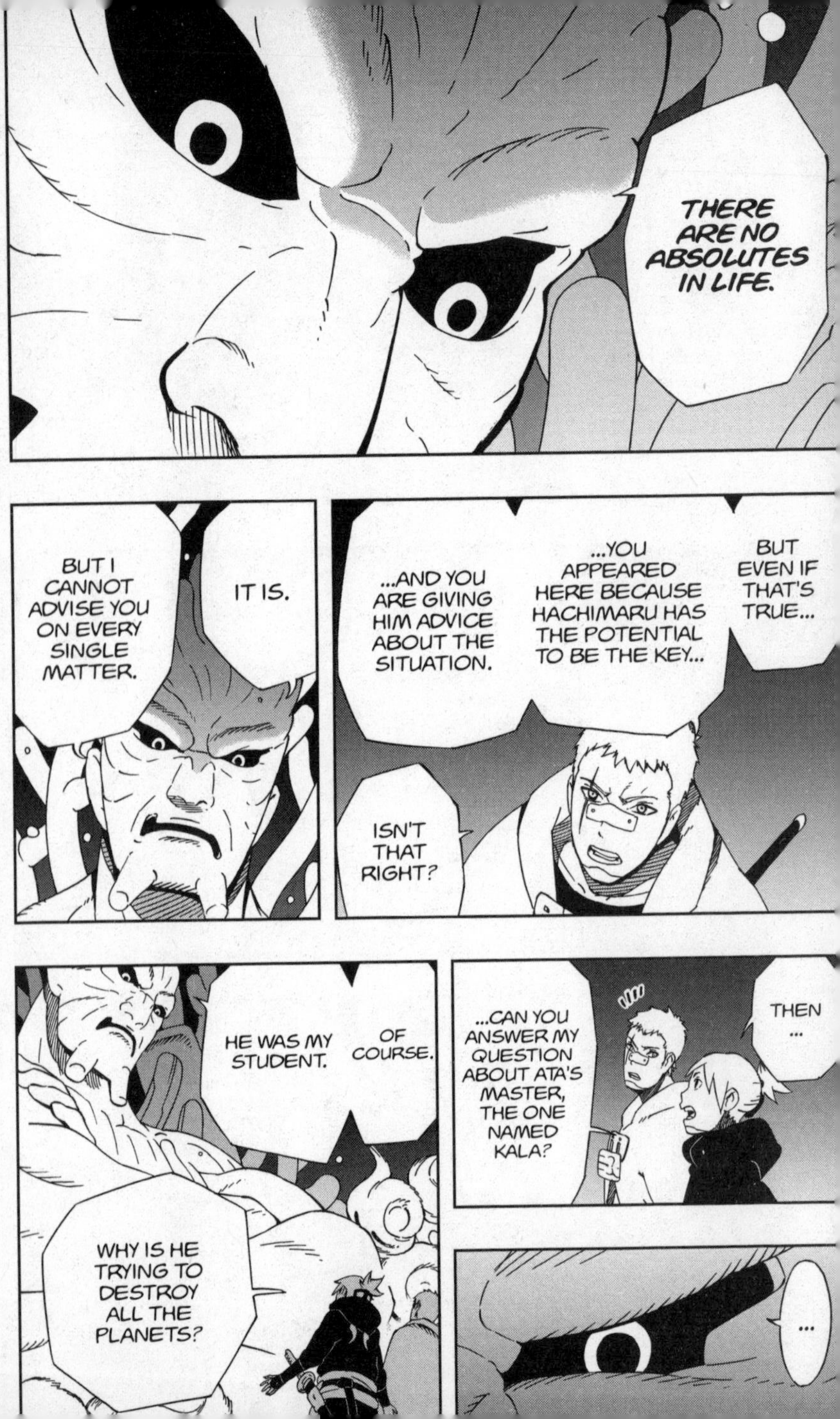
THERE ARE NO ABSOLUTES IN LIFE.
BUT EVEN IF THAT'S TRUE...
...YOU APPEARED HERE BECAUSE HACHIMARU HAS THE POTENTIAL TO BE THE KEY...
...AND YOU ARE GIVING HIM ADVICE ABOUT THE SITUATION.
ISN'T THAT RIGHT?
IT IS.
BUT I CANNOT ADVISE YOU ON EVERY SINGLE MATTER.
THEN...
...CAN YOU ANSWER MY QUESTION ABOUT ATA'S MASTER, THE ONE NAMED KALA?
...
OF COURSE.
HE WAS MY STUDENT.
WHY IS HE TRYING TO DESTROY ALL THE PLANETS?

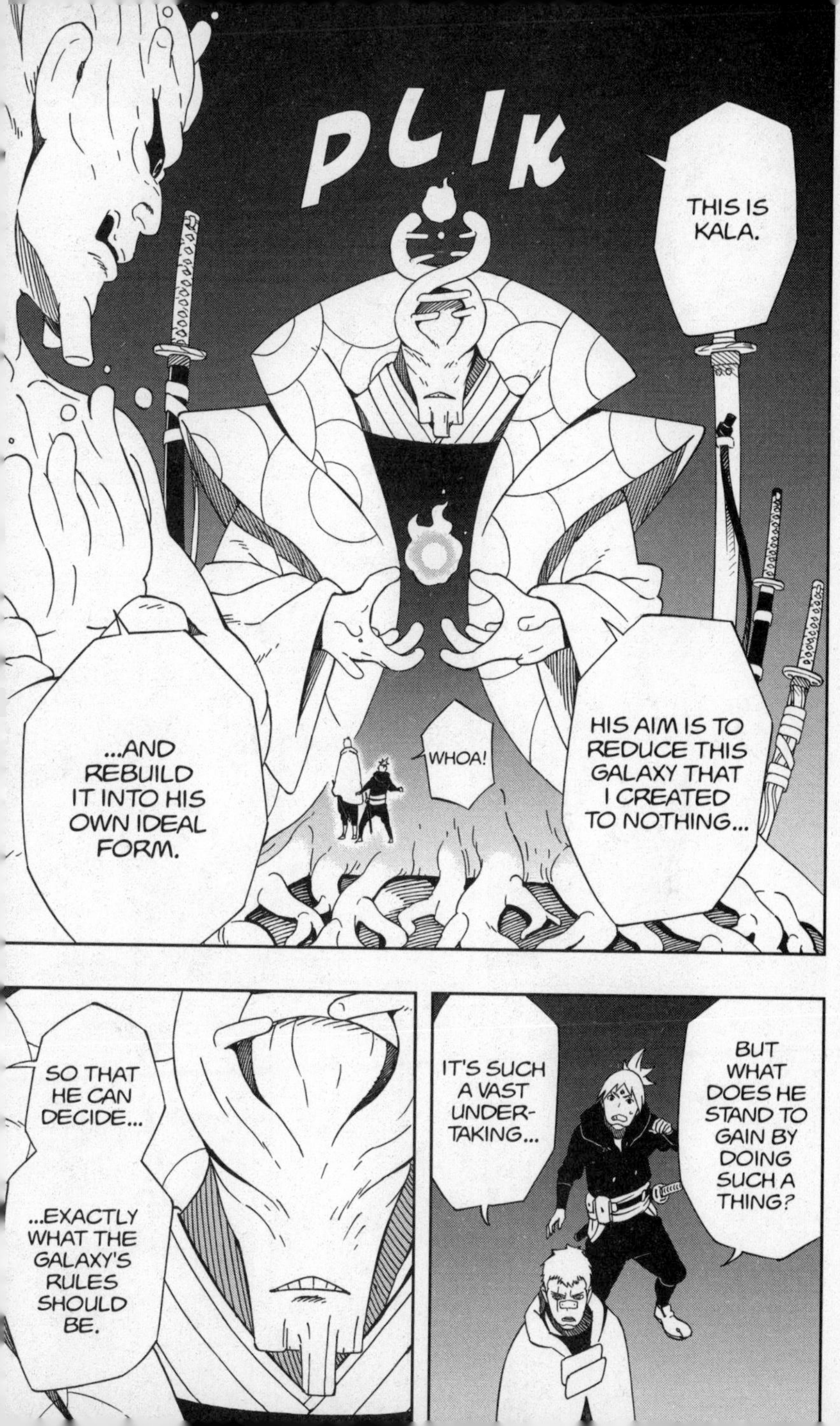
THIS IS KALA.
PLIK
HIS AIM IS TO REDUCE THIS GALAXY THAT I CREATED TO NOTHING...
WHOA!
...AND REBUILD IT INTO HIS OWN IDEAL FORM.
BUT WHAT DOES HE STAND TO GAIN BY DOING SUCH A THING?
IT'S SUCH A VAST UNDER-TAKING...
SO THAT HE CAN DECIDE...
...EXACTLY WHAT THE GALAXY'S RULES SHOULD BE.

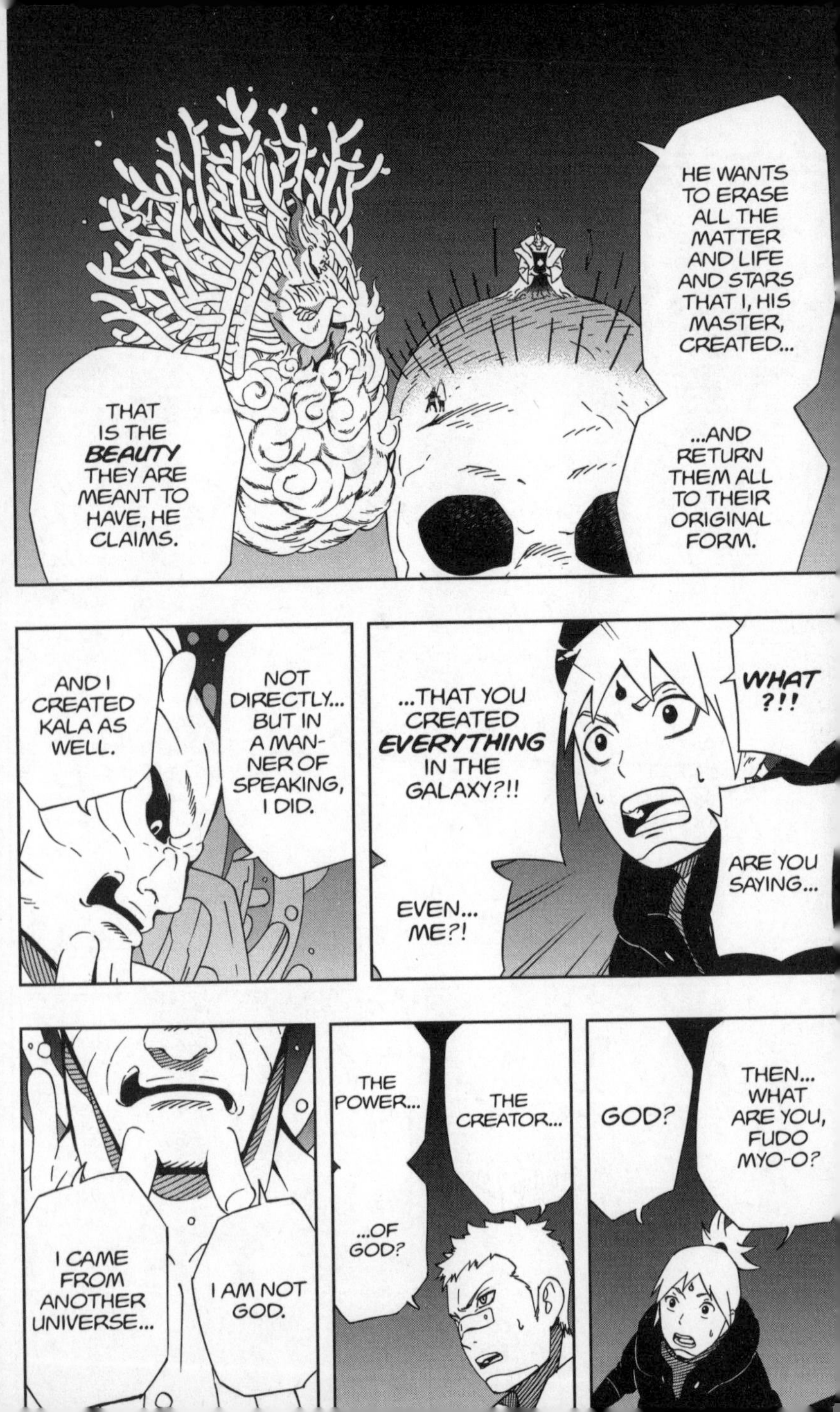
HE WANTS TO ERASE ALL THE MATTER AND LIFE AND STARS THAT I, HIS MASTER, CREATED...
...AND RETURN THEM ALL TO THEIR ORIGINAL FORM.
THAT IS THE *BEAUTY* THEY ARE MEANT TO HAVE, HE CLAIMS.
WHAT ?!!
ARE YOU SAYING...
...THAT YOU CREATED *EVERYTHING* IN THE GALAXY?!!
EVEN... ME?!
NOT DIRECTLY... BUT IN A MAN-NER OF SPEAKING, I DID.
AND I CREATED KALA AS WELL.
THEN... WHAT ARE YOU, FUDO MYO-O?
GOD?
THE CREATOR...
THE POWER...
...OF GOD?
I AM NOT GOD.
I CAME FROM ANOTHER UNIVERSE...

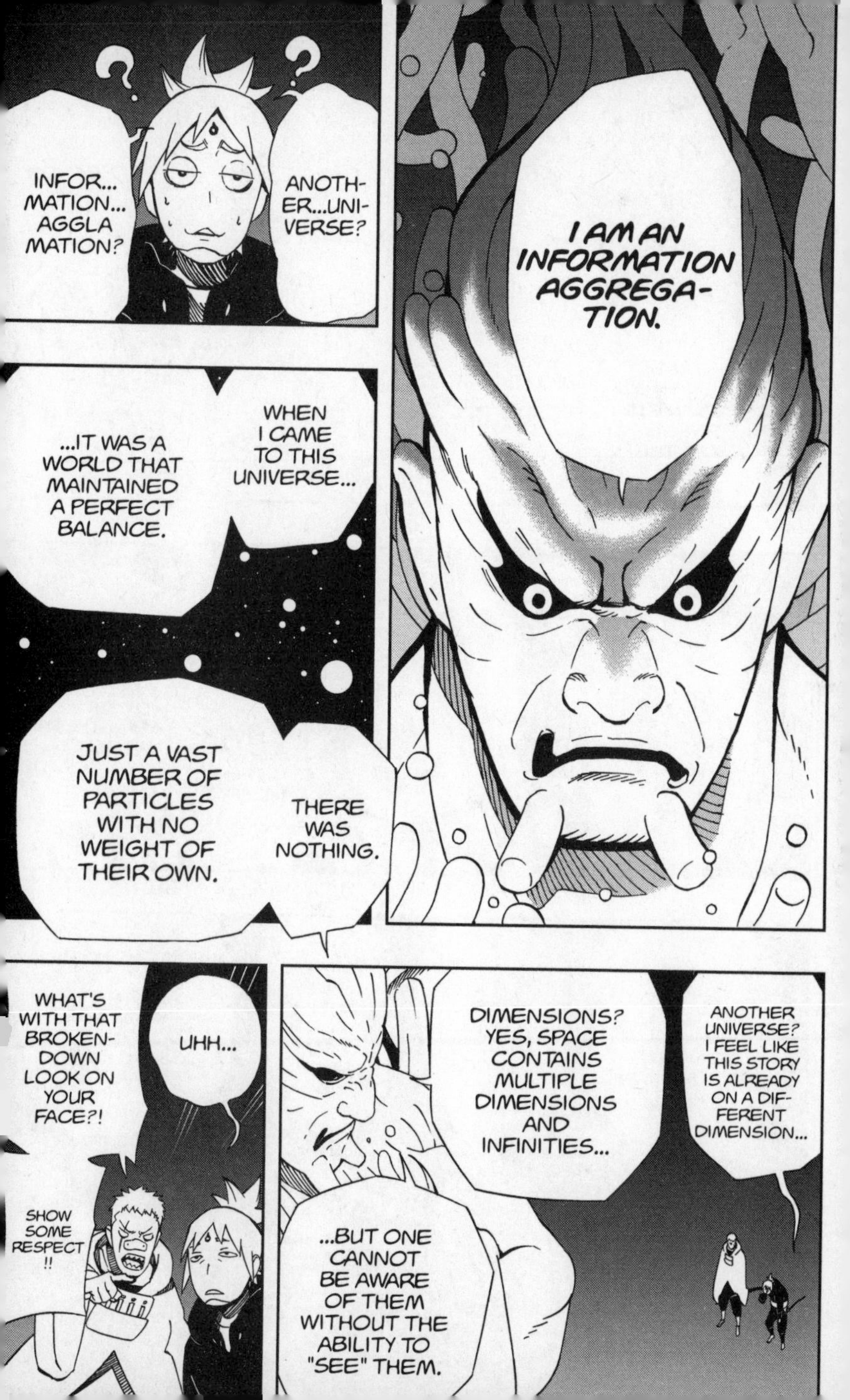
I AM AN INFORMATION AGGREGATION.
ANOTHER...UNIVERSE?
INFOR... MATION... AGGLA MATION?
WHEN I CAME TO THIS UNIVERSE...
...IT WAS A WORLD THAT MAINTAINED A PERFECT BALANCE.
THERE WAS NOTHING.
JUST A VAST NUMBER OF PARTICLES WITH NO WEIGHT OF THEIR OWN.
ANOTHER UNIVERSE? I FEEL LIKE THIS STORY IS ALREADY ON A DIFFERENT DIMENSION...
DIMENSIONS? YES, SPACE CONTAINS MULTIPLE DIMENSIONS AND INFINITIES...
...BUT ONE CANNOT BE AWARE OF THEM WITHOUT THE ABILITY TO "SEE" THEM.
UHH...
WHAT'S WITH THAT BROKEN-DOWN LOOK ON YOUR FACE?!
SHOW SOME RESPECT!!

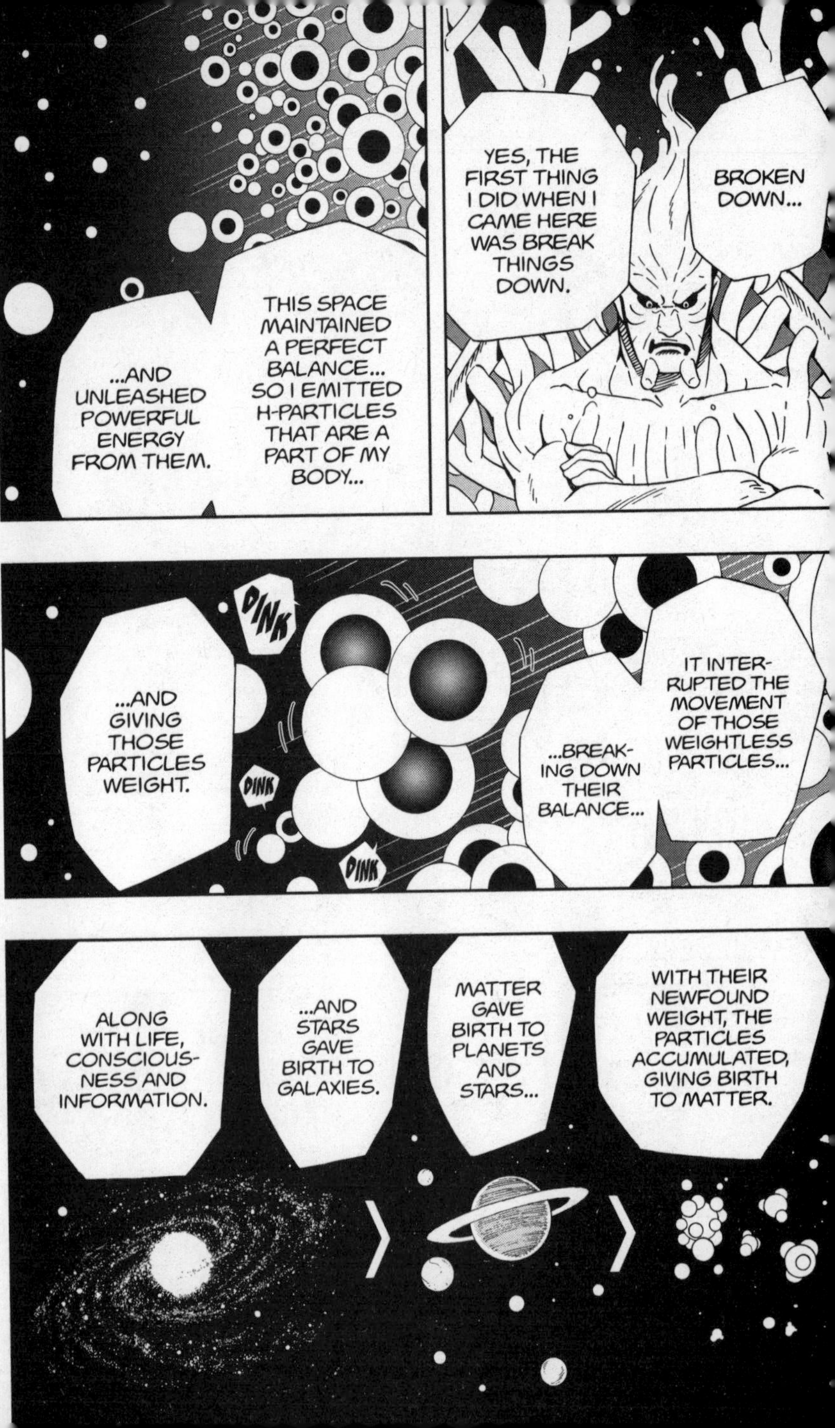
BROKEN DOWN...
YES, THE FIRST THING I DID WHEN I CAME HERE WAS BREAK THINGS DOWN.
THIS SPACE MAINTAINED A PERFECT BALANCE... SO I EMITTED H-PARTICLES THAT ARE A PART OF MY BODY...
...AND UNLEASHED POWERFUL ENERGY FROM THEM.
IT INTER-RUPTED THE MOVEMENT OF THOSE WEIGHTLESS PARTICLES...
...BREAK-ING DOWN THEIR BALANCE...
DINK
DINK
DINK
...AND GIVING THOSE PARTICLES WEIGHT.
WITH THEIR NEWFOUND WEIGHT, THE PARTICLES ACCUMULATED, GIVING BIRTH TO MATTER.
MATTER GAVE BIRTH TO PLANETS AND STARS...
...AND STARS GAVE BIRTH TO GALAXIES.
ALONG WITH LIFE, CONSCIOUS-NESS AND INFORMATION.

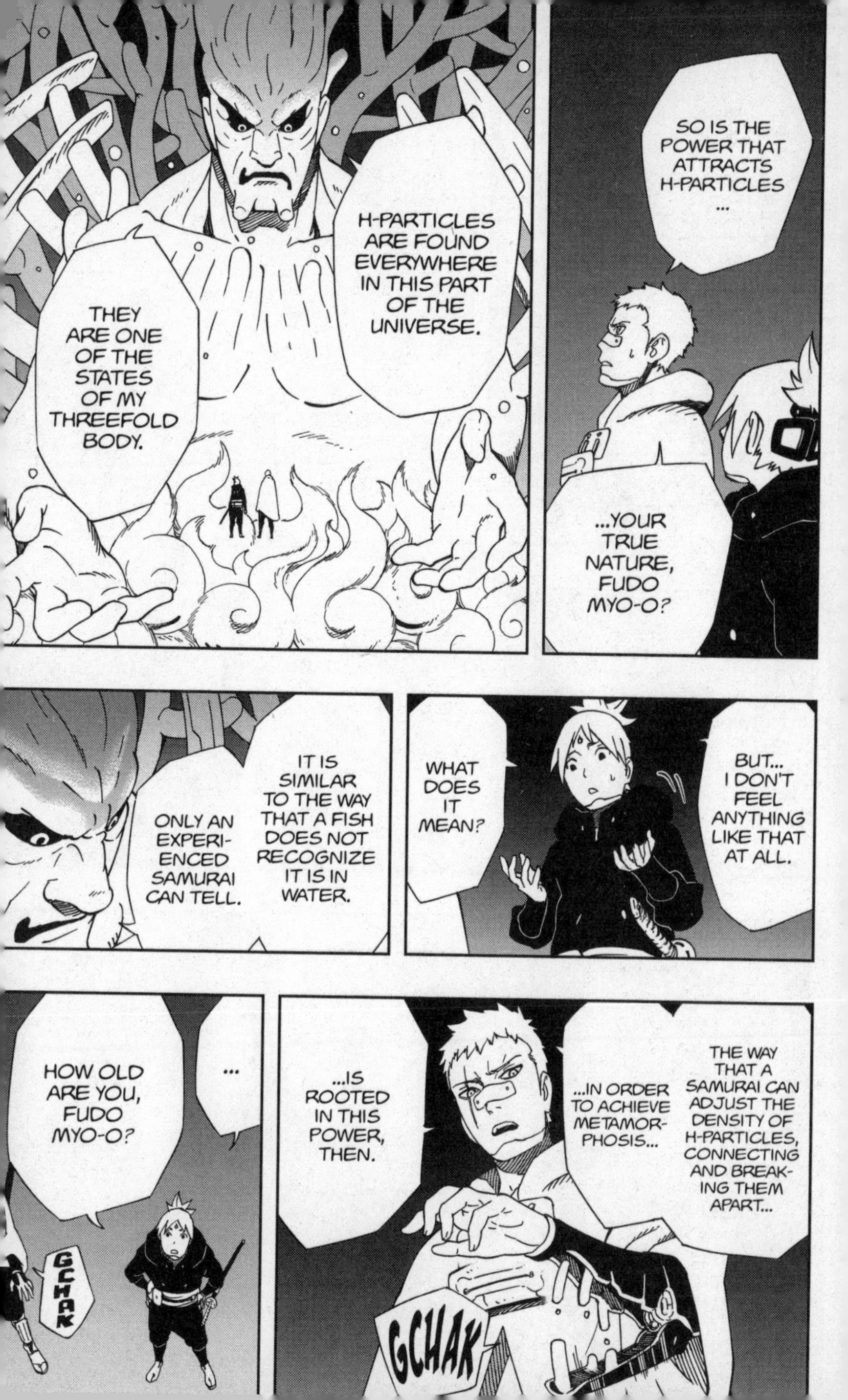

SO IS THE POWER THAT ATTRACTS H-PARTICLES ...
...YOUR TRUE NATURE, FUDO MYO-O?
H-PARTICLES ARE FOUND EVERYWHERE IN THIS PART OF THE UNIVERSE.
THEY ARE ONE OF THE STATES OF MY THREEFOLD BODY.
BUT... I DON'T FEEL ANYTHING LIKE THAT AT ALL.
WHAT DOES IT MEAN?
IT IS SIMILAR TO THE WAY THAT A FISH DOES NOT RECOGNIZE IT IS IN WATER.
ONLY AN EXPERI-ENCED SAMURAI CAN TELL.
THE WAY THAT A SAMURAI CAN ADJUST THE DENSITY OF H-PARTICLES, CONNECTING AND BREAK-ING THEM APART...
...IN ORDER TO ACHIEVE METAMOR-PHOSIS...
...IS ROOTED IN THIS POWER, THEN.
GCHAK
...
HOW OLD ARE YOU, FUDO MYO-O?
GCHAK

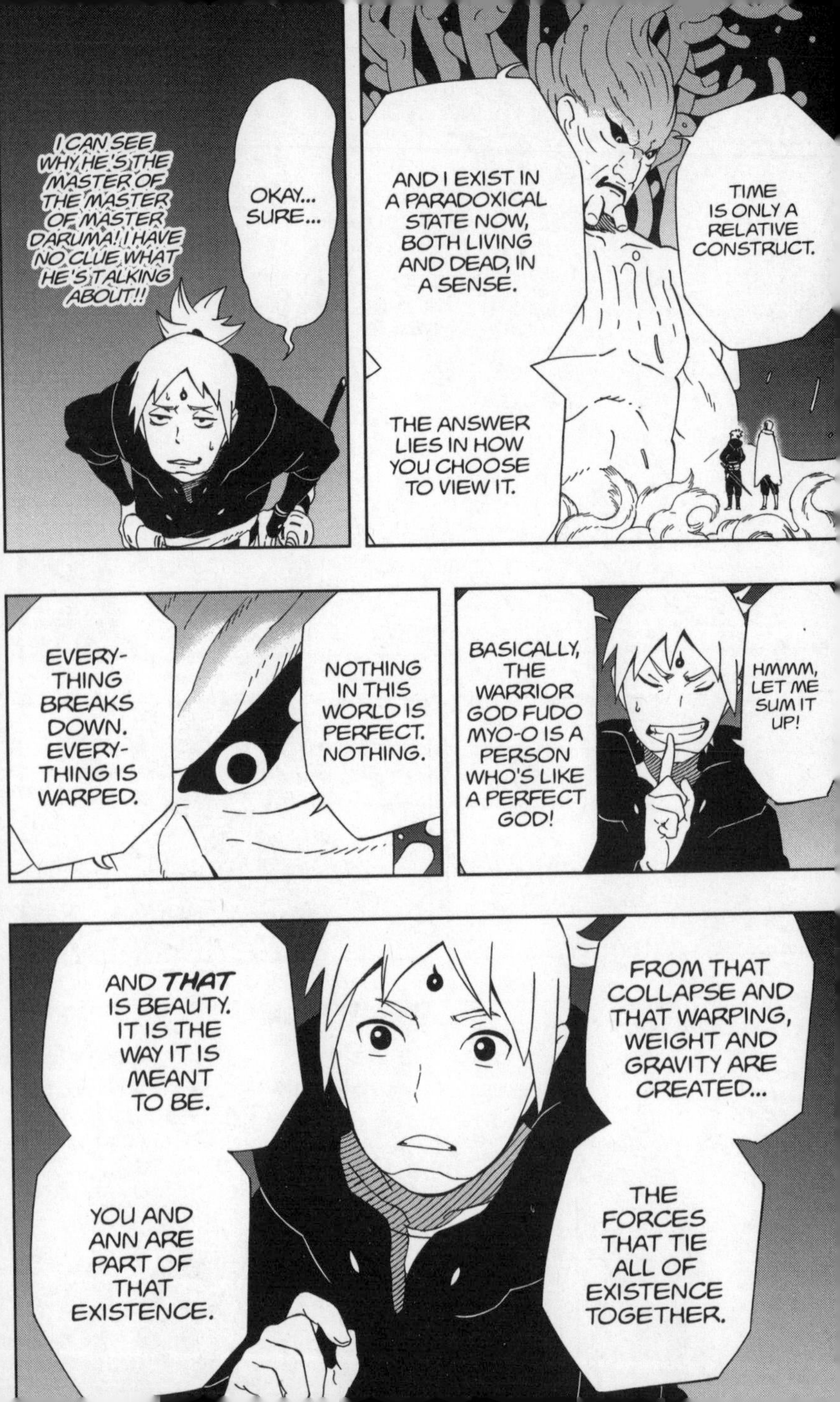
TIME IS ONLY A RELATIVE CONSTRUCT.
AND I EXIST IN A PARADOXICAL STATE NOW, BOTH LIVING AND DEAD, IN A SENSE.
THE ANSWER LIES IN HOW YOU CHOOSE TO VIEW IT.
OKAY... SURE...
I CAN SEE WHY HE'S THE MASTER OF THE MASTER OF MASTER DARUMA! I HAVE NO CLUE WHAT HE'S TALKING ABOUT!!
HMMM, LET ME SUM IT UP!
BASICALLY, THE WARRIOR GOD FUDO MYO-O IS A PERSON WHO'S LIKE A PERFECT GOD!
NOTHING IN THIS WORLD IS PERFECT. NOTHING.
EVERY-THING BREAKS DOWN. EVERY-THING IS WARPED.
FROM THAT COLLAPSE AND THAT WARPING, WEIGHT AND GRAVITY ARE CREATED...
AND *THAT* IS BEAUTY. IT IS THE WAY IT IS MEANT TO BE.
THE FORCES THAT TIE ALL OF EXISTENCE TOGETHER.
YOU AND ANN ARE PART OF THAT EXISTENCE.

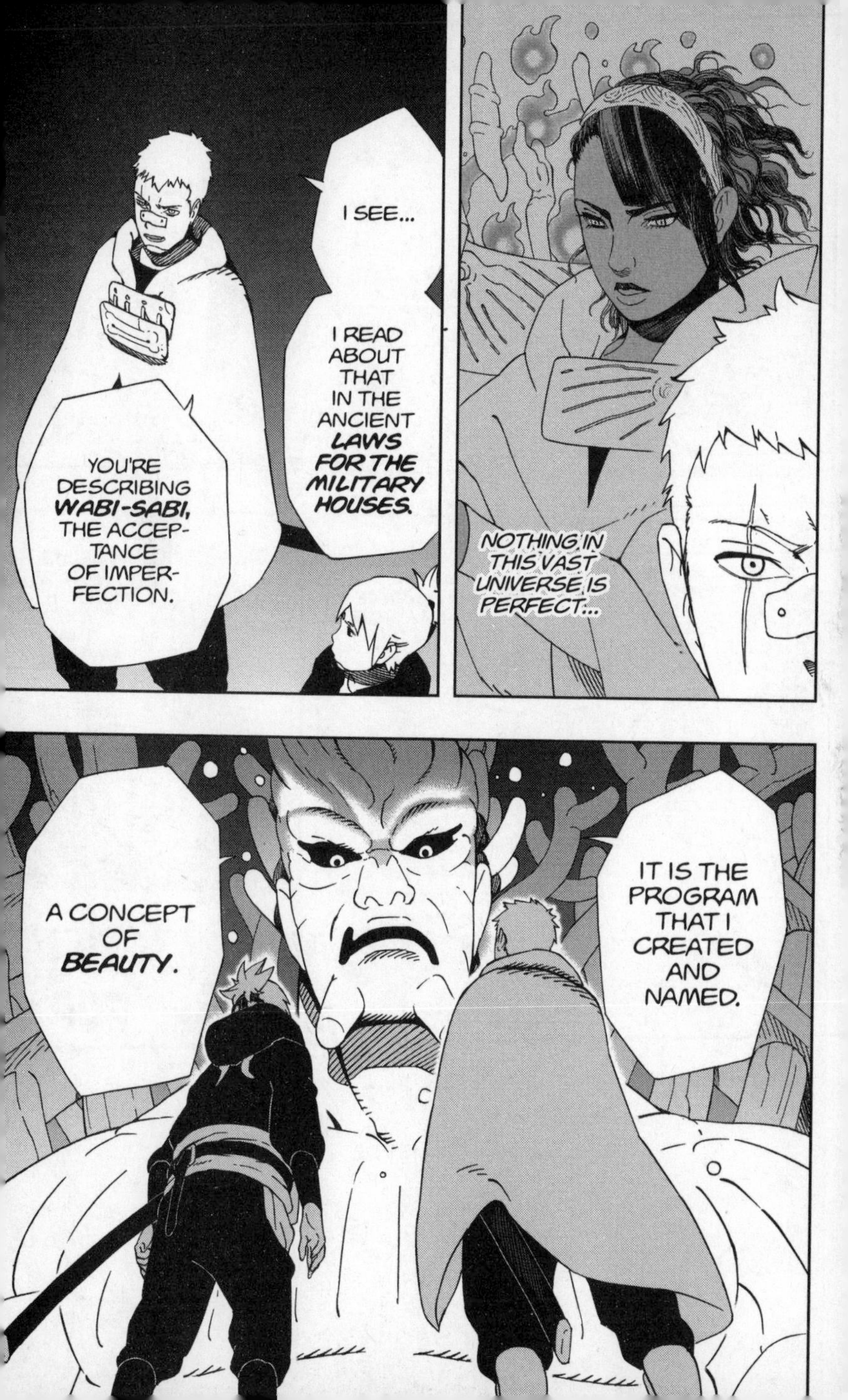

NOTHING IN THIS VAST UNIVERSE IS PERFECT...
I SEE...
I READ ABOUT THAT IN THE ANCIENT **LAWS FOR THE MILITARY HOUSES.**
YOU'RE DESCRIBING **WABI-SABI,** THE ACCEPTANCE OF IMPERFECTION.
IT IS THE PROGRAM THAT I CREATED AND NAMED.
A CONCEPT OF **BEAUTY.**

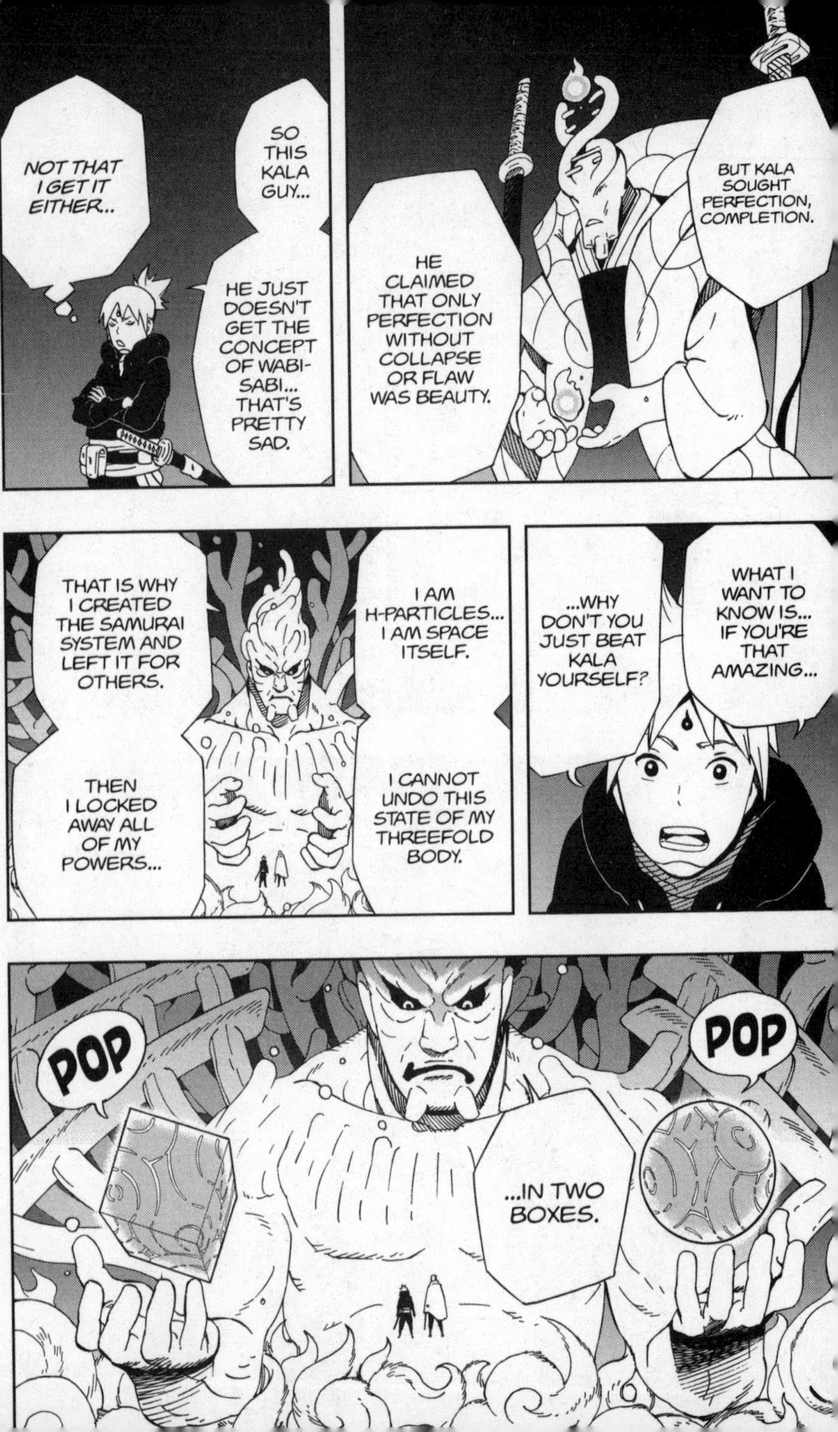
BUT KALA SOUGHT PERFECTION, COMPLETION.
HE CLAIMED THAT ONLY PERFECTION WITHOUT COLLAPSE OR FLAW WAS BEAUTY.
SO THIS KALA GUY...
HE JUST DOESN'T GET THE CONCEPT OF WABI-SABI... THAT'S PRETTY SAD.
NOT THAT I GET IT EITHER...
WHAT I WANT TO KNOW IS... IF YOU'RE THAT AMAZING...
...WHY DON'T YOU JUST BEAT KALA YOURSELF?
I AM H-PARTICLES... I AM SPACE ITSELF.
I CANNOT UNDO THIS STATE OF MY THREEFOLD BODY.
THAT IS WHY I CREATED THE SAMURAI SYSTEM AND LEFT IT FOR OTHERS.
THEN I LOCKED AWAY ALL OF MY POWERS...
POP
POP
...IN TWO BOXES.

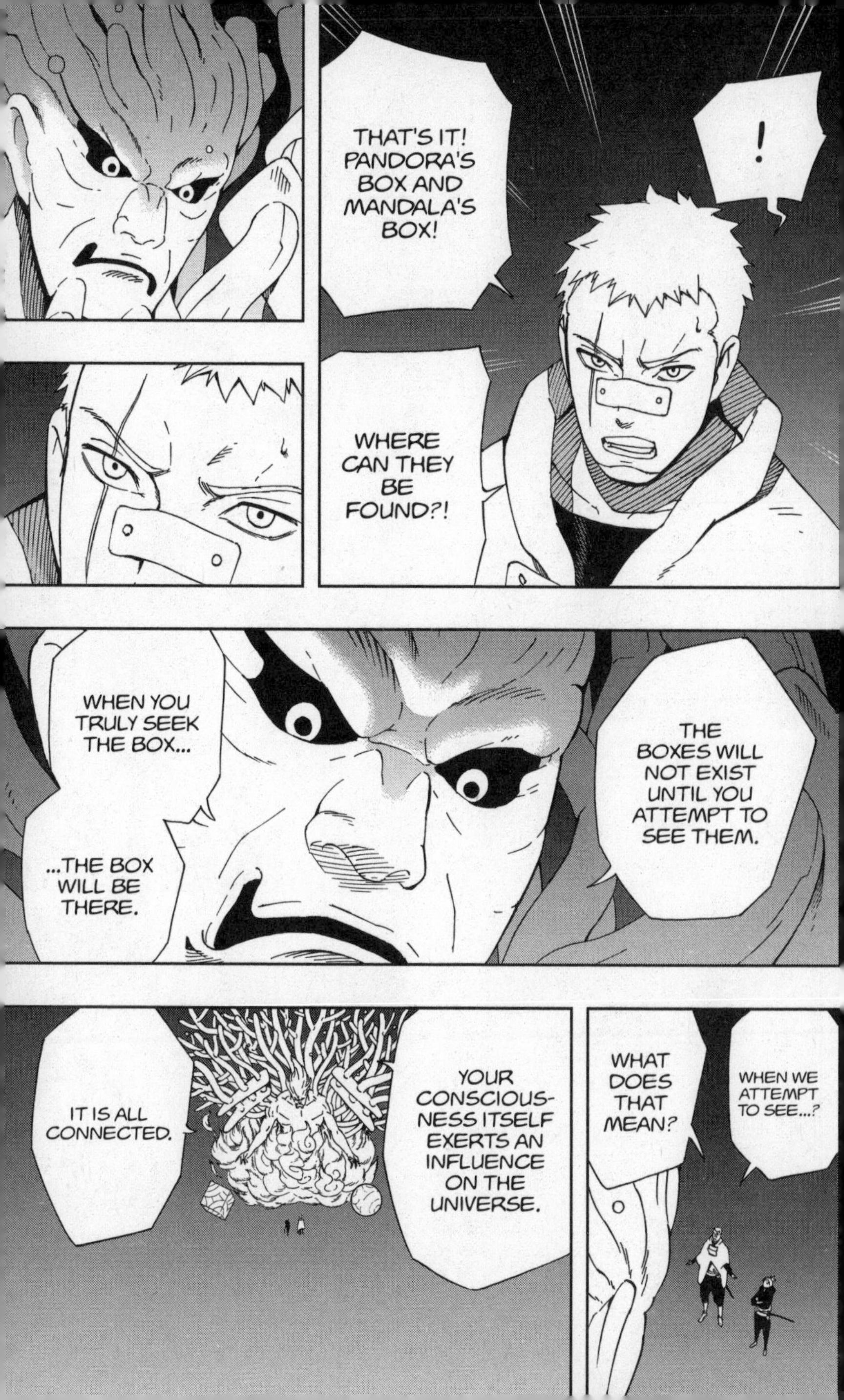
!
THAT'S IT! PANDORA'S BOX AND MANDALA'S BOX!
WHERE CAN THEY BE FOUND?!
THE BOXES WILL NOT EXIST UNTIL YOU ATTEMPT TO SEE THEM.
WHEN YOU TRULY SEEK THE BOX...
...THE BOX WILL BE THERE.
WHEN WE ATTEMPT TO SEE...?
WHAT DOES THAT MEAN?
YOUR CONSCIOUSNESS ITSELF EXERTS AN INFLUENCE ON THE UNIVERSE.
IT IS ALL CONNECTED.

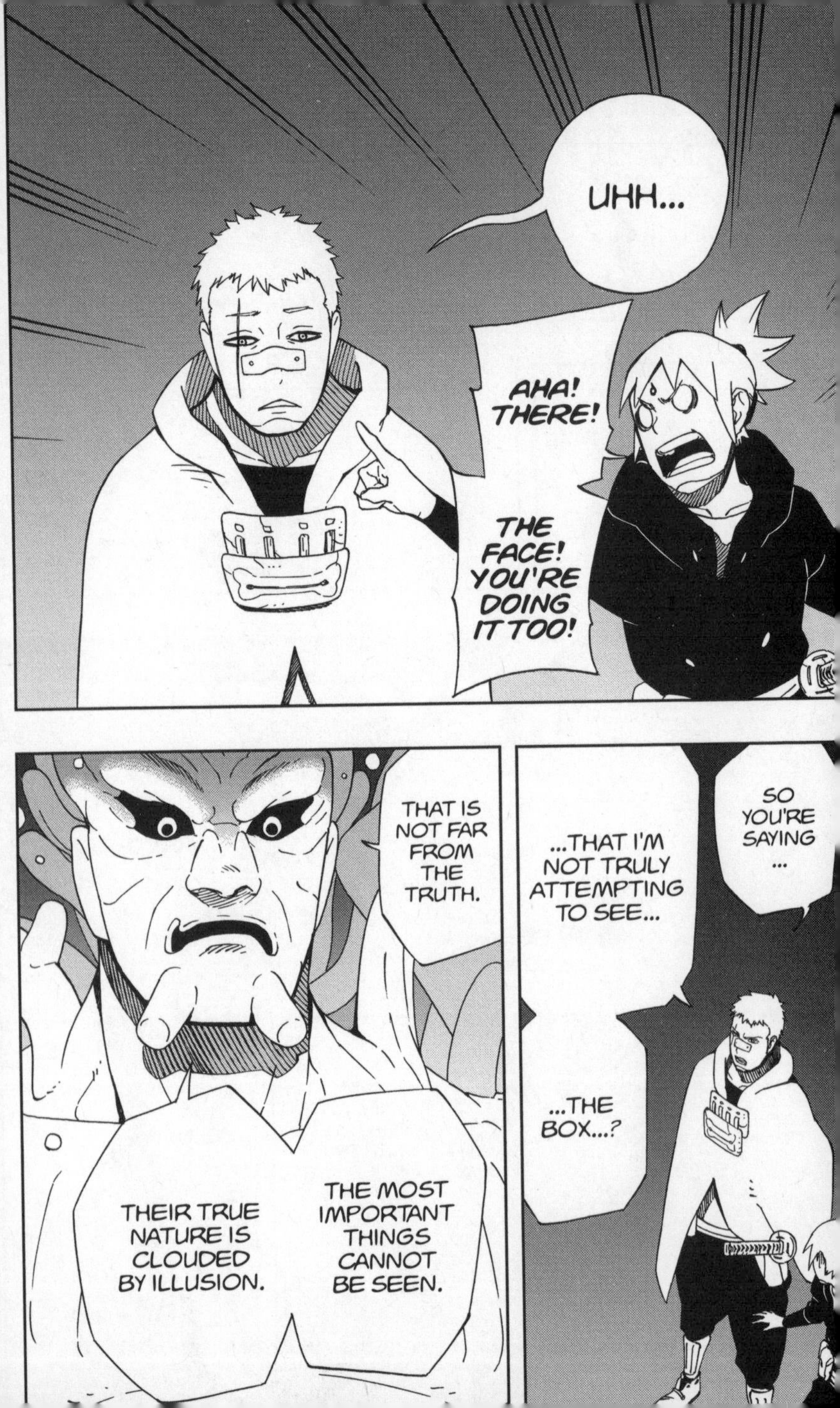
UHH...
AHA! THERE!
THE FACE! YOU'RE DOING IT TOO!
SO YOU'RE SAYING ...
...THAT I'M NOT TRULY ATTEMPTING TO SEE...
...THE BOX...?
THAT IS NOT FAR FROM THE TRUTH.
THE MOST IMPORTANT THINGS CANNOT BE SEEN.
THEIR TRUE NATURE IS CLOUDED BY ILLUSION.

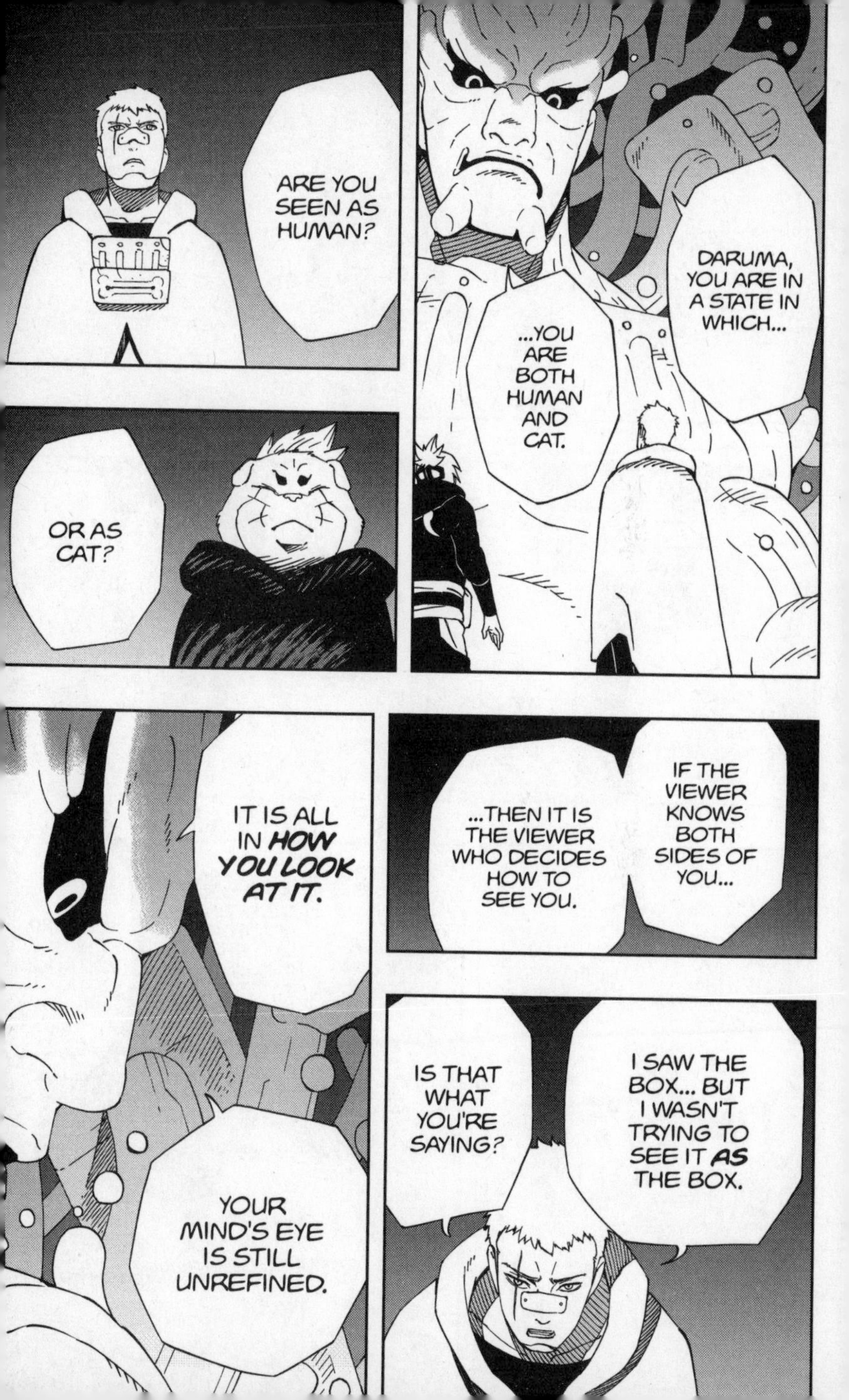
DARUMA, YOU ARE IN A STATE IN WHICH...
...YOU ARE BOTH HUMAN AND CAT.
ARE YOU SEEN AS HUMAN?
OR AS CAT?
IF THE VIEWER KNOWS BOTH SIDES OF YOU...
...THEN IT IS THE VIEWER WHO DECIDES HOW TO SEE YOU.
I SAW THE BOX... BUT I WASN'T TRYING TO SEE IT AS THE BOX.
IS THAT WHAT YOU'RE SAYING?
IT IS ALL IN HOW YOU LOOK AT IT.
YOUR MIND'S EYE IS STILL UNREFINED.

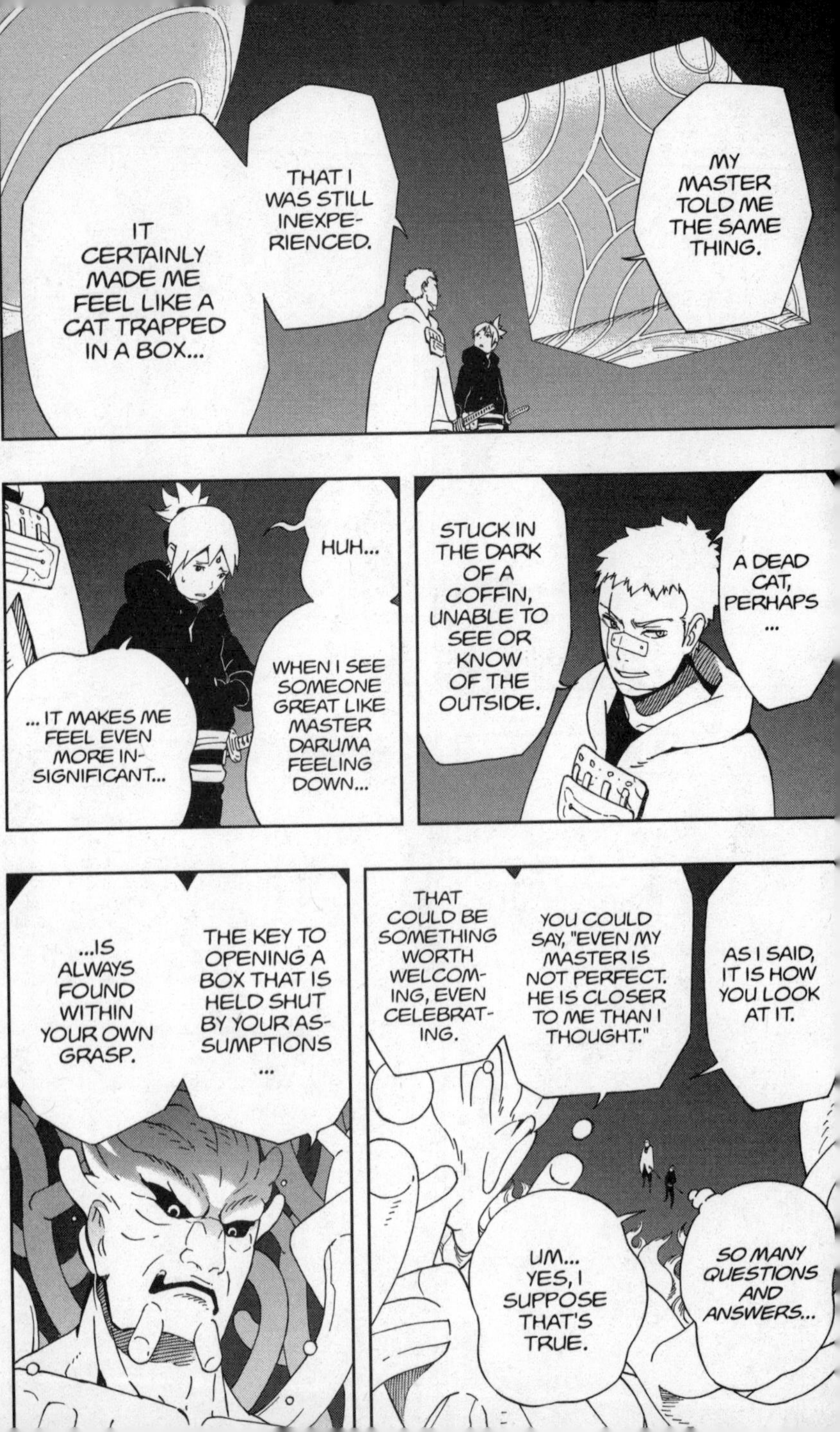
MY MASTER TOLD ME THE SAME THING.
THAT I WAS STILL INEXPERIENCED.
IT CERTAINLY MADE ME FEEL LIKE A CAT TRAPPED IN A BOX...
A DEAD CAT, PERHAPS ...
STUCK IN THE DARK OF A COFFIN, UNABLE TO SEE OR KNOW OF THE OUTSIDE.
HUH...
WHEN I SEE SOMEONE GREAT LIKE MASTER DARUMA FEELING DOWN...
... IT MAKES ME FEEL EVEN MORE INSIGNIFICANT...
AS I SAID, IT IS HOW YOU LOOK AT IT.
YOU COULD SAY, "EVEN MY MASTER IS NOT PERFECT. HE IS CLOSER TO ME THAN I THOUGHT."
THAT COULD BE SOMETHING WORTH WELCOMING, EVEN CELEBRATING.
SO MANY QUESTIONS AND ANSWERS...
UM... YES, I SUPPOSE THAT'S TRUE.
THE KEY TO OPENING A BOX THAT IS HELD SHUT BY YOUR ASSUMPTIONS ...
...IS ALWAYS FOUND WITHIN YOUR OWN GRASP.

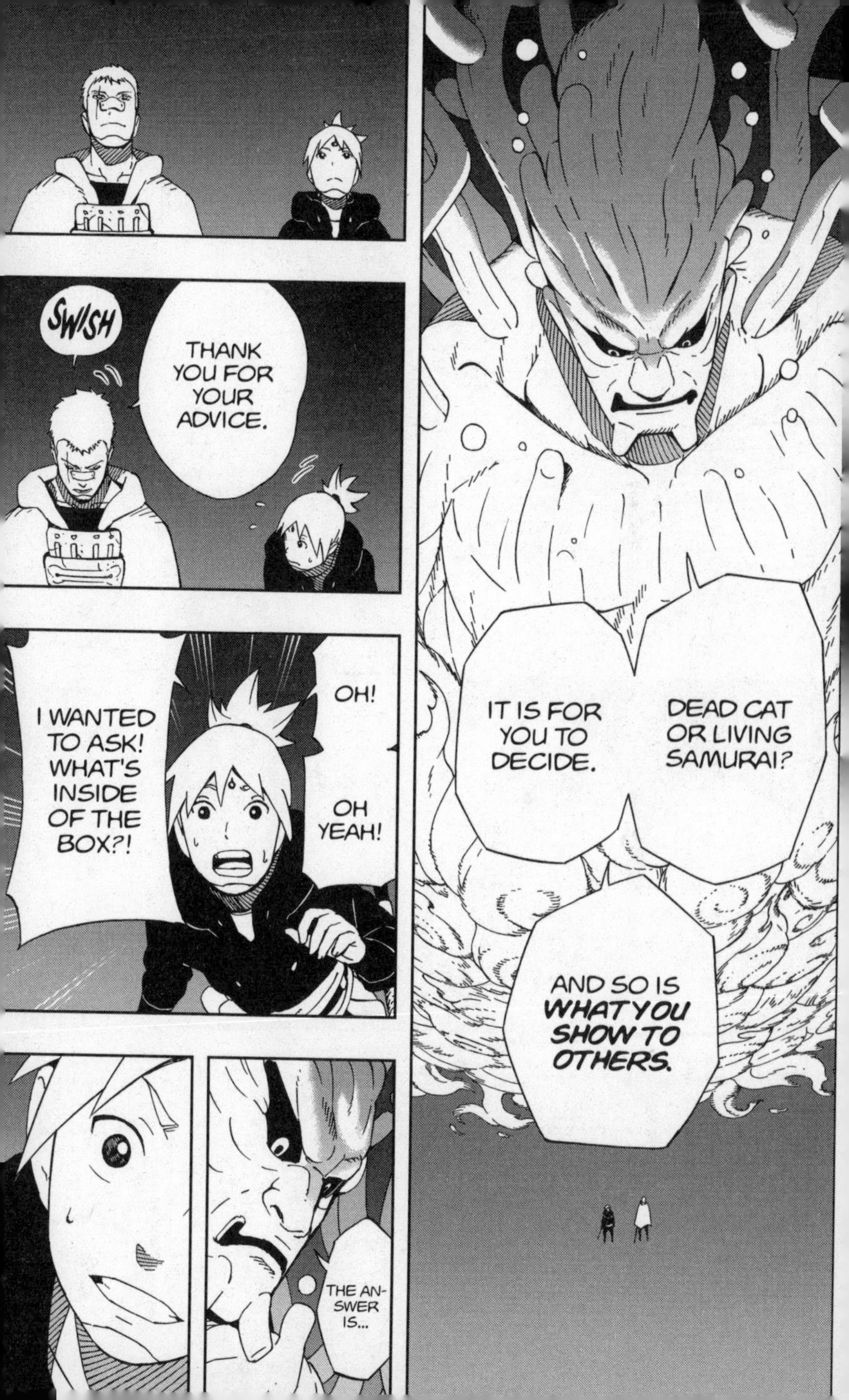
THANK YOU FOR YOUR ADVICE.
SWISH
OH!
OH YEAH!
I WANTED TO ASK! WHAT'S INSIDE OF THE BOX?!
THE AN-SWER IS...
DEAD CAT OR LIVING SAMURAI?
IT IS FOR YOU TO DECIDE.
AND SO IS **WHAT YOU SHOW TO OTHERS.**

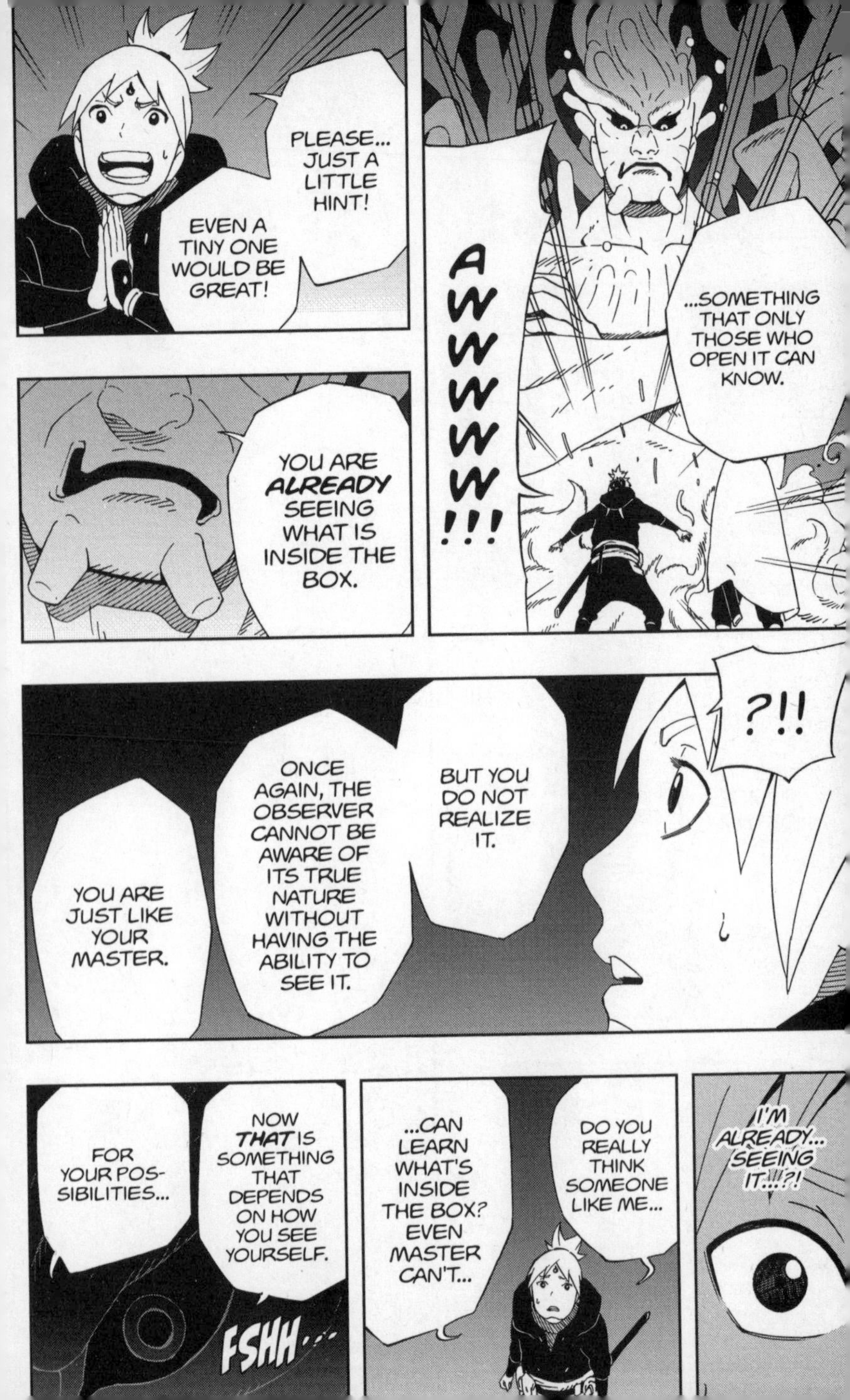

...SOMETHING THAT ONLY THOSE WHO OPEN IT CAN KNOW.
AWWWWWW!!!
PLEASE... JUST A LITTLE HINT!
EVEN A TINY ONE WOULD BE GREAT!
YOU ARE *ALREADY* SEEING WHAT IS INSIDE THE BOX.
?!!
BUT YOU DO NOT REALIZE IT.
ONCE AGAIN, THE OBSERVER CANNOT BE AWARE OF ITS TRUE NATURE WITHOUT HAVING THE ABILITY TO SEE IT.
YOU ARE JUST LIKE YOUR MASTER.
I'M ALREADY... SEEING IT...!?!
DO YOU REALLY THINK SOMEONE LIKE ME...
...CAN LEARN WHAT'S INSIDE THE BOX? EVEN MASTER CAN'T...
NOW *THAT* IS SOMETHING THAT DEPENDS ON HOW YOU SEE YOURSELF.
FOR YOUR POS-SIBILITIES...
FSHH...

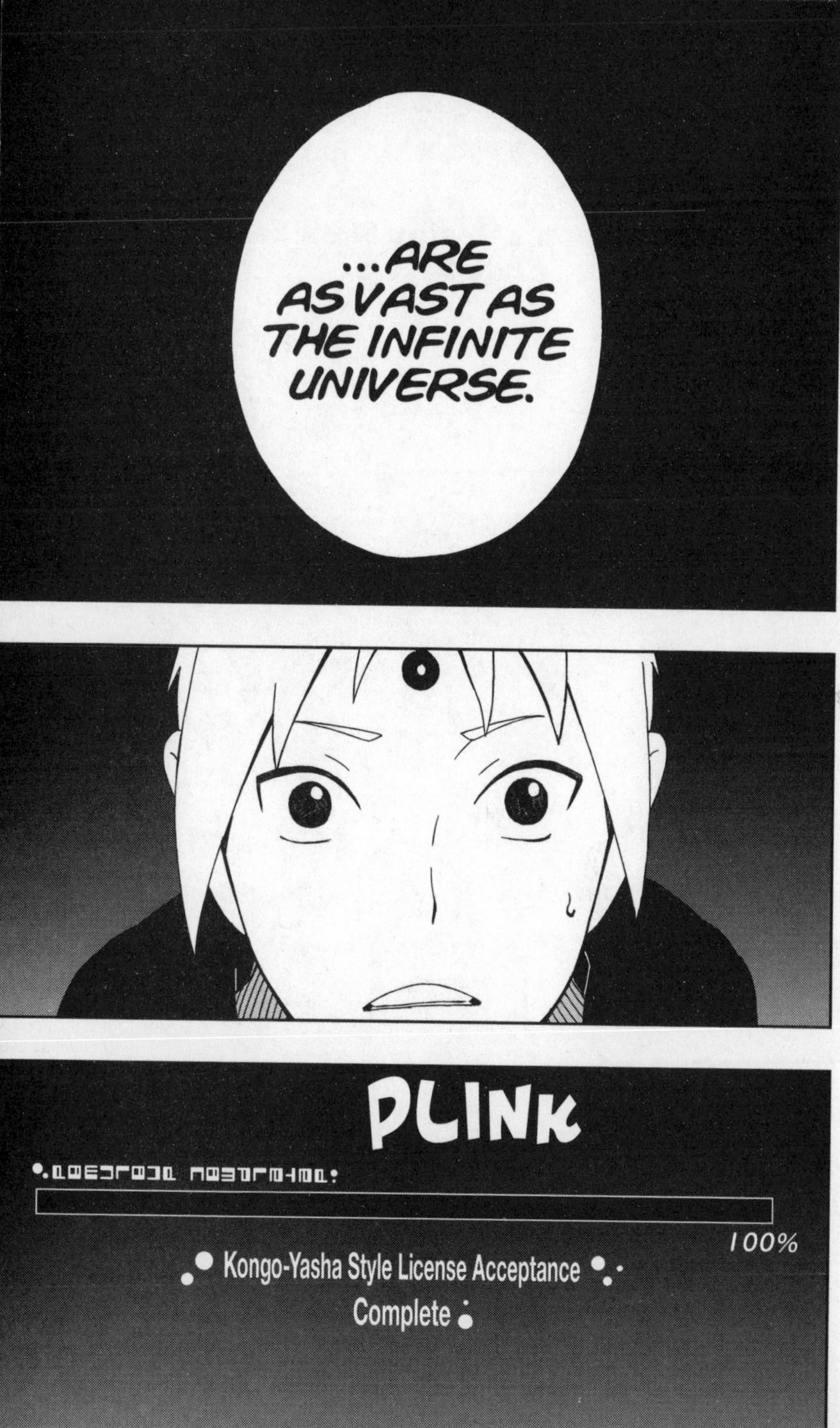
...ARE AS VAST AS THE INFINITE UNIVERSE.
PLINK
100%
Kongo-Yasha Style License Acceptance Complete

Character Design Sketches: Fudo Myo-o

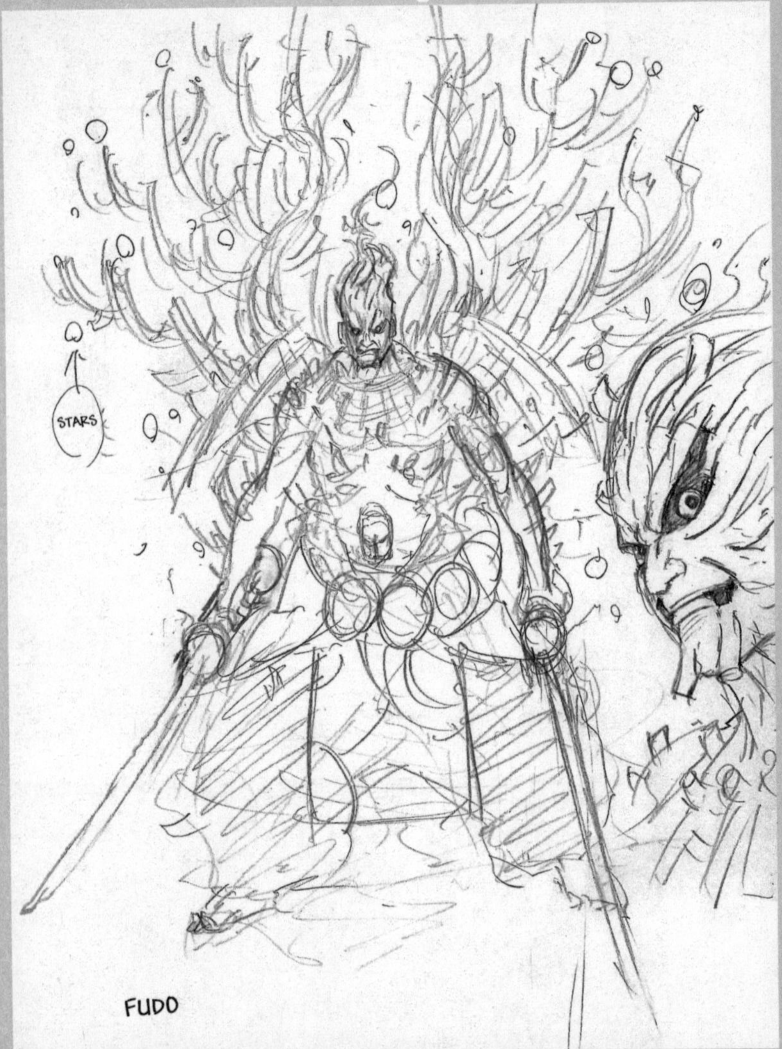
STARS
FUDO

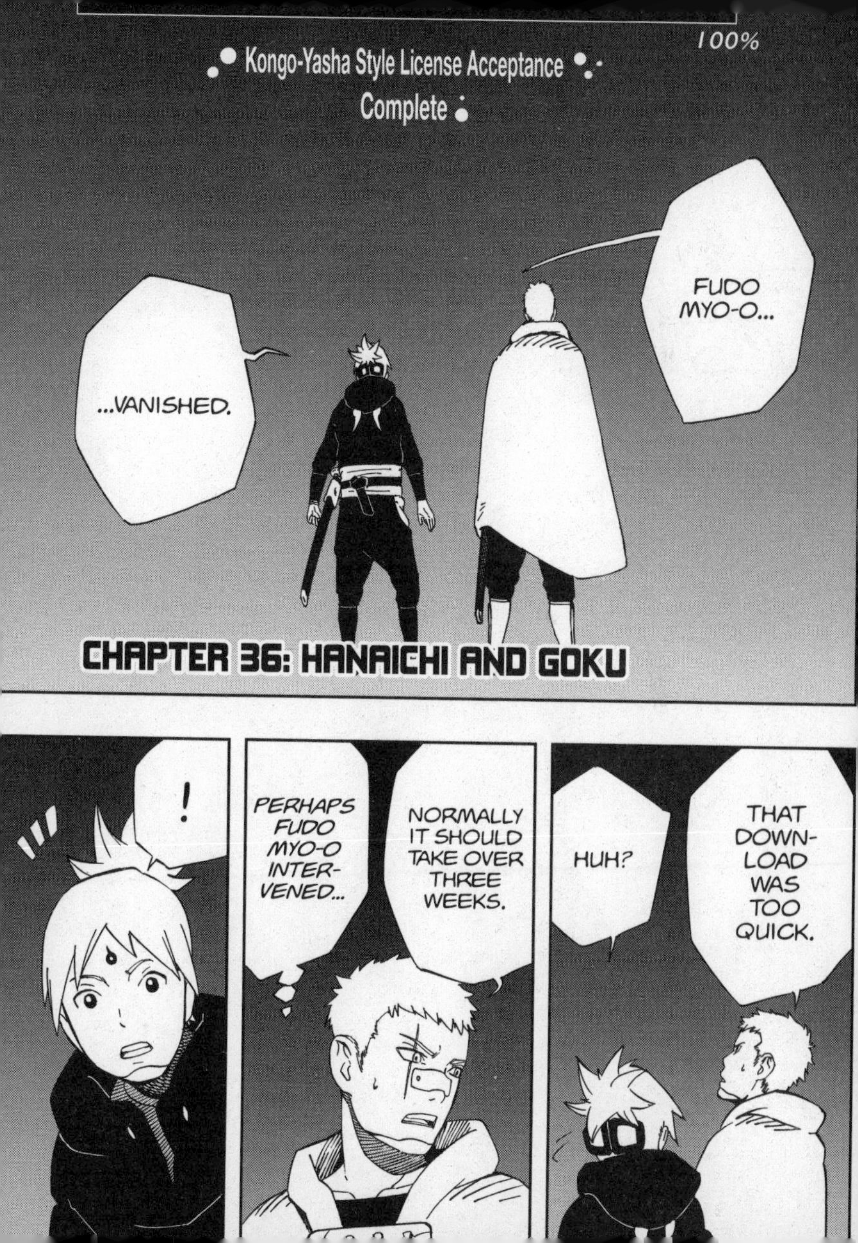
100%
Kongo-Yasha Style License Acceptance Complete
FUDO MYO-O...
...VANISHED.
CHAPTER 36: HANAICHI AND GOKU
THAT DOWNLOAD WAS TOO QUICK.
HUH?
NORMALLY IT SHOULD TAKE OVER THREE WEEKS.
PERHAPS FUDO MYO-O INTERVENED...
!

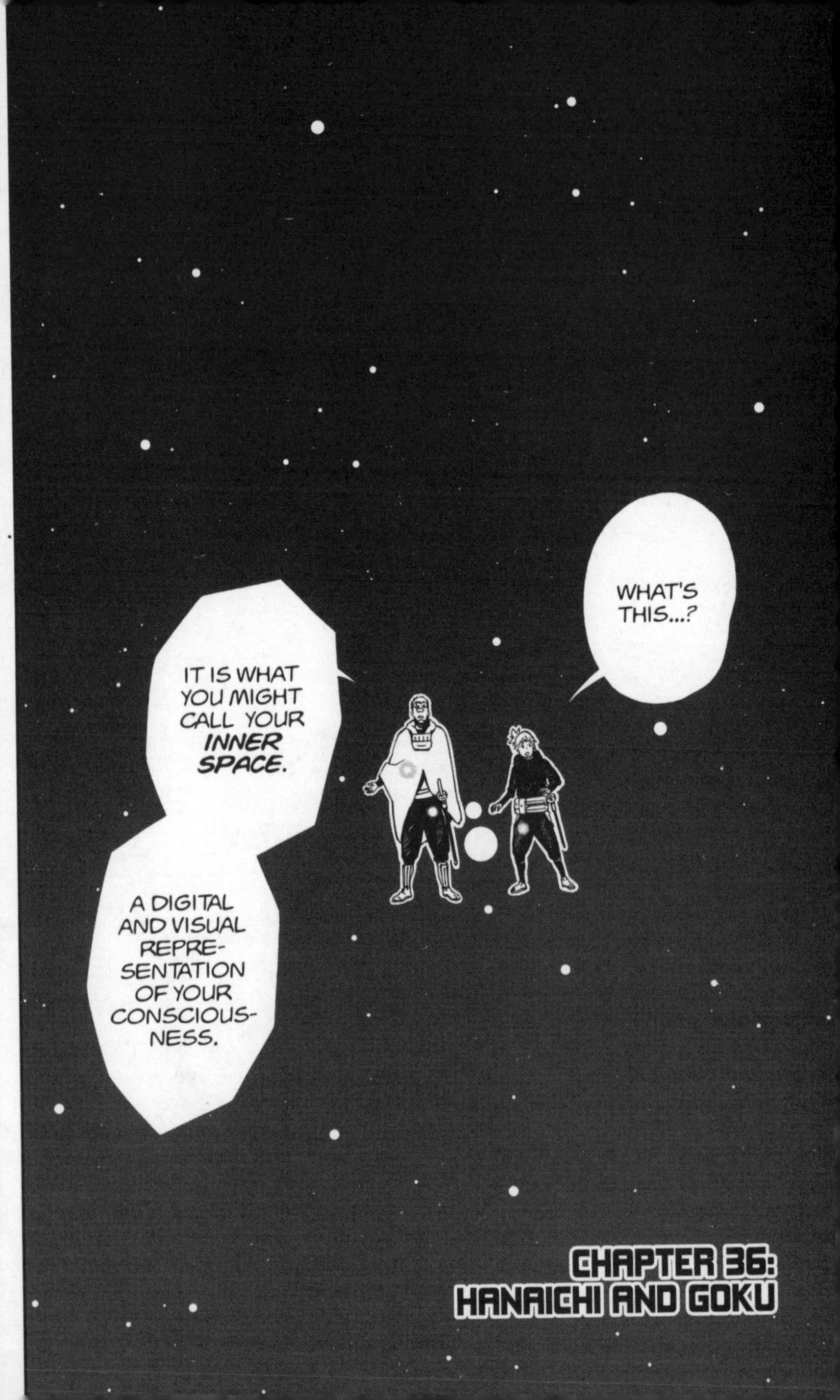
WHAT'S THIS...?
IT IS WHAT YOU MIGHT CALL YOUR *INNER SPACE*.
A DIGITAL AND VISUAL REPRE-SENTATION OF YOUR CONSCIOUS-NESS.
CHAPTER 36: HANAICHI AND GOKU

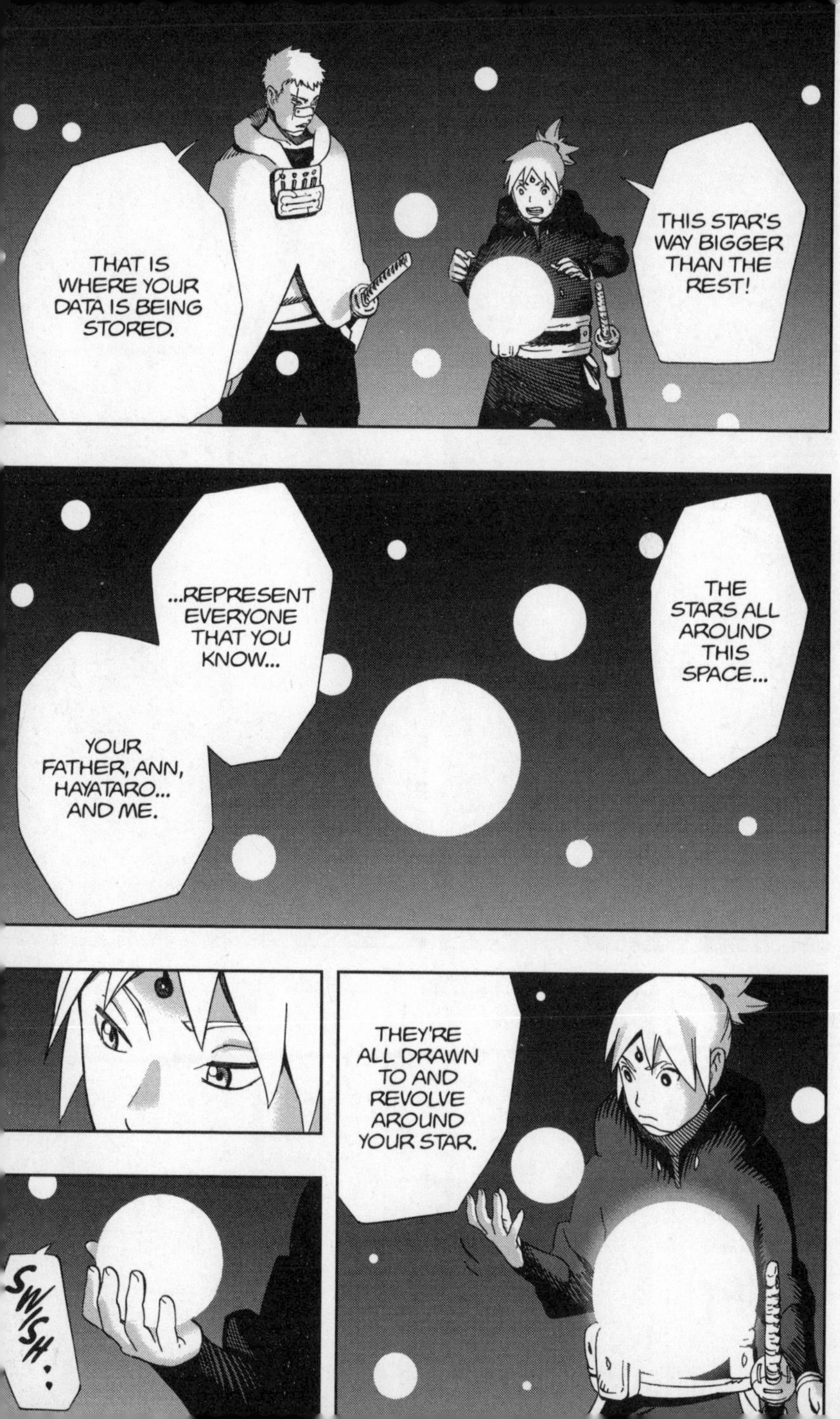
THIS STAR'S WAY BIGGER THAN THE REST!
THAT IS WHERE YOUR DATA IS BEING STORED.
THE STARS ALL AROUND THIS SPACE...
...REPRESENT EVERYONE THAT YOU KNOW...
YOUR FATHER, ANN, HAYATARO... AND ME.
THEY'RE ALL DRAWN TO AND REVOLVE AROUND YOUR STAR.
SWISH..

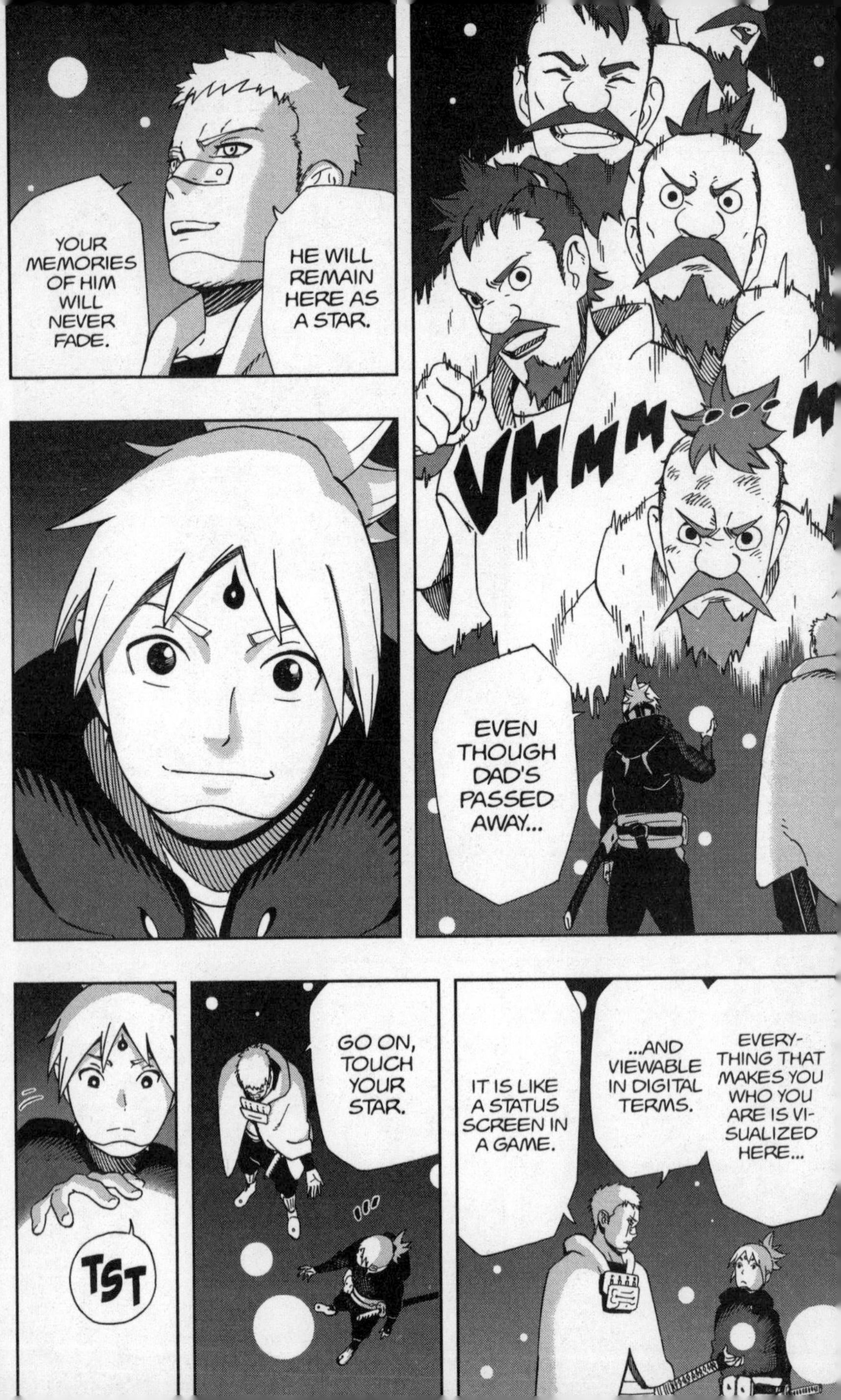
VMMMM...M
EVEN THOUGH DAD'S PASSED AWAY...
HE WILL REMAIN HERE AS A STAR.
YOUR MEMORIES OF HIM WILL NEVER FADE.
EVERY-THING THAT MAKES YOU WHO YOU ARE IS VI-SUALIZED HERE...
...AND VIEWABLE IN DIGITAL TERMS.
IT IS LIKE A STATUS SCREEN IN A GAME.
GO ON, TOUCH YOUR STAR.
TST

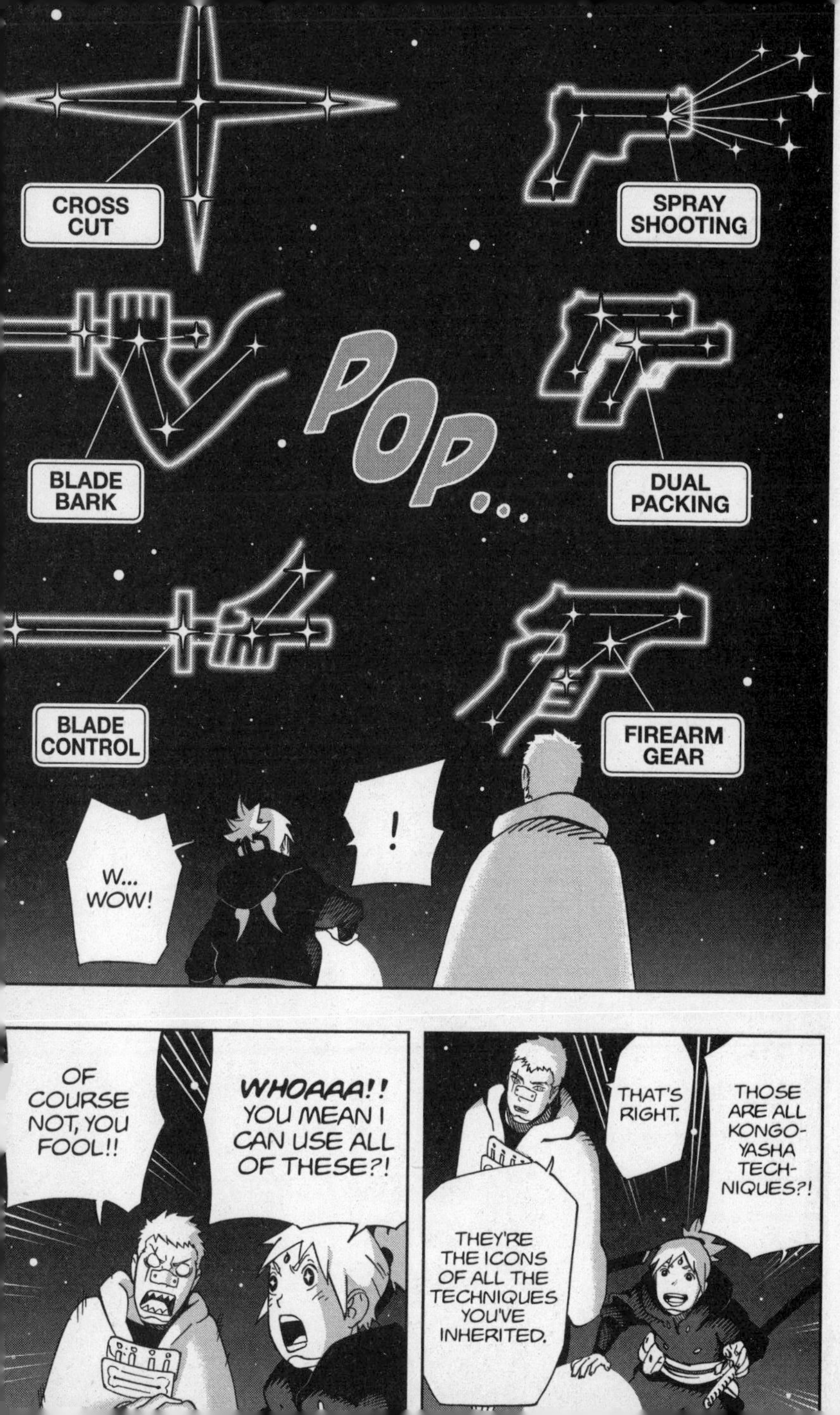
SPRAY SHOOTING
CROSS CUT
DUAL PACKING
BLADE BARK
POP...
FIREARM GEAR
BLADE CONTROL
!
W... WOW!
THOSE ARE ALL KONGO-YASHA TECH-NIQUES?!
THAT'S RIGHT.
THEY'RE THE ICONS OF ALL THE TECHNIQUES YOU'VE INHERITED.
WHOAAA!! YOU MEAN I CAN USE ALL OF THESE?!
OF COURSE NOT, YOU FOOL!!

ATMOS FANGS!

ATMOS FANGS

...THE ONE YOU TAUGHT ME EARLIER...?

UM, THAT SKILL UP THERE... IS THAT...

ALL SKILLS HAVE CERTAIN NECESSARY STATS BEFORE YOU CAN USE THEM.

YOU'VE ONLY *INHERITED* THE SKILLS, NOT *LEARNED* THEM.

THESE ARE THE STATISTICS YOU NEED IN ORDER TO USE ATMOS FANGS.

GLOW

BEEP

ATMOS FANGS

CHOPSCOTCH

Strength	900
Speed	900
Intelligence	900
Technical Sense	900
Gravity	900
Key Holder	900
Heroism	900
Charisma	0
Stress	900

LET'S TRY THAT ONE. LIFT YOUR HAND AND HOLD IT IN FRONT OF THE ATMOS FANGS CONSTELLATION.

SLASH GLOW

A FA

SWISH

...ONLY THEN WILL YOU GAIN USE OF ATMOS FANGS.

WHEN YOUR TRAINING HAS PUSHED ALL OF YOUR STATISTICS ABOVE A VALUE OF 900...

THEY'RE ALL 900, ASIDE FROM CHARISMA...

OHHHH...

THE REASON YOU WERE ABLE TO ACTIVATE THE TECHNIQUE BEFORE...

...IS BECAUSE YOU WERE LINKED TO MY KEY, AND I HAVE LEARNED ATMOS FANGS.

I HAVE SO FAR TO GO...

COMPARE THESE NUMBERS TO YOUR OWN NOW.

BUT IF YOUR STATS GO BEYOND 900, ITS POWER WILL INCREASE.

AND EVEN ONCE YOU HAVE LEARNED IT, IF ANY OF YOUR STATS EVER DIP BELOW 900...

...THEN THE TECHNIQUE MAY BE WEAKER, OR NOT ACTIVATE AT ALL.

Samurai: Hachimaru	
Strength — 7	Strength — 900
Speed — 12	Speed — 900
Intelligence — 33	Intelligence — 900
Technical Sense — 18	Technical Sense — 900
Gravity — 80,000	Gravity — 900
Key Holder — 35	Key Holder — 900
Heroism — 8	Heroism — 900
Charisma — 0	Charisma — 0
Key Life — 1,200	Stress — 900

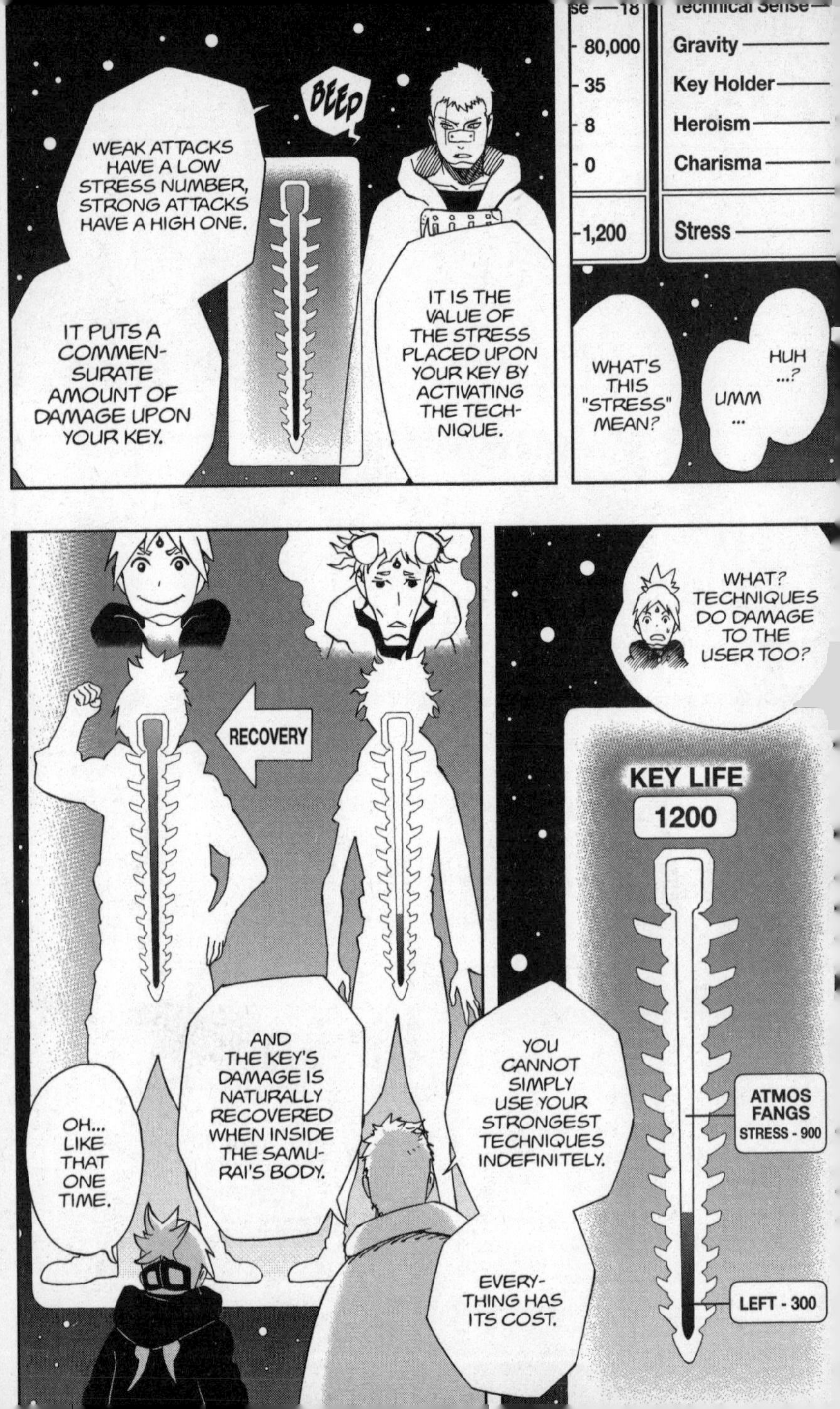
se — 18
Technical Sense
80,000
Gravity
35
Key Holder
8
Heroism
0
Charisma
1,200
Stress
HUH ...?
UMM ...
WHAT'S THIS "STRESS" MEAN?
BEEP
IT IS THE VALUE OF THE STRESS PLACED UPON YOUR KEY BY ACTIVATING THE TECHNIQUE.
IT PUTS A COMMENSURATE AMOUNT OF DAMAGE UPON YOUR KEY.
WEAK ATTACKS HAVE A LOW STRESS NUMBER, STRONG ATTACKS HAVE A HIGH ONE.
WHAT? TECHNIQUES DO DAMAGE TO THE USER TOO?
KEY LIFE
1200
ATMOS FANGS
STRESS - 900
LEFT - 300
YOU CANNOT SIMPLY USE YOUR STRONGEST TECHNIQUES INDEFINITELY.
EVERYTHING HAS ITS COST.
RECOVERY
AND THE KEY'S DAMAGE IS NATURALLY RECOVERED WHEN INSIDE THE SAMURAI'S BODY.
OH... LIKE THAT ONE TIME.

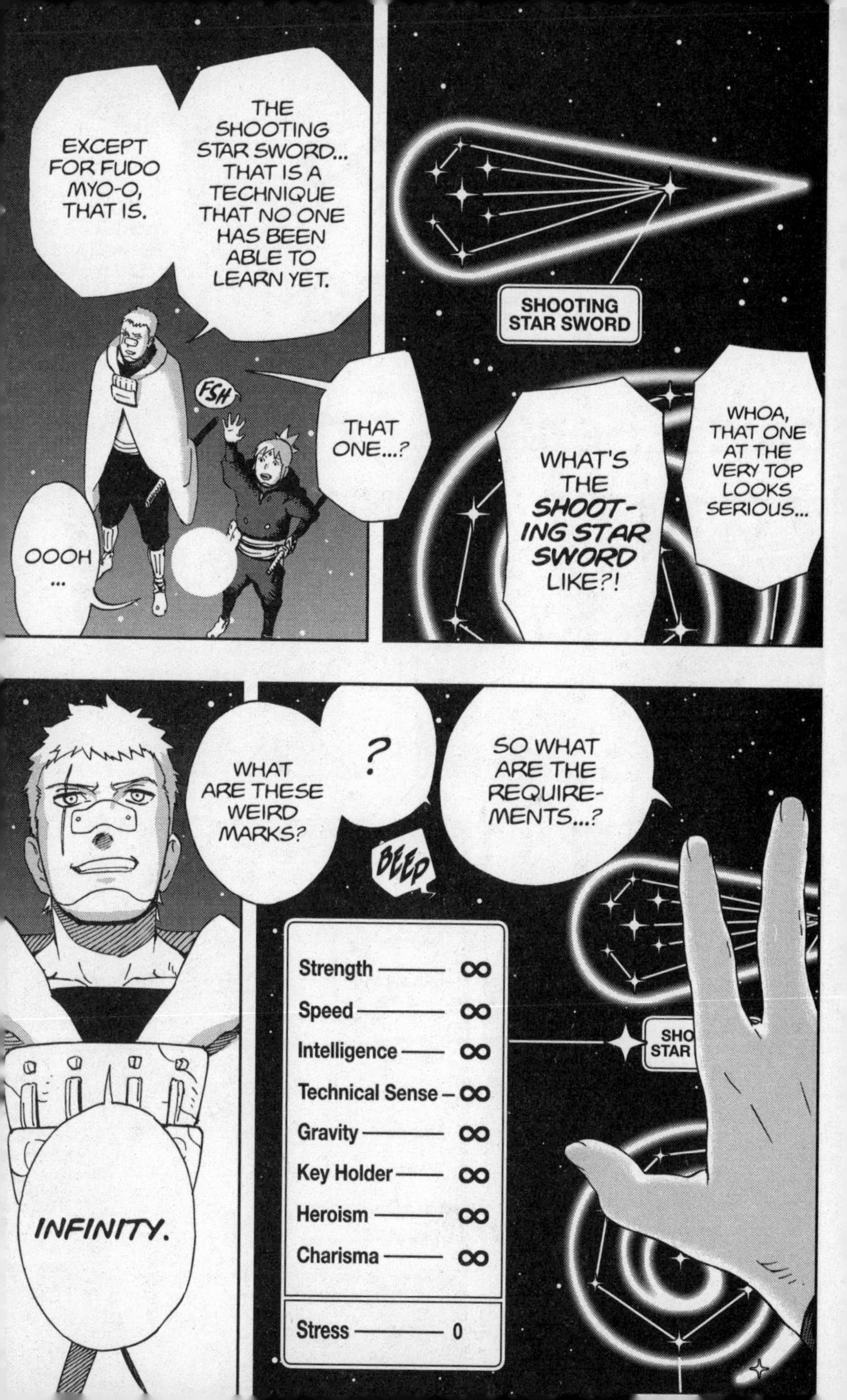
SHOOTING STAR SWORD
WHOA, THAT ONE AT THE VERY TOP LOOKS SERIOUS...
WHAT'S THE *SHOOTING STAR SWORD* LIKE?!
THE SHOOTING STAR SWORD... THAT IS A TECHNIQUE THAT NO ONE HAS BEEN ABLE TO LEARN YET.
EXCEPT FOR FUDO MYO-O, THAT IS.
THAT ONE...?
FSH
OOOH ...
SO WHAT ARE THE REQUIRE-MENTS...?
?
WHAT ARE THESE WEIRD MARKS?
BEEP
Strength — ∞
Speed — ∞
Intelligence — ∞
Technical Sense — ∞
Gravity — ∞
Key Holder — ∞
Heroism — ∞
Charisma — ∞
Stress — 0
INFINITY.

ength ———————— ∞

eed ———————— ∞

ellig ———————— ∞

IN OTHER WORDS, IT IS IMPOSSIBLE TO OBTAIN.

chnical Sense — ∞

TO UNLOCK THIS TECHNIQUE, YOU MUST HAVE INFINITE STAT VALUES.

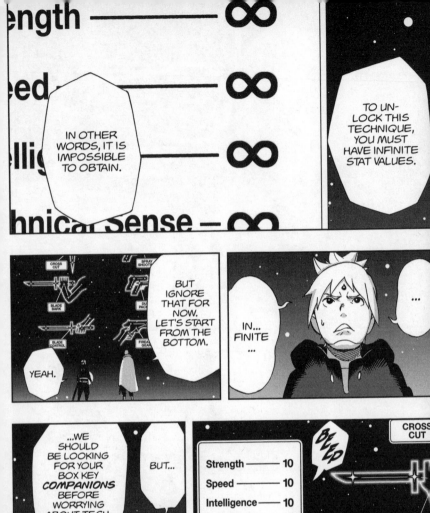

BUT IGNORE THAT FOR NOW. LET'S START FROM THE BOTTOM.

YEAH.

IN... FINITE...

...

CROSS CUT

SPRAY SHOOT

BLADE BARK

DU... PAC...

BLADE CONTROL

FIREA... GEAR

...WE SHOULD BE LOOKING FOR YOUR BOX KEY **COMPANIONS** BEFORE WORRYING ABOUT TECHNIQUES.

BUT...

BEEP

CROSS CUT

Strength	10
Speed	10
Intelligence	10
Technical Sense	10
Gravity	10
Key Holder	10
Heroism	10
Charisma	0
Stress	10

BLADE BARK

SO IT LOOKS LIKE THE BEST I CAN DO RIGHT NOW IS...BLADE BARK.

BLADE CONTROL

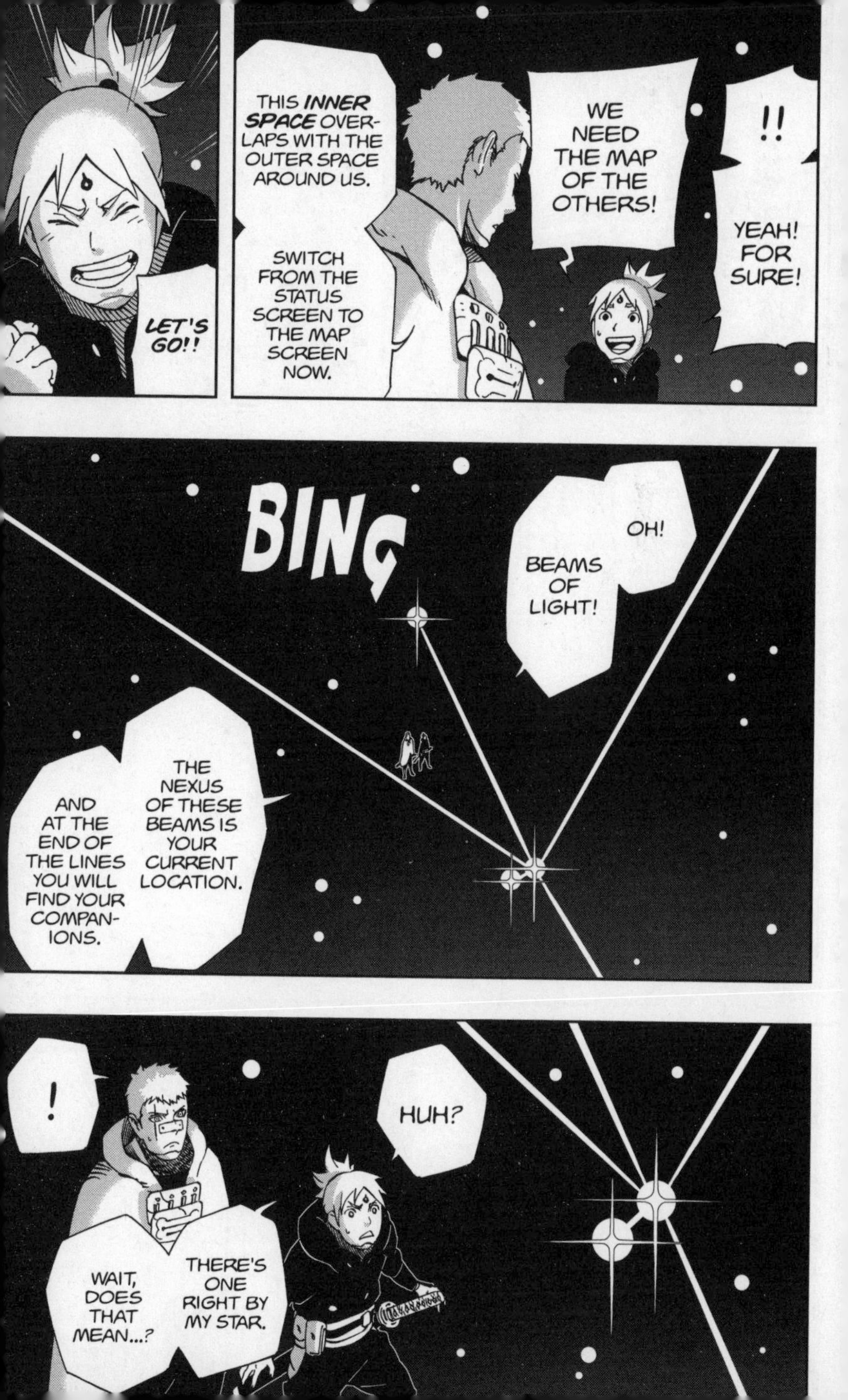
!!
YEAH! FOR SURE!
WE NEED THE MAP OF THE OTHERS!
THIS *INNER SPACE* OVER-LAPS WITH THE OUTER SPACE AROUND US.
SWITCH FROM THE STATUS SCREEN TO THE MAP SCREEN NOW.
LET'S GO!!
BING
OH!
BEAMS OF LIGHT!
THE NEXUS OF THESE BEAMS IS YOUR CURRENT LOCATION.
AND AT THE END OF THE LINES YOU WILL FIND YOUR COMPAN-IONS.
HUH?
!
THERE'S ONE RIGHT BY MY STAR.
WAIT, DOES THAT MEAN...?

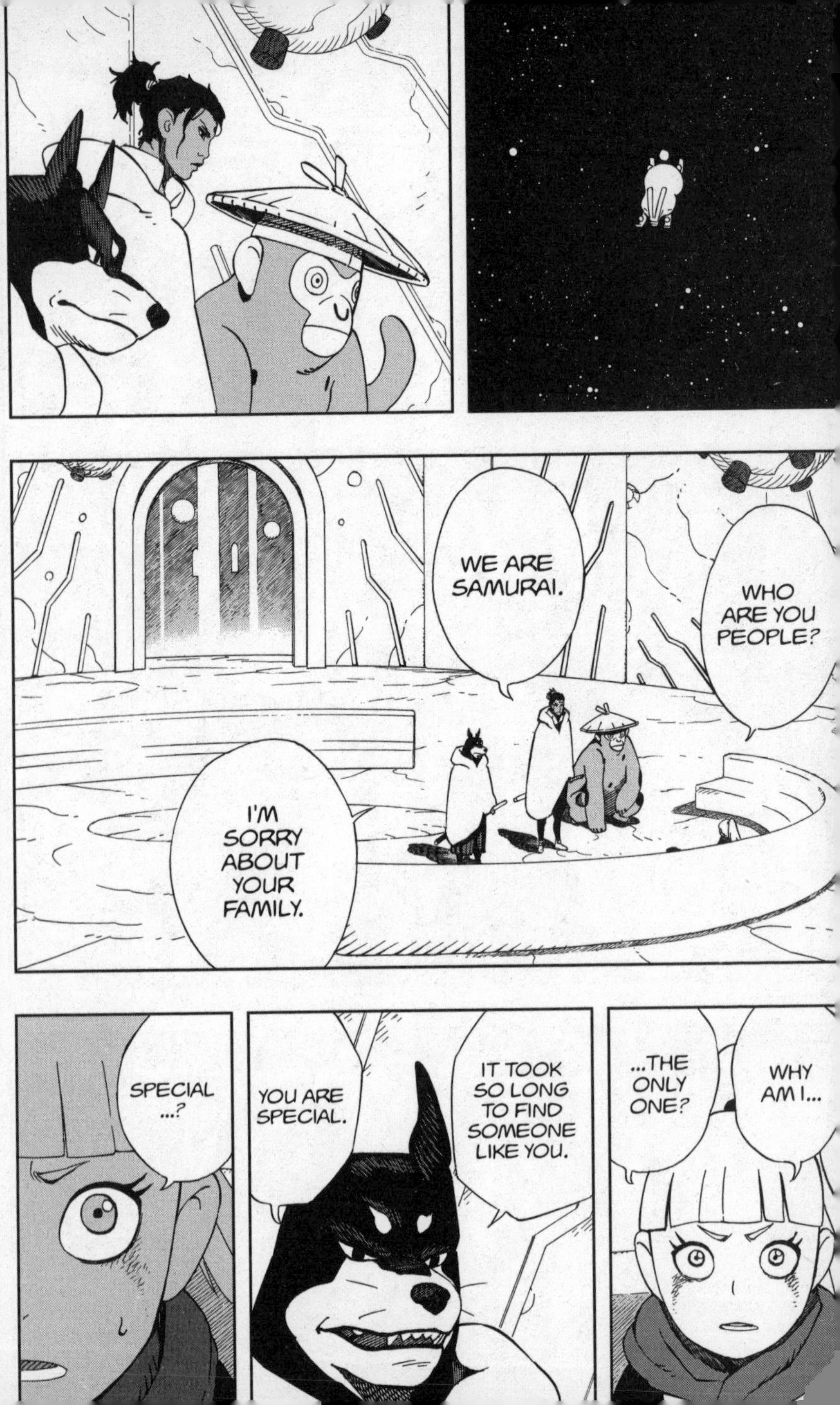
WHO ARE YOU PEOPLE?
WE ARE SAMURAI.
I'M SORRY ABOUT YOUR FAMILY.
WHY AM I...
...THE ONLY ONE?
IT TOOK SO LONG TO FIND SOMEONE LIKE YOU.
YOU ARE SPECIAL.
SPECIAL ...?

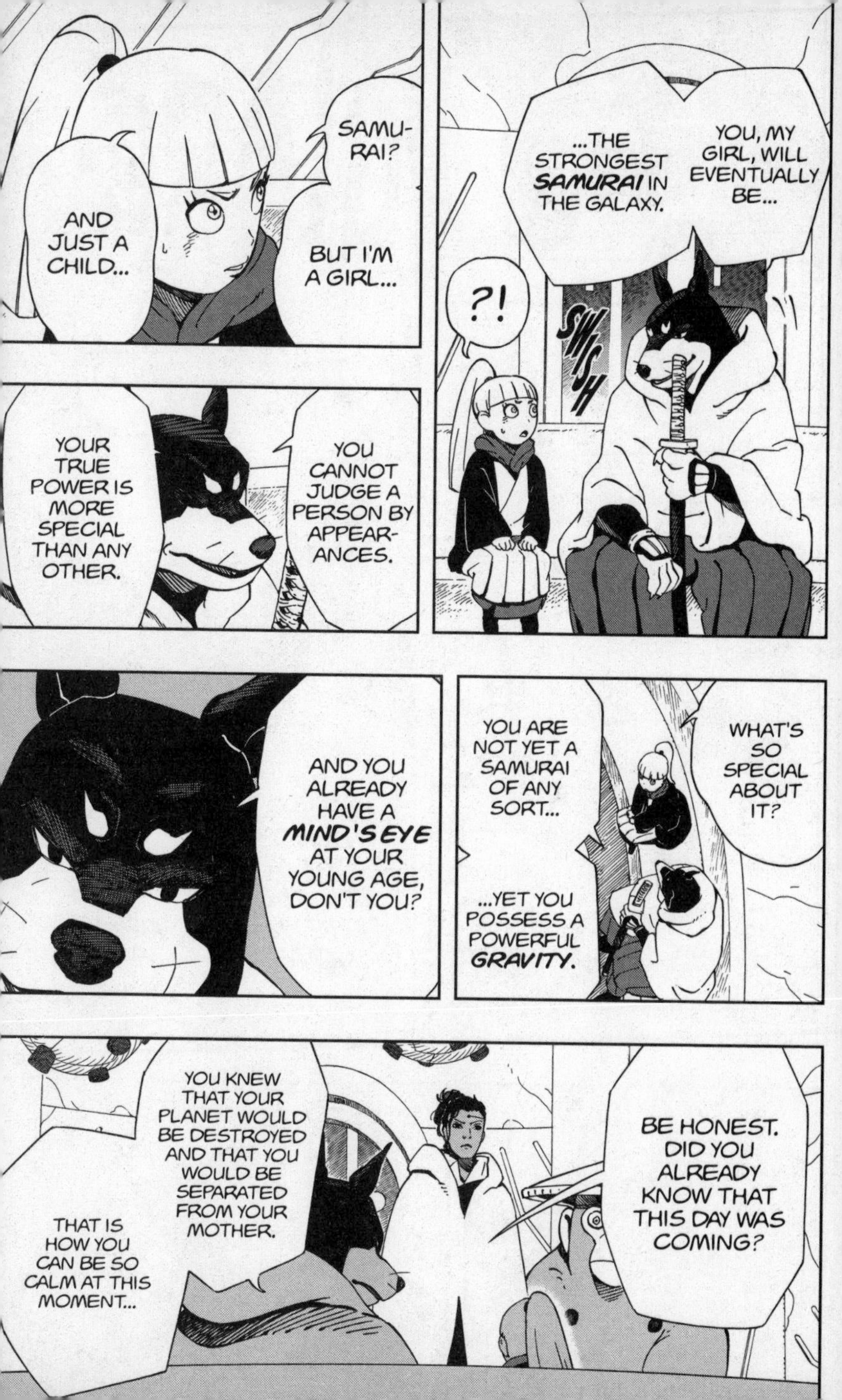
YOU, MY GIRL, WILL EVENTUALLY BE...
...THE STRONGEST SAMURAI IN THE GALAXY.
?!
SWISH
SAMURAI?
BUT I'M A GIRL...
AND JUST A CHILD...
YOU CANNOT JUDGE A PERSON BY APPEARANCES.
YOUR TRUE POWER IS MORE SPECIAL THAN ANY OTHER.
WHAT'S SO SPECIAL ABOUT IT?
YOU ARE NOT YET A SAMURAI OF ANY SORT...
...YET YOU POSSESS A POWERFUL GRAVITY.
AND YOU ALREADY HAVE A MIND'S EYE AT YOUR YOUNG AGE, DON'T YOU?
BE HONEST. DID YOU ALREADY KNOW THAT THIS DAY WAS COMING?
YOU KNEW THAT YOUR PLANET WOULD BE DESTROYED AND THAT YOU WOULD BE SEPARATED FROM YOUR MOTHER.
THAT IS HOW YOU CAN BE SO CALM AT THIS MOMENT...

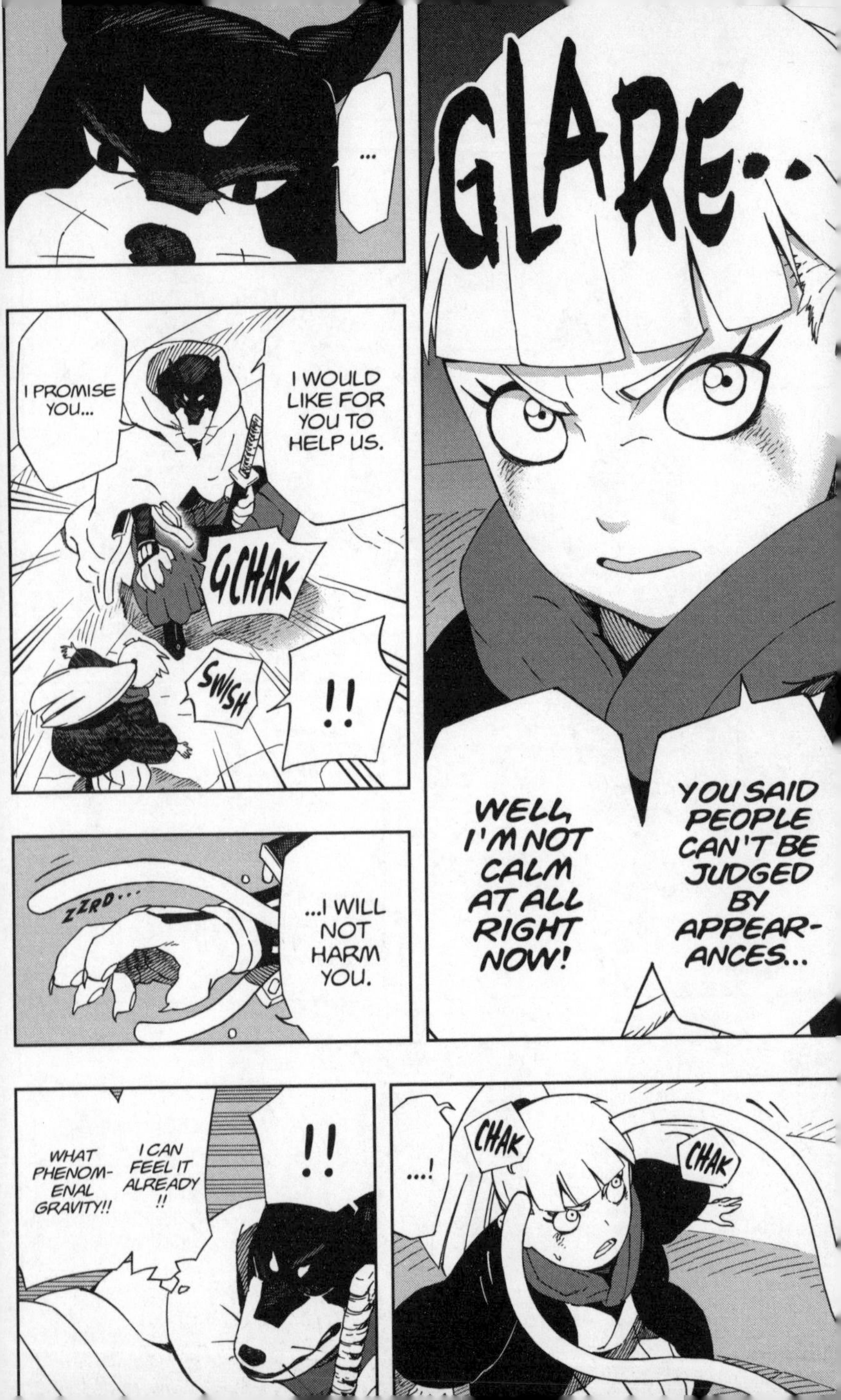
GLARE...
YOU SAID PEOPLE CAN'T BE JUDGED BY APPEARANCES...
WELL, I'M NOT CALM AT ALL RIGHT NOW!
...
I WOULD LIKE FOR YOU TO HELP US.
I PROMISE YOU...
GCHAK
!!
SWISH
...I WILL NOT HARM YOU.
ZZRD...
CHAK
CHAK
...!
!!
I CAN FEEL IT ALREADY!!
WHAT PHENOMENAL GRAVITY!!

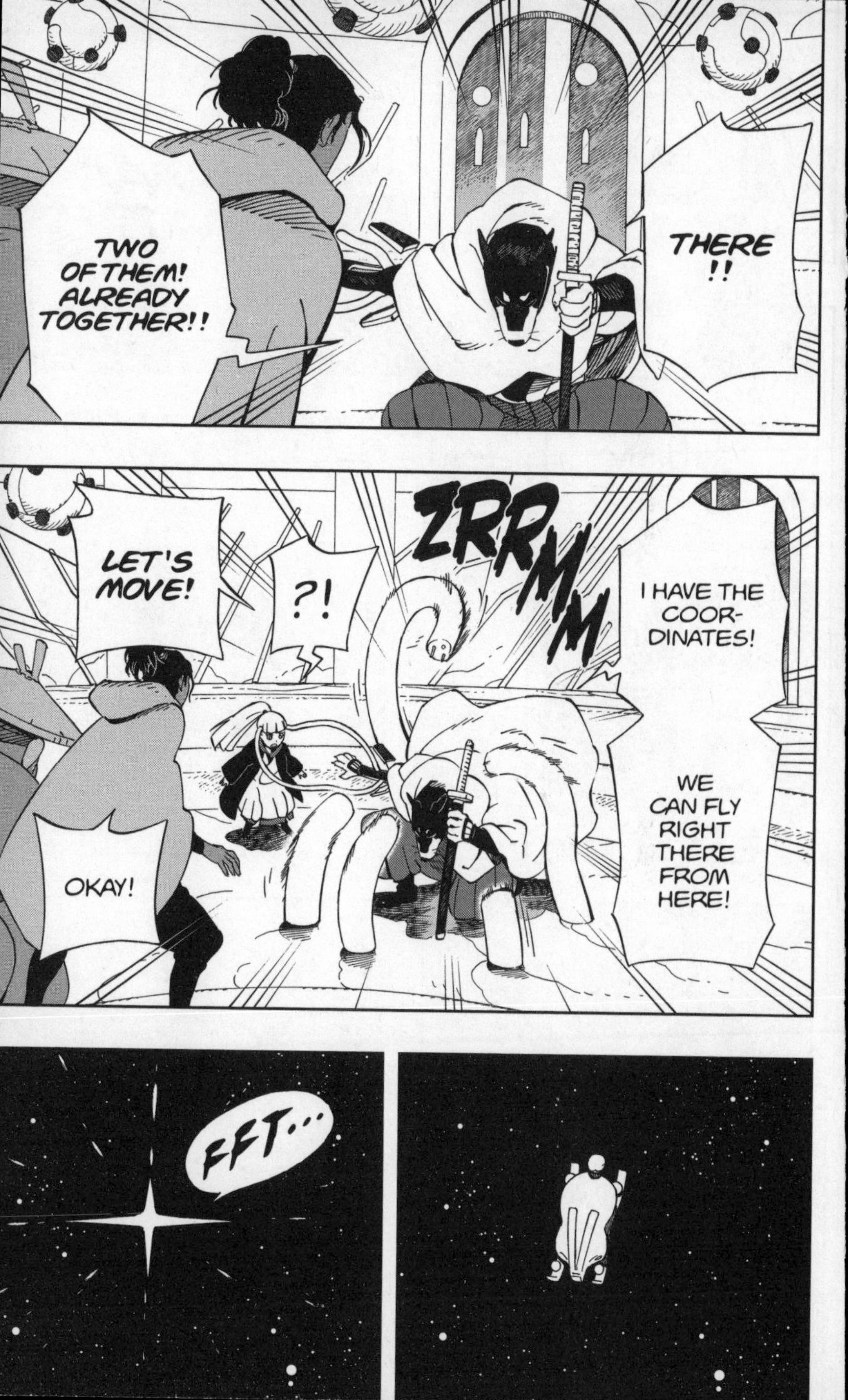
THERE !!
TWO OF THEM! ALREADY TOGETHER!!
I HAVE THE COOR-DINATES!
WE CAN FLY RIGHT THERE FROM HERE!
ZRRMMM
?!
LET'S MOVE!
OKAY!
FFT...

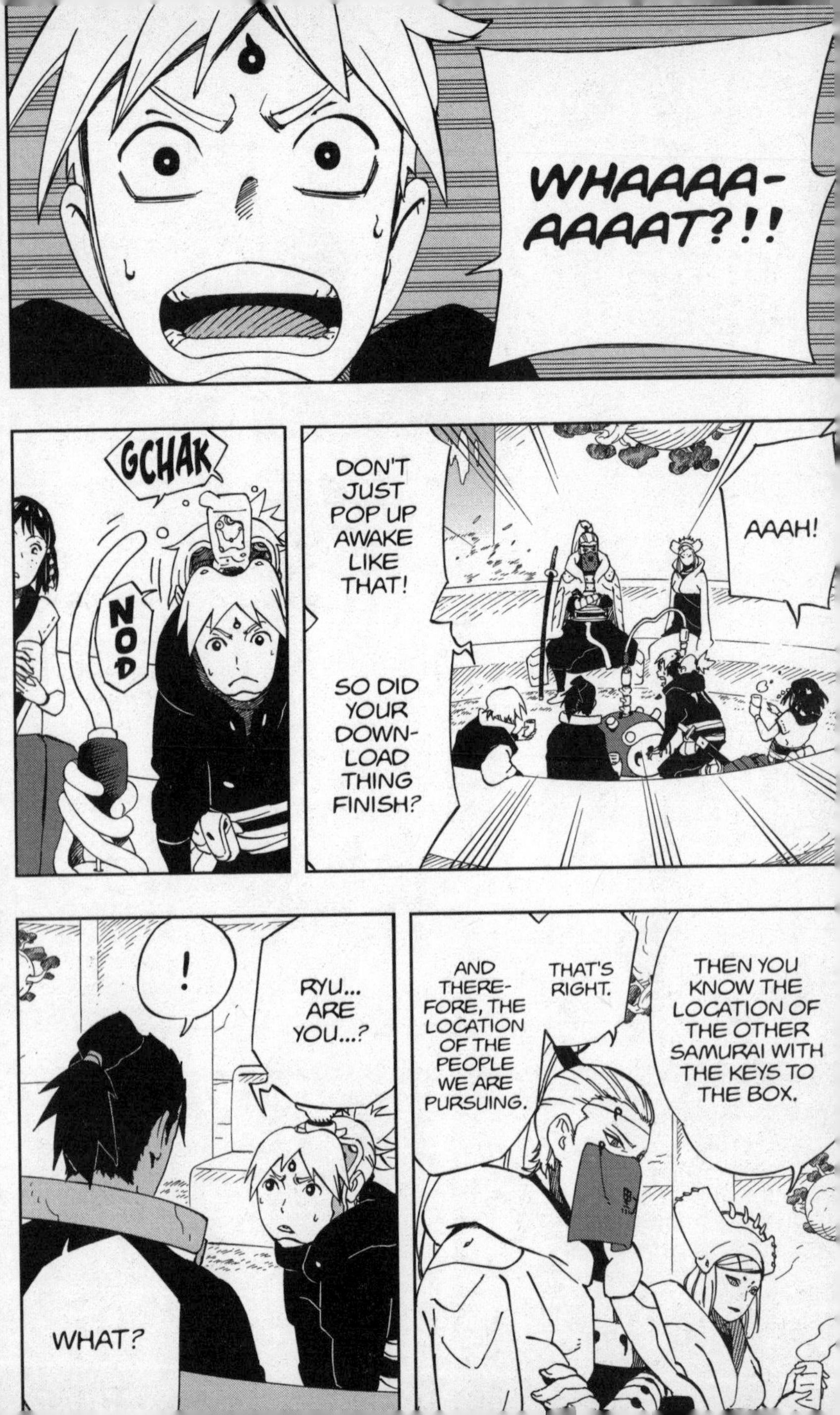
WHAAAA-AAAAT?!!
AAAH!
DON'T JUST POP UP AWAKE LIKE THAT!
SO DID YOUR DOWN-LOAD THING FINISH?
GCHAK
NOD
THEN YOU KNOW THE LOCATION OF THE OTHER SAMURAI WITH THE KEYS TO THE BOX.
THAT'S RIGHT.
AND THERE-FORE, THE LOCATION OF THE PEOPLE WE ARE PURSUING.
RYU... ARE YOU...?
!
WHAT?

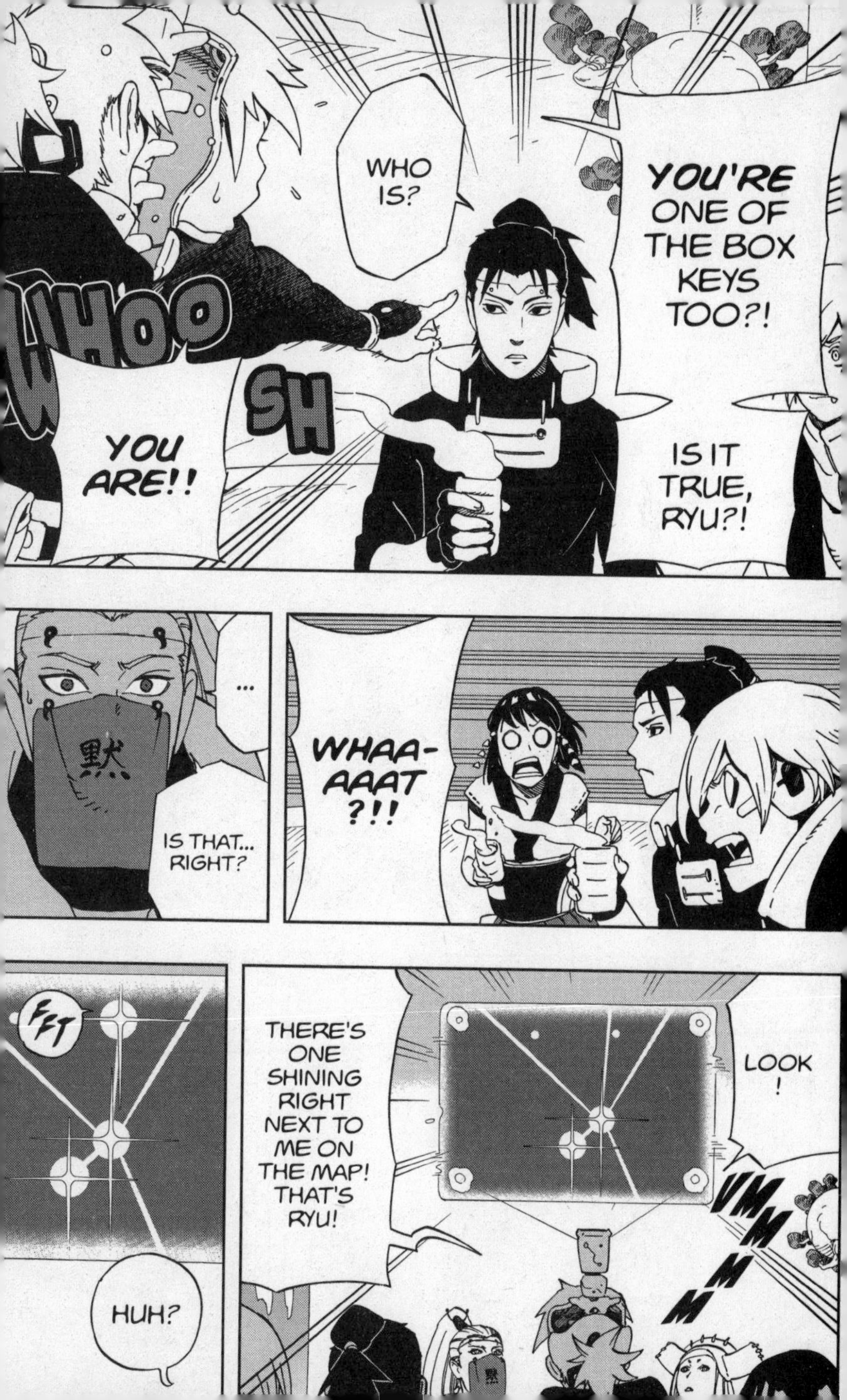
YOU'RE ONE OF THE BOX KEYS TOO?!
IS IT TRUE, RYU?!
WHO IS?
YOU ARE!!
WHOOSH
WHAA-AAAT?!!
...
默
IS THAT... RIGHT?
LOOK!
VMMMMM
THERE'S ONE SHINING RIGHT NEXT TO ME ON THE MAP! THAT'S RYU!
FFT
HUH?

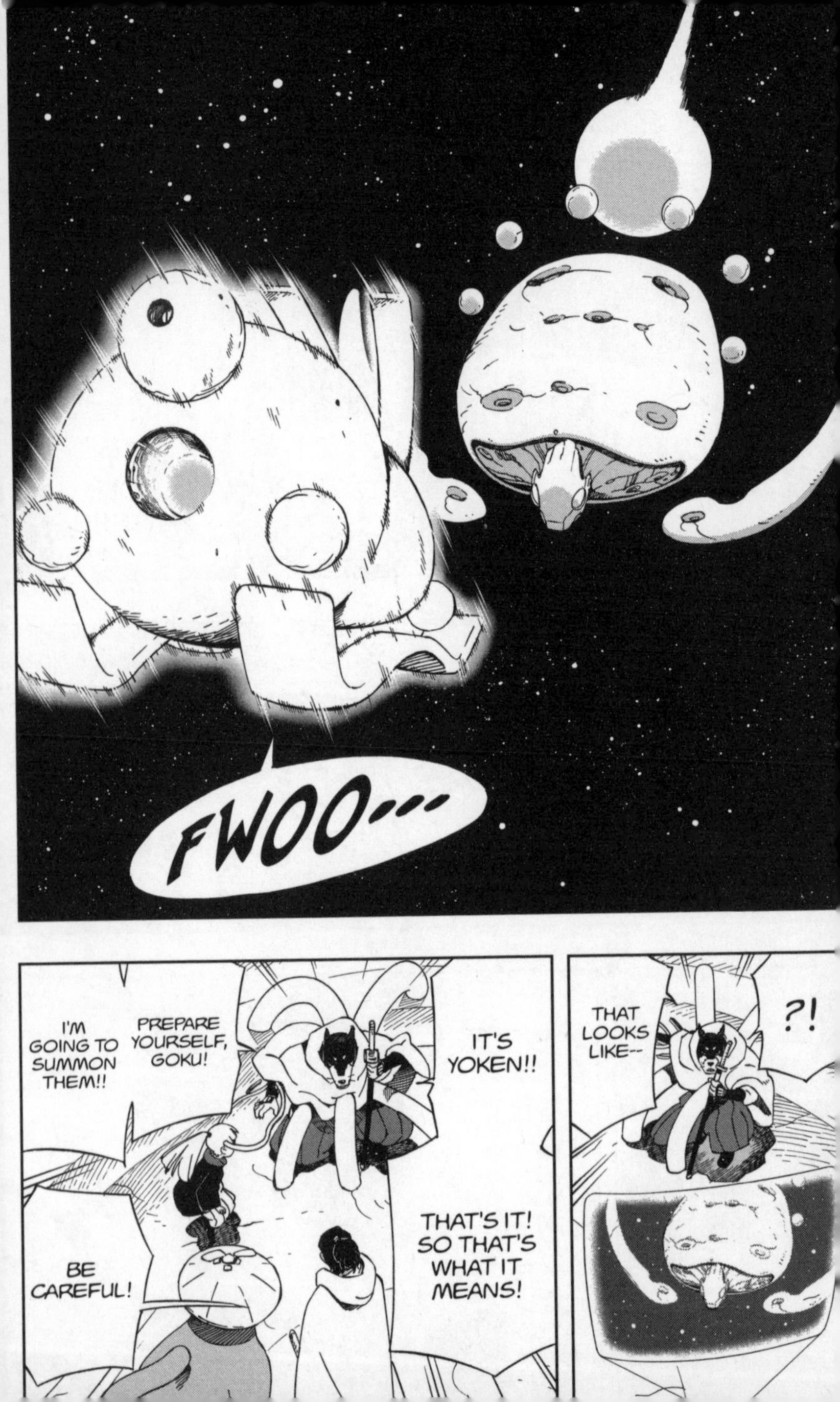
FWOO...
?!
THAT LOOKS LIKE--
IT'S YOKEN!!
PREPARE YOURSELF, GOKU!
I'M GOING TO SUMMON THEM!!
THAT'S IT! SO THAT'S WHAT IT MEANS!
BE CAREFUL!

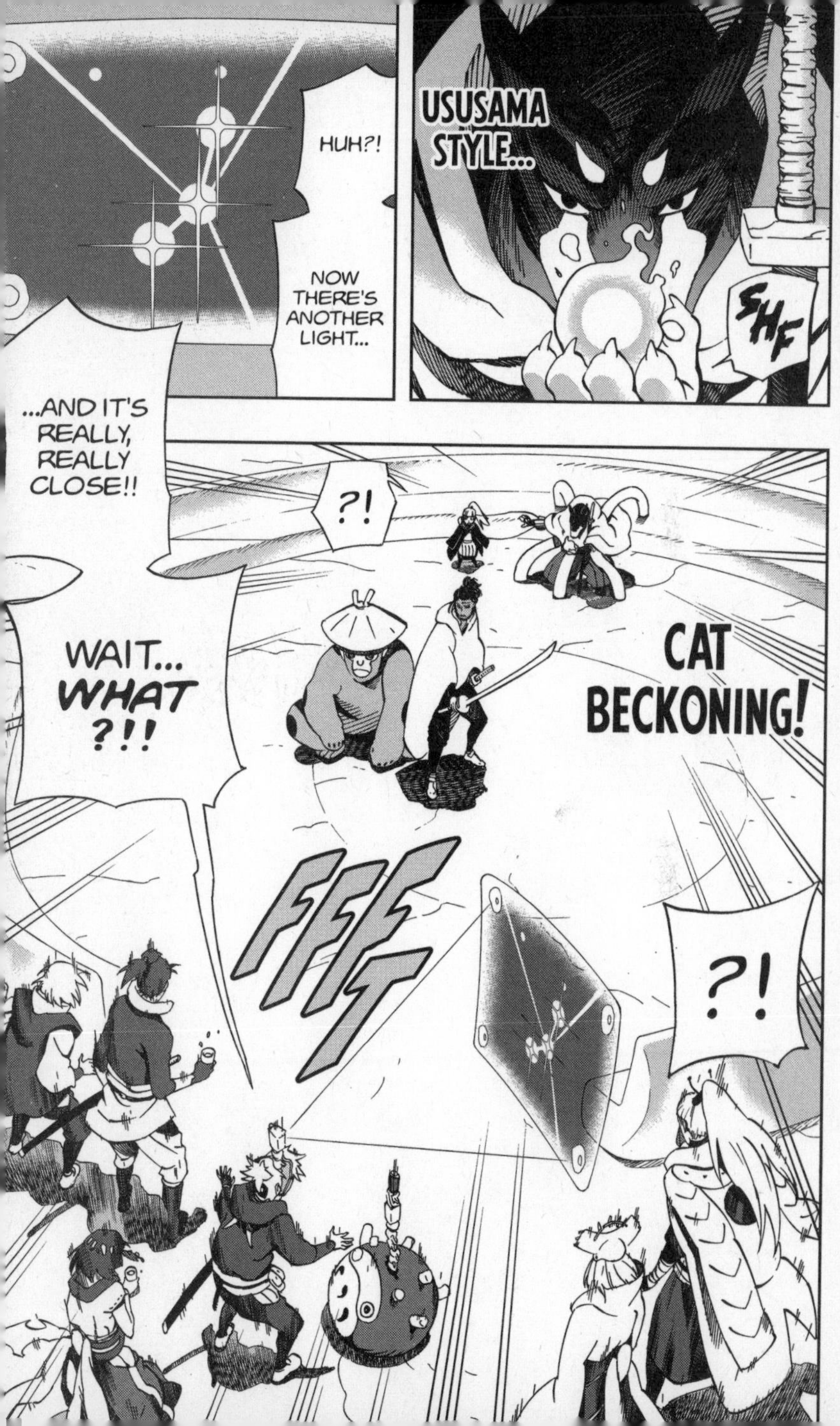
USUSAMA STYLE...
SHF
HUH?!
NOW THERE'S ANOTHER LIGHT...
...AND IT'S REALLY, REALLY CLOSE!!
?!
CAT BECKONING!
WAIT... WHAT?!!
FFFT
?!

Pre-Series Rough Designs (Okubo)

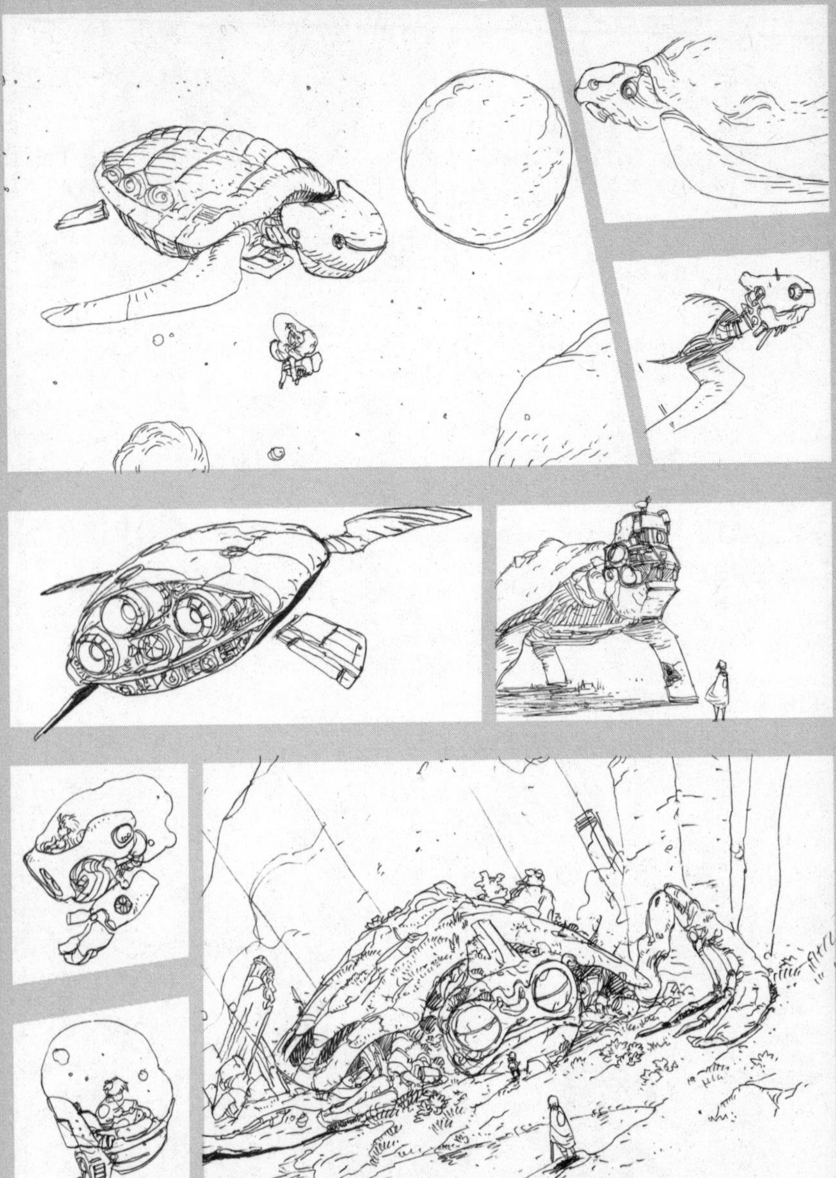

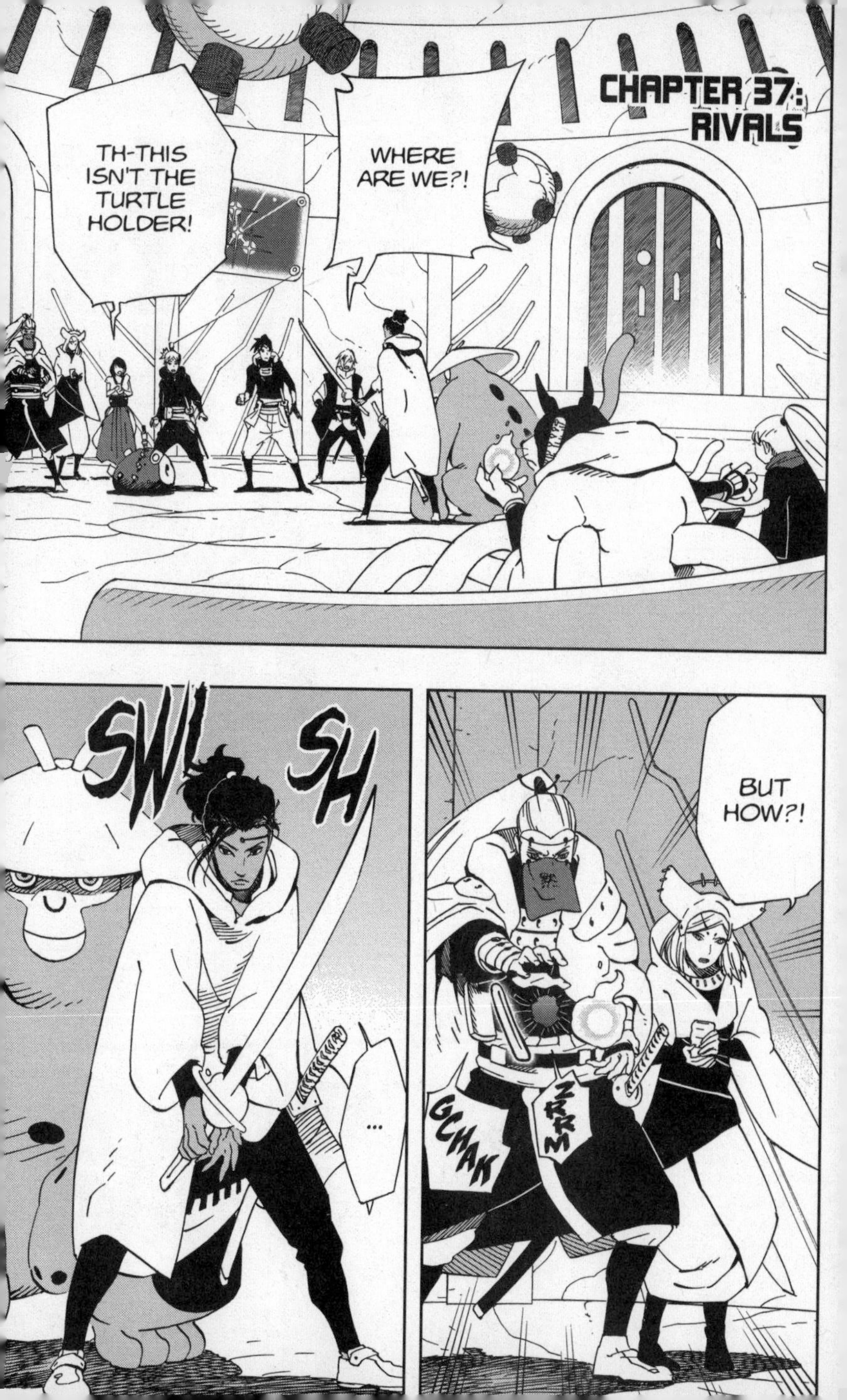
CHAPTER 37: RIVALS
WHERE ARE WE?!
TH-THIS ISN'T THE TURTLE HOLDER!
BUT HOW?!
ZRRM
GCHAK
SWISH
...

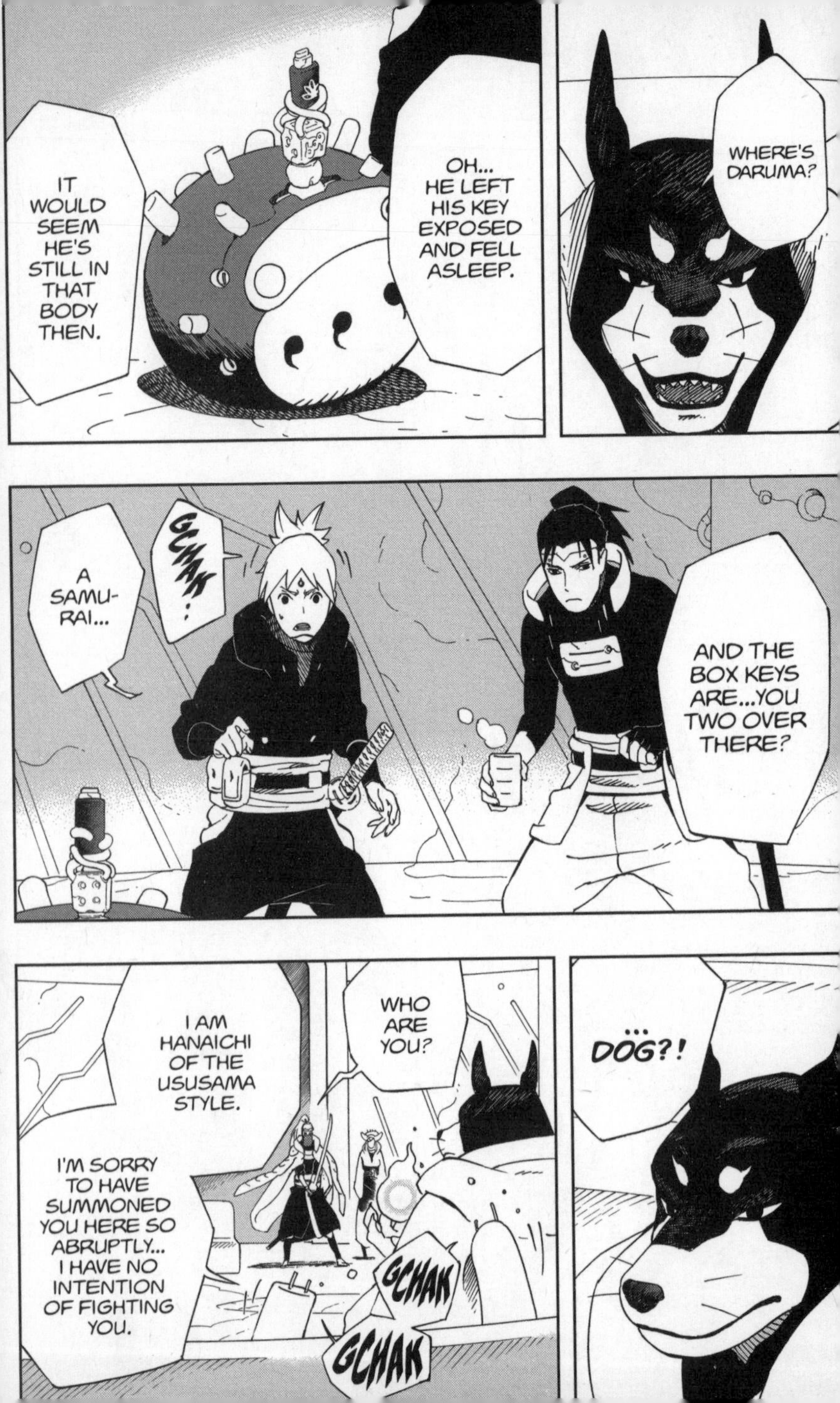
WHERE'S DARUMA?
OH... HE LEFT HIS KEY EXPOSED AND FELL ASLEEP.
IT WOULD SEEM HE'S STILL IN THAT BODY THEN.
AND THE BOX KEYS ARE...YOU TWO OVER THERE?
GCHAK
A SAMU-RAI...
...DOG?!
WHO ARE YOU?
I AM HANAICHI OF THE USUSAMA STYLE.
I'M SORRY TO HAVE SUMMONED YOU HERE SO ABRUPTLY... I HAVE NO INTENTION OF FIGHTING YOU.
GCHAK
GCHAK

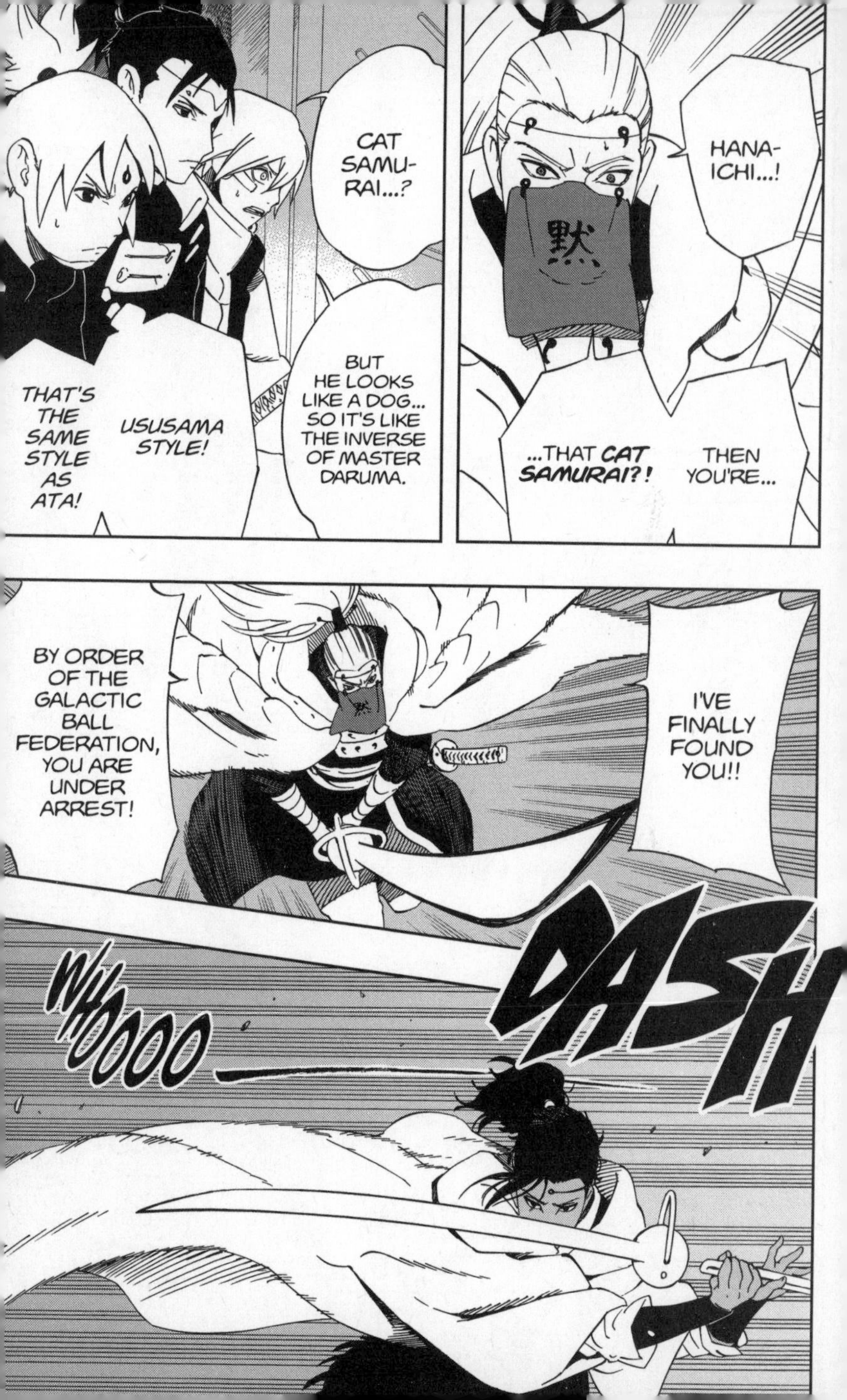
HANA-ICHI...!
THEN YOU'RE...
...THAT CAT SAMURAI?!
CAT SAMU-RAI...?
BUT HE LOOKS LIKE A DOG... SO IT'S LIKE THE INVERSE OF MASTER DARUMA.
USUSAMA STYLE!
THAT'S THE SAME STYLE AS ATA!
I'VE FINALLY FOUND YOU!!
BY ORDER OF THE GALACTIC BALL FEDERATION, YOU ARE UNDER ARREST!
DASH
WHOOOO

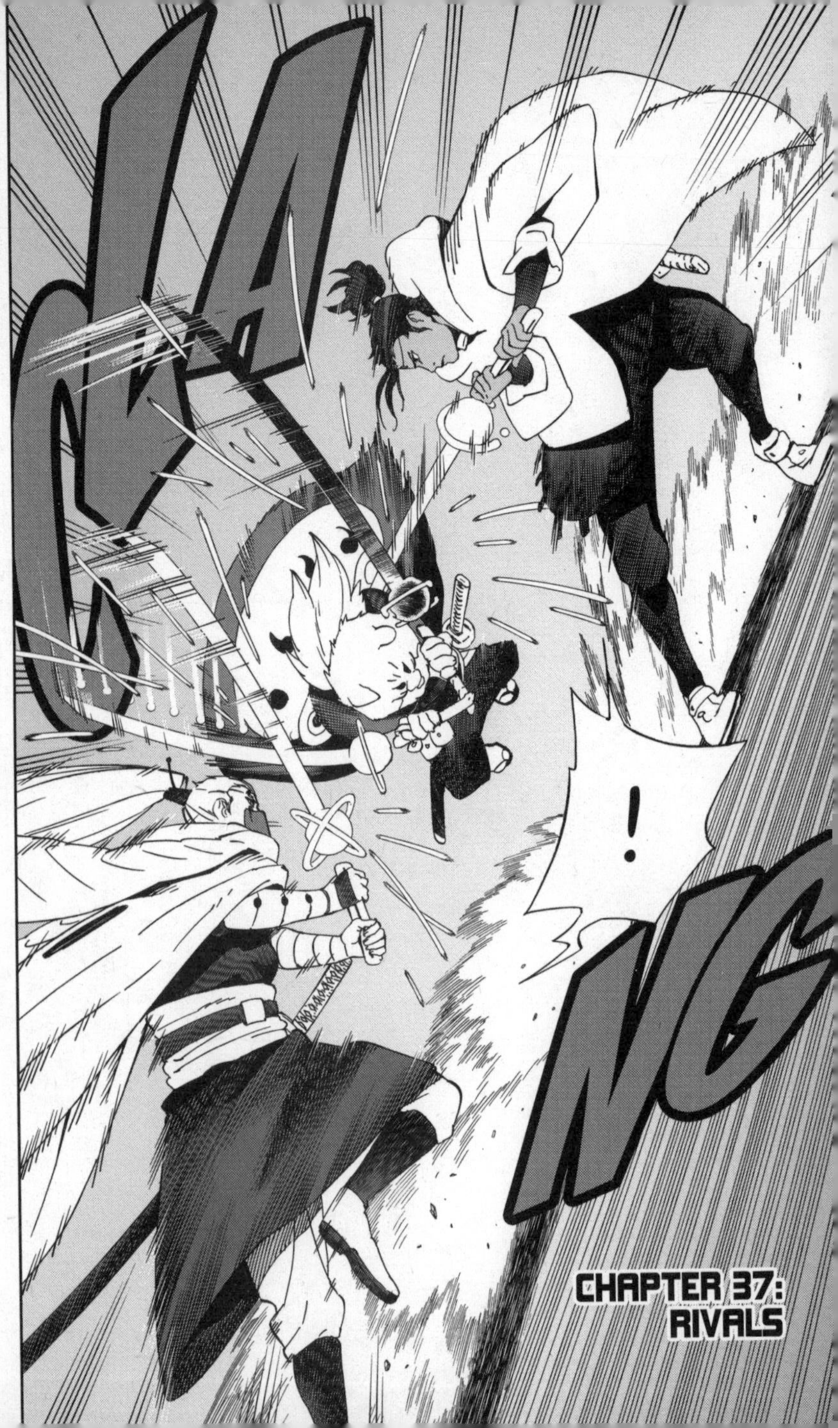

CLA
!
NG
CHAPTER 37:
RIVALS

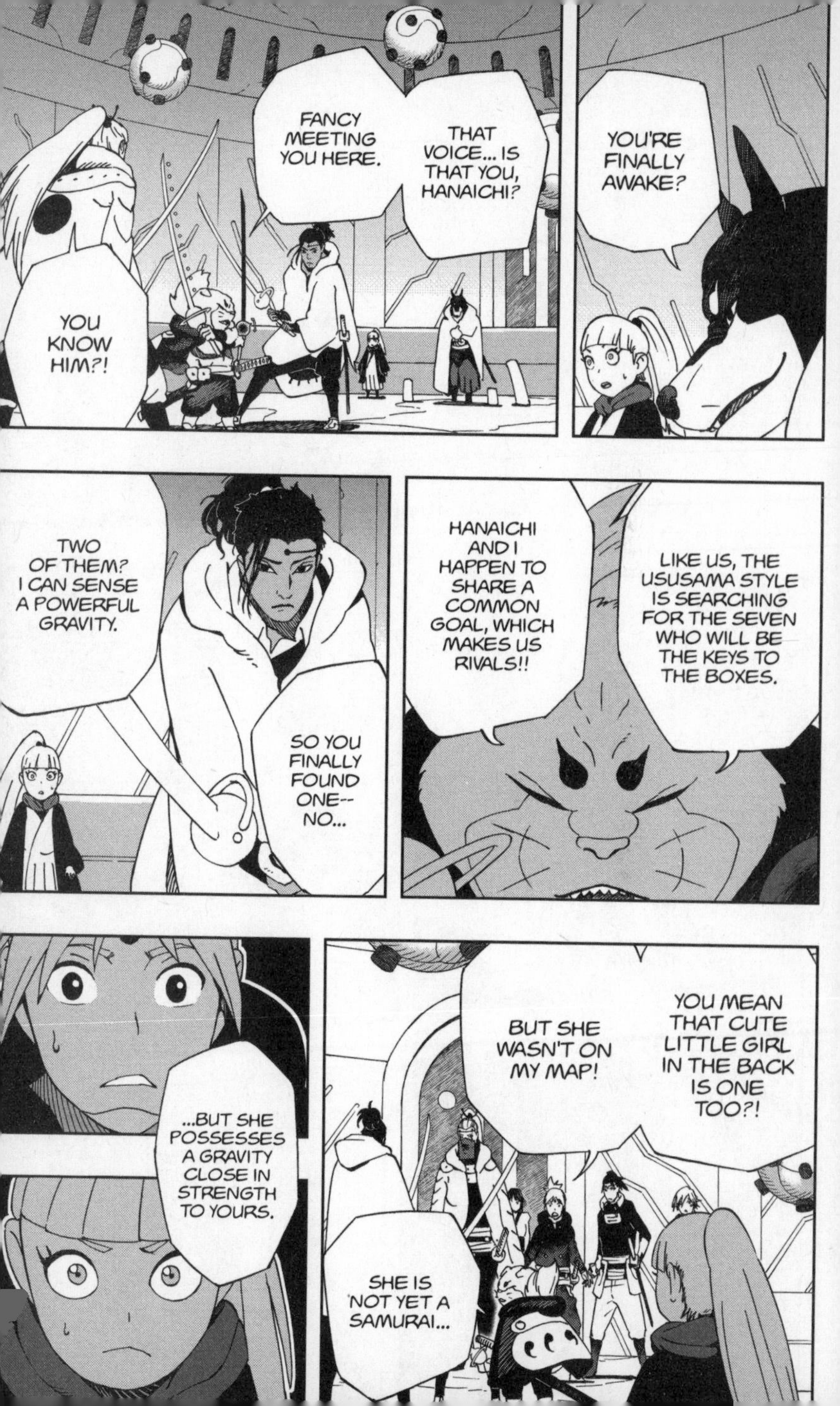
YOU'RE FINALLY AWAKE?
THAT VOICE... IS THAT YOU, HANAICHI?
FANCY MEETING YOU HERE.
YOU KNOW HIM?!
LIKE US, THE USUSAMA STYLE IS SEARCHING FOR THE SEVEN WHO WILL BE THE KEYS TO THE BOXES.
HANAICHI AND I HAPPEN TO SHARE A COMMON GOAL, WHICH MAKES US RIVALS!!
SO YOU FINALLY FOUND ONE-- NO...
TWO OF THEM? I CAN SENSE A POWERFUL GRAVITY.
YOU MEAN THAT CUTE LITTLE GIRL IN THE BACK IS ONE TOO?!
BUT SHE WASN'T ON MY MAP!
SHE IS NOT YET A SAMURAI...
...BUT SHE POSSESSES A GRAVITY CLOSE IN STRENGTH TO YOURS.

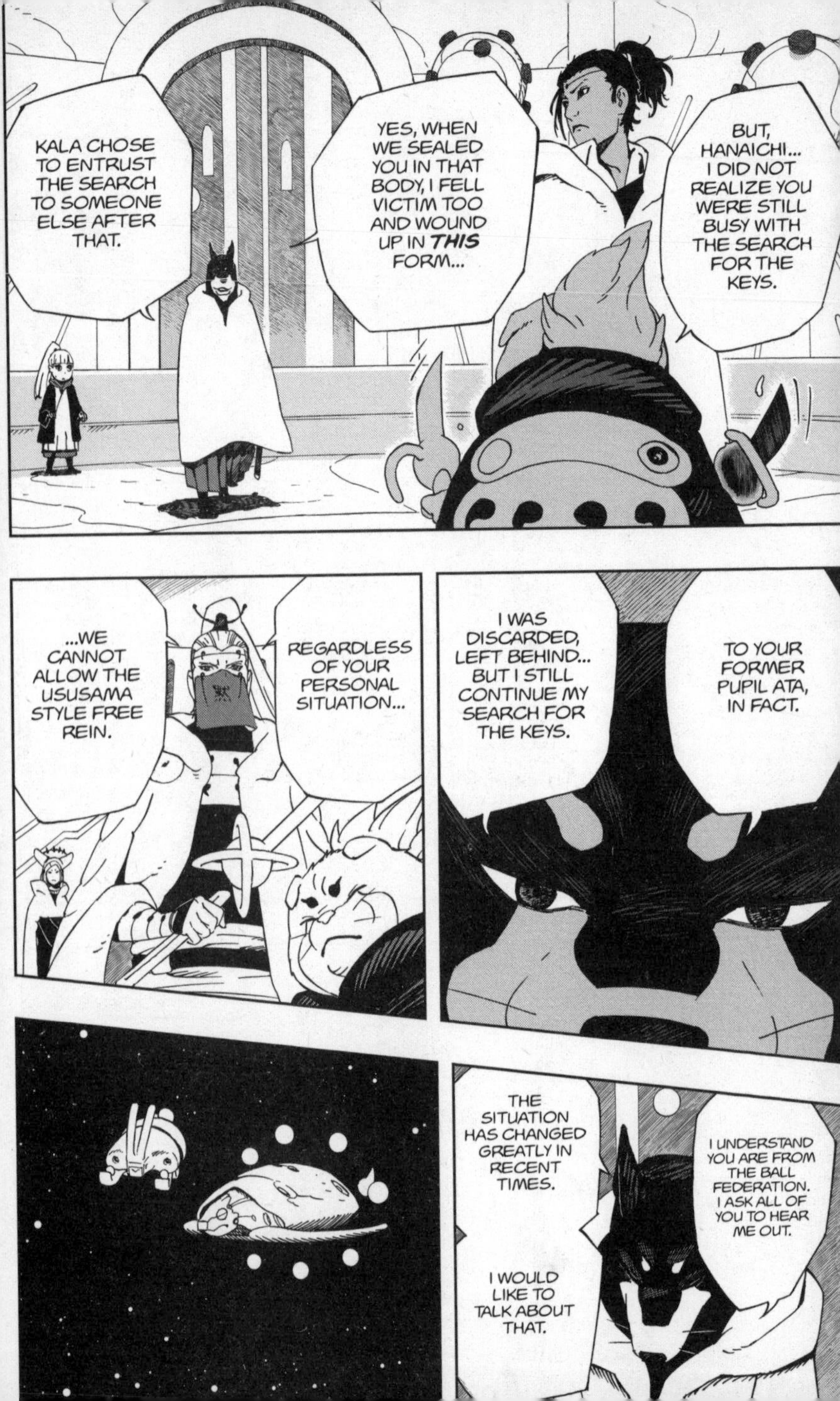
BUT, HANAICHI... I DID NOT REALIZE YOU WERE STILL BUSY WITH THE SEARCH FOR THE KEYS.
YES, WHEN WE SEALED YOU IN THAT BODY, I FELL VICTIM TOO AND WOUND UP IN ***THIS*** FORM...
KALA CHOSE TO ENTRUST THE SEARCH TO SOMEONE ELSE AFTER THAT.
TO YOUR FORMER PUPIL ATA, IN FACT.
I WAS DISCARDED, LEFT BEHIND... BUT I STILL CONTINUE MY SEARCH FOR THE KEYS.
REGARDLESS OF YOUR PERSONAL SITUATION...
...WE CANNOT ALLOW THE USUSAMA STYLE FREE REIN.
I UNDERSTAND YOU ARE FROM THE BALL FEDERATION. I ASK ALL OF YOU TO HEAR ME OUT.
THE SITUATION HAS CHANGED GREATLY IN RECENT TIMES.
I WOULD LIKE TO TALK ABOUT THAT.

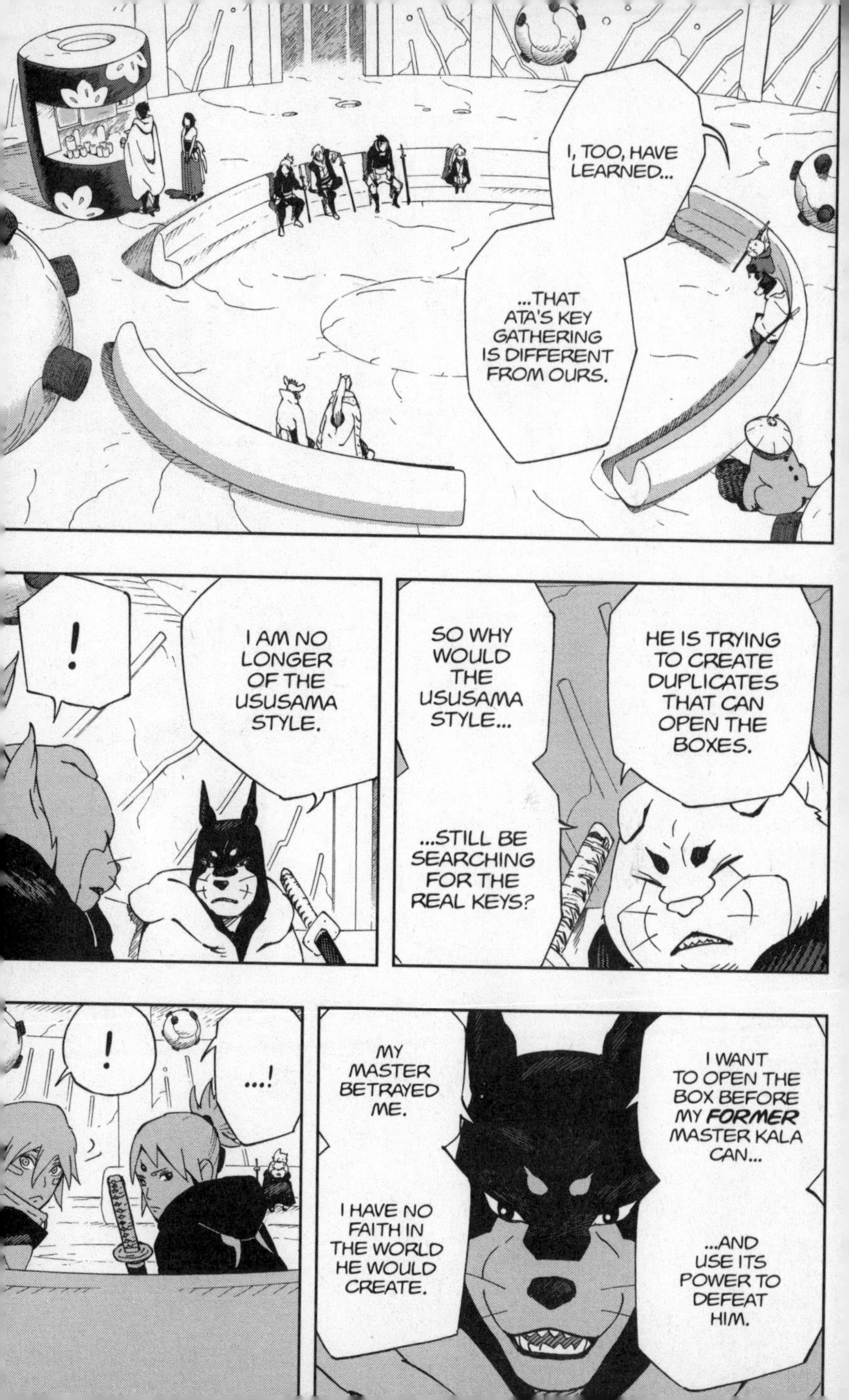

I, TOO, HAVE LEARNED...
...THAT ATA'S KEY GATHERING IS DIFFERENT FROM OURS.
HE IS TRYING TO CREATE DUPLICATES THAT CAN OPEN THE BOXES.
SO WHY WOULD THE USUSAMA STYLE...
...STILL BE SEARCHING FOR THE REAL KEYS?
I AM NO LONGER OF THE USUSAMA STYLE.
!
I WANT TO OPEN THE BOX BEFORE MY **FORMER** MASTER KALA CAN...
...AND USE ITS POWER TO DEFEAT HIM.
MY MASTER BETRAYED ME.
I HAVE NO FAITH IN THE WORLD HE WOULD CREATE.
...!
!

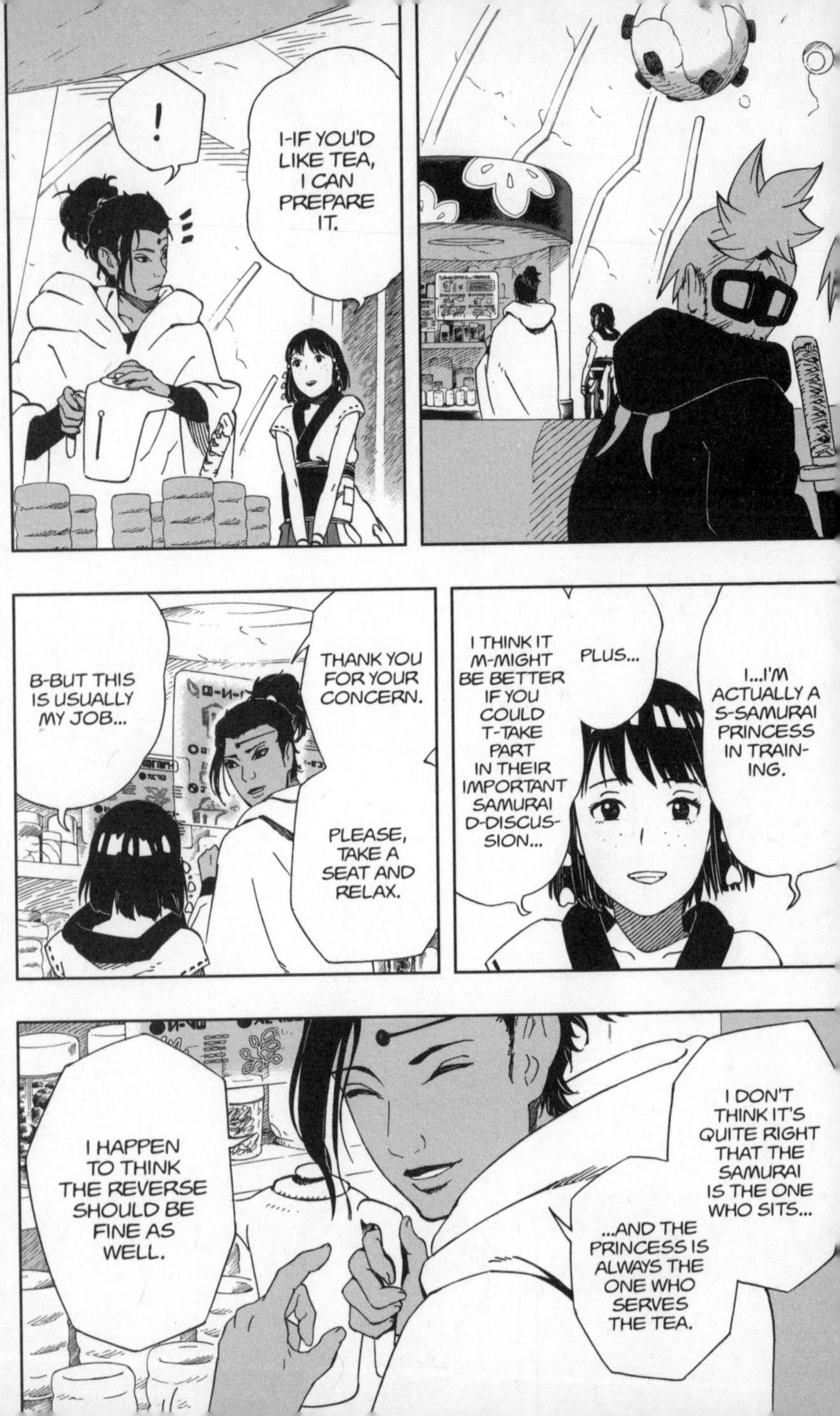
I-IF YOU'D LIKE TEA, I CAN PREPARE IT.
!
I...I'M ACTUALLY A S-SAMURAI PRINCESS IN TRAINING.
PLUS...
I THINK IT M-MIGHT BE BETTER IF YOU COULD T-TAKE PART IN THEIR IMPORTANT SAMURAI D-DISCUSSION...
THANK YOU FOR YOUR CONCERN.
PLEASE, TAKE A SEAT AND RELAX.
B-BUT THIS IS USUALLY MY JOB...
I DON'T THINK IT'S QUITE RIGHT THAT THE SAMURAI IS THE ONE WHO SITS...
...AND THE PRINCESS IS ALWAYS THE ONE WHO SERVES THE TEA.
I HAPPEN TO THINK THE REVERSE SHOULD BE FINE AS WELL.

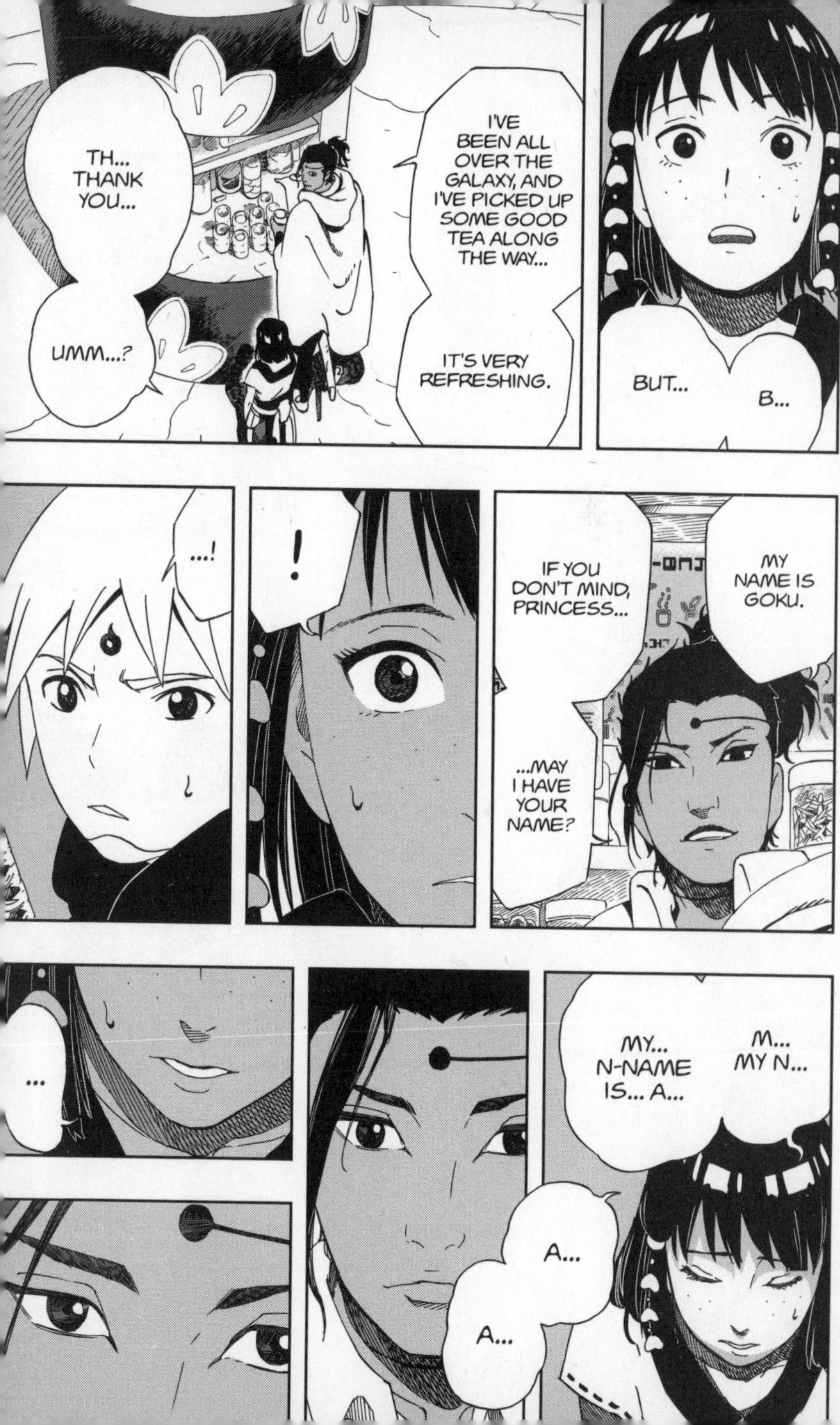
BUT...
B...
I'VE BEEN ALL OVER THE GALAXY, AND I'VE PICKED UP SOME GOOD TEA ALONG THE WAY...
IT'S VERY REFRESHING.
TH... THANK YOU...
UMM...?
MY NAME IS GOKU.
IF YOU DON'T MIND, PRINCESS...
...MAY I HAVE YOUR NAME?
!
...!
M... MY N...
MY... N-NAME IS... A...
A...
A...
...

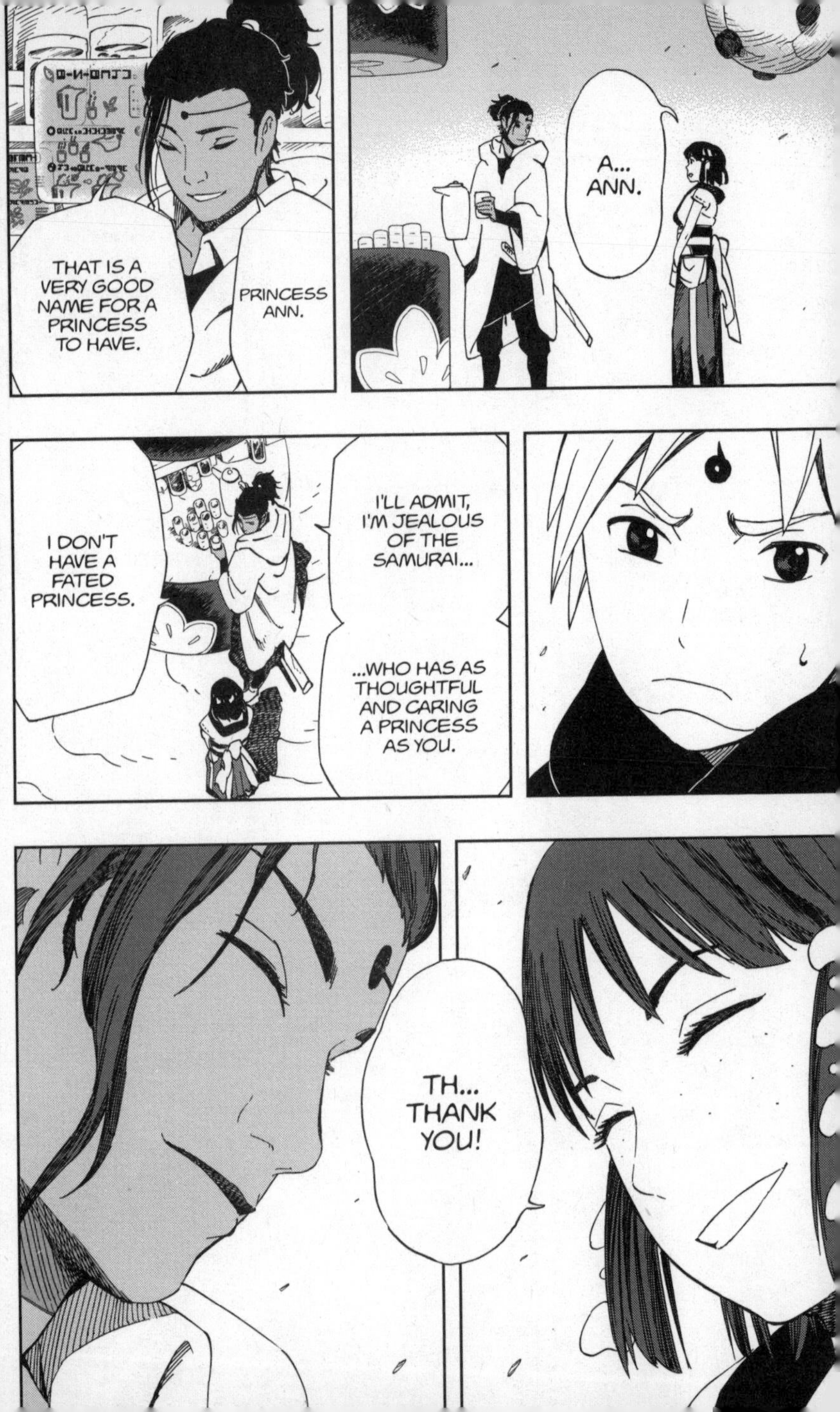
A...
ANN.
PRINCESS ANN.
THAT IS A VERY GOOD NAME FOR A PRINCESS TO HAVE.
I'LL ADMIT, I'M JEALOUS OF THE SAMURAI...
...WHO HAS AS THOUGHTFUL AND CARING A PRINCESS AS YOU.
I DON'T HAVE A FATED PRINCESS.
TH... THANK YOU!

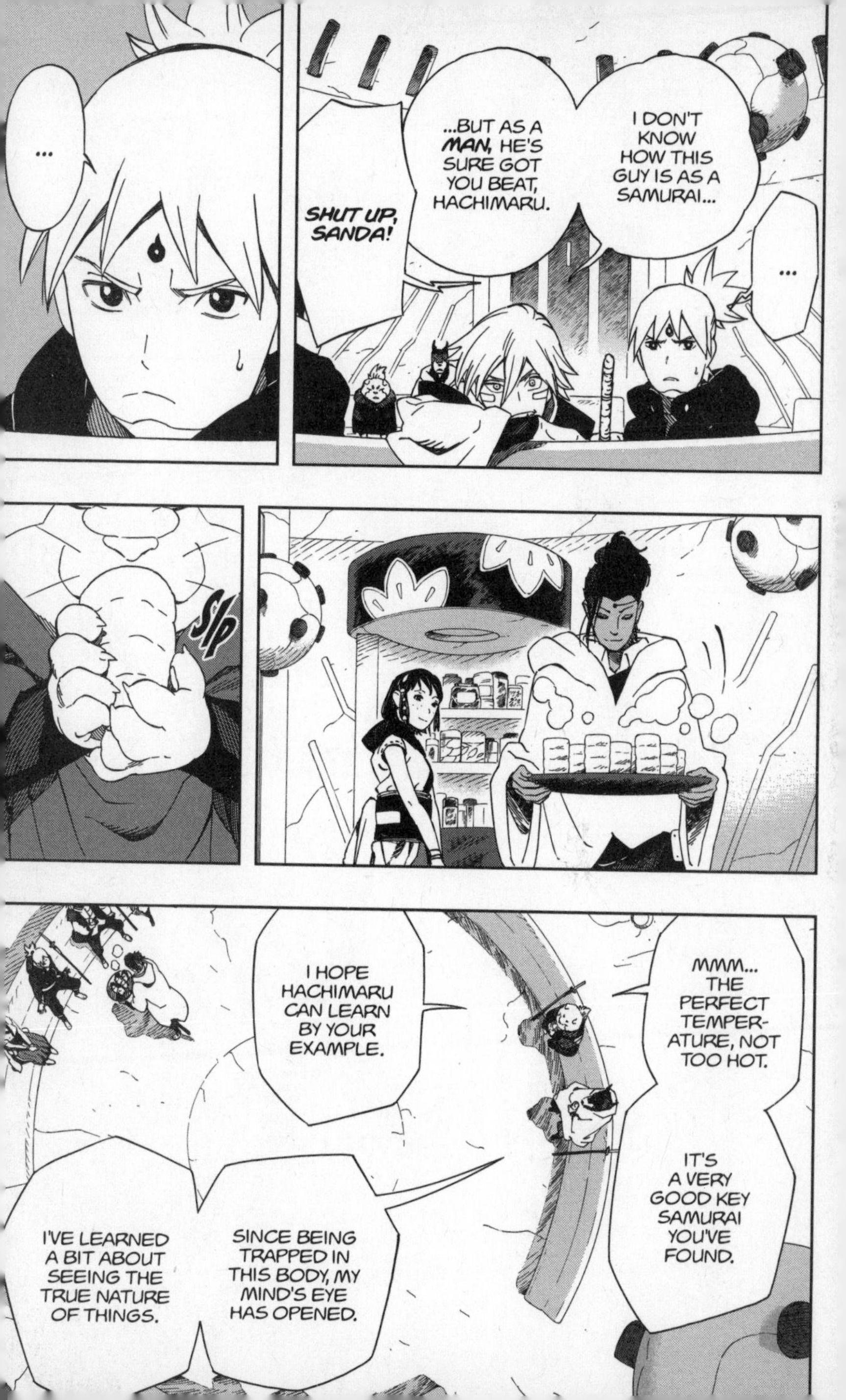
I DON'T KNOW HOW THIS GUY IS AS A SAMURAI...
...BUT AS A MAN, HE'S SURE GOT YOU BEAT, HACHIMARU.
...
SHUT UP, SANDA!
...
SIP
MMM... THE PERFECT TEMPER-ATURE, NOT TOO HOT.
IT'S A VERY GOOD KEY SAMURAI YOU'VE FOUND.
I HOPE HACHIMARU CAN LEARN BY YOUR EXAMPLE.
SINCE BEING TRAPPED IN THIS BODY, MY MIND'S EYE HAS OPENED.
I'VE LEARNED A BIT ABOUT SEEING THE TRUE NATURE OF THINGS.

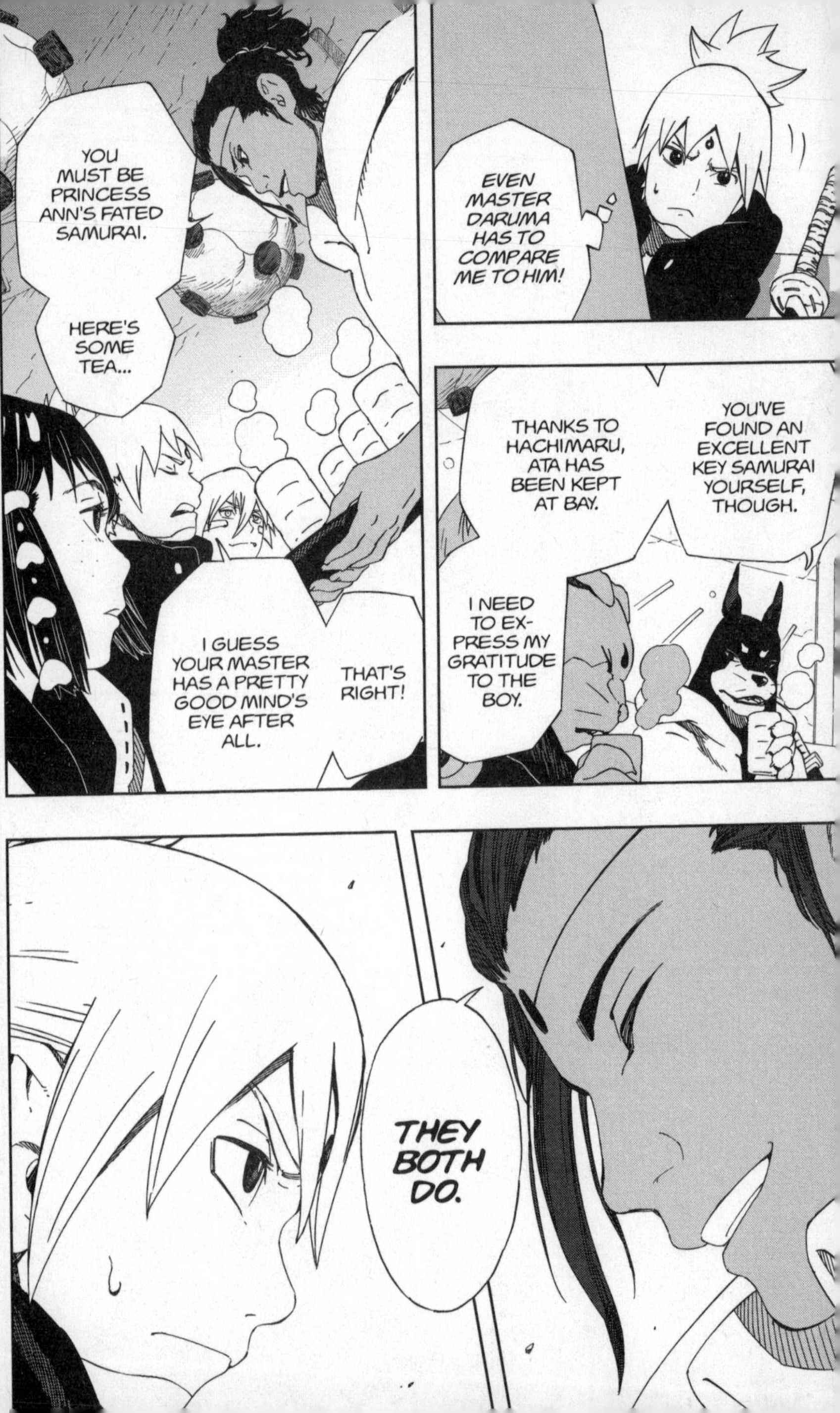
EVEN MASTER DARUMA HAS TO COMPARE ME TO HIM!
YOU'VE FOUND AN EXCELLENT KEY SAMURAI YOURSELF, THOUGH.
THANKS TO HACHIMARU, ATA HAS BEEN KEPT AT BAY.
I NEED TO EX-PRESS MY GRATITUDE TO THE BOY.
YOU MUST BE PRINCESS ANN'S FATED SAMURAI.
HERE'S SOME TEA...
THAT'S RIGHT!
I GUESS YOUR MASTER HAS A PRETTY GOOD MIND'S EYE AFTER ALL.
THEY BOTH DO.

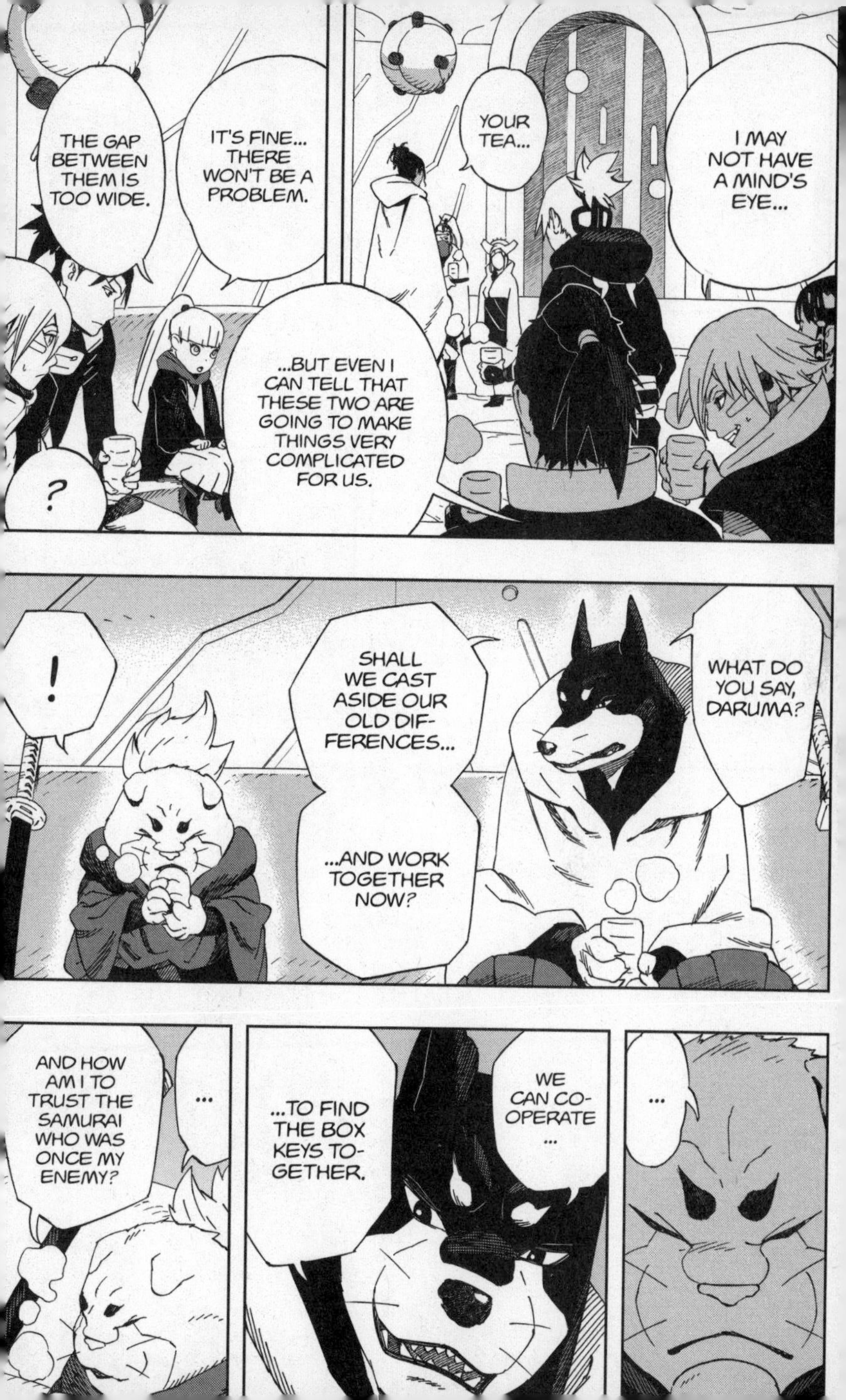
I MAY NOT HAVE A MIND'S EYE...
YOUR TEA...
...BUT EVEN I CAN TELL THAT THESE TWO ARE GOING TO MAKE THINGS VERY COMPLICATED FOR US.
IT'S FINE... THERE WON'T BE A PROBLEM.
THE GAP BETWEEN THEM IS TOO WIDE.
?
WHAT DO YOU SAY, DARUMA?
SHALL WE CAST ASIDE OUR OLD DIF-FERENCES...
...AND WORK TOGETHER NOW?
!
...
WE CAN CO-OPERATE ...
...TO FIND THE BOX KEYS TO-GETHER.
...
AND HOW AM I TO TRUST THE SAMURAI WHO WAS ONCE MY ENEMY?

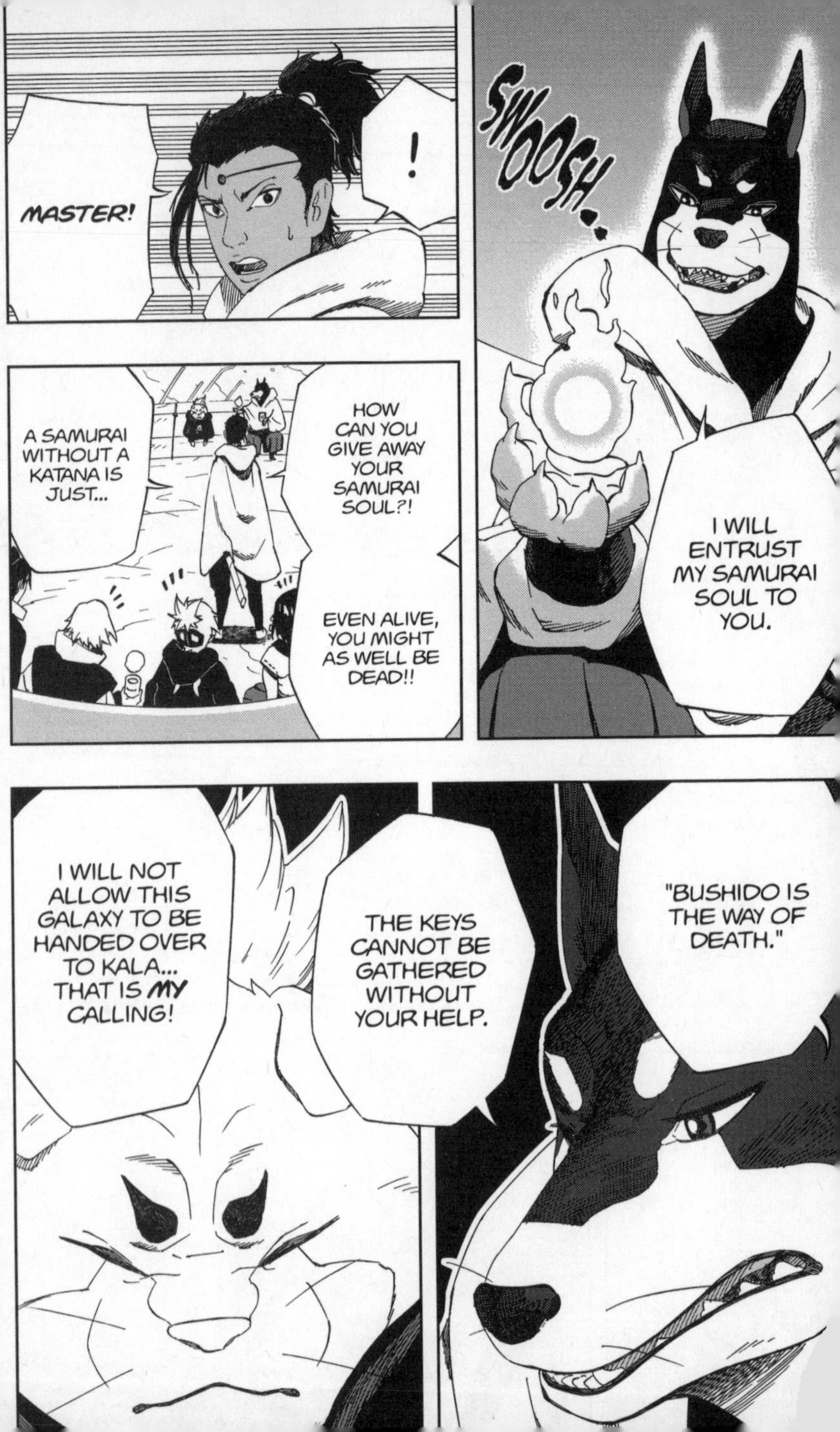
SWOOSH..
I WILL ENTRUST MY SAMURAI SOUL TO YOU.
!
MASTER!
HOW CAN YOU GIVE AWAY YOUR SAMURAI SOUL?!
A SAMURAI WITHOUT A KATANA IS JUST...
EVEN ALIVE, YOU MIGHT AS WELL BE DEAD!!
"BUSHIDO IS THE WAY OF DEATH."
THE KEYS CANNOT BE GATHERED WITHOUT YOUR HELP.
I WILL NOT ALLOW THIS GALAXY TO BE HANDED OVER TO KALA... THAT IS MY CALLING!

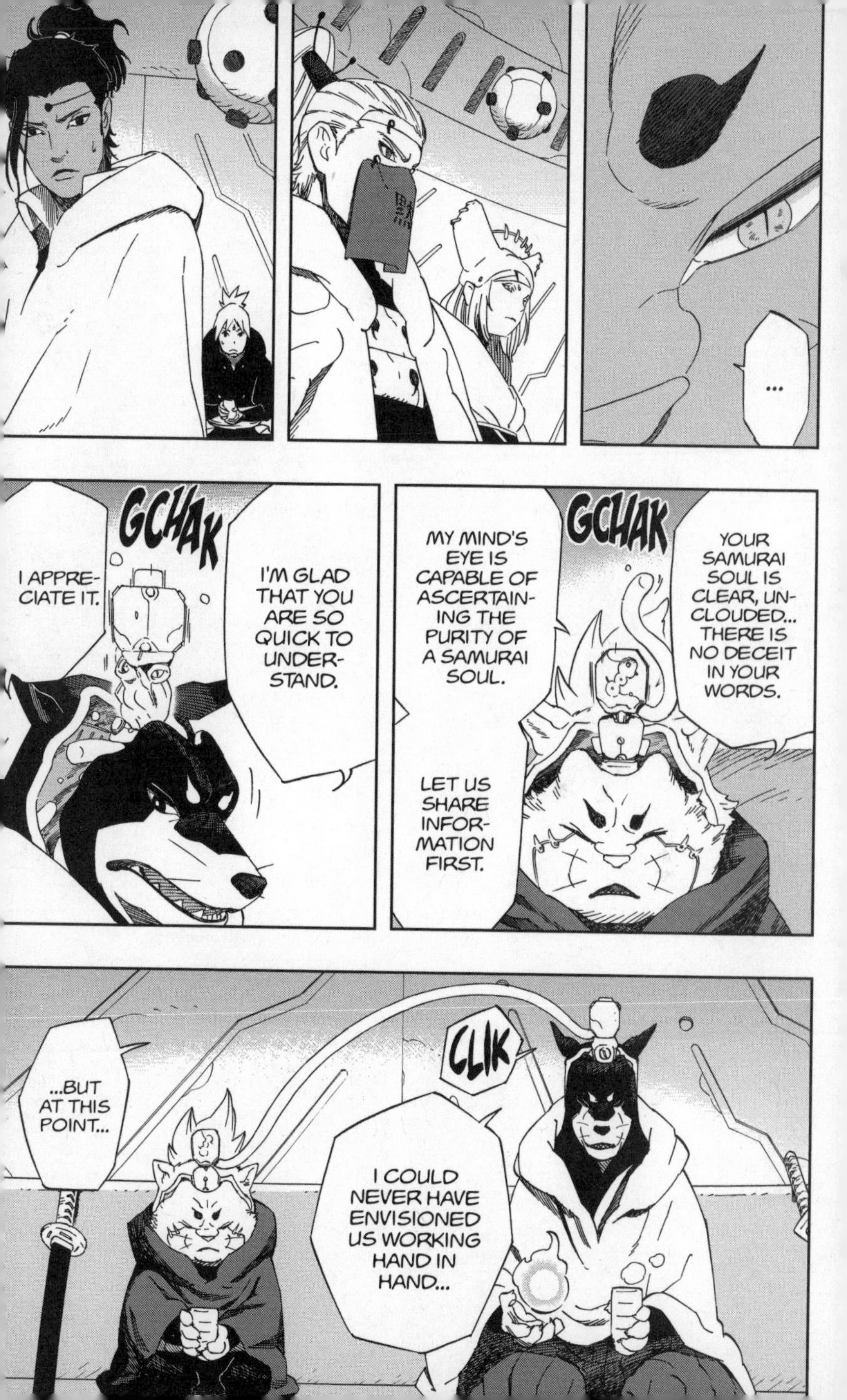
...
GCHAK
YOUR SAMURAI SOUL IS CLEAR, UNCLOUDED... THERE IS NO DECEIT IN YOUR WORDS.
MY MIND'S EYE IS CAPABLE OF ASCERTAINING THE PURITY OF A SAMURAI SOUL.
LET US SHARE INFORMATION FIRST.
GCHAK
I'M GLAD THAT YOU ARE SO QUICK TO UNDERSTAND.
I APPRECIATE IT.
CLIK
I COULD NEVER HAVE ENVISIONED US WORKING HAND IN HAND...
...BUT AT THIS POINT...

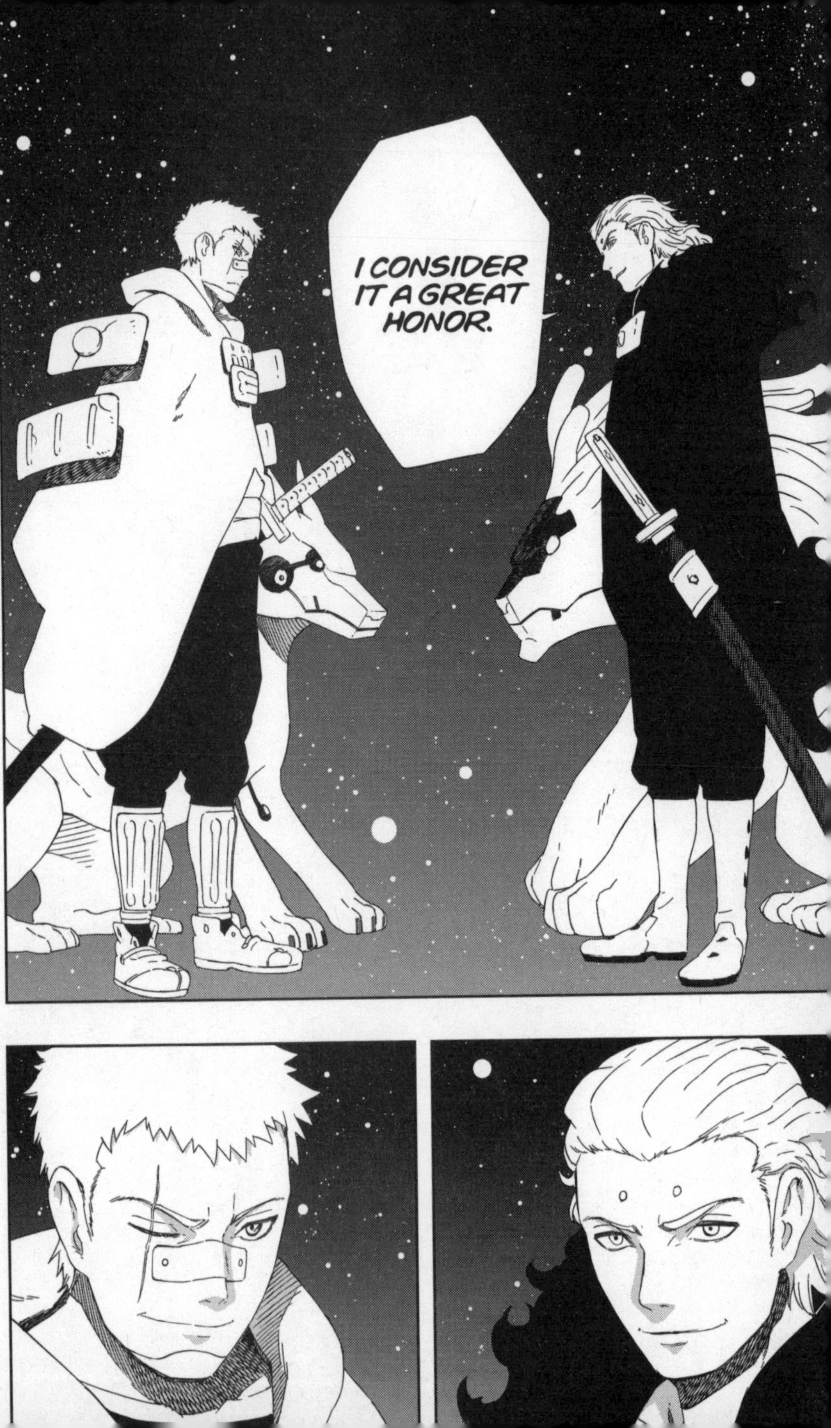
I CONSIDER IT A GREAT HONOR.

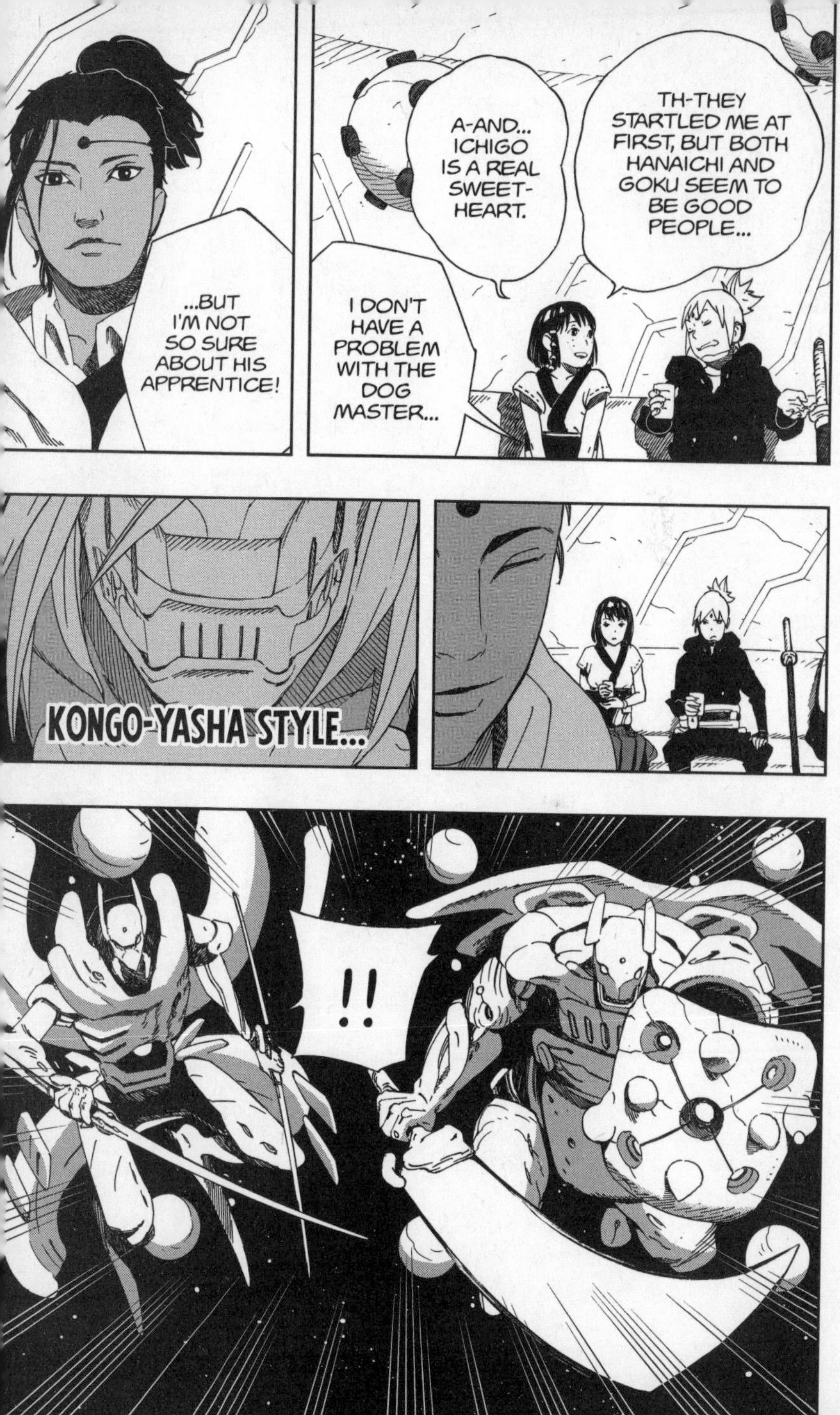
TH-THEY STARTLED ME AT FIRST, BUT BOTH HANAICHI AND GOKU SEEM TO BE GOOD PEOPLE...
A-AND... ICHIGO IS A REAL SWEET-HEART.
I DON'T HAVE A PROBLEM WITH THE DOG MASTER...
...BUT I'M NOT SO SURE ABOUT HIS APPRENTICE!
KONGO-YASHA STYLE...
!!

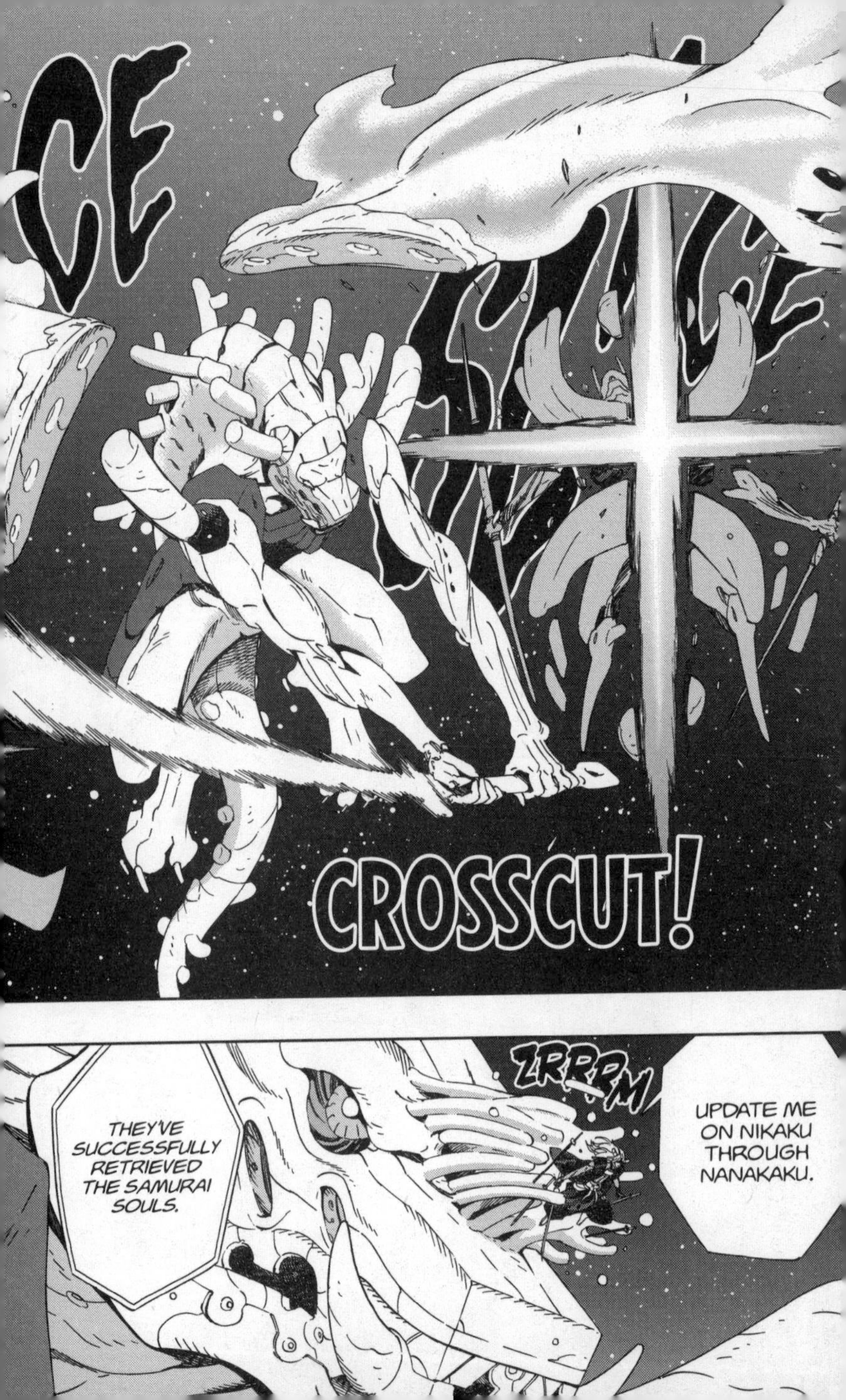
CE
CROSSCUT!
ZRRRM
UPDATE ME ON NIKAKU THROUGH NANAKAKU.
THEY'VE SUCCESSFULLY RETRIEVED THE SAMURAI SOULS.

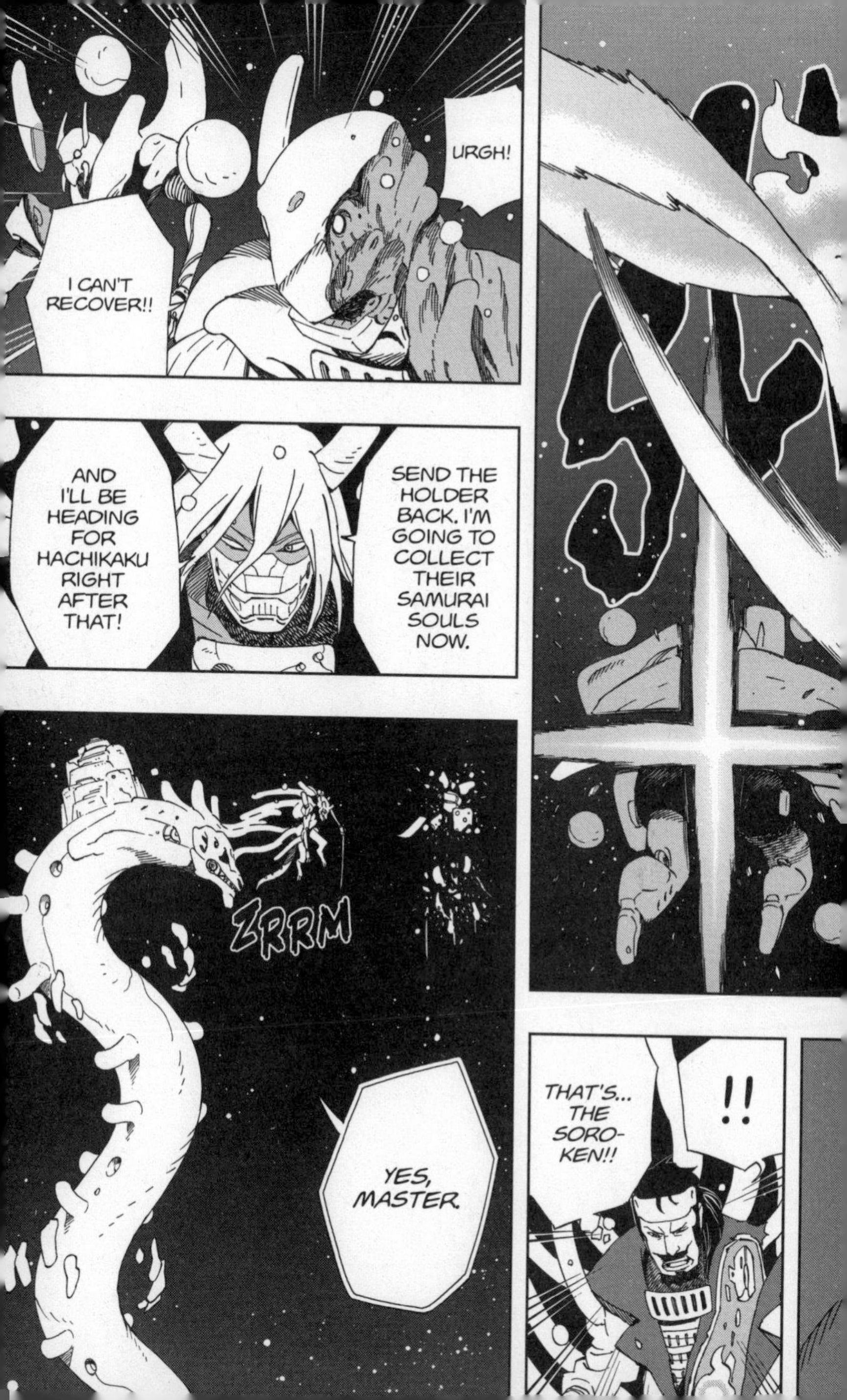
URGH!
I CAN'T RECOVER!!
SEND THE HOLDER BACK. I'M GOING TO COLLECT THEIR SAMURAI SOULS NOW.
AND I'LL BE HEADING FOR HACHIKAKU RIGHT AFTER THAT!
ZRRM
YES, MASTER.
!!
THAT'S... THE SORO-KEN!!

Character Design Sketches: Ichigo

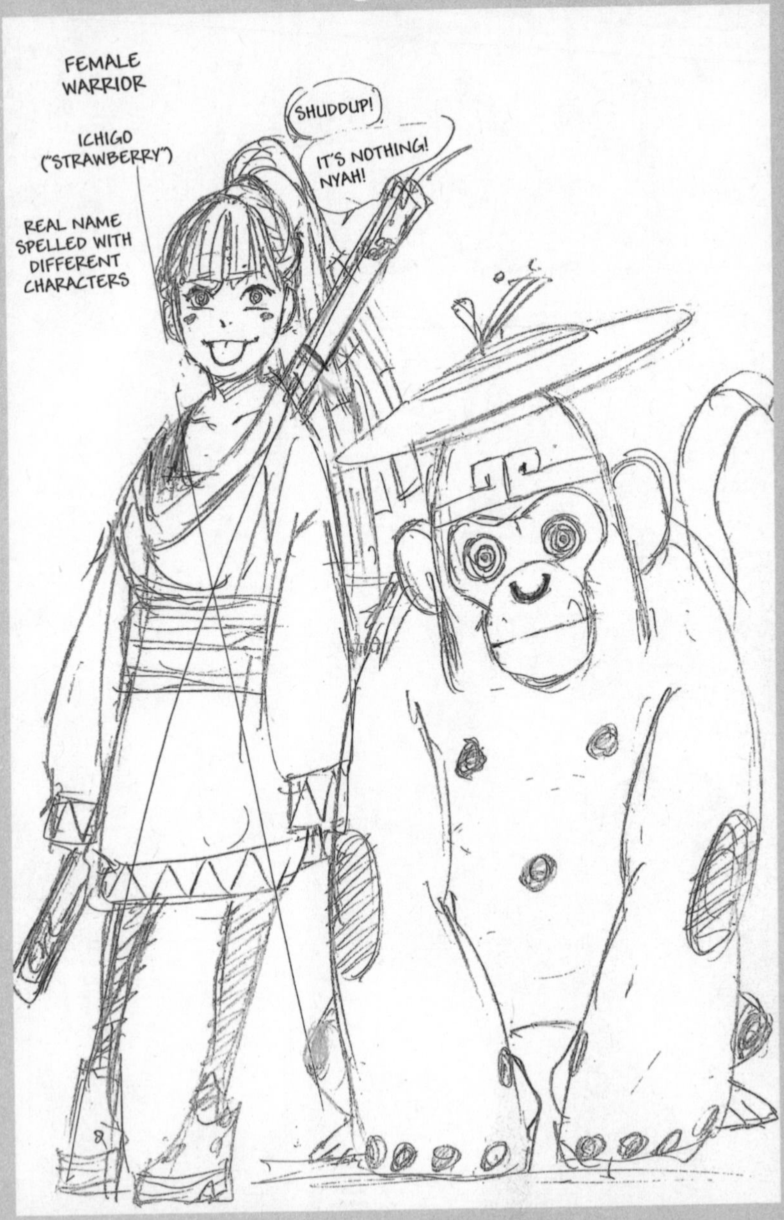

FEMALE WARRIOR
ICHIGO ("STRAWBERRY")
REAL NAME SPELLED WITH DIFFERENT CHARACTERS
SHUDDUP!
IT'S NOTHING! NYAH!

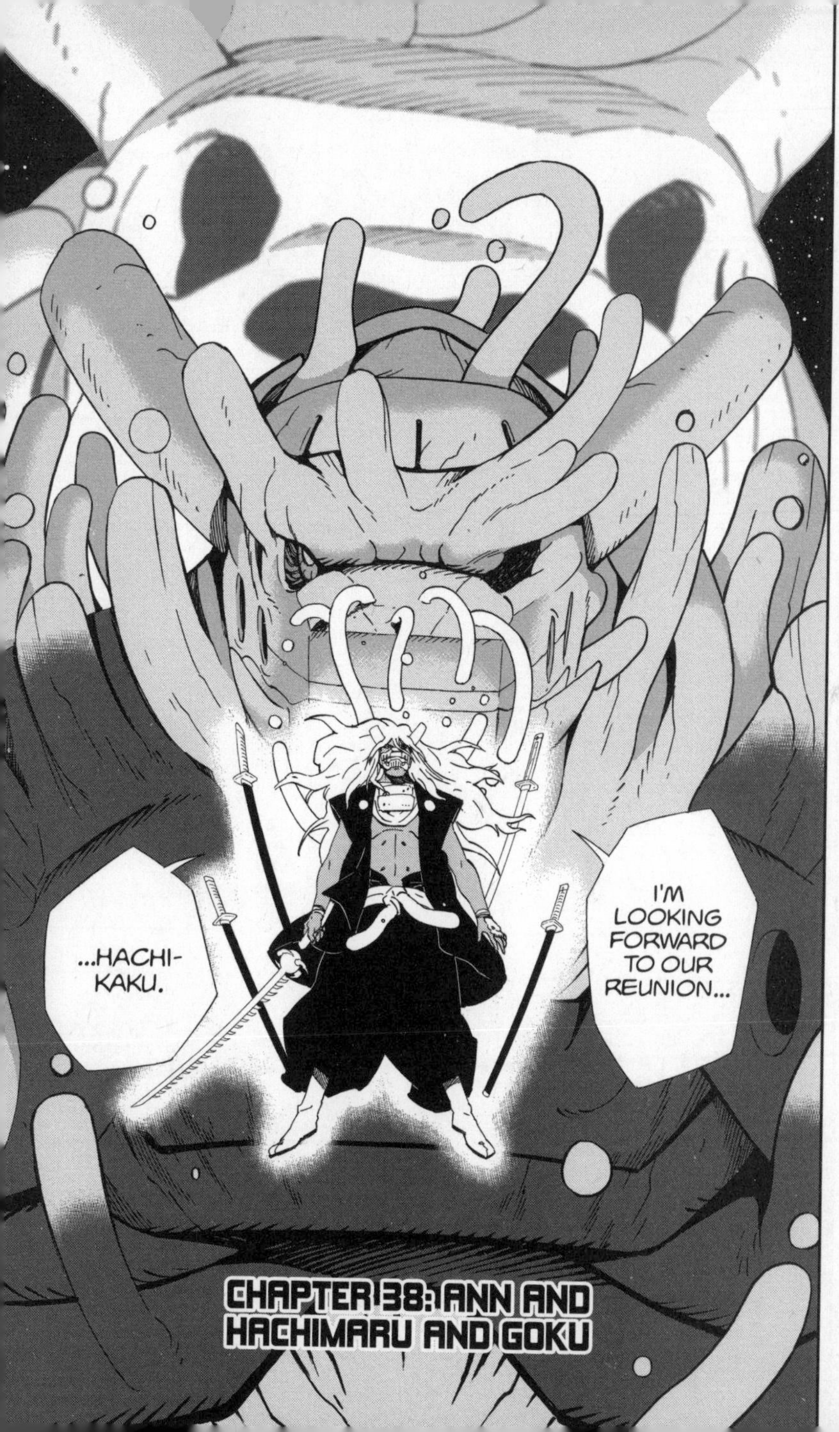
I'M LOOKING FORWARD TO OUR REUNION...
...HACHI-KAKU.
CHAPTER 38: ANN AND HACHIMARU AND GOKU

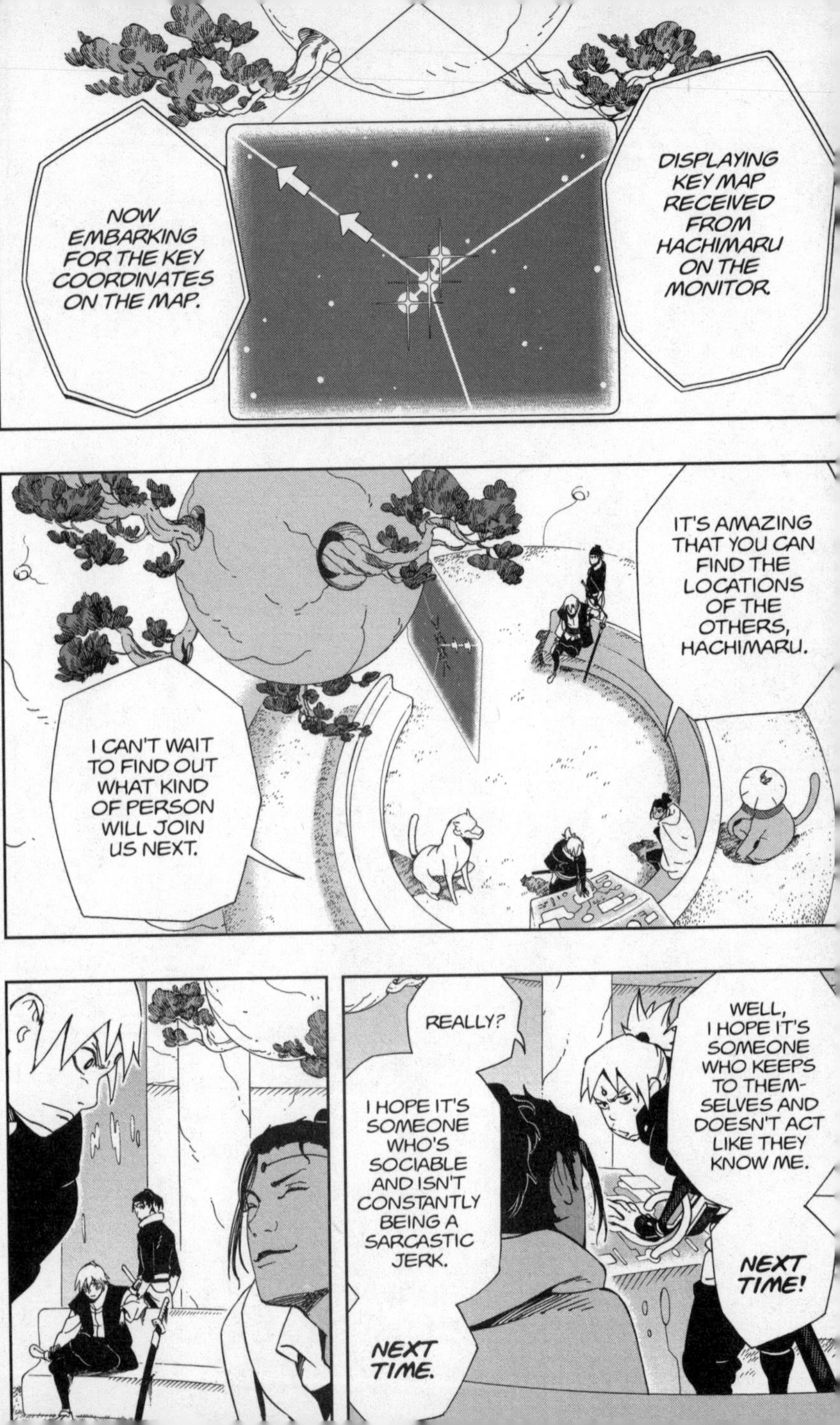
DISPLAYING KEY MAP RECEIVED FROM HACHIMARU ON THE MONITOR.
NOW EMBARKING FOR THE KEY COORDINATES ON THE MAP.
IT'S AMAZING THAT YOU CAN FIND THE LOCATIONS OF THE OTHERS, HACHIMARU.
I CAN'T WAIT TO FIND OUT WHAT KIND OF PERSON WILL JOIN US NEXT.
WELL, I HOPE IT'S SOMEONE WHO KEEPS TO THEM-SELVES AND DOESN'T ACT LIKE THEY KNOW ME.
REALLY?
I HOPE IT'S SOMEONE WHO'S SOCIABLE AND ISN'T CONSTANTLY BEING A SARCASTIC JERK.
NEXT TIME!
NEXT TIME.

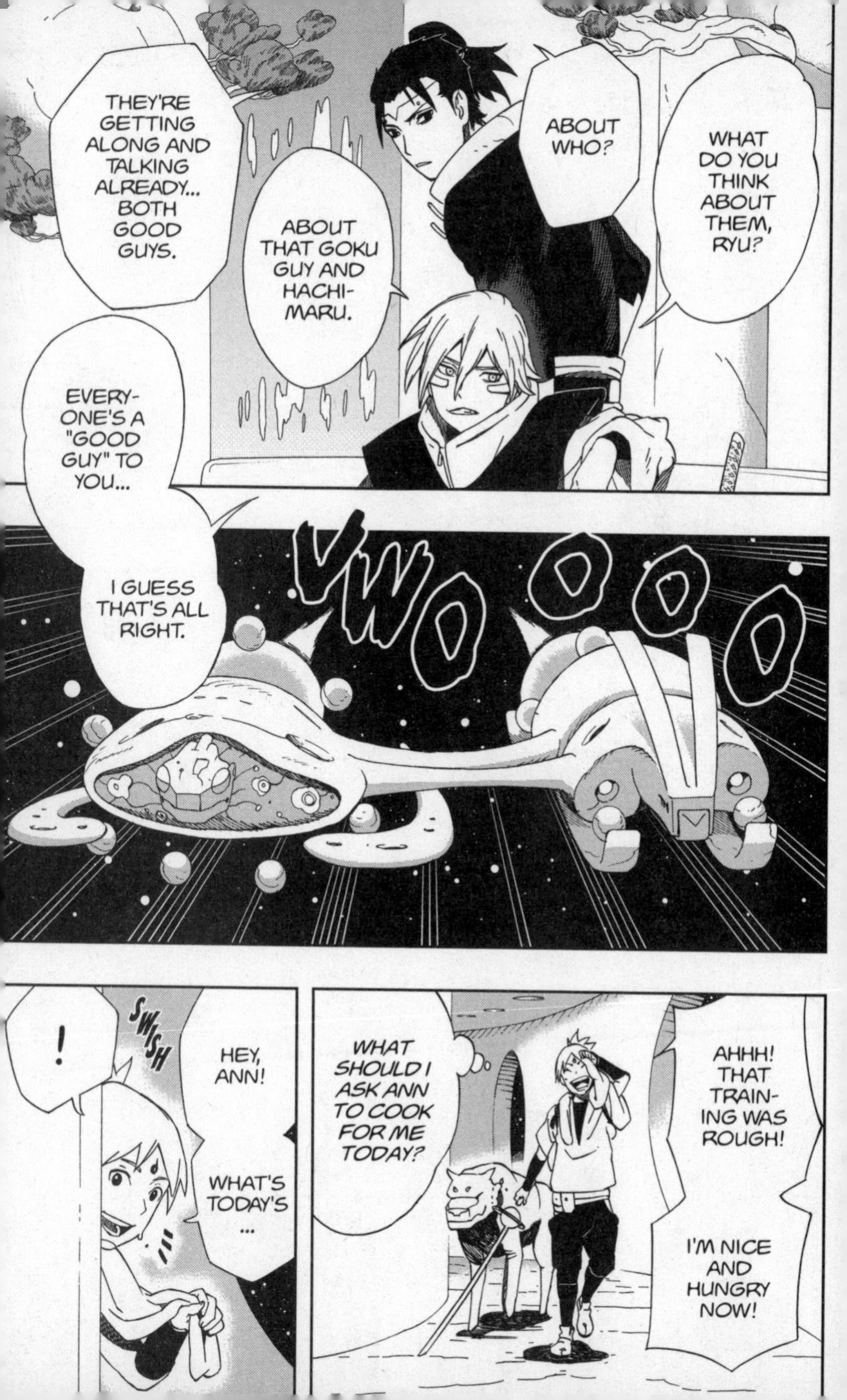
WHAT DO YOU THINK ABOUT THEM, RYU?
ABOUT WHO?
ABOUT THAT GOKU GUY AND HACHI-MARU.
THEY'RE GETTING ALONG AND TALKING ALREADY... BOTH GOOD GUYS.
EVERY-ONE'S A "GOOD GUY" TO YOU...
I GUESS THAT'S ALL RIGHT.
VWOOOOO
AHHH! THAT TRAIN-ING WAS ROUGH!
I'M NICE AND HUNGRY NOW!
WHAT SHOULD I ASK ANN TO COOK FOR ME TODAY?
HEY, ANN!
WHAT'S TODAY'S ...
SWISH
!

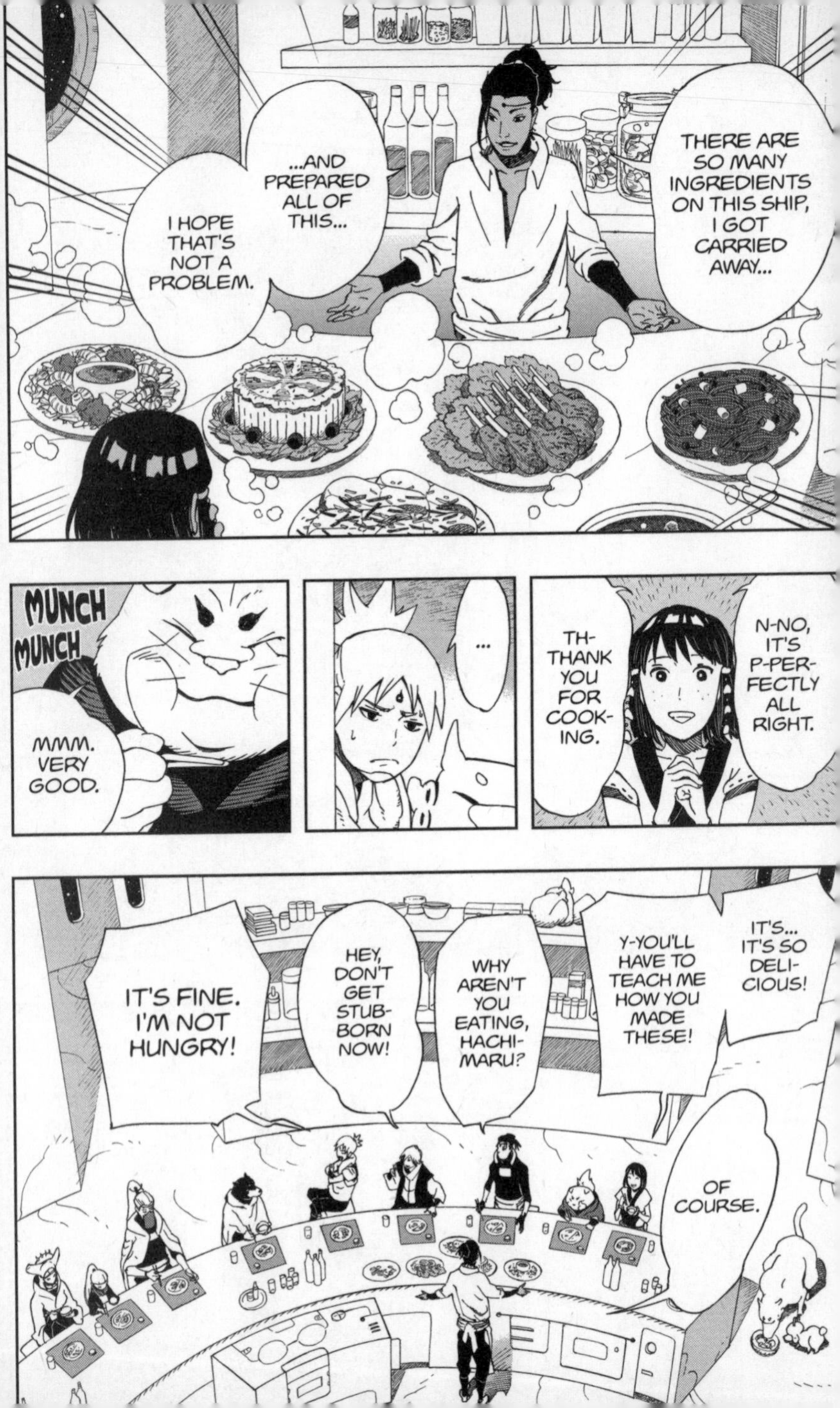
THERE ARE SO MANY INGREDIENTS ON THIS SHIP, I GOT CARRIED AWAY...
...AND PREPARED ALL OF THIS...
I HOPE THAT'S NOT A PROBLEM.
N-NO, IT'S P-PERFECTLY ALL RIGHT.
TH-THANK YOU FOR COOKING.
...
MUNCH MUNCH
MMM. VERY GOOD.
IT'S... IT'S SO DELICIOUS!
Y-YOU'LL HAVE TO TEACH ME HOW YOU MADE THESE!
WHY AREN'T YOU EATING, HACHIMARU?
HEY, DON'T GET STUBBORN NOW!
IT'S FINE. I'M NOT HUNGRY!
OF COURSE.

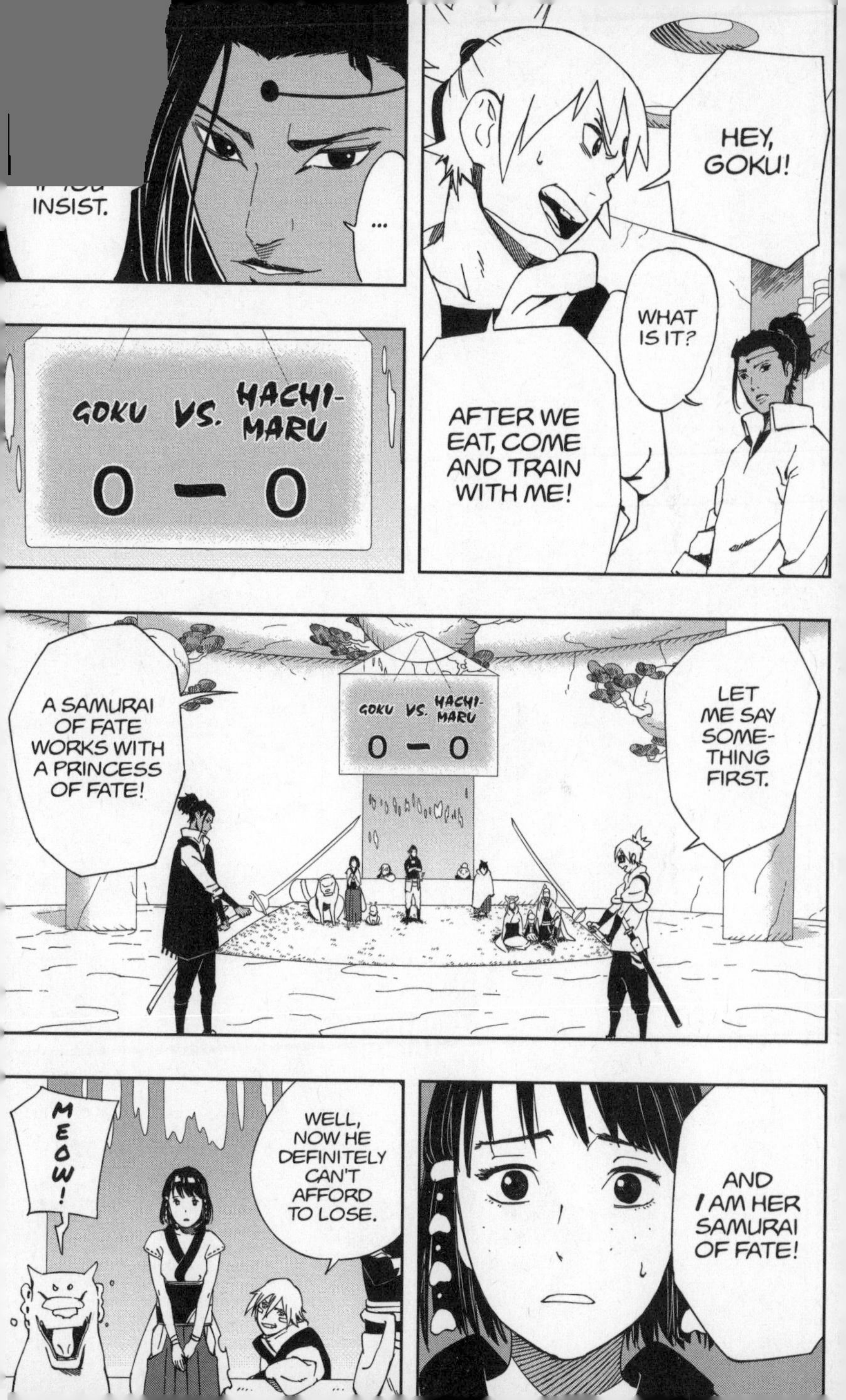
HEY, GOKU!
WHAT IS IT?
AFTER WE EAT, COME AND TRAIN WITH ME!
...
INSIST.
GOKU VS. HACHI-MARU
0 — 0
LET ME SAY SOME-THING FIRST.
GOKU VS. HACHI-MARU
0 — 0
A SAMURAI OF FATE WORKS WITH A PRINCESS OF FATE!
AND I AM HER SAMURAI OF FATE!
WELL, NOW HE DEFINITELY CAN'T AFFORD TO LOSE.
MEOW!

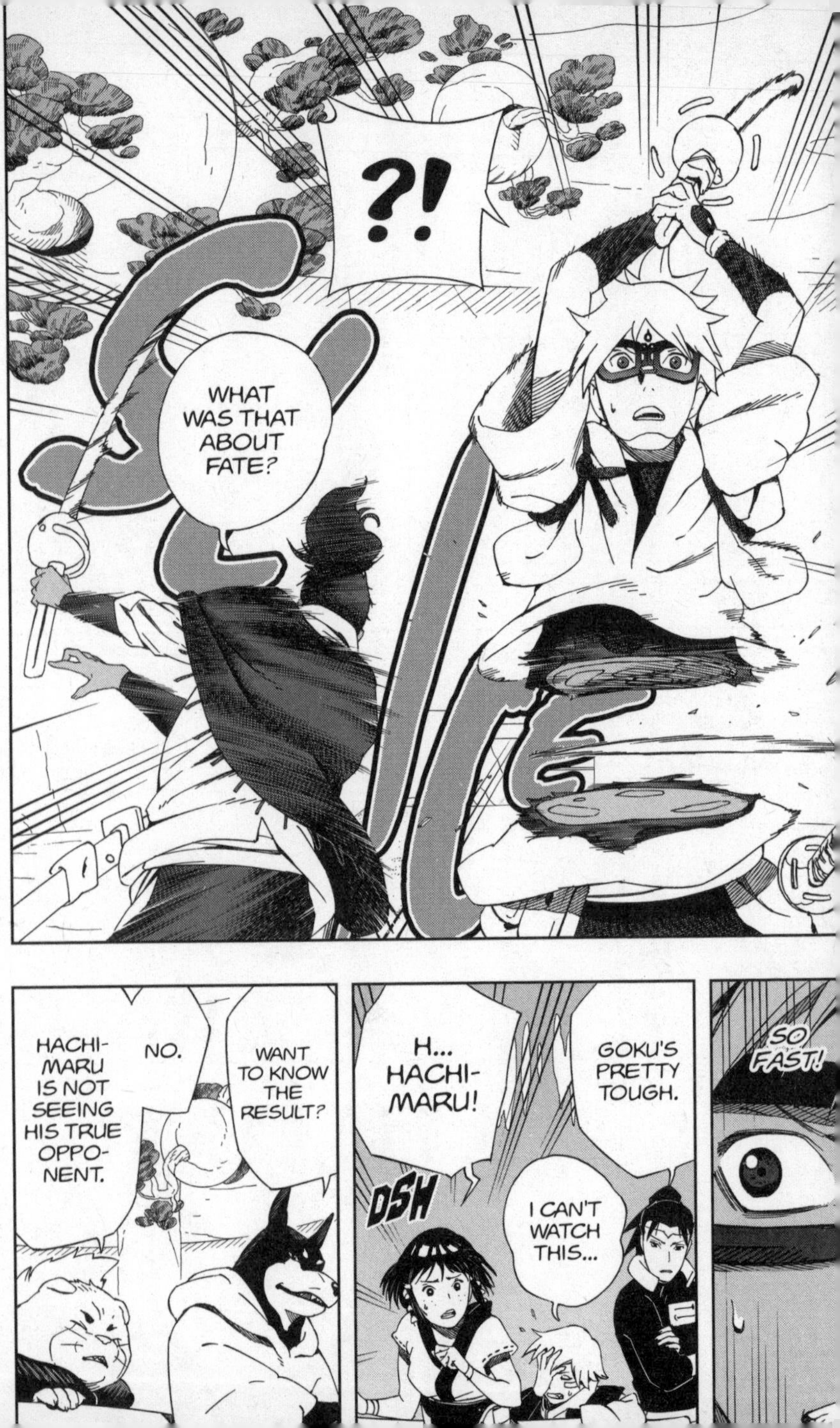
?!
WHAT WAS THAT ABOUT FATE?
SO FAST!
GOKU'S PRETTY TOUGH.
H... HACHIMARU!
DSH
I CAN'T WATCH THIS...
WANT TO KNOW THE RESULT?
NO.
HACHIMARU IS NOT SEEING HIS TRUE OPPONENT.

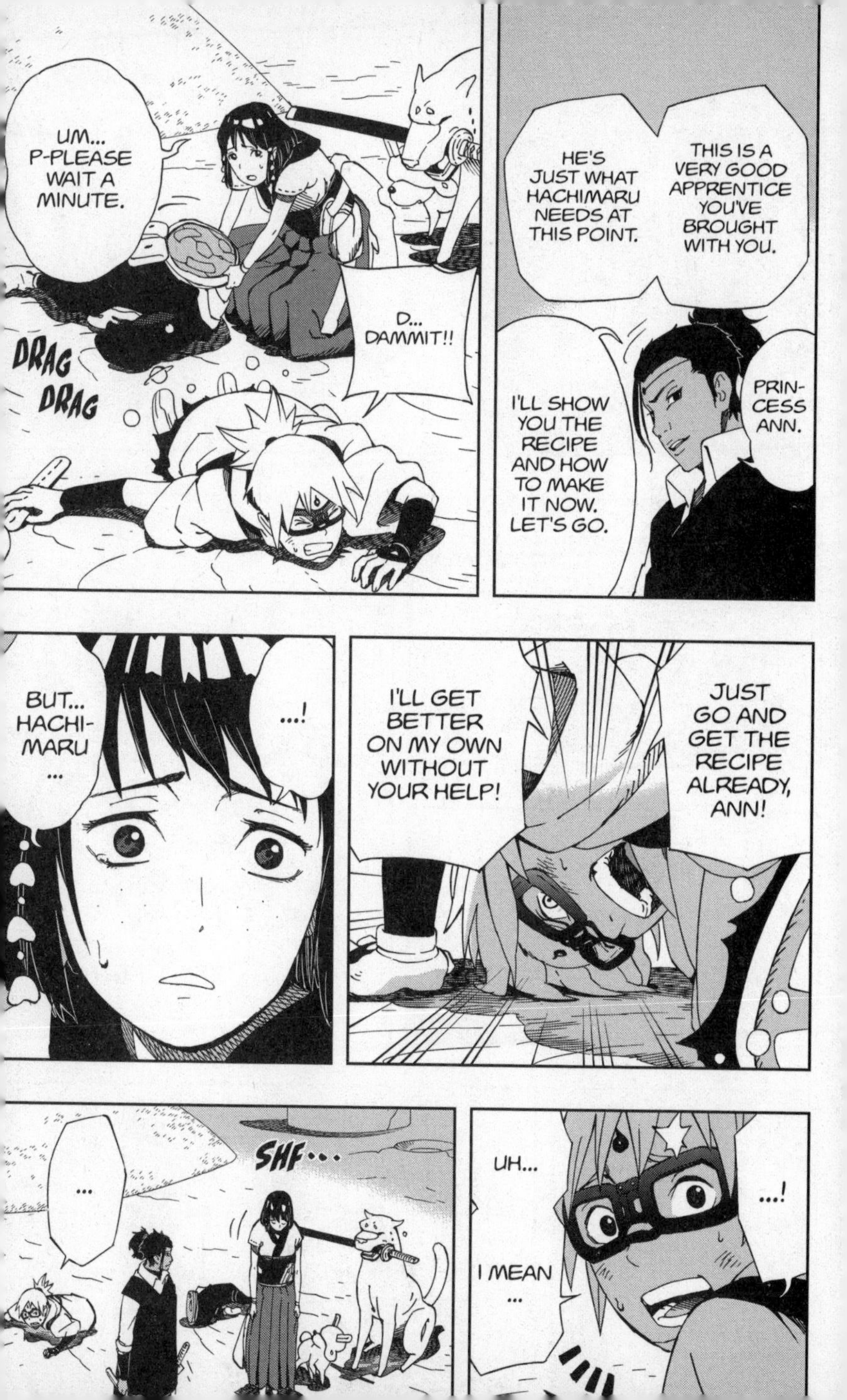

THIS IS A VERY GOOD APPRENTICE YOU'VE BROUGHT WITH YOU.
HE'S JUST WHAT HACHIMARU NEEDS AT THIS POINT.
PRINCESS ANN.
I'LL SHOW YOU THE RECIPE AND HOW TO MAKE IT NOW. LET'S GO.
D... DAMMIT!!
UM... P-PLEASE WAIT A MINUTE.
DRAG DRAG
JUST GO AND GET THE RECIPE ALREADY, ANN!
I'LL GET BETTER ON MY OWN WITHOUT YOUR HELP!
...!
BUT... HACHIMARU...
...!
UH...
I MEAN...
SHF...
...

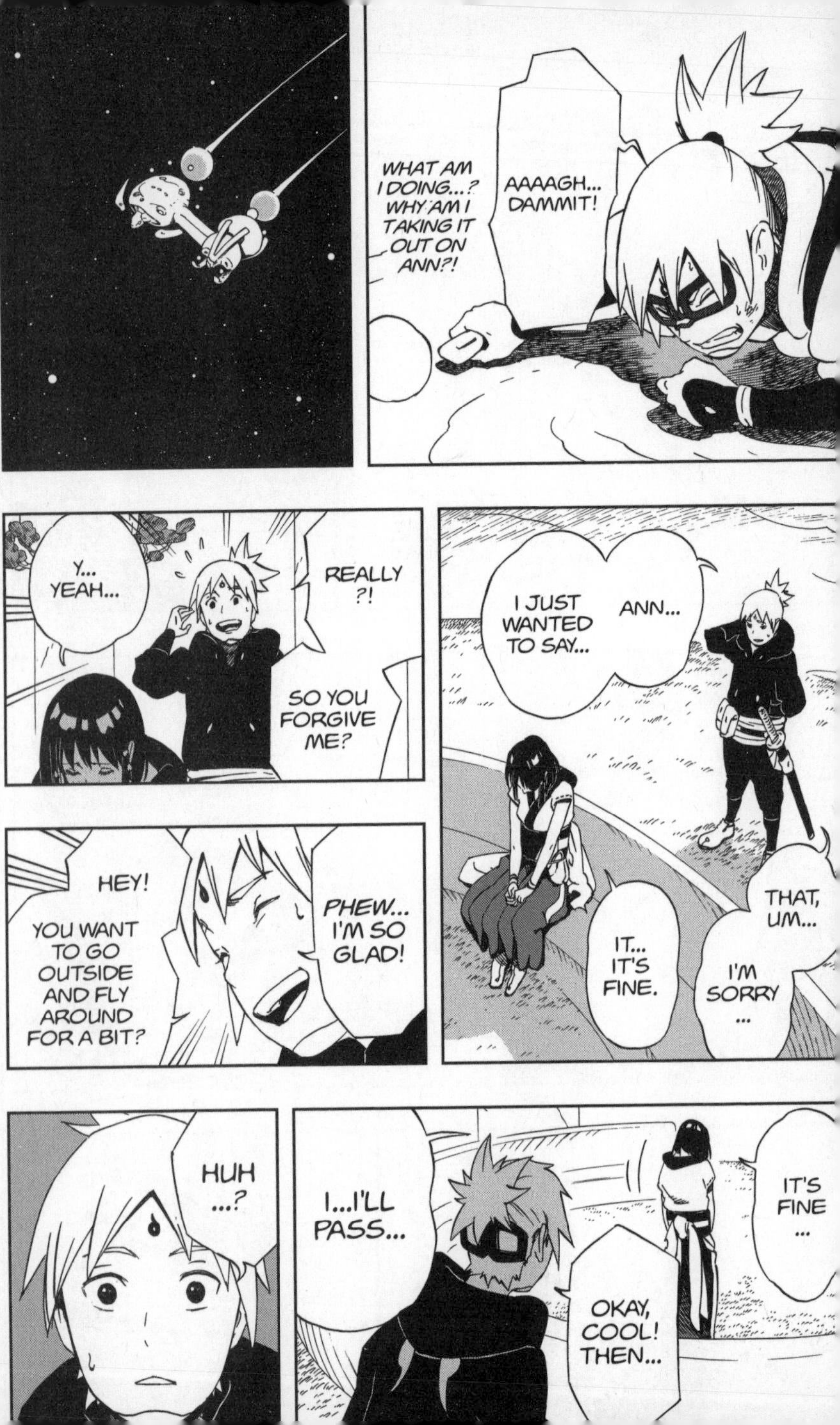
AAAAGH... DAMMIT!
WHAT AM I DOING...? WHY AM I TAKING IT OUT ON ANN?!
ANN...
I JUST WANTED TO SAY...
THAT, UM...
I'M SORRY ...
IT... IT'S FINE.
REALLY ?!
SO YOU FORGIVE ME?
Y... YEAH...
PHEW... I'M SO GLAD!
HEY!
YOU WANT TO GO OUTSIDE AND FLY AROUND FOR A BIT?
IT'S FINE ...
I...I'LL PASS...
OKAY, COOL! THEN...
HUH ...?

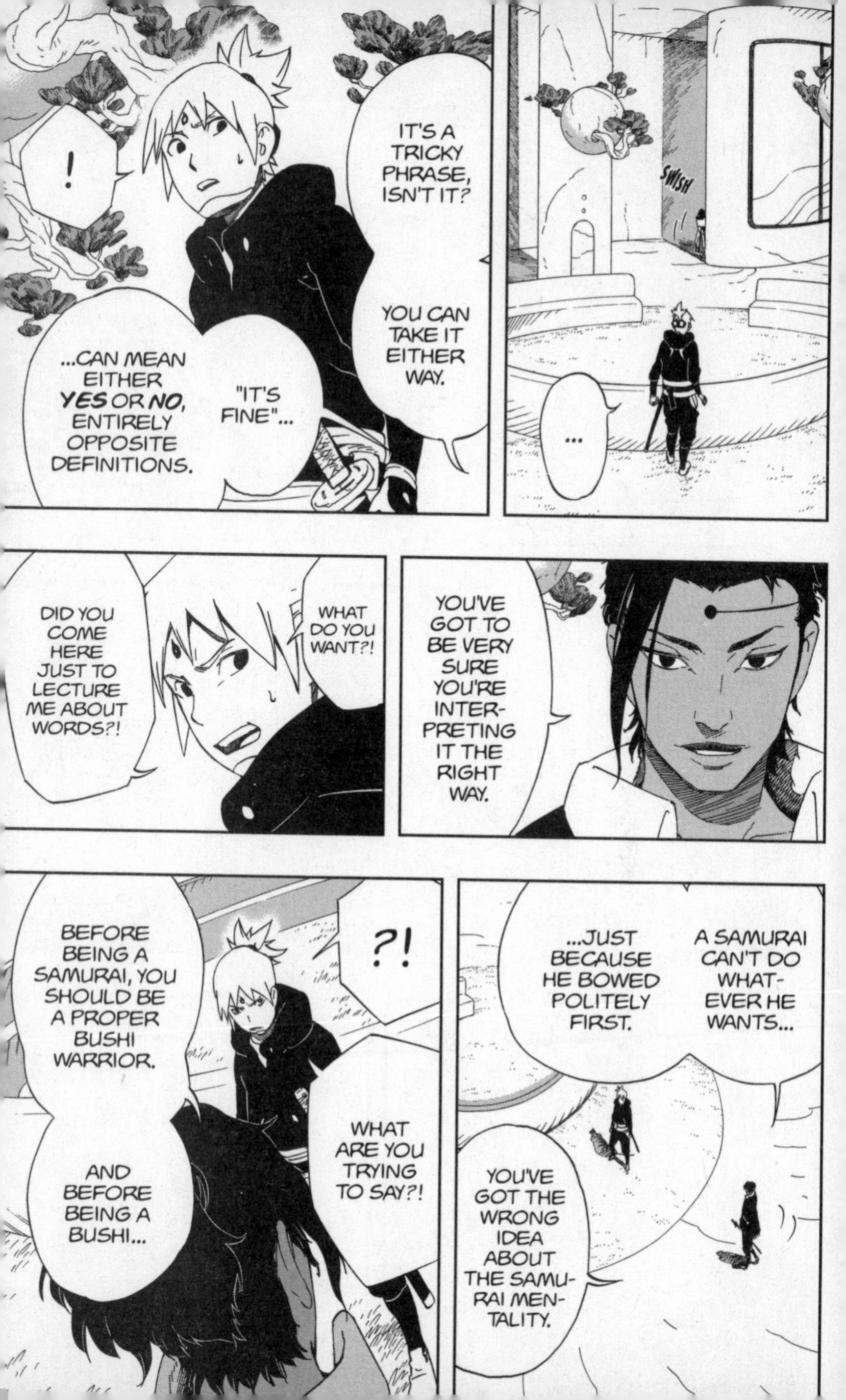
SWISH
...
IT'S A TRICKY PHRASE, ISN'T IT?
YOU CAN TAKE IT EITHER WAY.
!
"IT'S FINE"...
...CAN MEAN EITHER **YES** OR **NO**, ENTIRELY OPPOSITE DEFINITIONS.
YOU'VE GOT TO BE VERY SURE YOU'RE INTER-PRETING IT THE RIGHT WAY.
WHAT DO YOU WANT?!
DID YOU COME HERE JUST TO LECTURE ME ABOUT WORDS?!
A SAMURAI CAN'T DO WHAT-EVER HE WANTS...
...JUST BECAUSE HE BOWED POLITELY FIRST.
YOU'VE GOT THE WRONG IDEA ABOUT THE SAMU-RAI MEN-TALITY.
?!
BEFORE BEING A SAMURAI, YOU SHOULD BE A PROPER BUSHI WARRIOR.
WHAT ARE YOU TRYING TO SAY?!
AND BEFORE BEING A BUSHI...

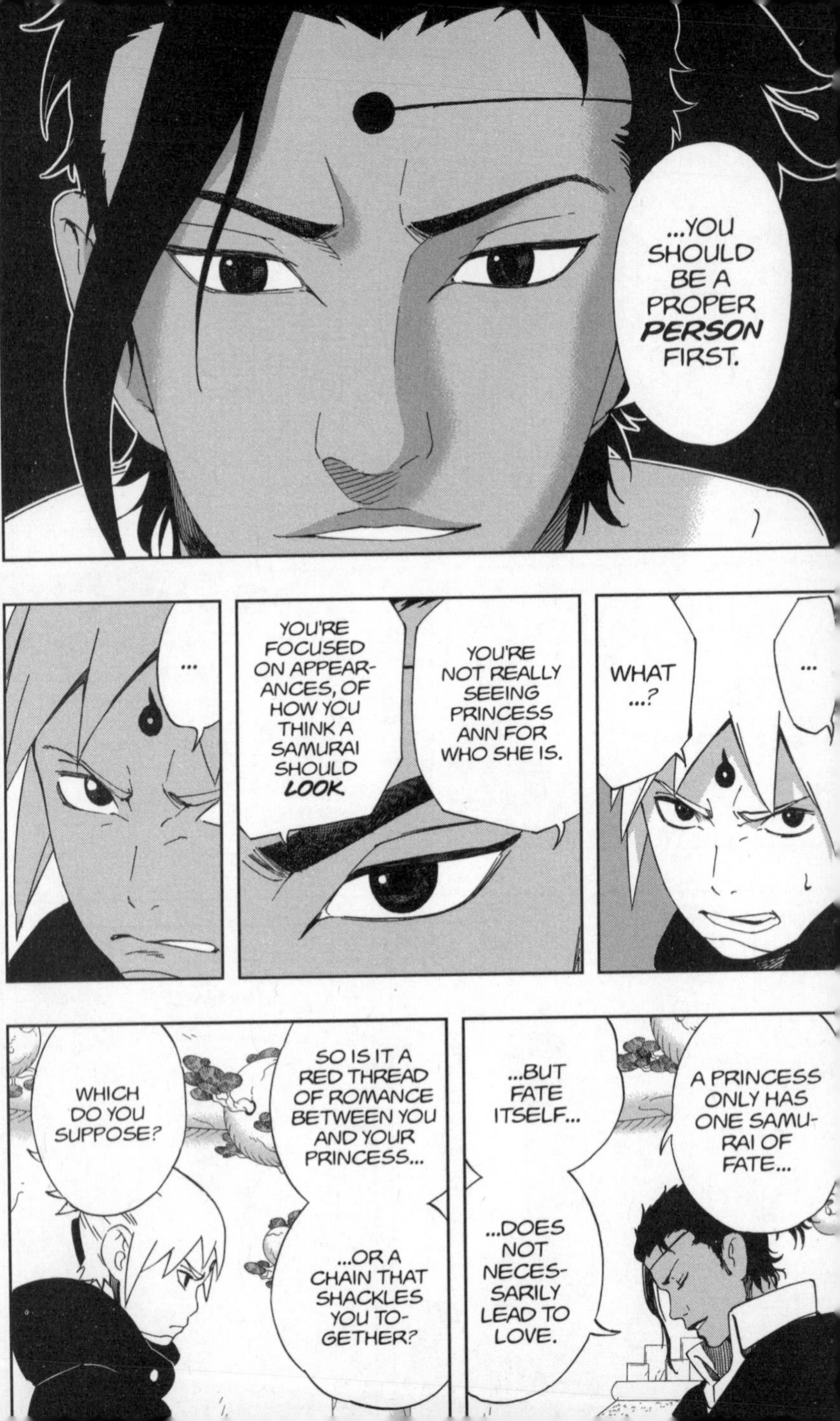
...YOU SHOULD BE A PROPER **PERSON** FIRST.
...
WHAT ...?
YOU'RE NOT REALLY SEEING PRINCESS ANN FOR WHO SHE IS.
YOU'RE FOCUSED ON APPEARANCES, OF HOW YOU THINK A SAMURAI SHOULD **LOOK**
...
A PRINCESS ONLY HAS ONE SAMURAI OF FATE...
...BUT FATE ITSELF...
...DOES NOT NECESSARILY LEAD TO LOVE.
SO IS IT A RED THREAD OF ROMANCE BETWEEN YOU AND YOUR PRINCESS...
...OR A CHAIN THAT SHACKLES YOU TOGETHER?
WHICH DO YOU SUPPOSE?

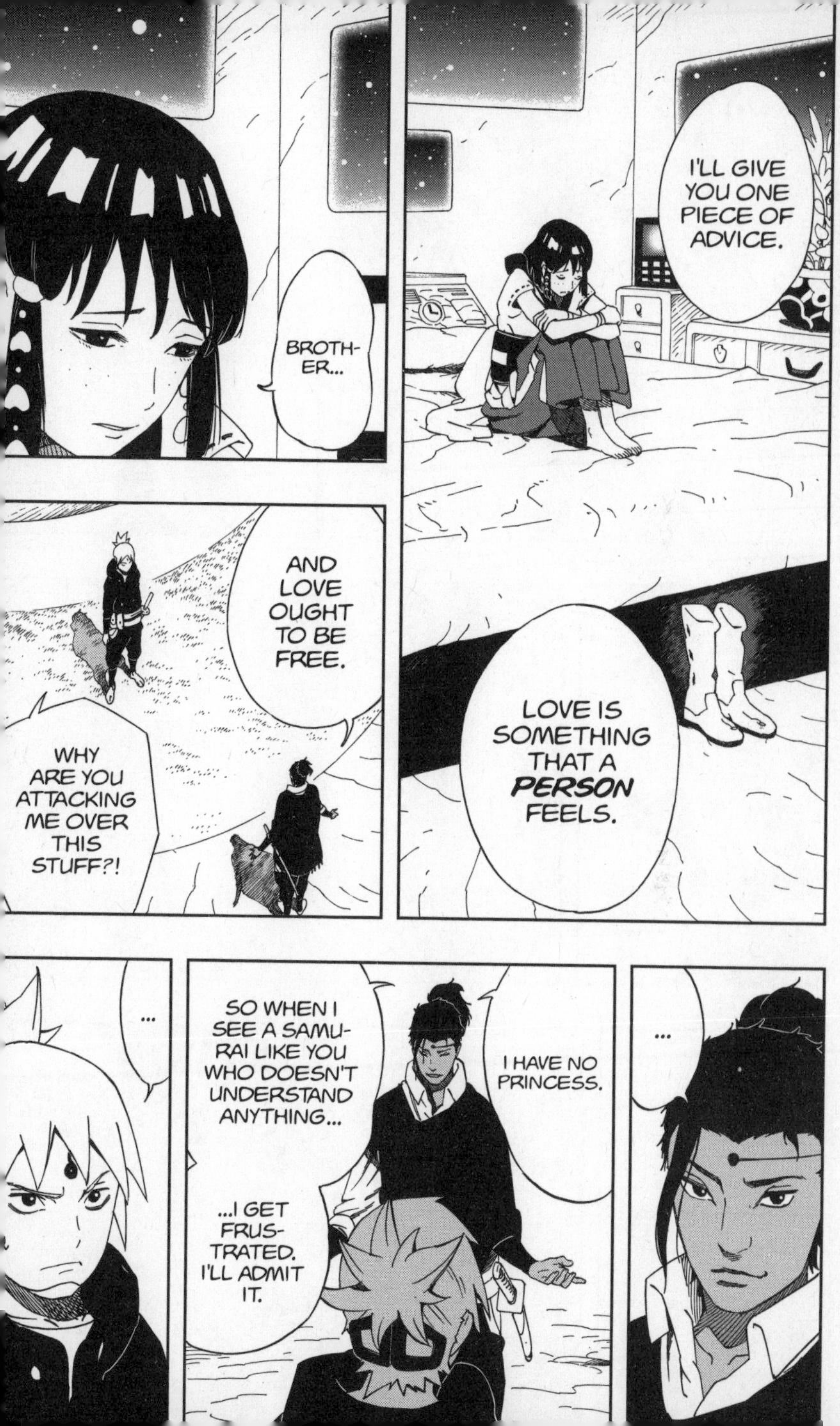
I'LL GIVE YOU ONE PIECE OF ADVICE.
BROTHER...
LOVE IS SOMETHING THAT A ***PERSON*** FEELS.
AND LOVE OUGHT TO BE FREE.
WHY ARE YOU ATTACKING ME OVER THIS STUFF?!
...
I HAVE NO PRINCESS.
SO WHEN I SEE A SAMURAI LIKE YOU WHO DOESN'T UNDERSTAND ANYTHING...
...I GET FRUSTRATED. I'LL ADMIT IT.
...

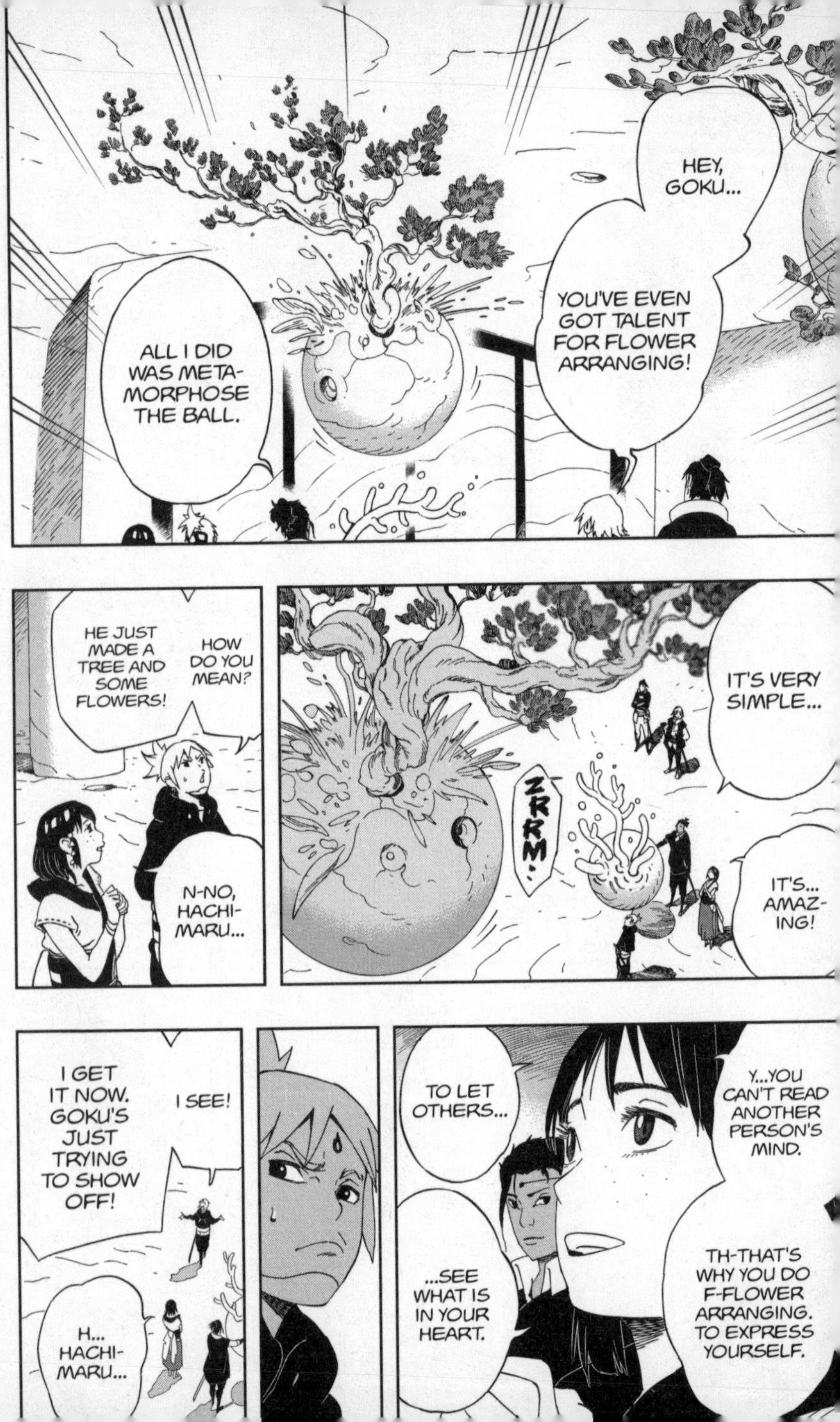
HEY, GOKU...
YOU'VE EVEN GOT TALENT FOR FLOWER ARRANGING!
ALL I DID WAS META-MORPHOSE THE BALL.
IT'S VERY SIMPLE...
ZRRM
IT'S... AMAZ-ING!
HOW DO YOU MEAN?
HE JUST MADE A TREE AND SOME FLOWERS!
N-NO, HACHI-MARU...
Y...YOU CAN'T READ ANOTHER PERSON'S MIND.
TH-THAT'S WHY YOU DO F-FLOWER ARRANGING. TO EXPRESS YOURSELF.
TO LET OTHERS...
...SEE WHAT IS IN YOUR HEART.
I SEE!
I GET IT NOW. GOKU'S JUST TRYING TO SHOW OFF!
H... HACHI-MARU...

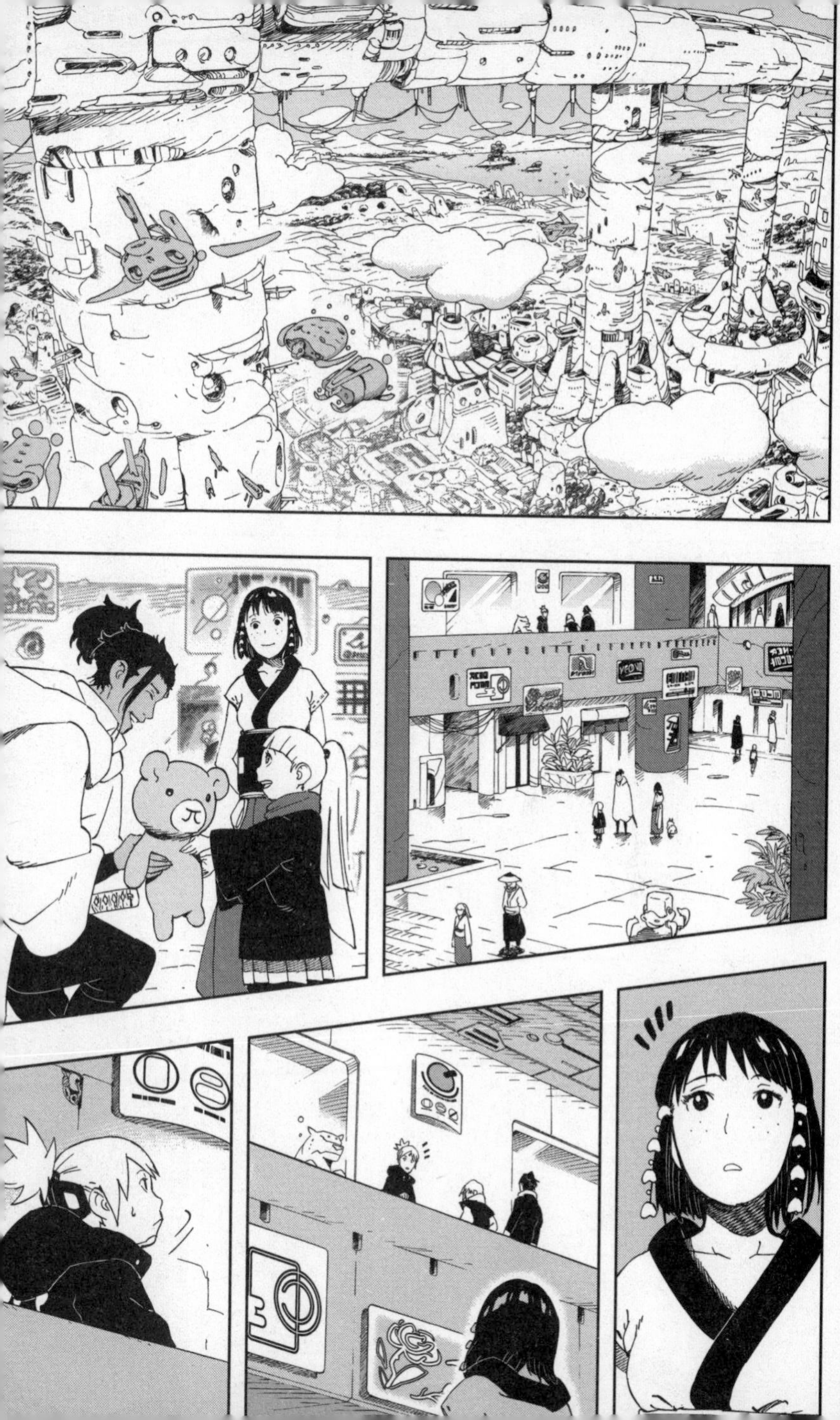

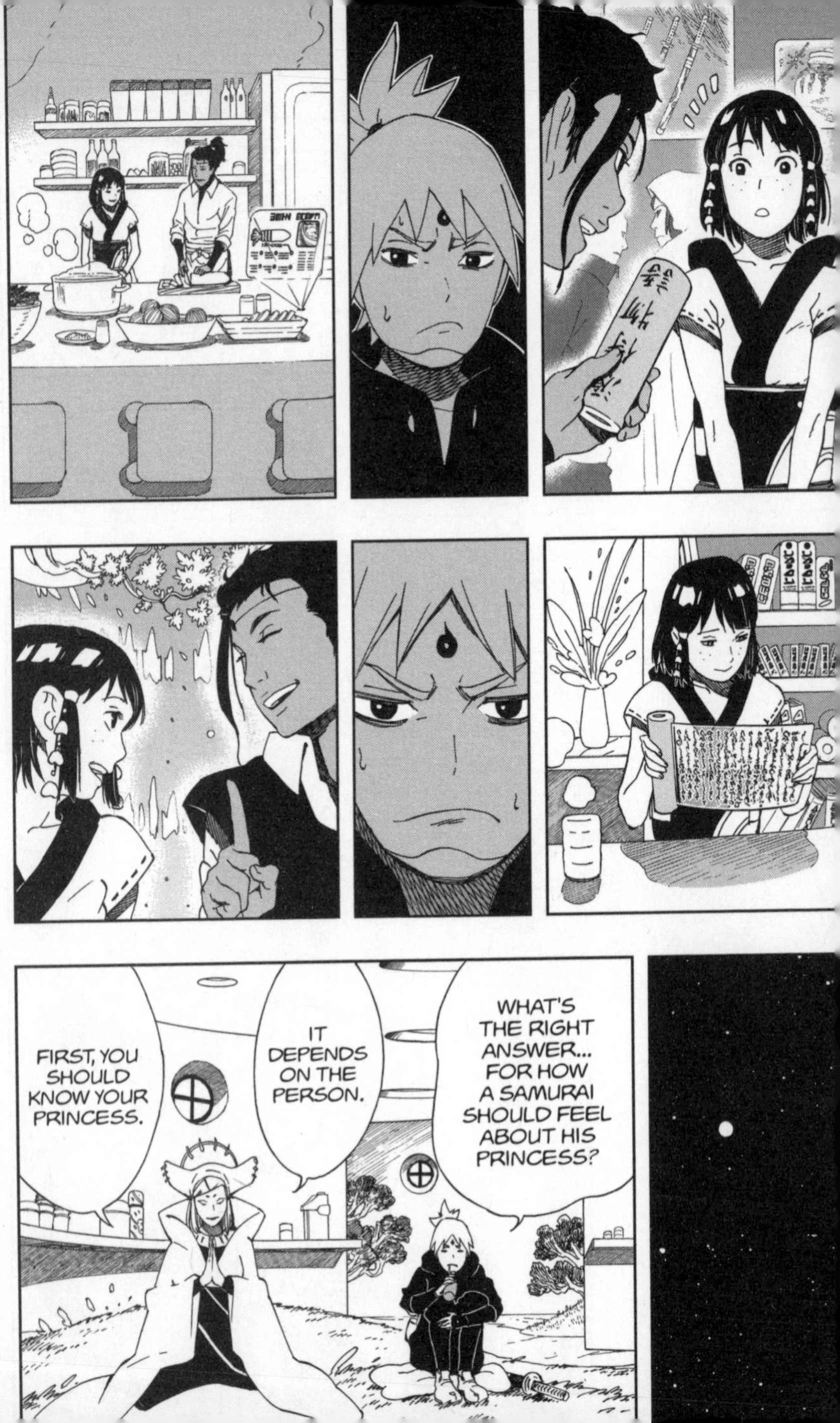
WHAT'S THE RIGHT ANSWER... FOR HOW A SAMURAI SHOULD FEEL ABOUT HIS PRINCESS?
IT DEPENDS ON THE PERSON.
FIRST, YOU SHOULD KNOW YOUR PRINCESS.

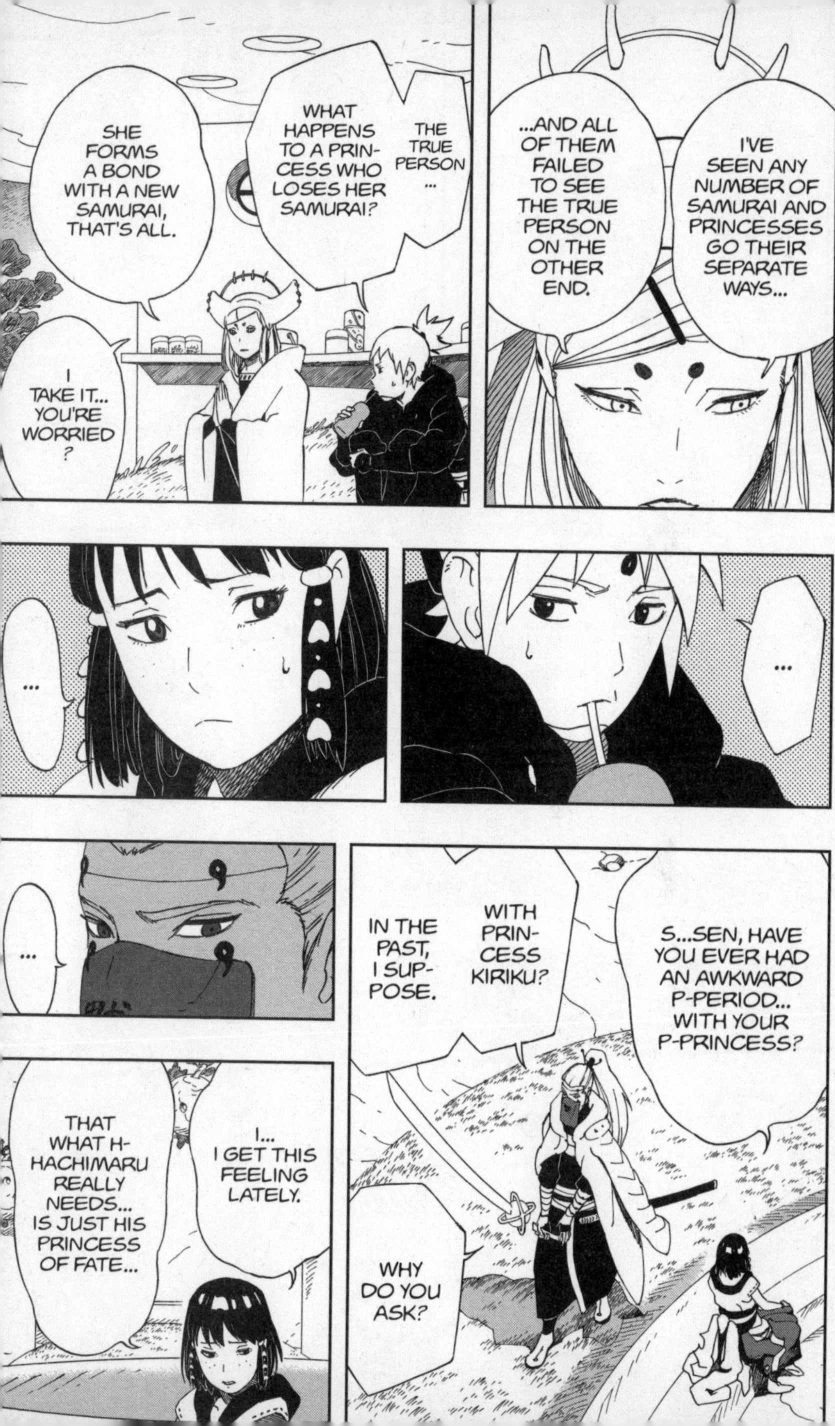
I'VE SEEN ANY NUMBER OF SAMURAI AND PRINCESSES GO THEIR SEPARATE WAYS...
...AND ALL OF THEM FAILED TO SEE THE TRUE PERSON ON THE OTHER END.
THE TRUE PERSON ...
WHAT HAPPENS TO A PRIN-CESS WHO LOSES HER SAMURAI?
SHE FORMS A BOND WITH A NEW SAMURAI, THAT'S ALL.
I TAKE IT... YOU'RE WORRIED?
...
...
S...SEN, HAVE YOU EVER HAD AN AWKWARD P-PERIOD... WITH YOUR P-PRINCESS?
WITH PRIN-CESS KIRIKU?
IN THE PAST, I SUP-POSE.
WHY DO YOU ASK?
...
I... I GET THIS FEELING LATELY.
THAT WHAT H-HACHIMARU REALLY NEEDS... IS JUST HIS PRINCESS OF FATE...

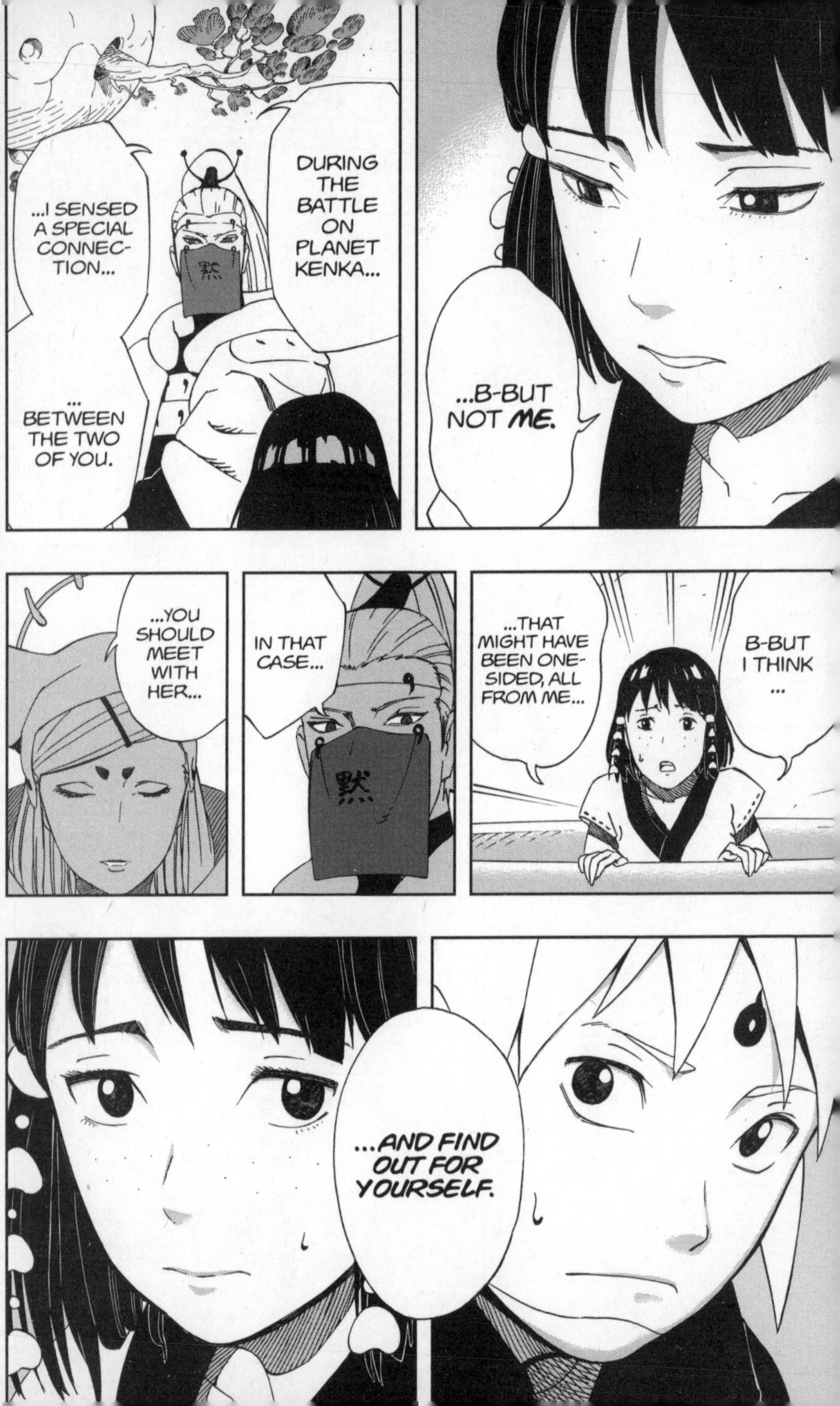
...B-BUT NOT ME.
DURING THE BATTLE ON PLANET KENKA...
...I SENSED A SPECIAL CONNECTION...
...BETWEEN THE TWO OF YOU.
B-BUT I THINK...
...THAT MIGHT HAVE BEEN ONE-SIDED, ALL FROM ME...
IN THAT CASE...
...YOU SHOULD MEET WITH HER...
...AND FIND OUT FOR YOURSELF.

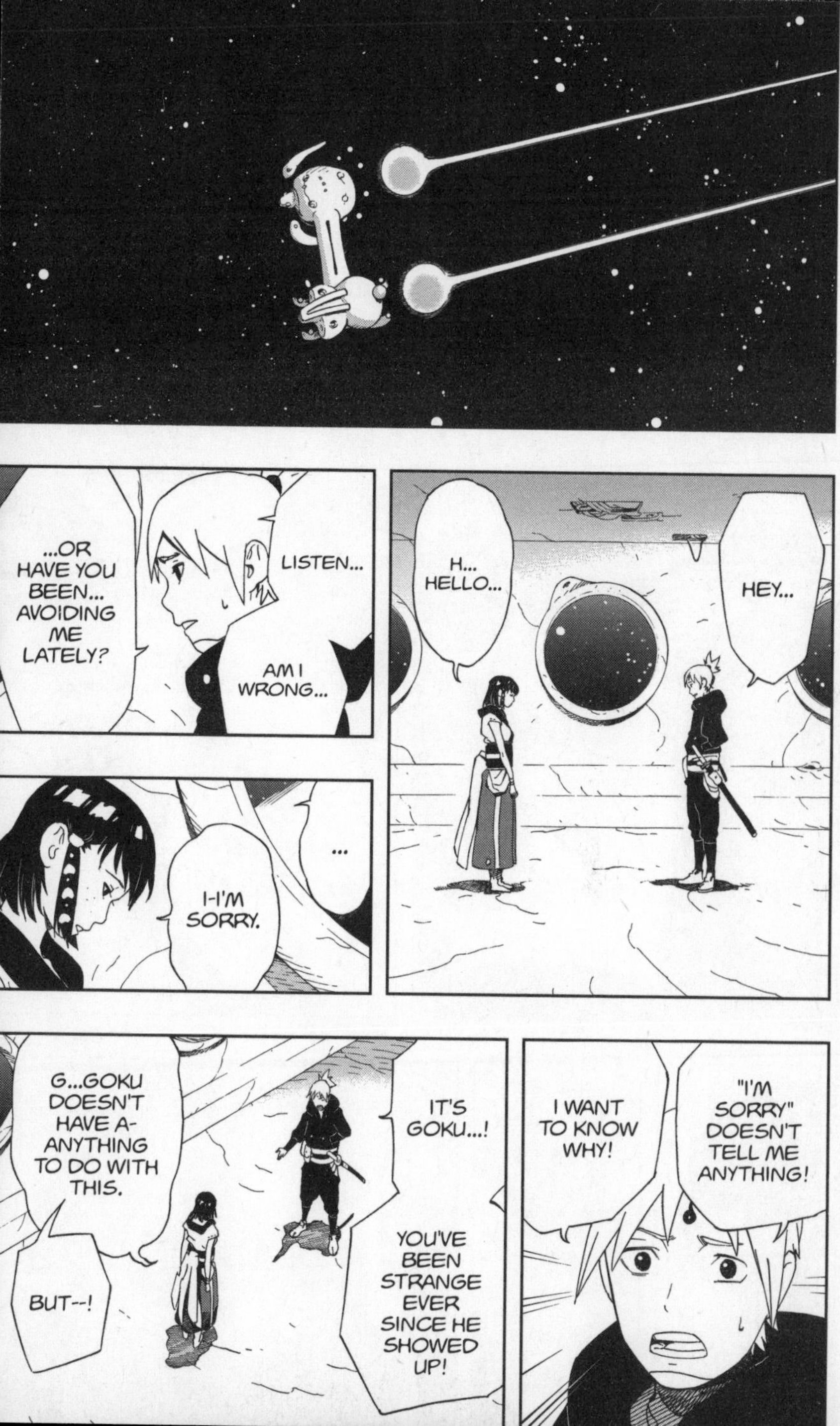
HEY...
H... HELLO...
LISTEN...
AM I WRONG...
...OR HAVE YOU BEEN... AVOIDING ME LATELY?
...
I-I'M SORRY.
"I'M SORRY" DOESN'T TELL ME ANYTHING!
I WANT TO KNOW WHY!
IT'S GOKU...!
YOU'VE BEEN STRANGE EVER SINCE HE SHOWED UP!
G...GOKU DOESN'T HAVE A-ANYTHING TO DO WITH THIS.
BUT--!

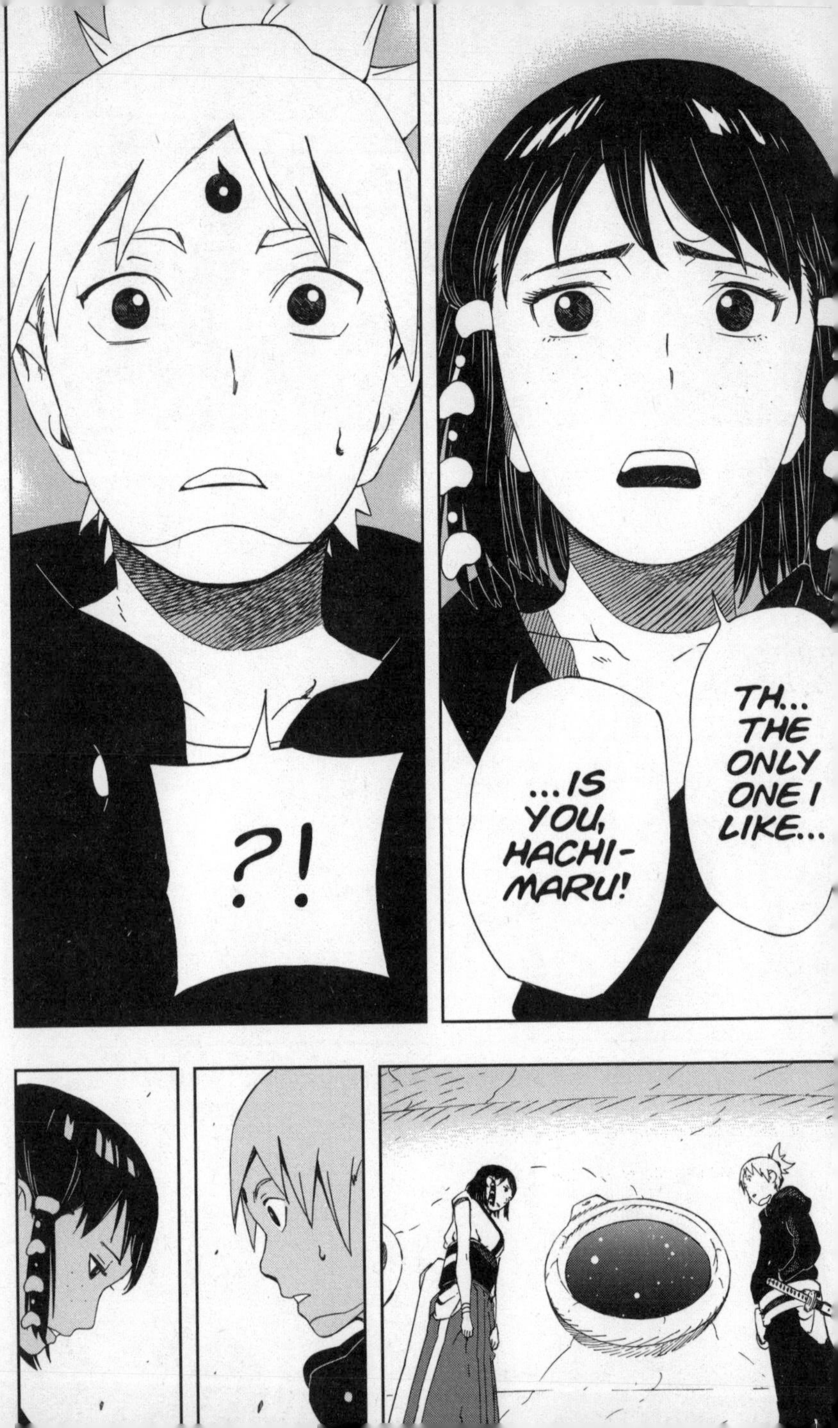
TH... THE ONLY ONE I LIKE...
...IS YOU, HACHI-MARU!
?!

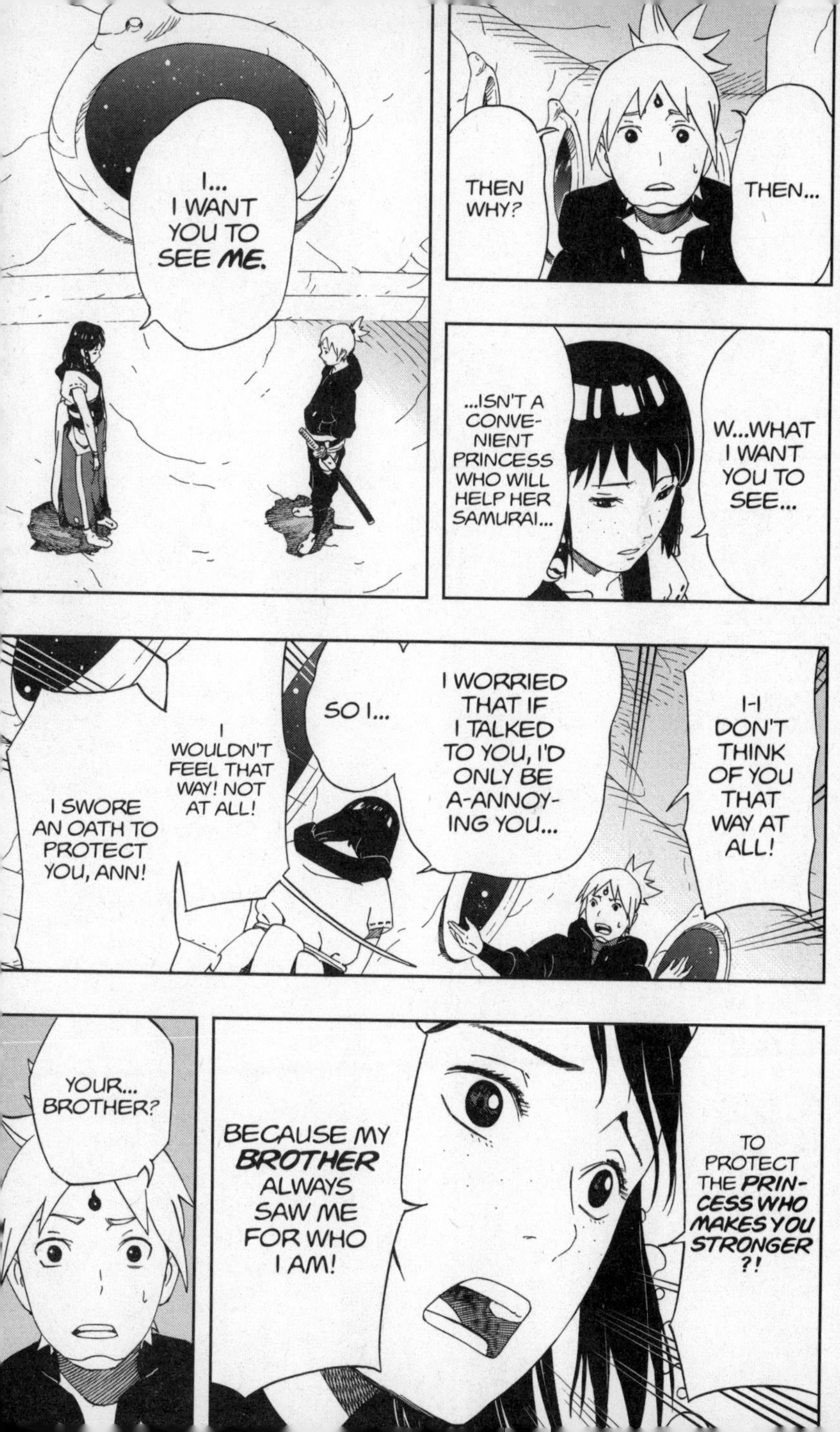
THEN...
THEN WHY?
W...WHAT I WANT YOU TO SEE...
...ISN'T A CONVENIENT PRINCESS WHO WILL HELP HER SAMURAI...
I... I WANT YOU TO SEE ME.
I-I DON'T THINK OF YOU THAT WAY AT ALL!
I WORRIED THAT IF I TALKED TO YOU, I'D ONLY BE A-ANNOYING YOU...
SO I...
I WOULDN'T FEEL THAT WAY! NOT AT ALL!
I SWORE AN OATH TO PROTECT YOU, ANN!
TO PROTECT THE PRINCESS WHO MAKES YOU STRONGER?!
BECAUSE MY BROTHER ALWAYS SAW ME FOR WHO I AM!
YOUR... BROTHER?

Pre-Series Rough Designs (Okubo)

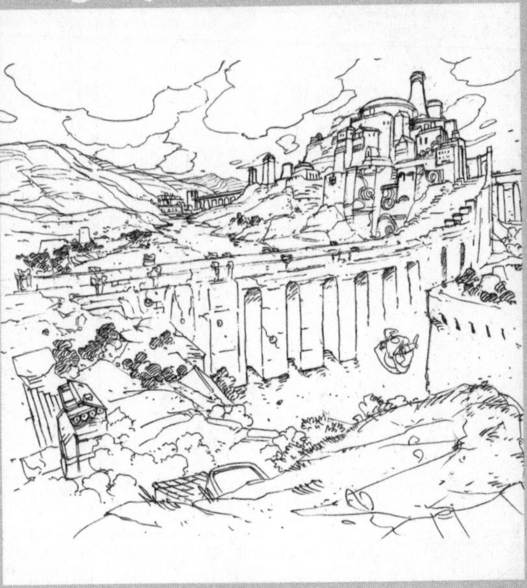

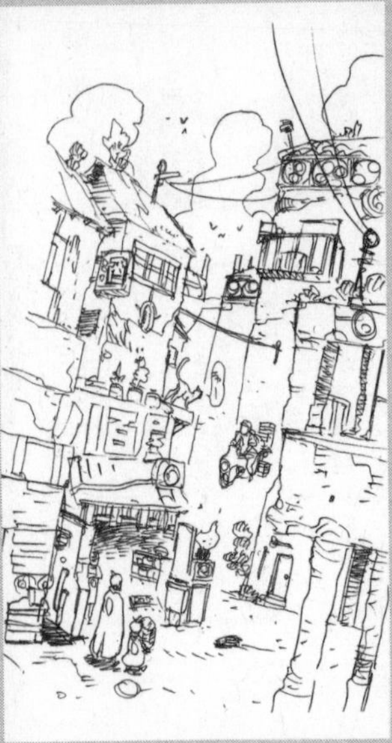

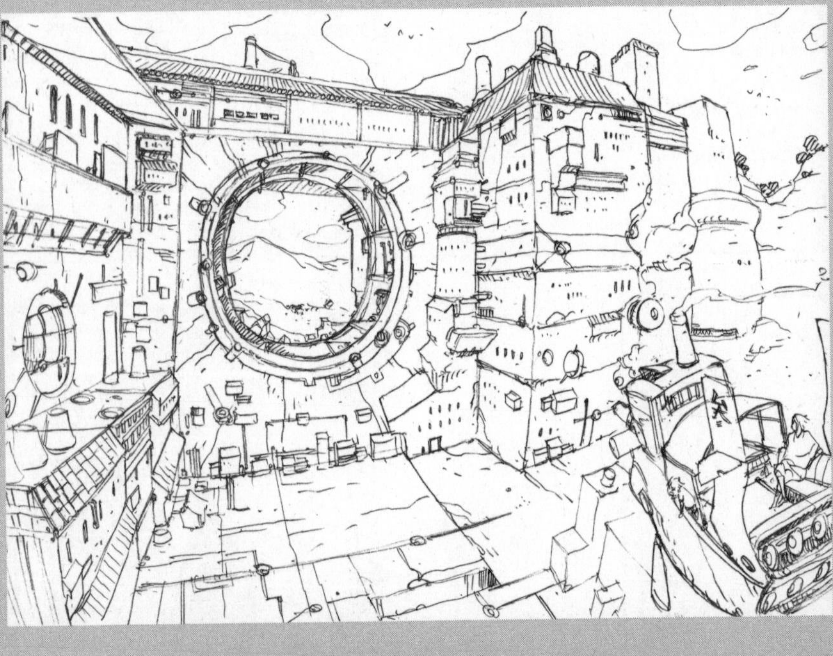

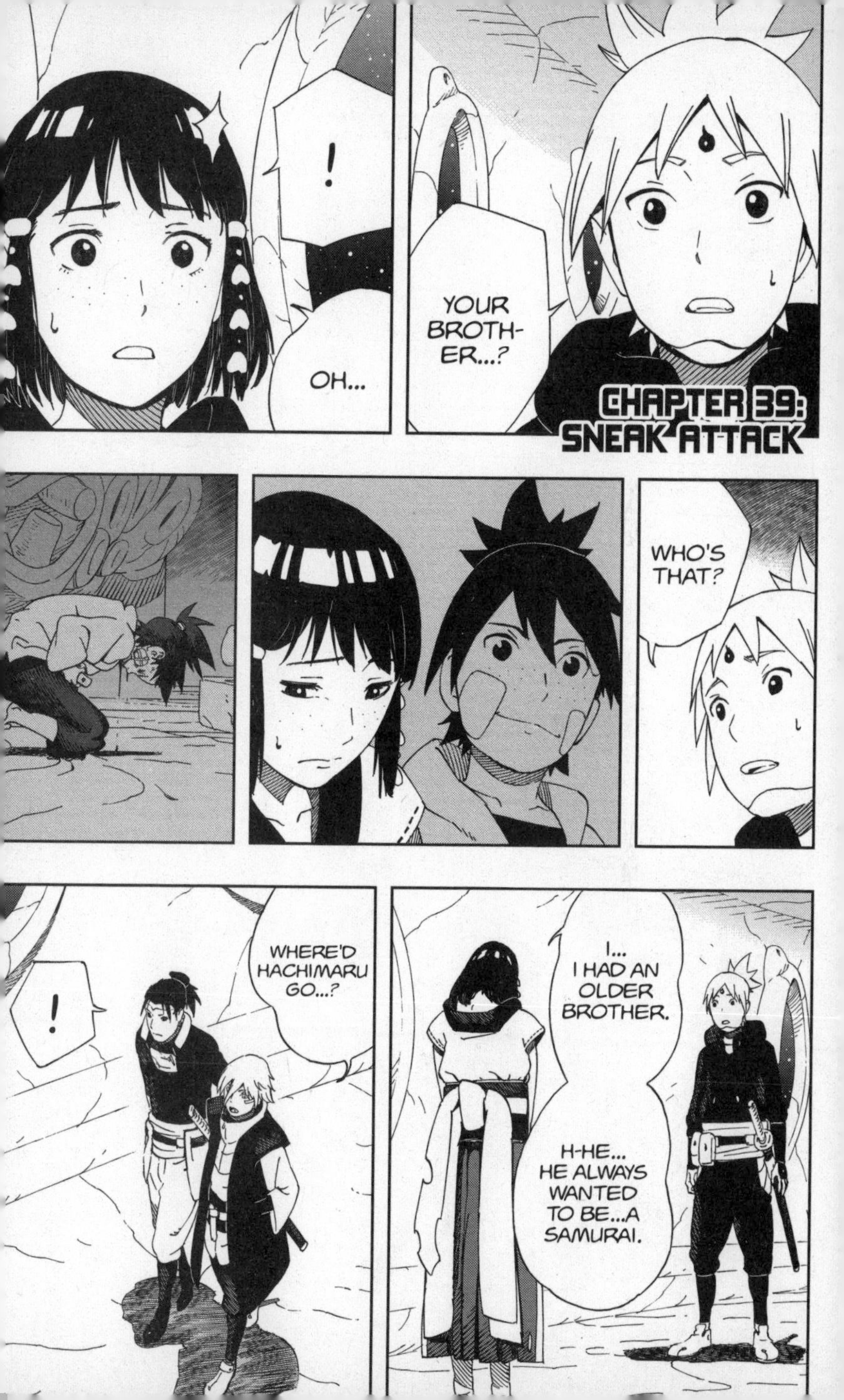
YOUR BROTHER-ER...?
CHAPTER 39: SNEAK ATTACK
!
OH...
WHO'S THAT?
I... I HAD AN OLDER BROTHER.
H-HE... HE ALWAYS WANTED TO BE...A SAMURAI.
WHERE'D HACHIMARU GO...?
!

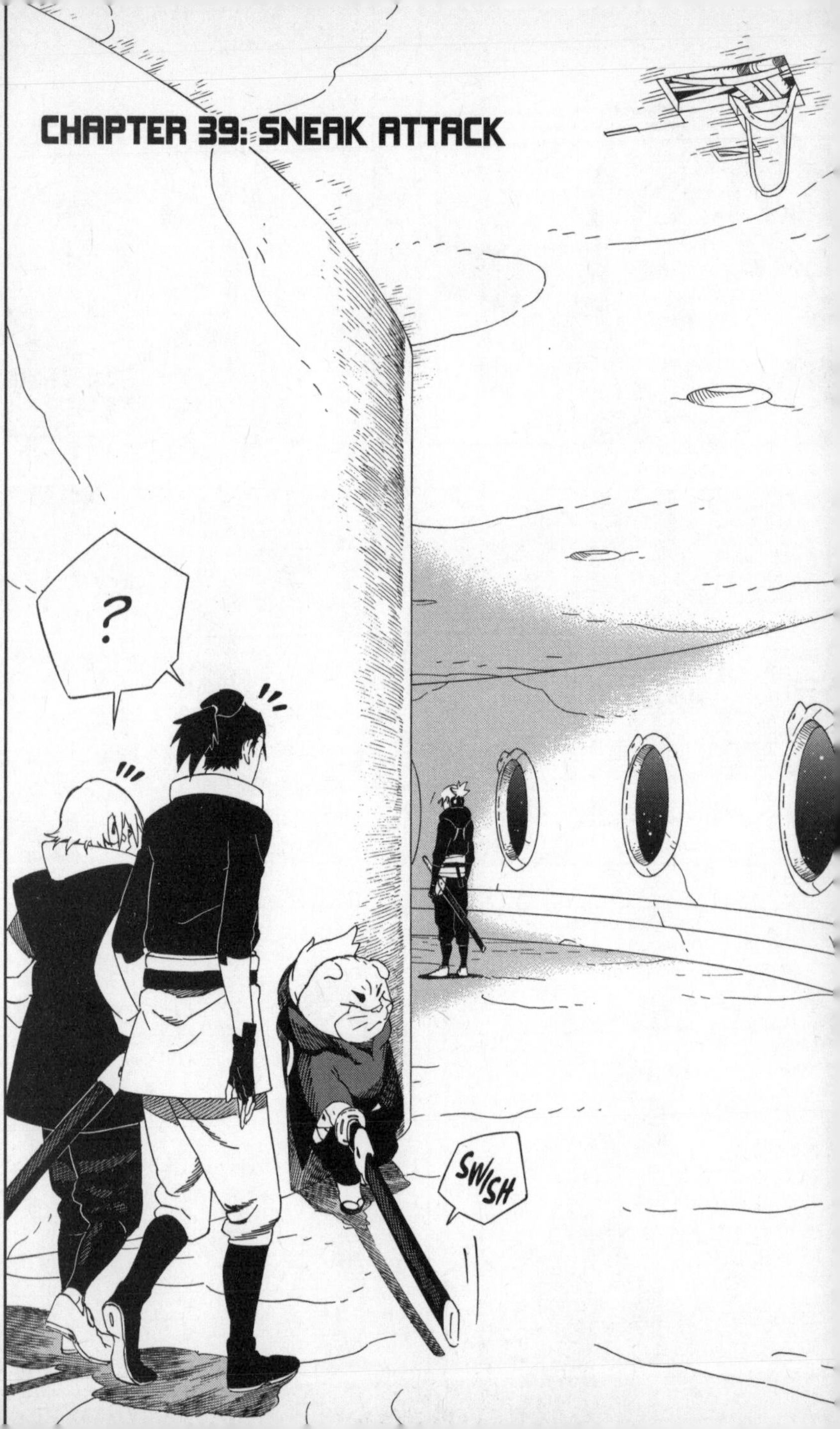
CHAPTER 39: SNEAK ATTACK
?
SWISH

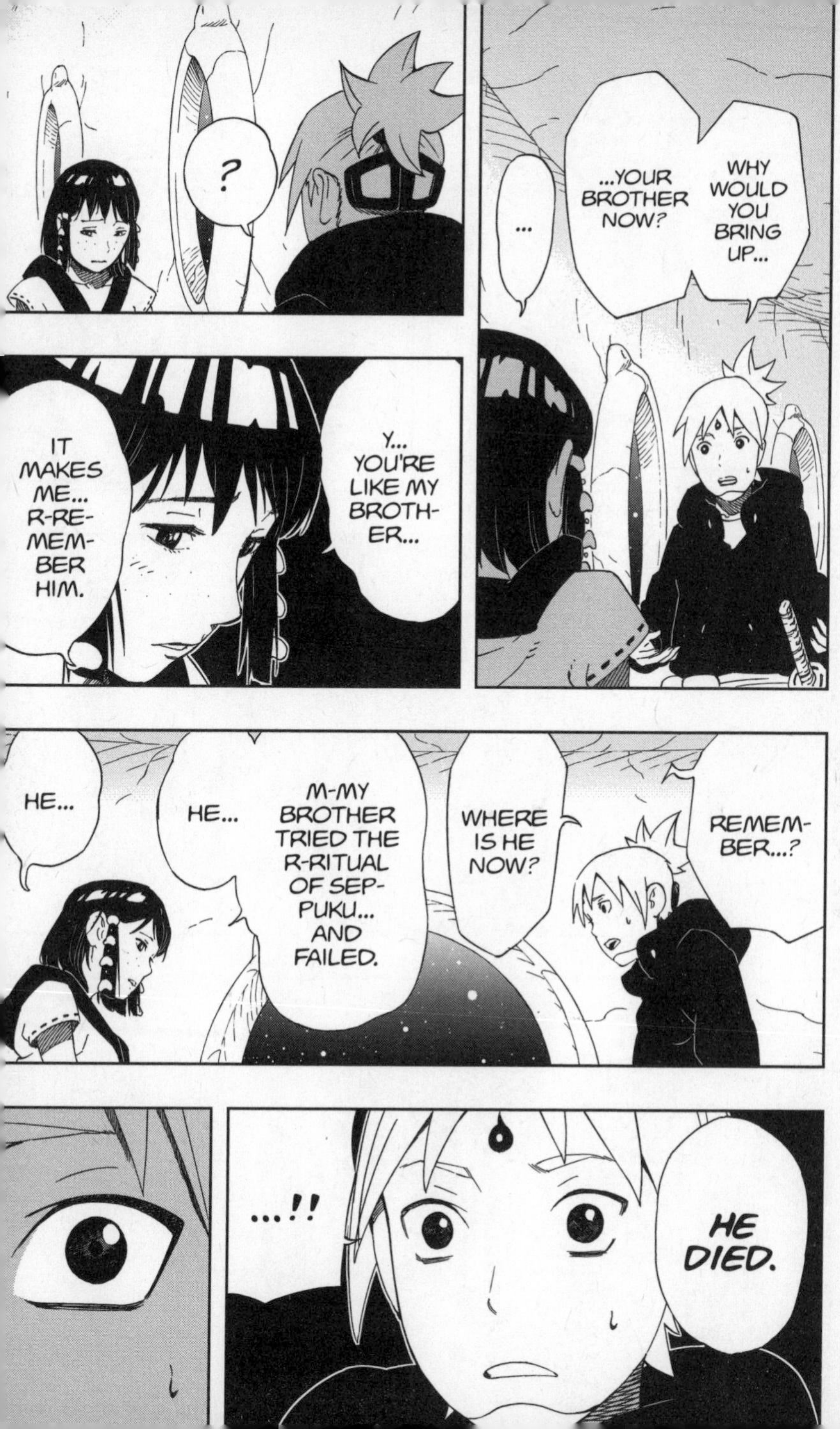
WHY WOULD YOU BRING UP...
...YOUR BROTHER NOW?
...
?
Y... YOU'RE LIKE MY BROTHER...
IT MAKES ME... R-REMEMBER HIM.
REMEMBER...?
WHERE IS HE NOW?
M-MY BROTHER TRIED THE R-RITUAL OF SEPPUKU... AND FAILED.
HE...
HE...
HE DIED.
...!!

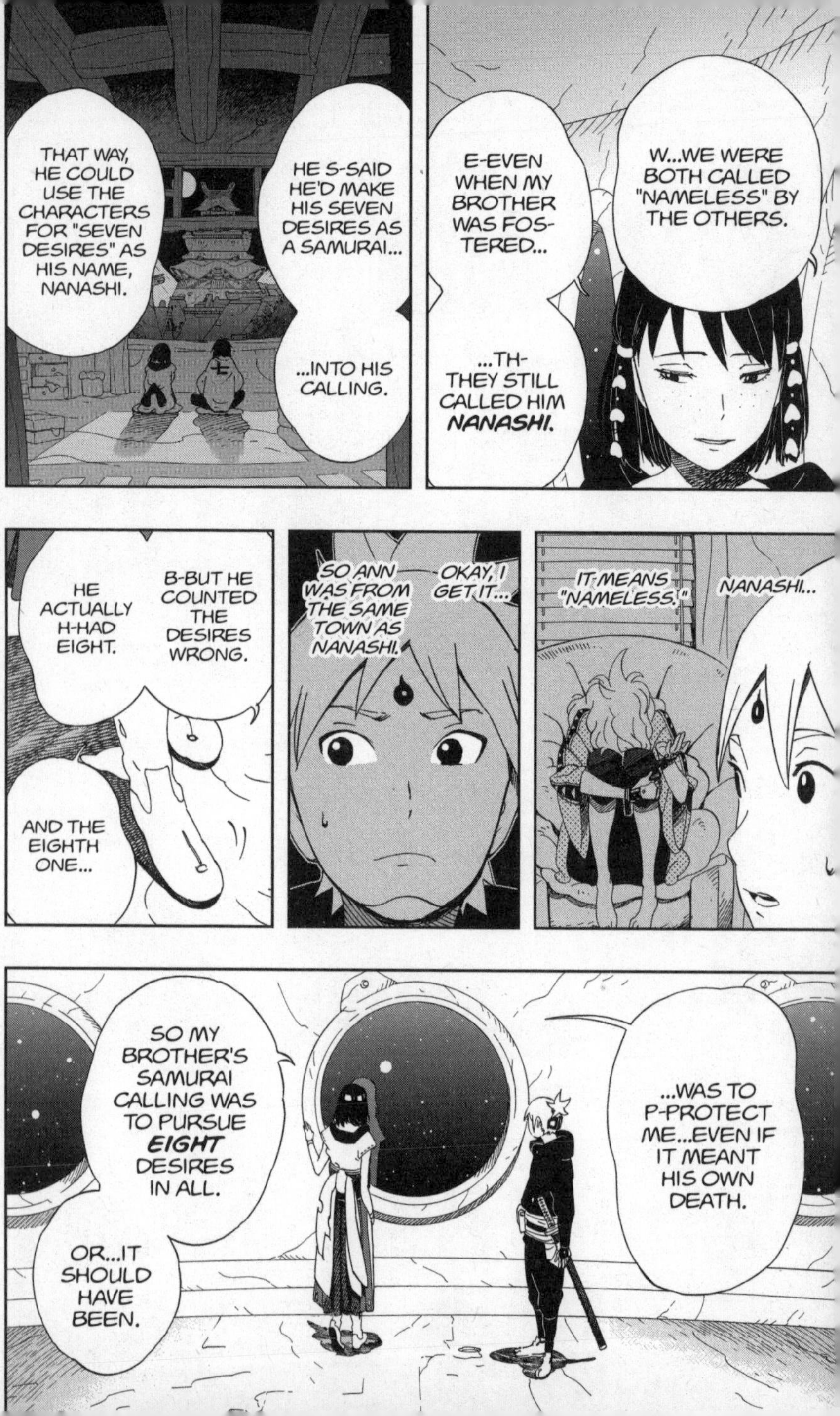
W...WE WERE BOTH CALLED "NAMELESS" BY THE OTHERS.
E-EVEN WHEN MY BROTHER WAS FOSTERED...
...TH-THEY STILL CALLED HIM ***NANASHI.***
HE S-SAID HE'D MAKE HIS SEVEN DESIRES AS A SAMURAI...
...INTO HIS CALLING.
THAT WAY, HE COULD USE THE CHARACTERS FOR "SEVEN DESIRES" AS HIS NAME, NANASHI.
NANASHI...
IT MEANS "NAMELESS."
OKAY, I GET IT...
SO ANN WAS FROM THE SAME TOWN AS NANASHI.
B-BUT HE COUNTED THE DESIRES WRONG.
HE ACTUALLY H-HAD EIGHT.
AND THE EIGHTH ONE...
...WAS TO P-PROTECT ME...EVEN IF IT MEANT HIS OWN DEATH.
SO MY BROTHER'S SAMURAI CALLING WAS TO PURSUE ***EIGHT*** DESIRES IN ALL.
OR...IT SHOULD HAVE BEEN.

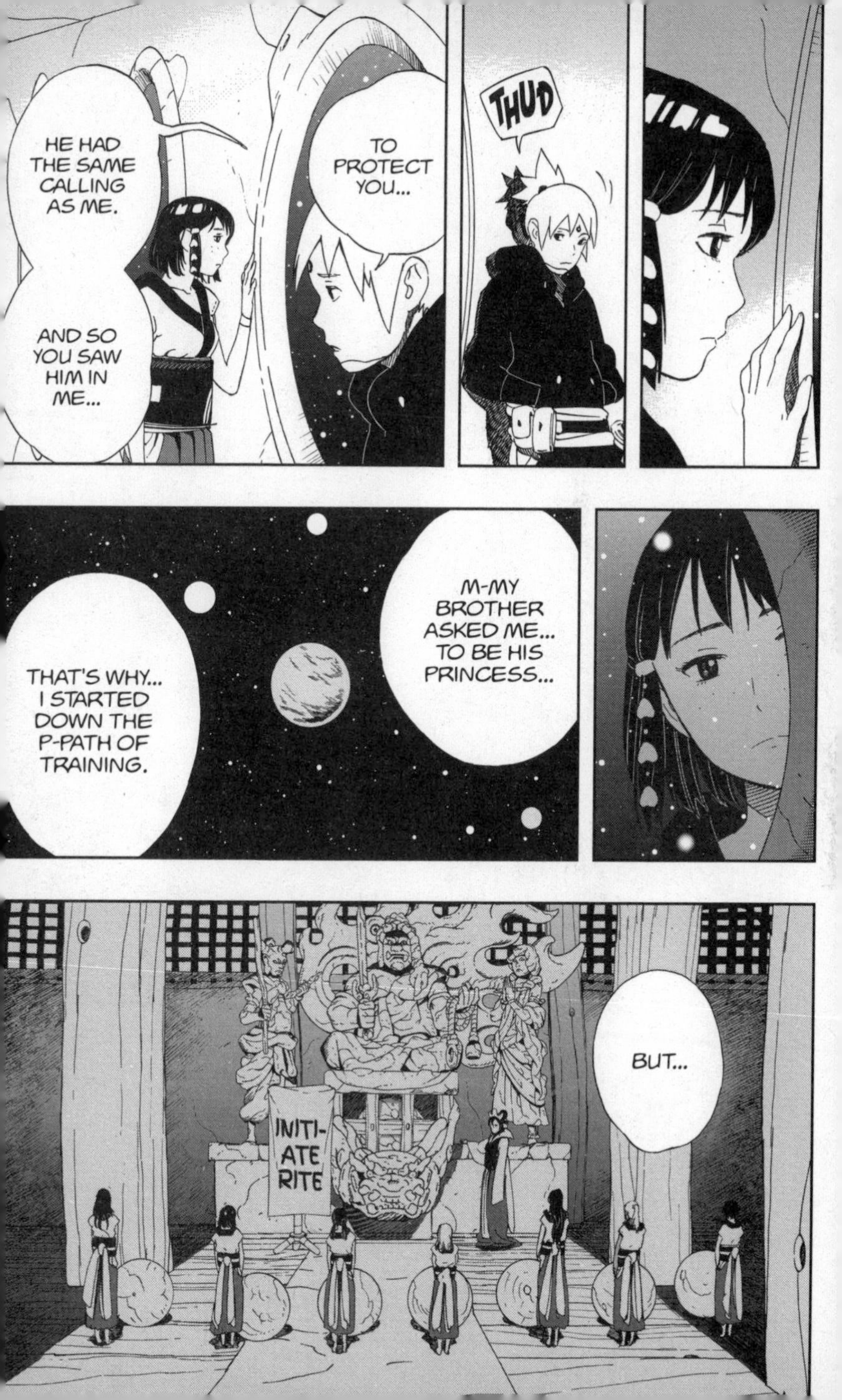
THUD
TO PROTECT YOU...
HE HAD THE SAME CALLING AS ME.
AND SO YOU SAW HIM IN ME...
M-MY BROTHER ASKED ME... TO BE HIS PRINCESS...
THAT'S WHY... I STARTED DOWN THE P-PATH OF TRAINING.
BUT...
INITI-ATE RITE

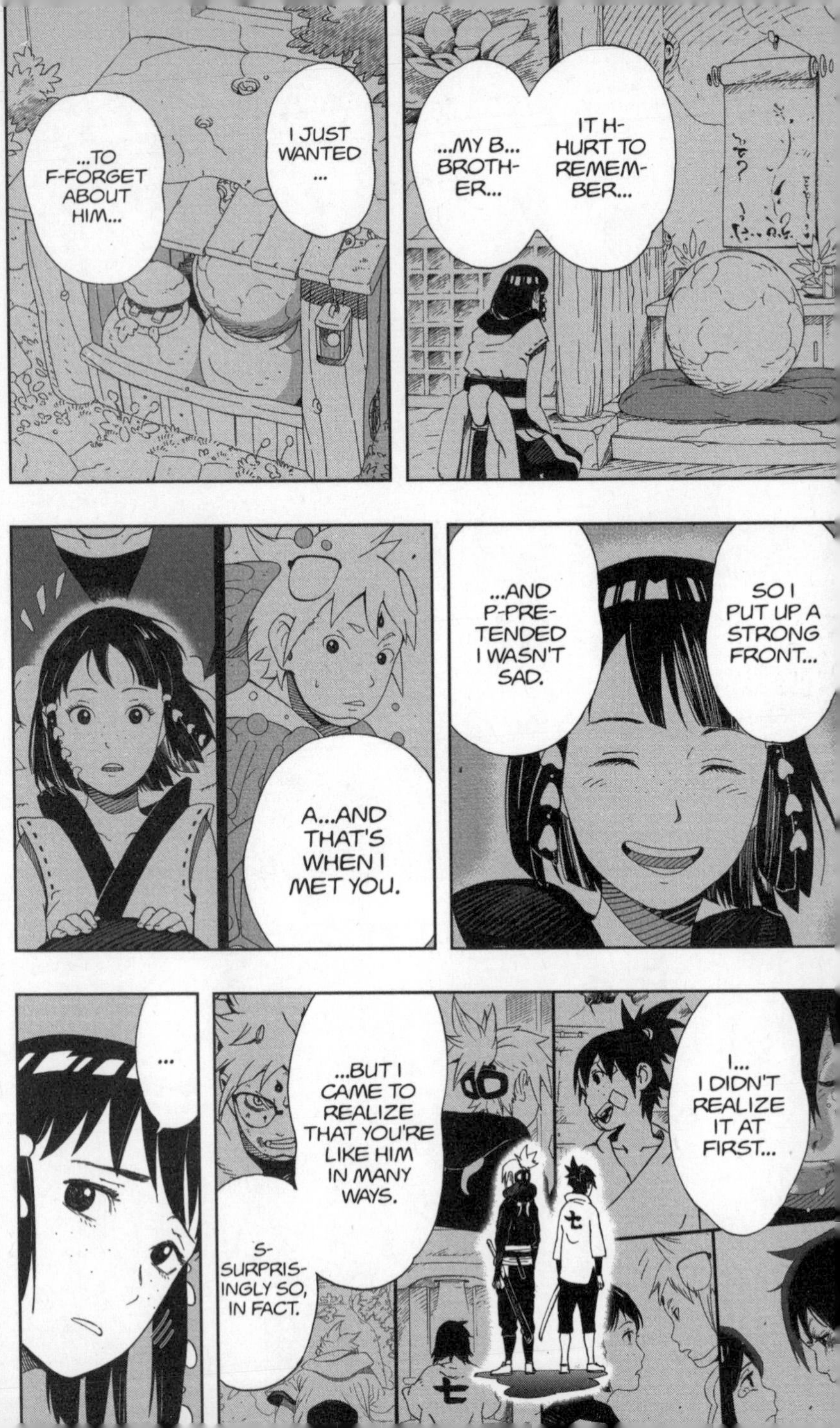
IT H-HURT TO REMEMBER...
...MY B... BROTHER...
I JUST WANTED ...
...TO F-FORGET ABOUT HIM...
SO I PUT UP A STRONG FRONT...
...AND P-PRETENDED I WASN'T SAD.
A...AND THAT'S WHEN I MET YOU.
I... I DIDN'T REALIZE IT AT FIRST...
...BUT I CAME TO REALIZE THAT YOU'RE LIKE HIM IN MANY WAYS.
S-SURPRISINGLY SO, IN FACT.
...

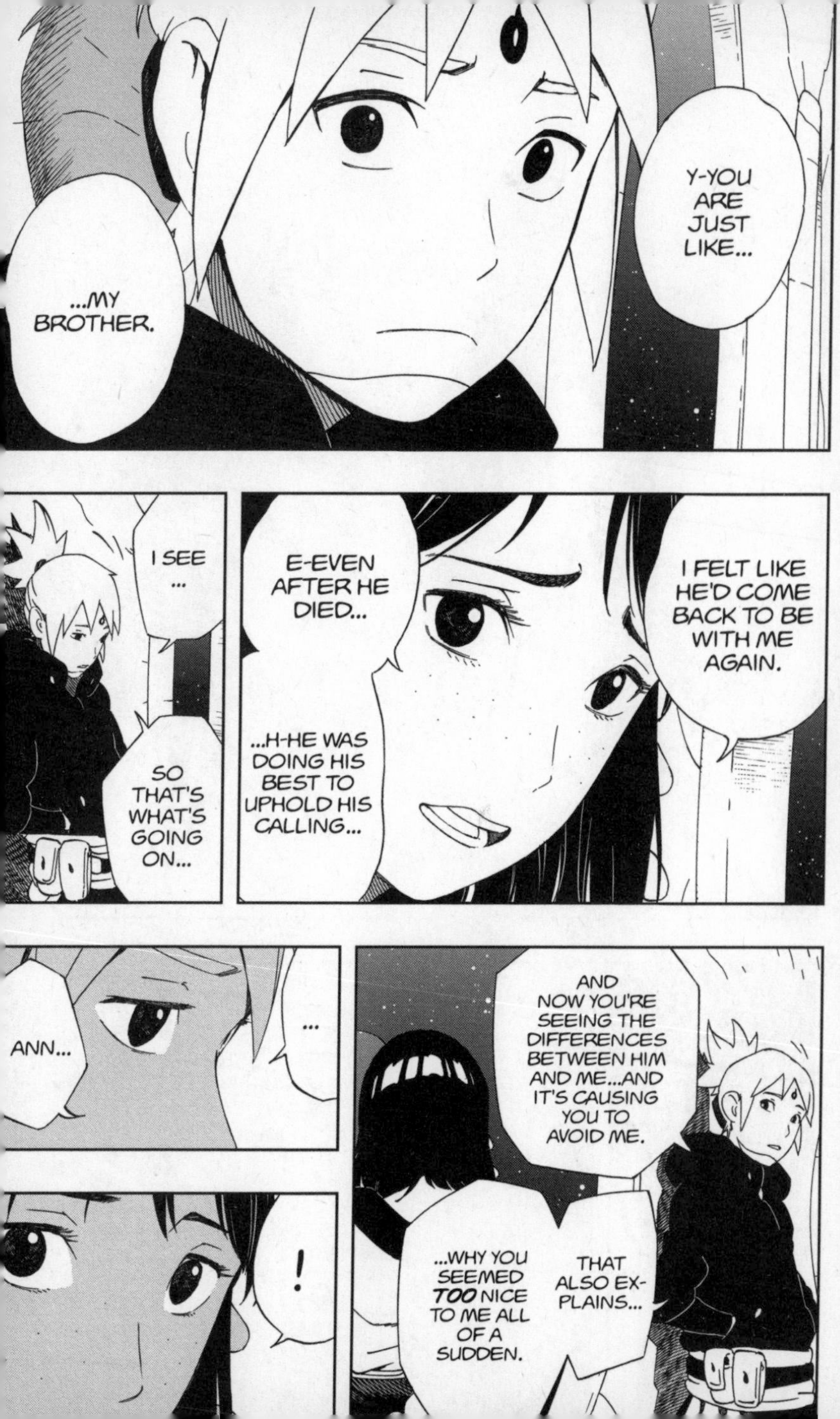
Y-YOU ARE JUST LIKE...
...MY BROTHER.
I FELT LIKE HE'D COME BACK TO BE WITH ME AGAIN.
E-EVEN AFTER HE DIED...
...H-HE WAS DOING HIS BEST TO UPHOLD HIS CALLING...
I SEE ...
SO THAT'S WHAT'S GOING ON...
AND NOW YOU'RE SEEING THE DIFFERENCES BETWEEN HIM AND ME...AND IT'S CAUSING YOU TO AVOID ME.
THAT ALSO EX-PLAINS...
...WHY YOU SEEMED TOO NICE TO ME ALL OF A SUDDEN.
...
ANN...
!

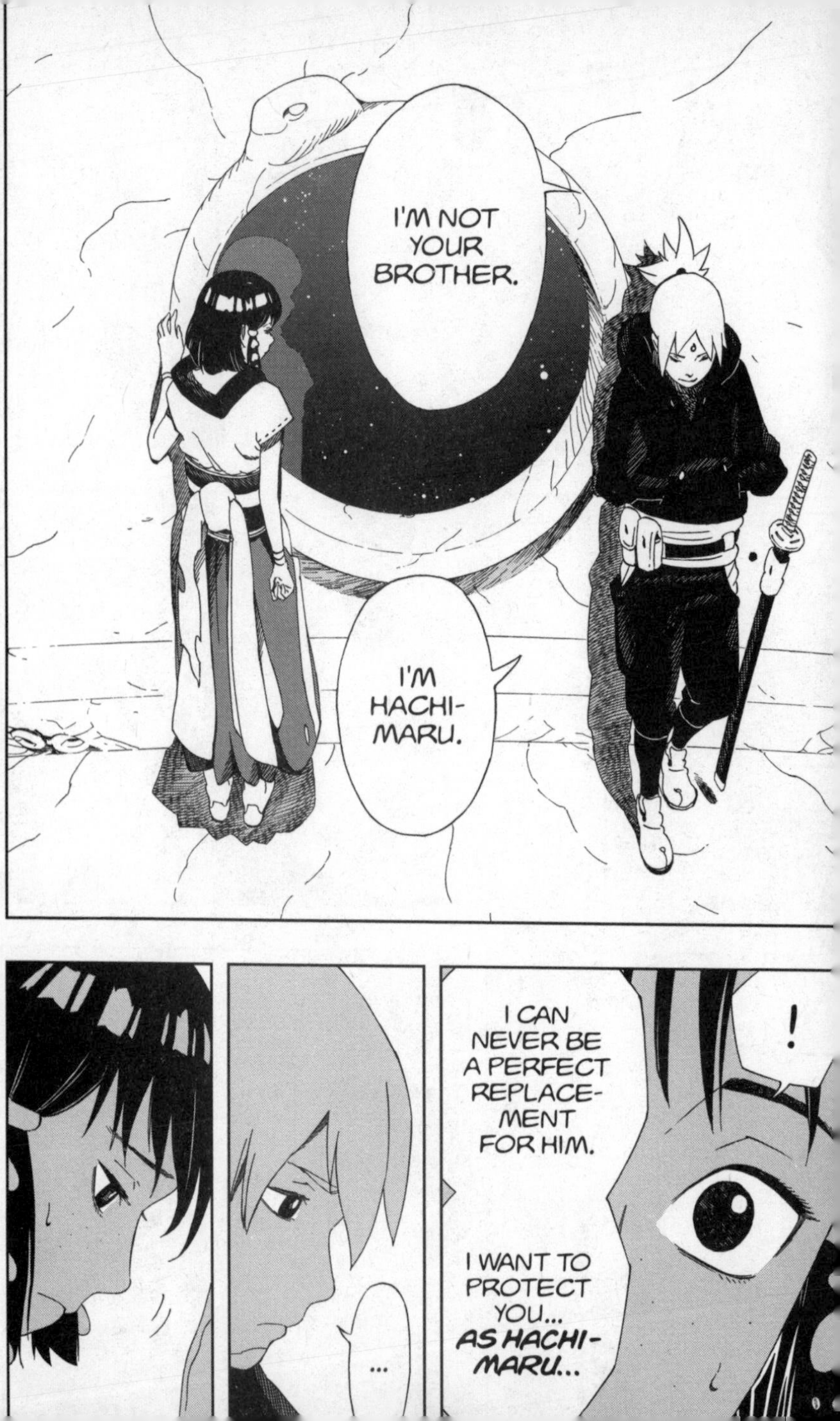
I'M NOT YOUR BROTHER.
I'M HACHI-MARU.
!
I CAN NEVER BE A PERFECT REPLACE-MENT FOR HIM.
I WANT TO PROTECT YOU... ***AS HACHI-MARU...***
...

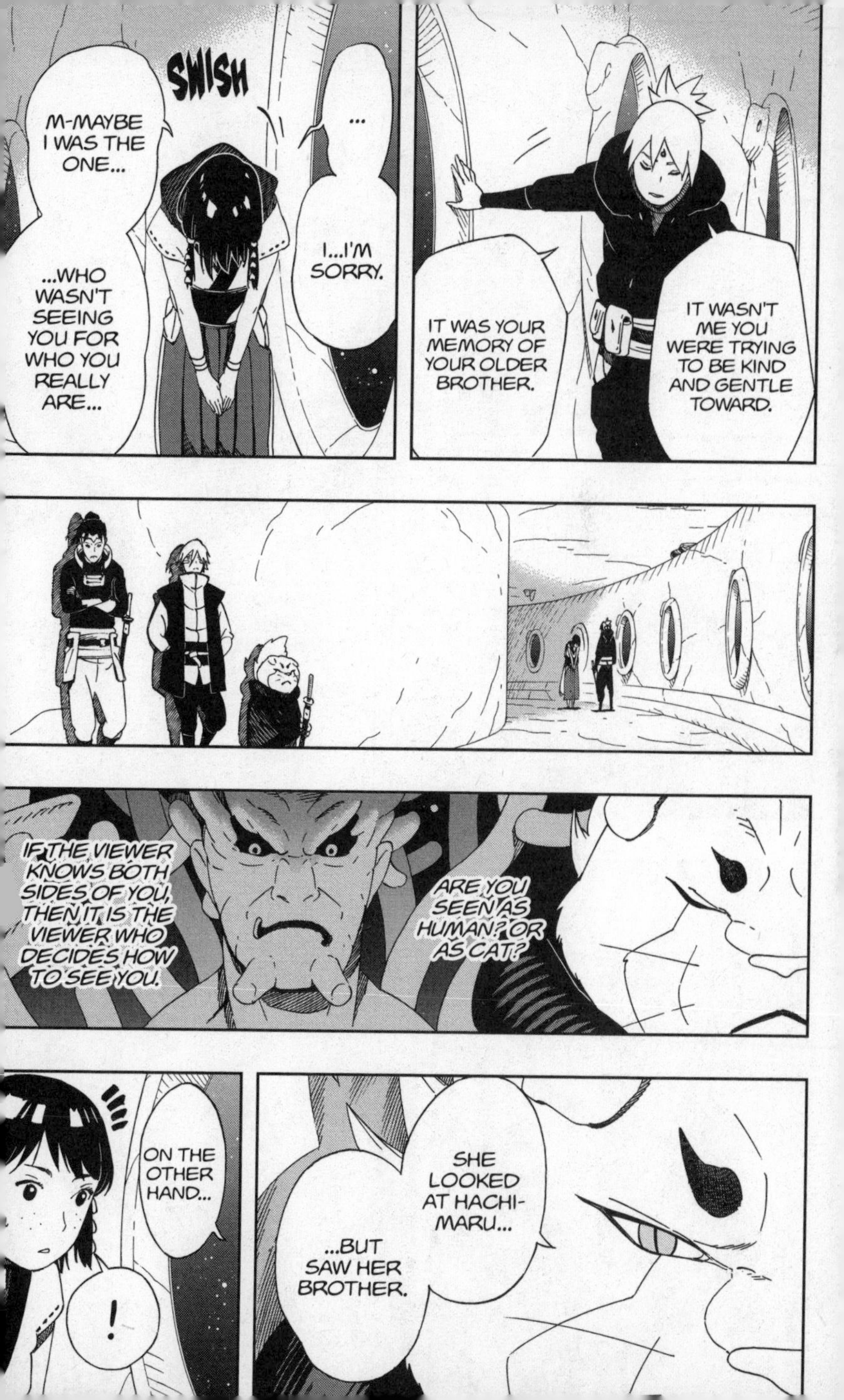
IT WASN'T ME YOU WERE TRYING TO BE KIND AND GENTLE TOWARD.
IT WAS YOUR MEMORY OF YOUR OLDER BROTHER.
...
I...I'M SORRY.
SWISH
M-MAYBE I WAS THE ONE...
...WHO WASN'T SEEING YOU FOR WHO YOU REALLY ARE...
ARE YOU SEEN AS HUMAN? OR AS CAT?
IF THE VIEWER KNOWS BOTH SIDES OF YOU, THEN IT IS THE VIEWER WHO DECIDES HOW TO SEE YOU.
SHE LOOKED AT HACHI-MARU...
...BUT SAW HER BROTHER.
ON THE OTHER HAND...
!

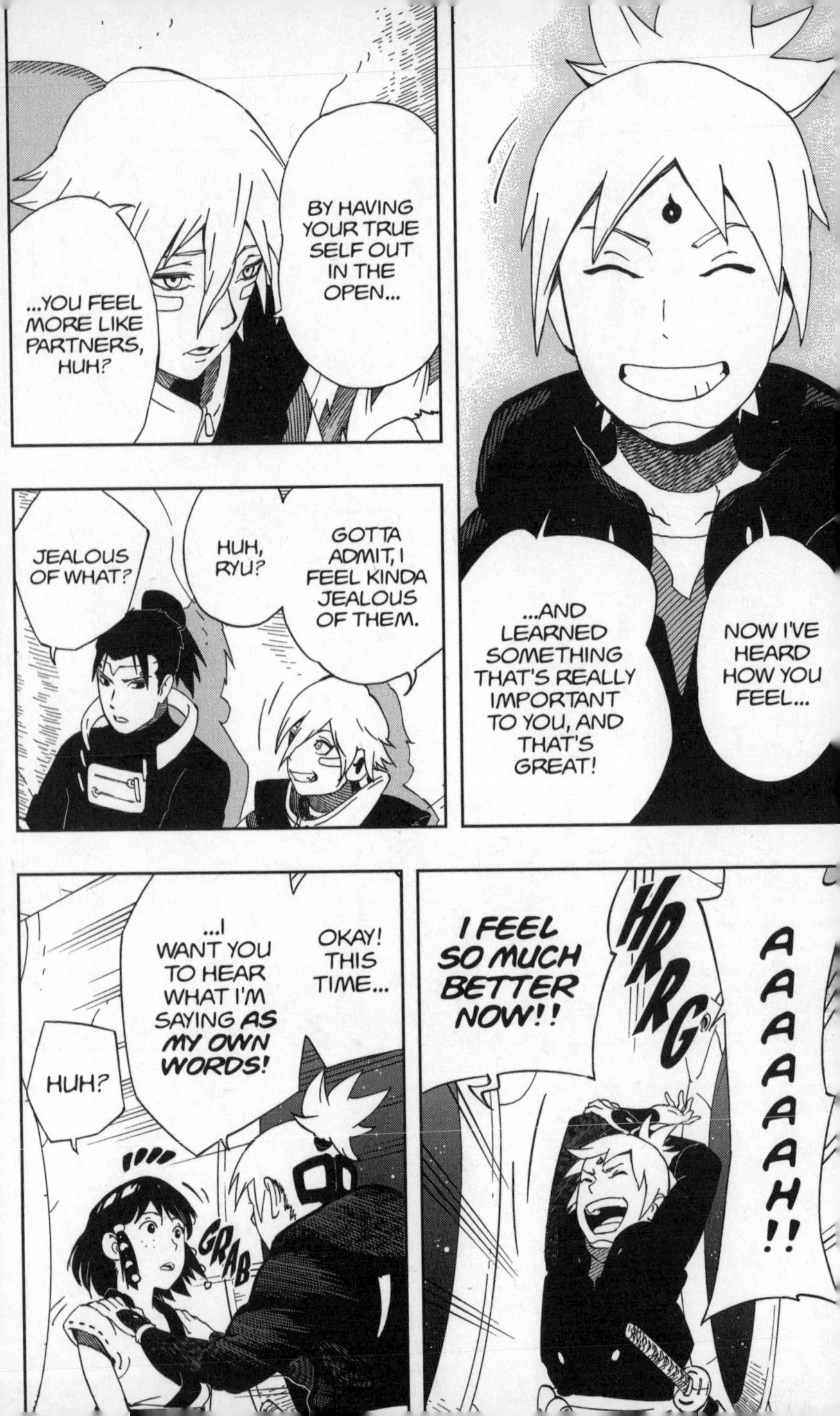
NOW I'VE HEARD HOW YOU FEEL...
...AND LEARNED SOMETHING THAT'S REALLY IMPORTANT TO YOU, AND THAT'S GREAT!
BY HAVING YOUR TRUE SELF OUT IN THE OPEN...
...YOU FEEL MORE LIKE PARTNERS, HUH?
GOTTA ADMIT, I FEEL KINDA JEALOUS OF THEM.
HUH, RYU?
JEALOUS OF WHAT?
AAAAAAAH!!
HRRG
I FEEL SO MUCH BETTER NOW!!
OKAY! THIS TIME...
...I WANT YOU TO HEAR WHAT I'M SAYING AS MY OWN WORDS!
GRAB
HUH?

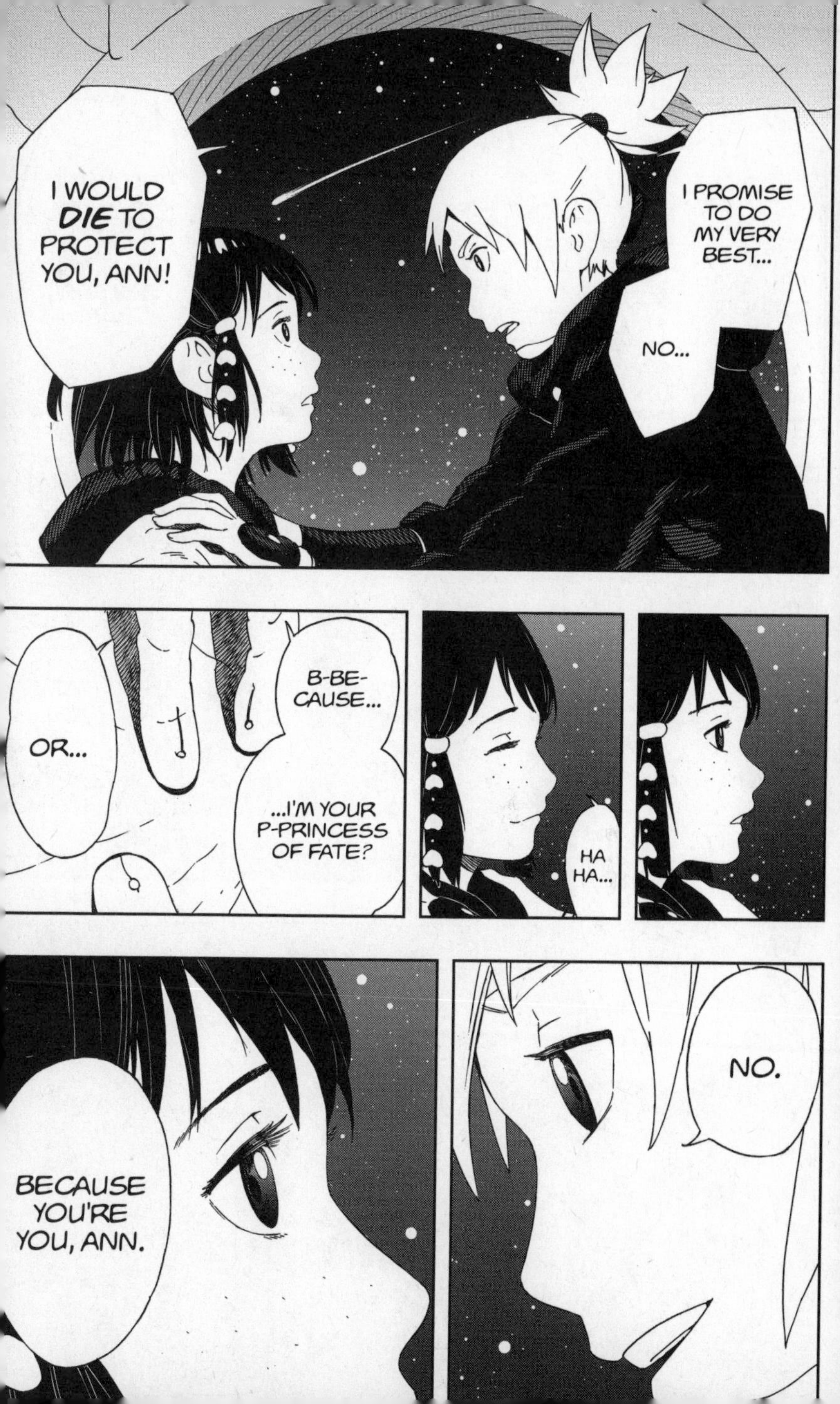
I PROMISE TO DO MY VERY BEST...
NO...
I WOULD **DIE** TO PROTECT YOU, ANN!
HA HA...
B-BE-CAUSE...
...I'M YOUR P-PRINCESS OF FATE?
OR...
NO.
BECAUSE YOU'RE YOU, ANN.

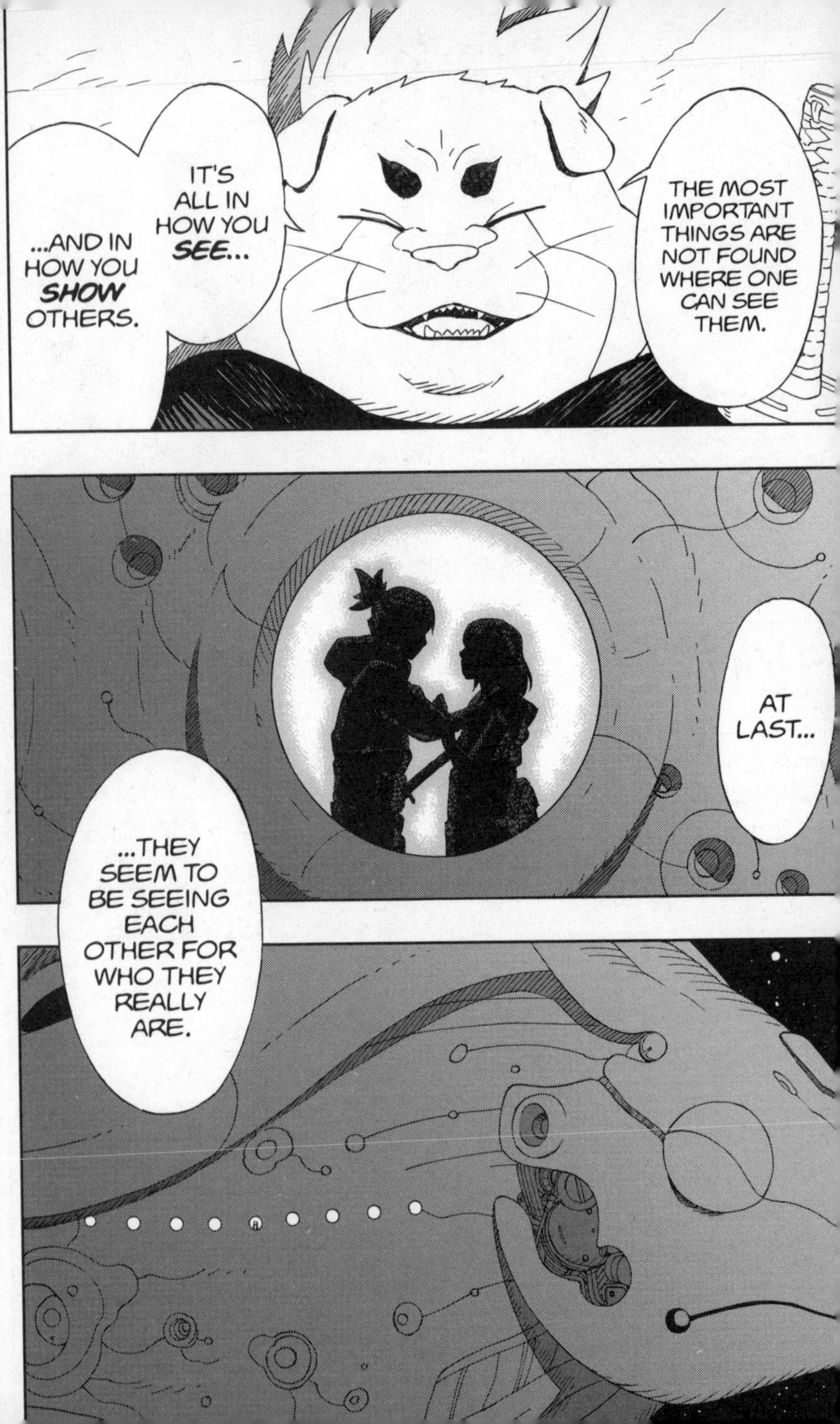
THE MOST IMPORTANT THINGS ARE NOT FOUND WHERE ONE CAN SEE THEM.
IT'S ALL IN HOW YOU SEE...
...AND IN HOW YOU SHOW OTHERS.
AT LAST...
...THEY SEEM TO BE SEEING EACH OTHER FOR WHO THEY REALLY ARE.

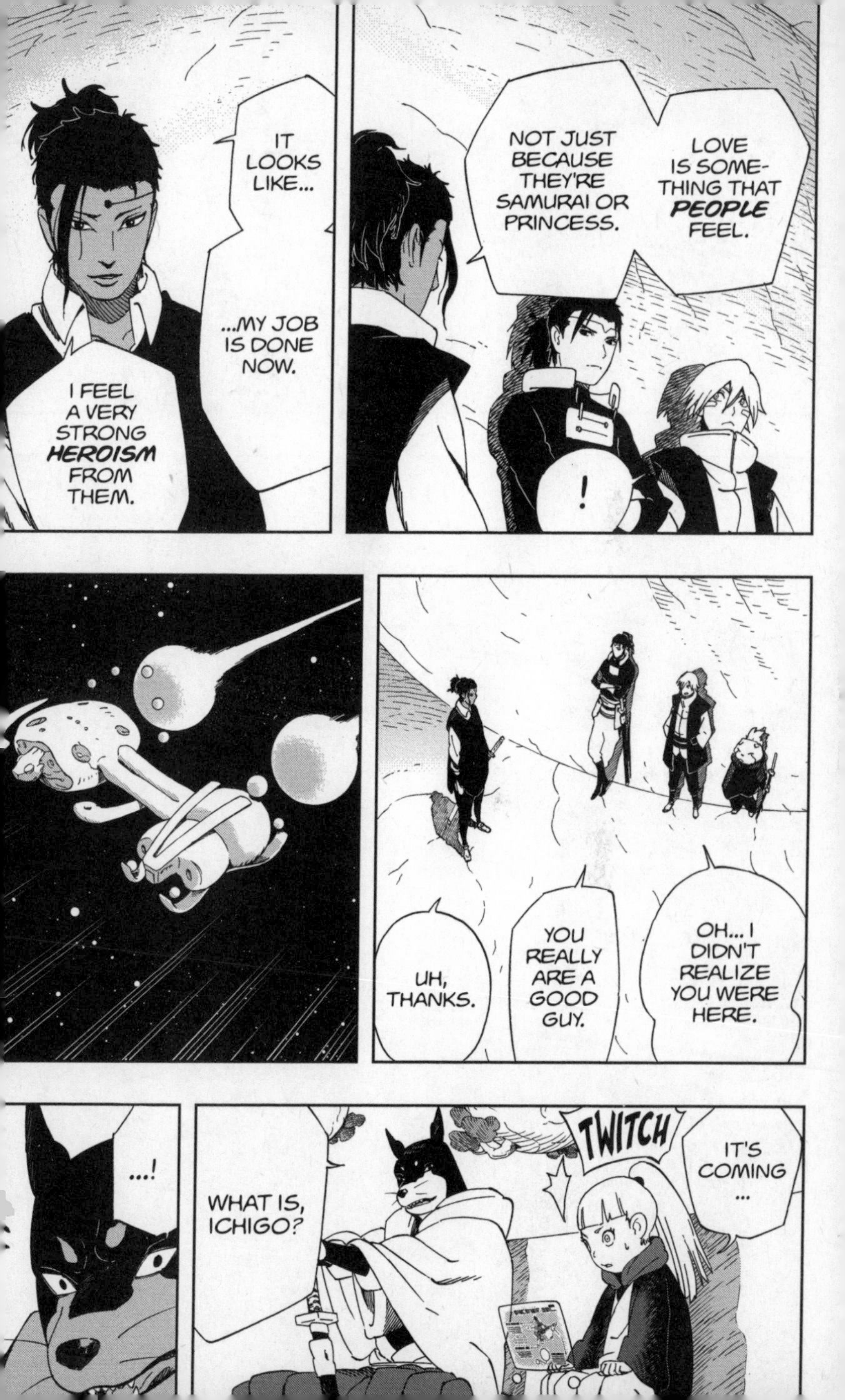
LOVE IS SOMETHING THAT PEOPLE FEEL.
NOT JUST BECAUSE THEY'RE SAMURAI OR PRINCESS.
!
IT LOOKS LIKE...
...MY JOB IS DONE NOW.
I FEEL A VERY STRONG HEROISM FROM THEM.
OH... I DIDN'T REALIZE YOU WERE HERE.
YOU REALLY ARE A GOOD GUY.
UH, THANKS.
IT'S COMING...
TWITCH
WHAT IS, ICHIGO?
...!

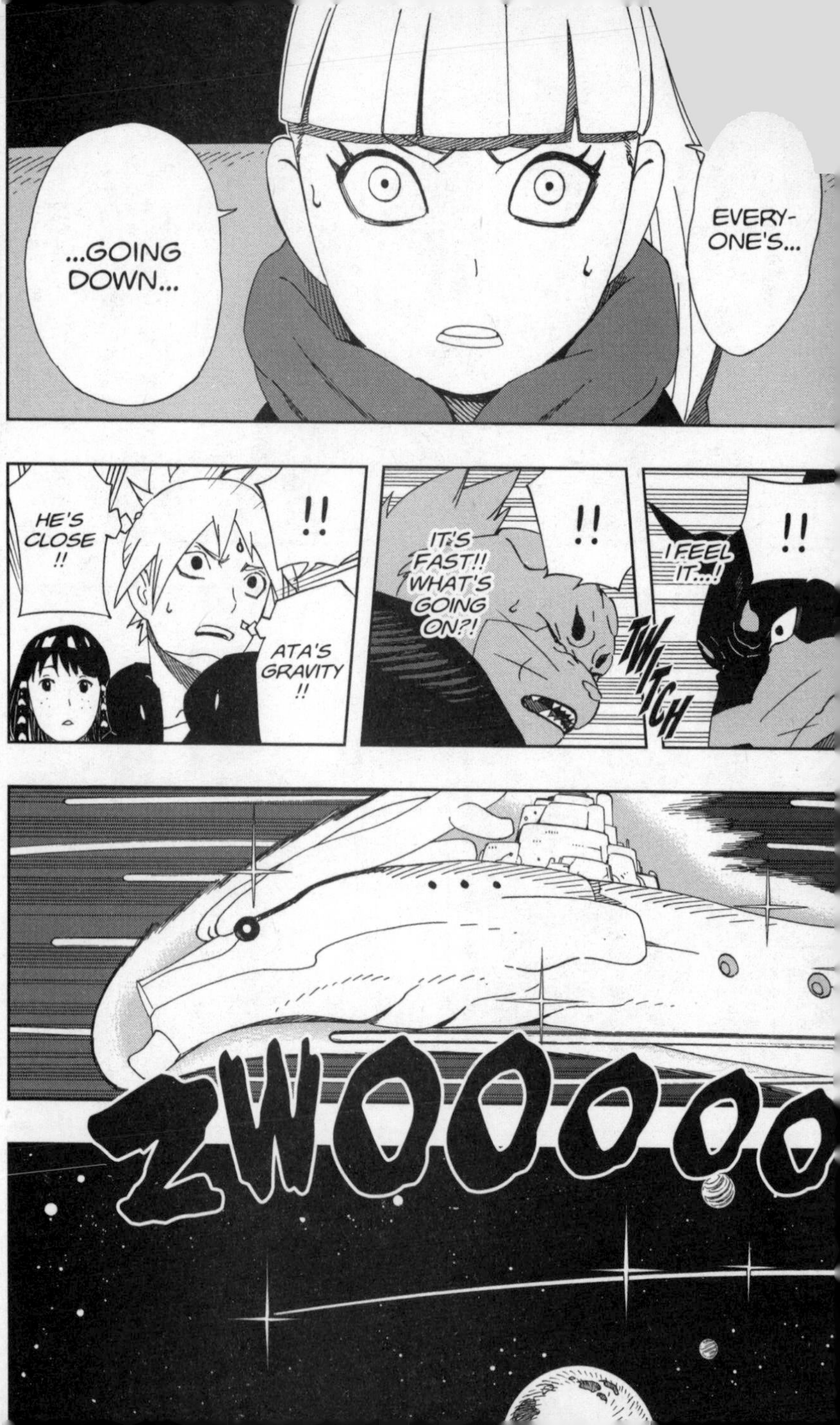
EVERY-ONE'S...
...GOING DOWN...
!!
I FEEL IT...!
TWITCH
!!
IT'S FAST!! WHAT'S GOING ON?!
!!
HE'S CLOSE !!
ATA'S GRAVITY !!
ZWOOOOO

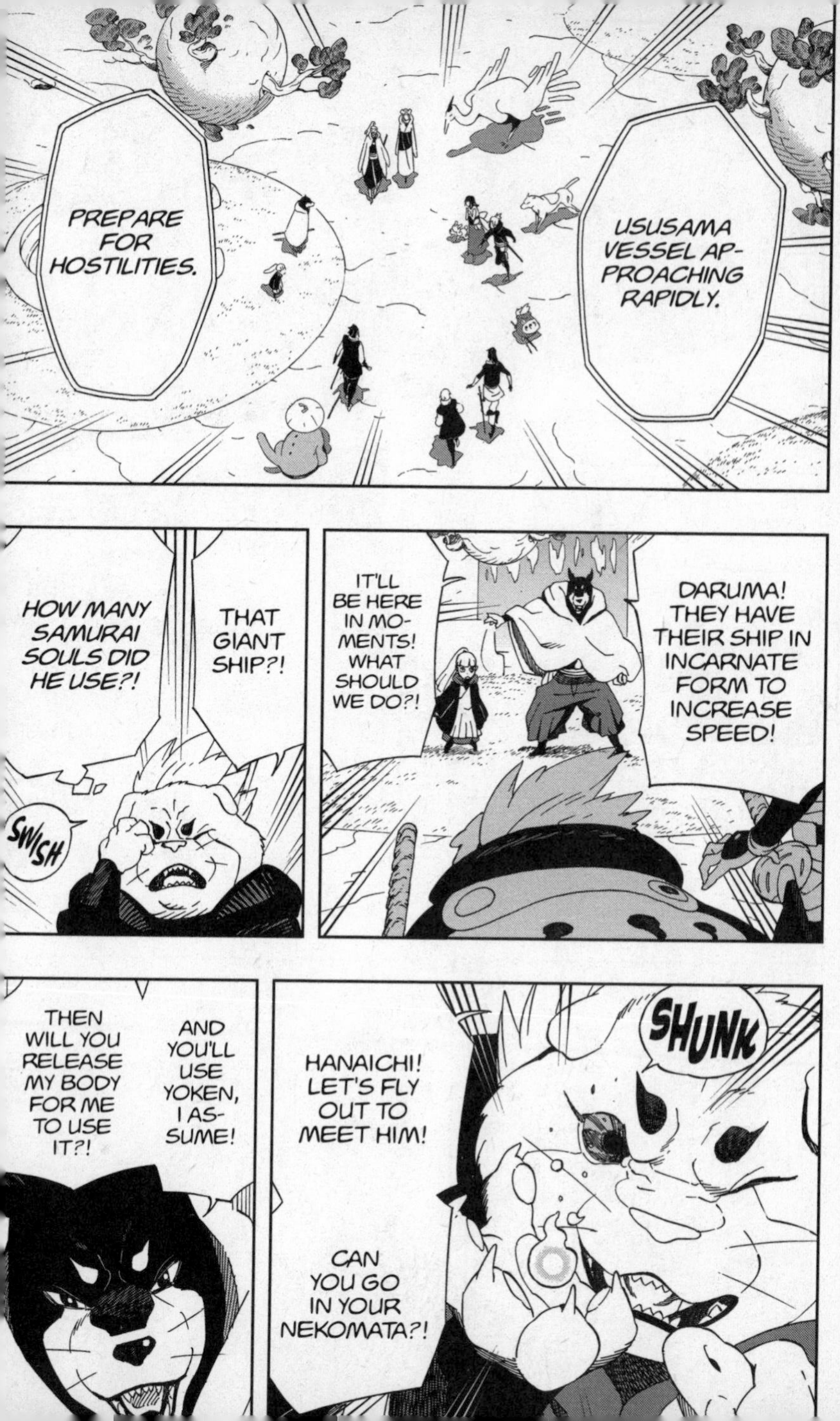
USUSAMA VESSEL AP-PROACHING RAPIDLY.
PREPARE FOR HOSTILITIES.
DARUMA! THEY HAVE THEIR SHIP IN INCARNATE FORM TO INCREASE SPEED!
IT'LL BE HERE IN MO-MENTS! WHAT SHOULD WE DO?!
THAT GIANT SHIP?!
HOW MANY SAMURAI SOULS DID HE USE?!
SWISH
SHUNK
HANAICHI! LET'S FLY OUT TO MEET HIM!
CAN YOU GO IN YOUR NEKOMATA?!
AND YOU'LL USE YOKEN, I AS-SUME!
THEN WILL YOU RELEASE MY BODY FOR ME TO USE IT?!

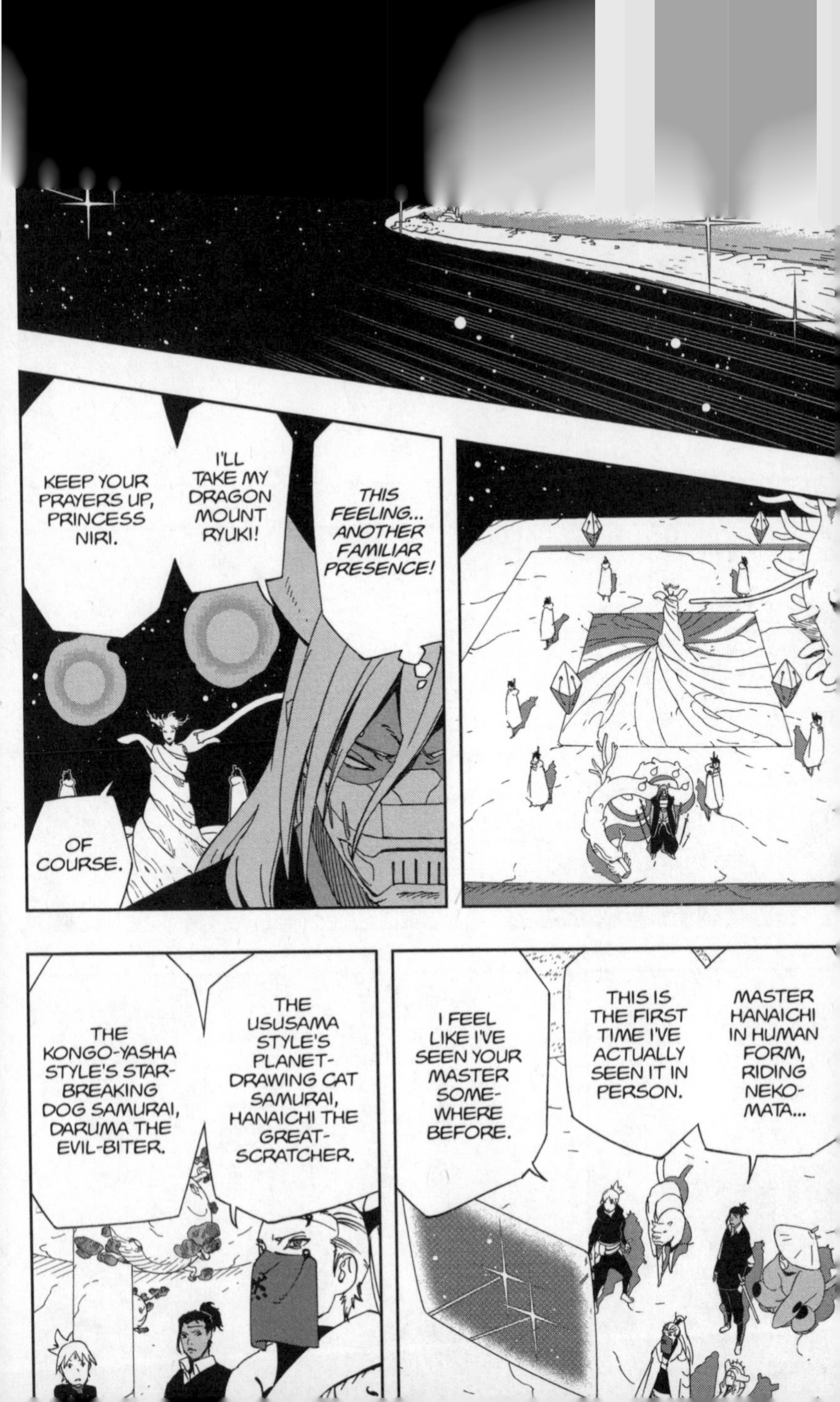
THIS FEELING... ANOTHER FAMILIAR PRESENCE!
I'LL TAKE MY DRAGON MOUNT RYUKI!
KEEP YOUR PRAYERS UP, PRINCESS NIRI.
OF COURSE.
MASTER HANAICHI IN HUMAN FORM, RIDING NEKO-MATA...
THIS IS THE FIRST TIME I'VE ACTUALLY SEEN IT IN PERSON.
I FEEL LIKE I'VE SEEN YOUR MASTER SOME-WHERE BEFORE.
THE USUSAMA STYLE'S PLANET-DRAWING CAT SAMURAI, HANAICHI THE GREAT-SCRATCHER.
THE KONGO-YASHA STYLE'S STAR-BREAKING DOG SAMURAI, DARUMA THE EVIL-BITER.

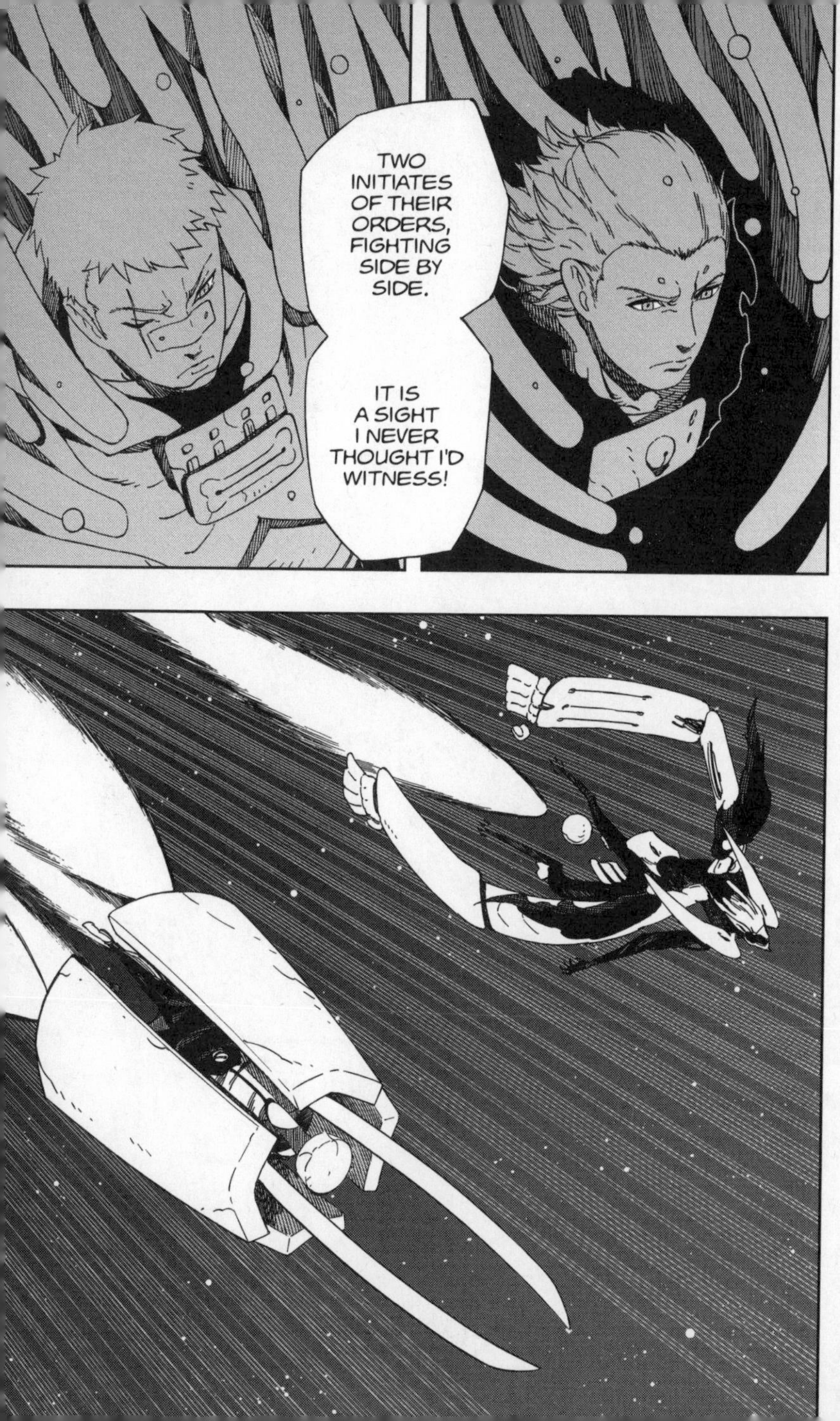
TWO INITIATES OF THEIR ORDERS, FIGHTING SIDE BY SIDE.
IT IS A SIGHT I NEVER THOUGHT I'D WITNESS!

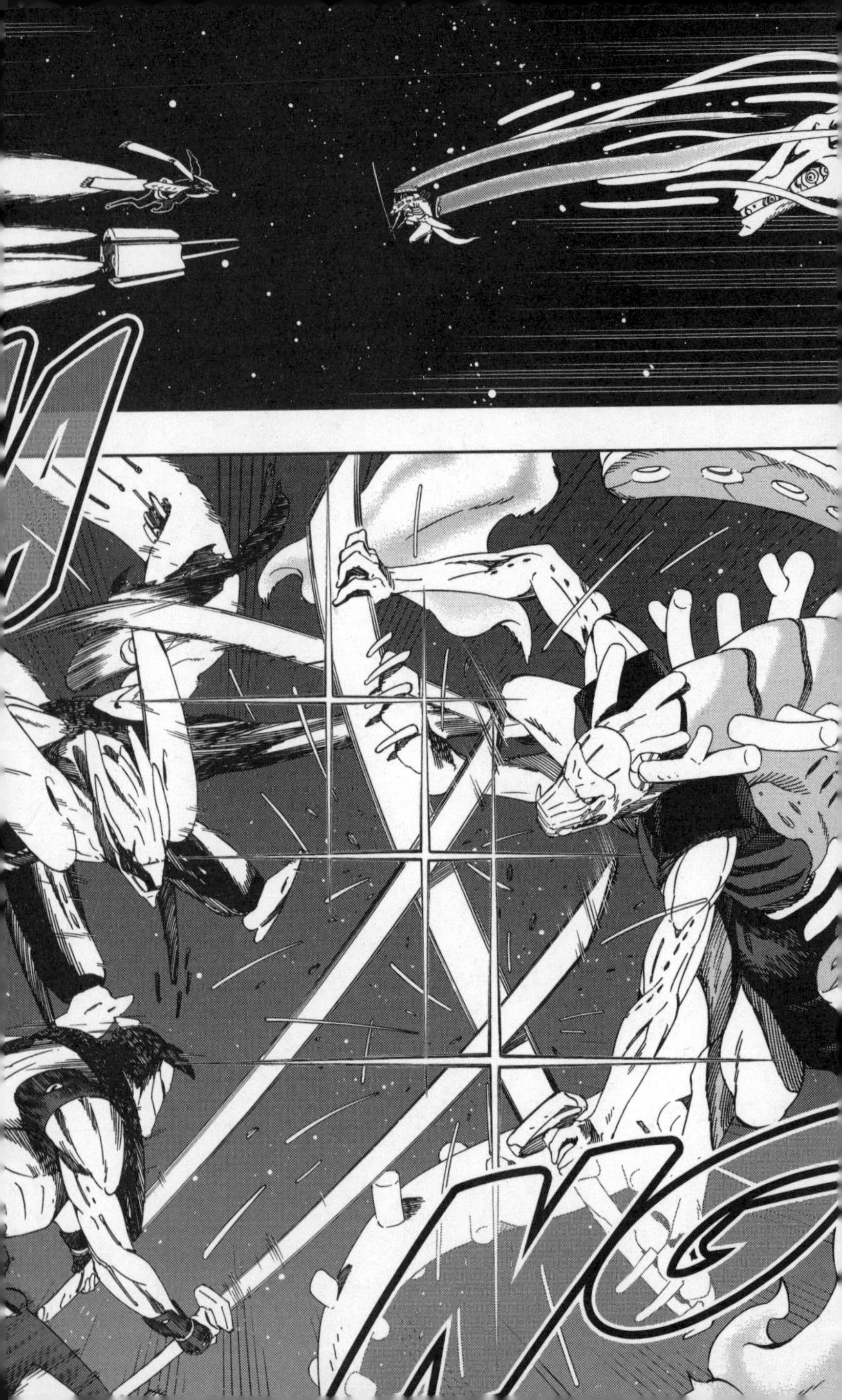

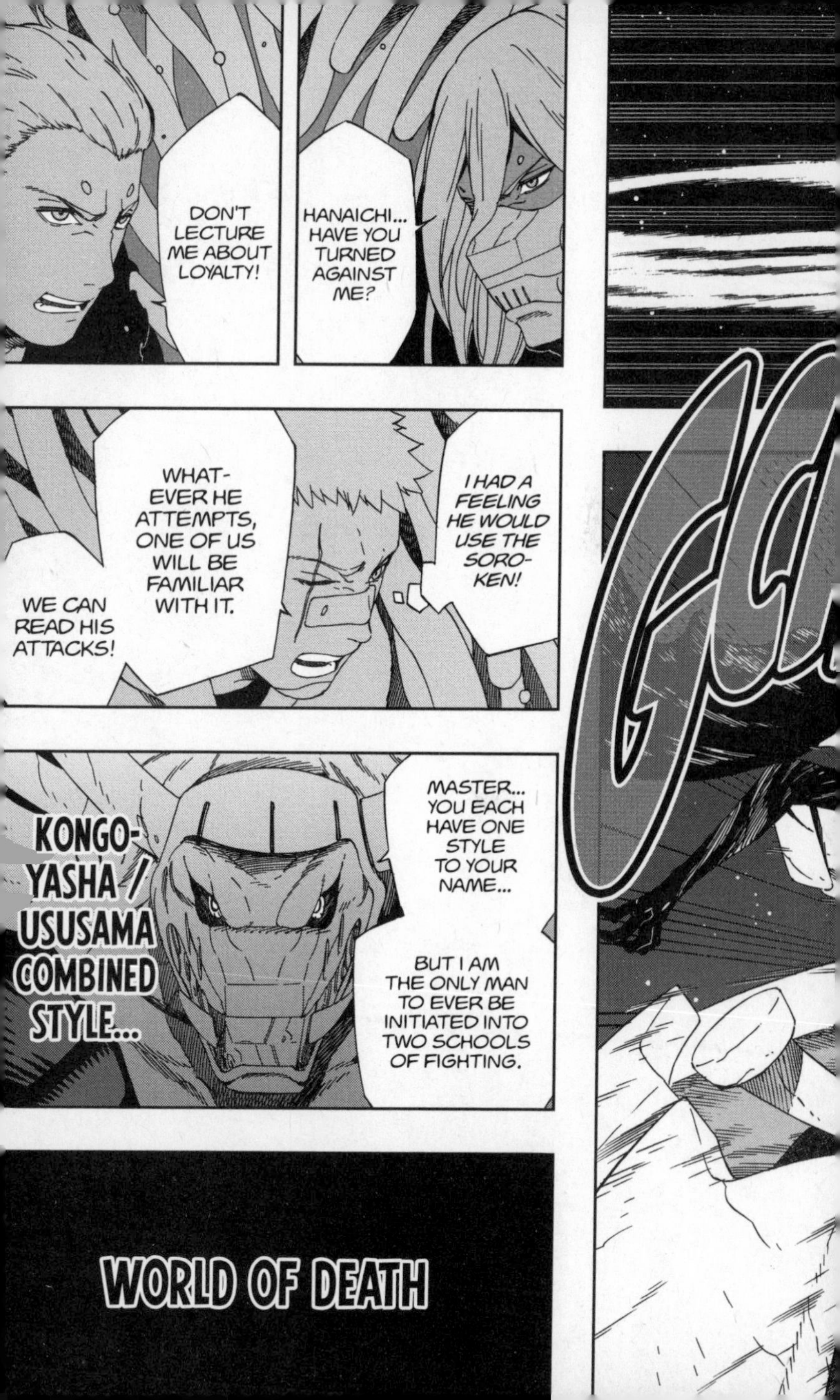
HANAICHI... HAVE YOU TURNED AGAINST ME?
DON'T LECTURE ME ABOUT LOYALTY!
I HAD A FEELING HE WOULD USE THE SORO-KEN!
WHAT-EVER HE ATTEMPTS, ONE OF US WILL BE FAMILIAR WITH IT.
WE CAN READ HIS ATTACKS!
MASTER... YOU EACH HAVE ONE STYLE TO YOUR NAME...
BUT I AM THE ONLY MAN TO EVER BE INITIATED INTO TWO SCHOOLS OF FIGHTING.
KONGO-YASHA / USUSAMA COMBINED STYLE...
WORLD OF DEATH

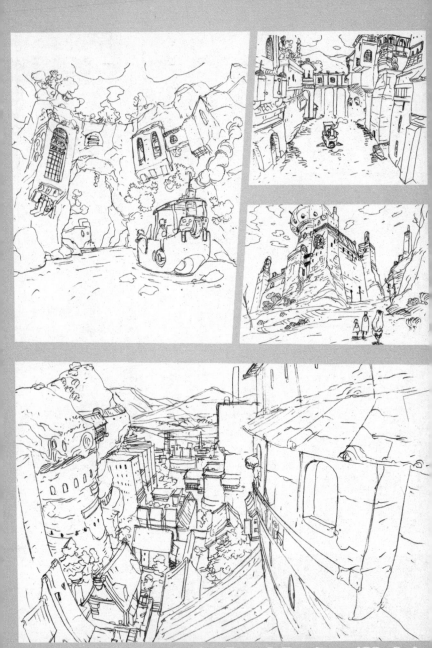

Pre-Series Rough Designs (Okubo)

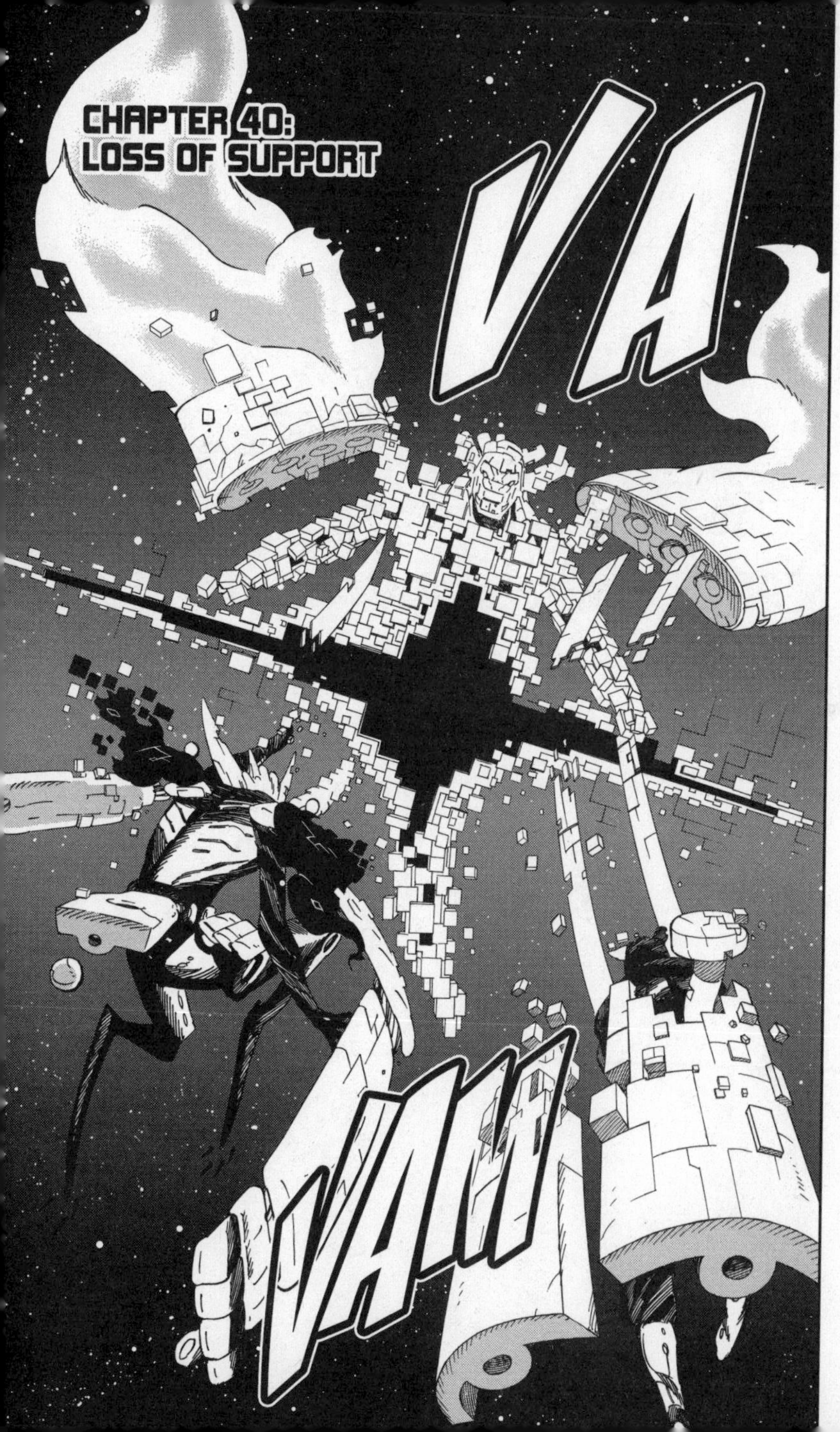
CHAPTER 40:
LOSS OF SUPPORT
VA
VAM

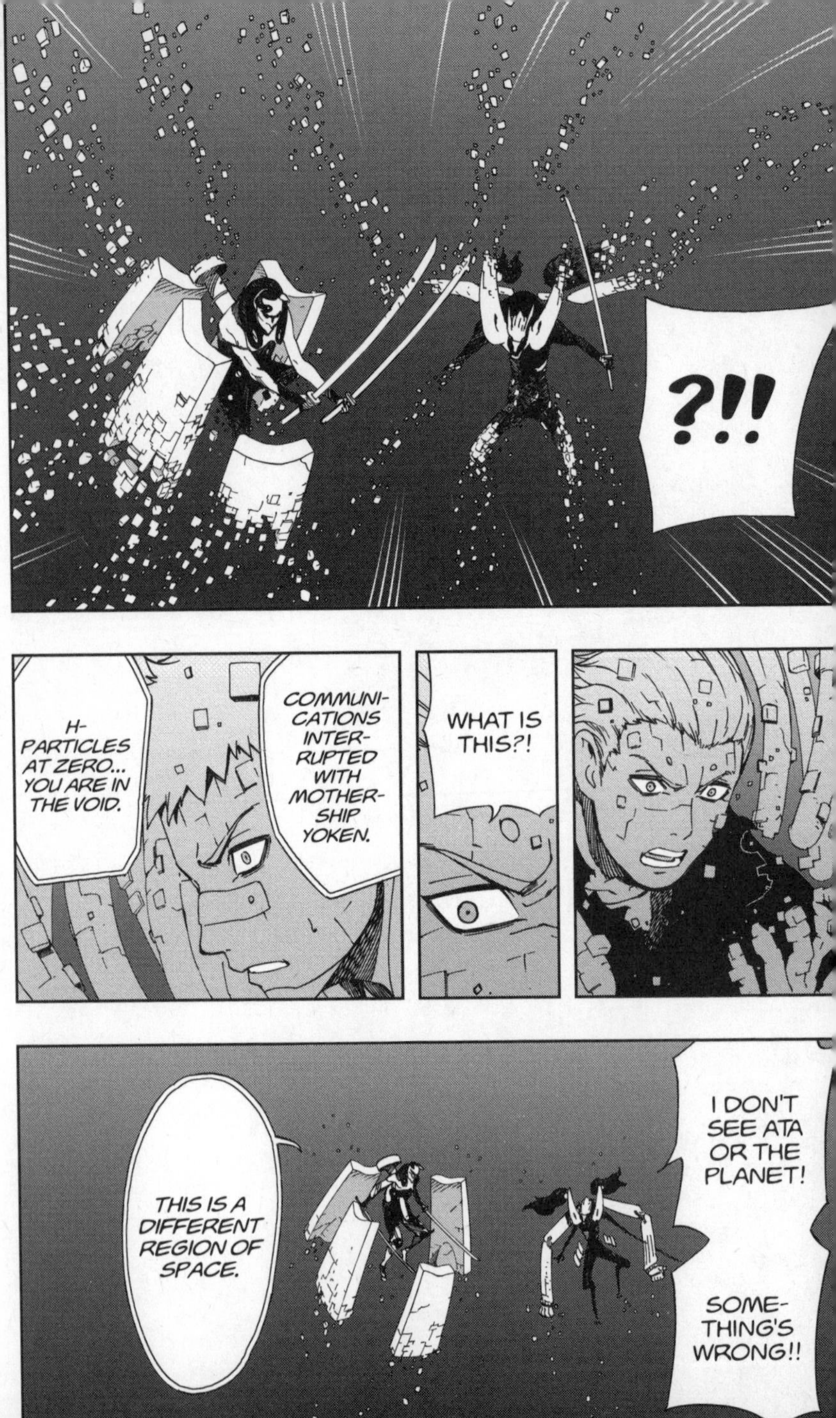
?!!
WHAT IS THIS?!
COMMUNICATIONS INTERRUPTED WITH MOTHERSHIP YOKEN.
H-PARTICLES AT ZERO... YOU ARE IN THE VOID.
I DON'T SEE ATA OR THE PLANET!
SOMETHING'S WRONG!!
THIS IS A DIFFERENT REGION OF SPACE.

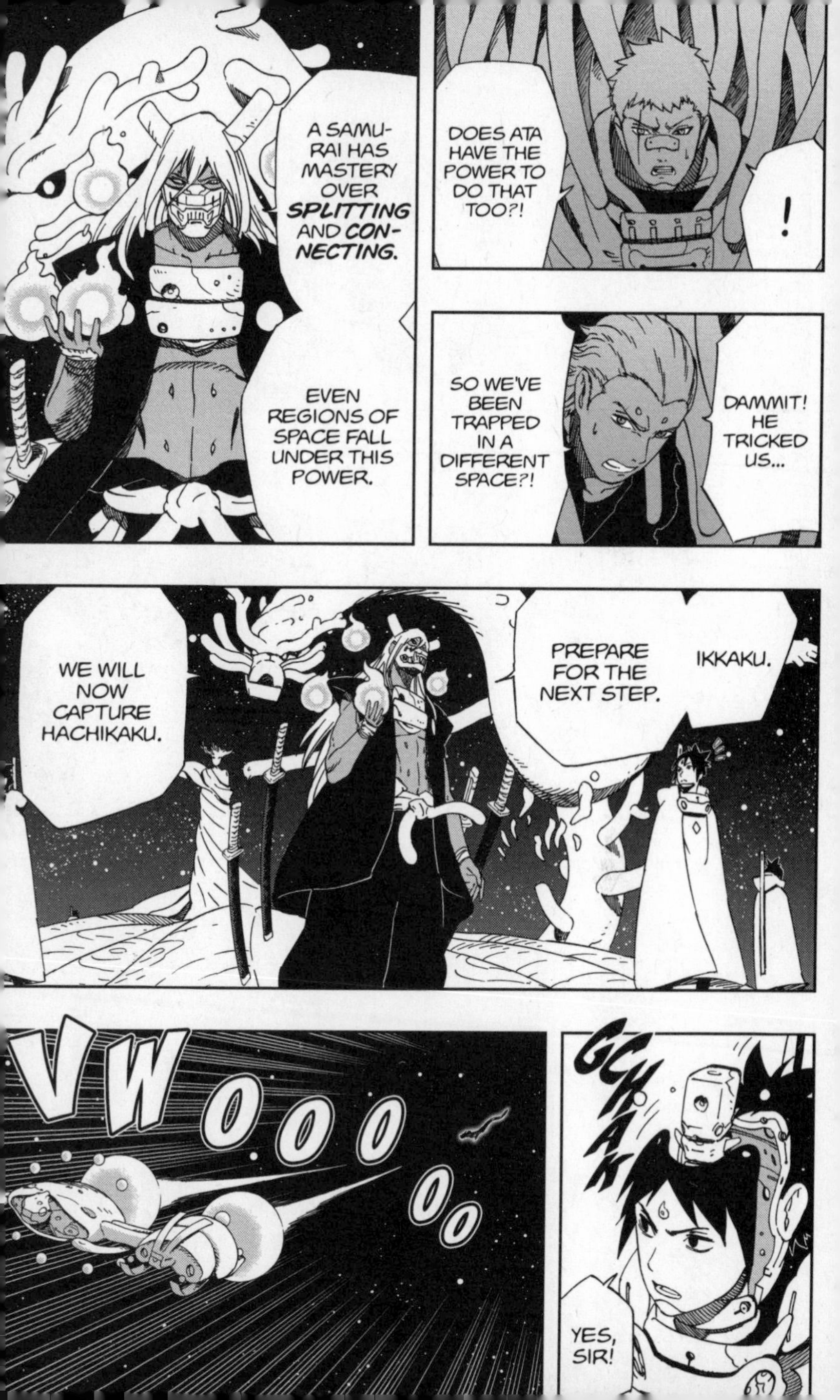
!
DOES ATA HAVE THE POWER TO DO THAT TOO?!
DAMMIT! HE TRICKED US...
SO WE'VE BEEN TRAPPED IN A DIFFERENT SPACE?!
A SAMURAI HAS MASTERY OVER **SPLITTING** AND **CONNECTING.**
EVEN REGIONS OF SPACE FALL UNDER THIS POWER.
IKKAKU.
PREPARE FOR THE NEXT STEP.
WE WILL NOW CAPTURE HACHIKAKU.
GCHAK
YES, SIR!
VWOOOOOO

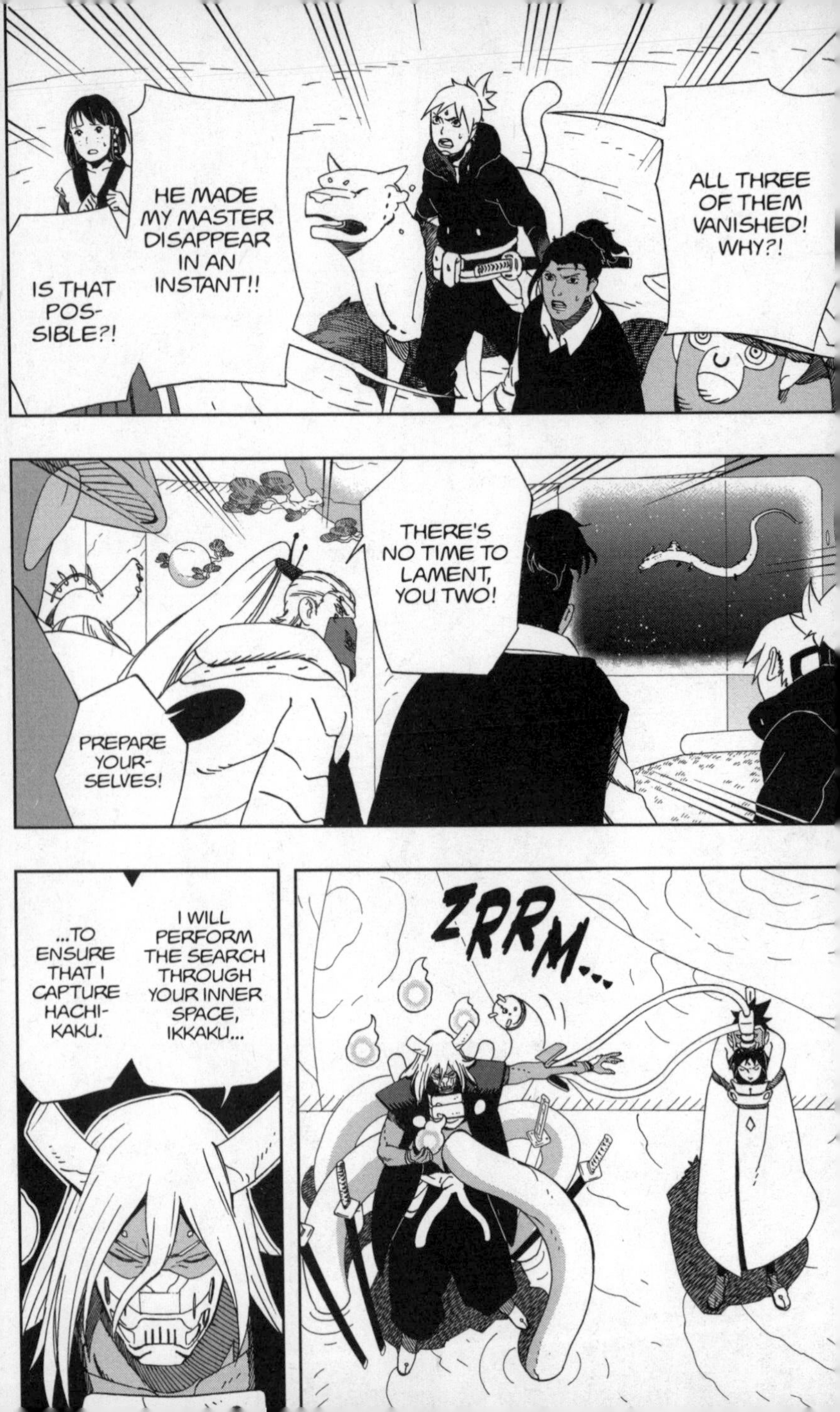
ALL THREE OF THEM VANISHED! WHY?!
HE MADE MY MASTER DISAPPEAR IN AN INSTANT!!
IS THAT POSSIBLE?!
THERE'S NO TIME TO LAMENT, YOU TWO!
PREPARE YOURSELVES!
ZRRM...
I WILL PERFORM THE SEARCH THROUGH YOUR INNER SPACE, IKKAKU...
...TO ENSURE THAT I CAPTURE HACHIKAKU.

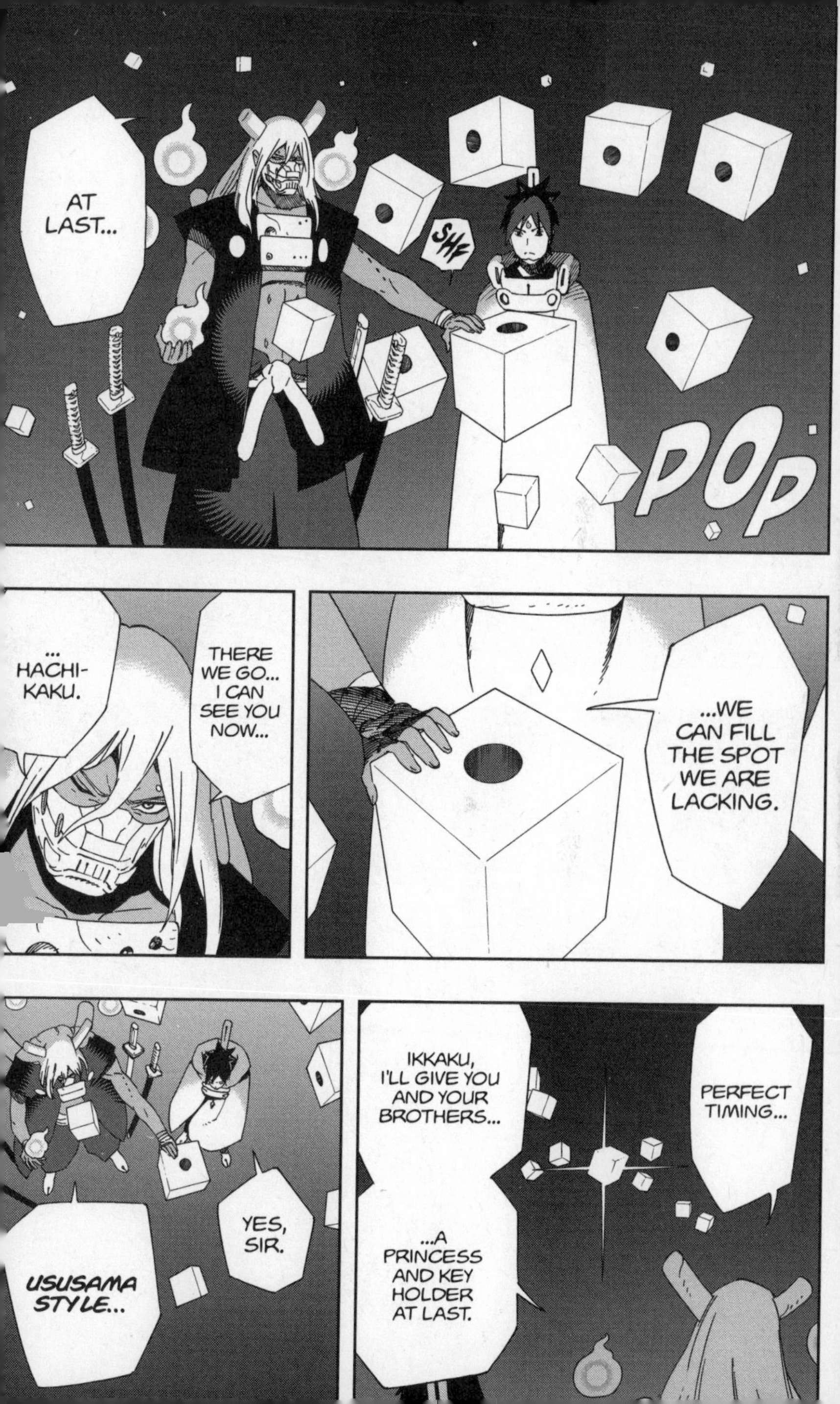
SHF
AT LAST...
POP
...WE CAN FILL THE SPOT WE ARE LACKING.
THERE WE GO... I CAN SEE YOU NOW...
... HACHIKAKU.
PERFECT TIMING...
IKKAKU, I'LL GIVE YOU AND YOUR BROTHERS...
...A PRINCESS AND KEY HOLDER AT LAST.
YES, SIR.
USUSAMA STYLE...

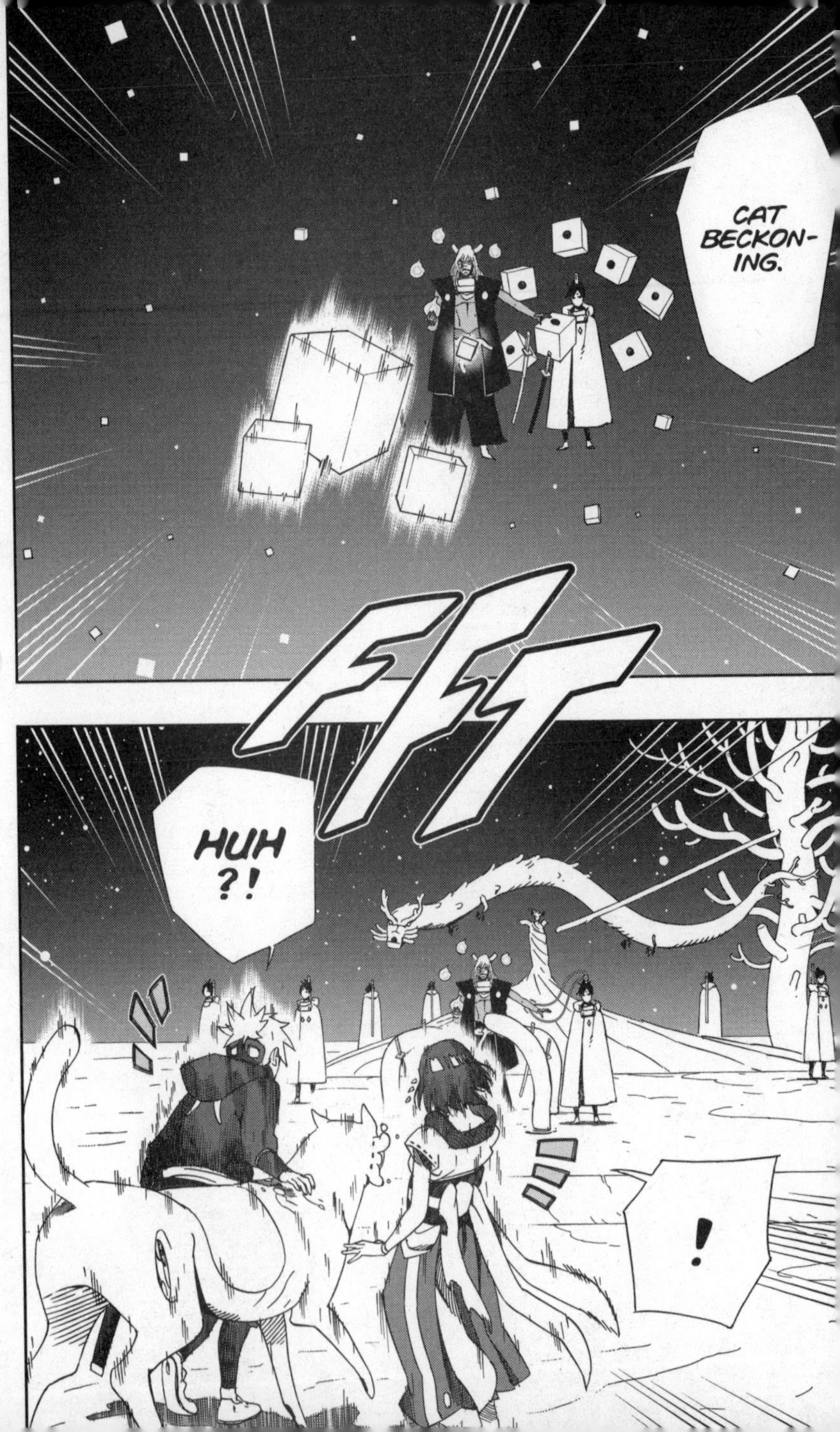
CAT BECKON-ING.
FFT
HUH ?!
!

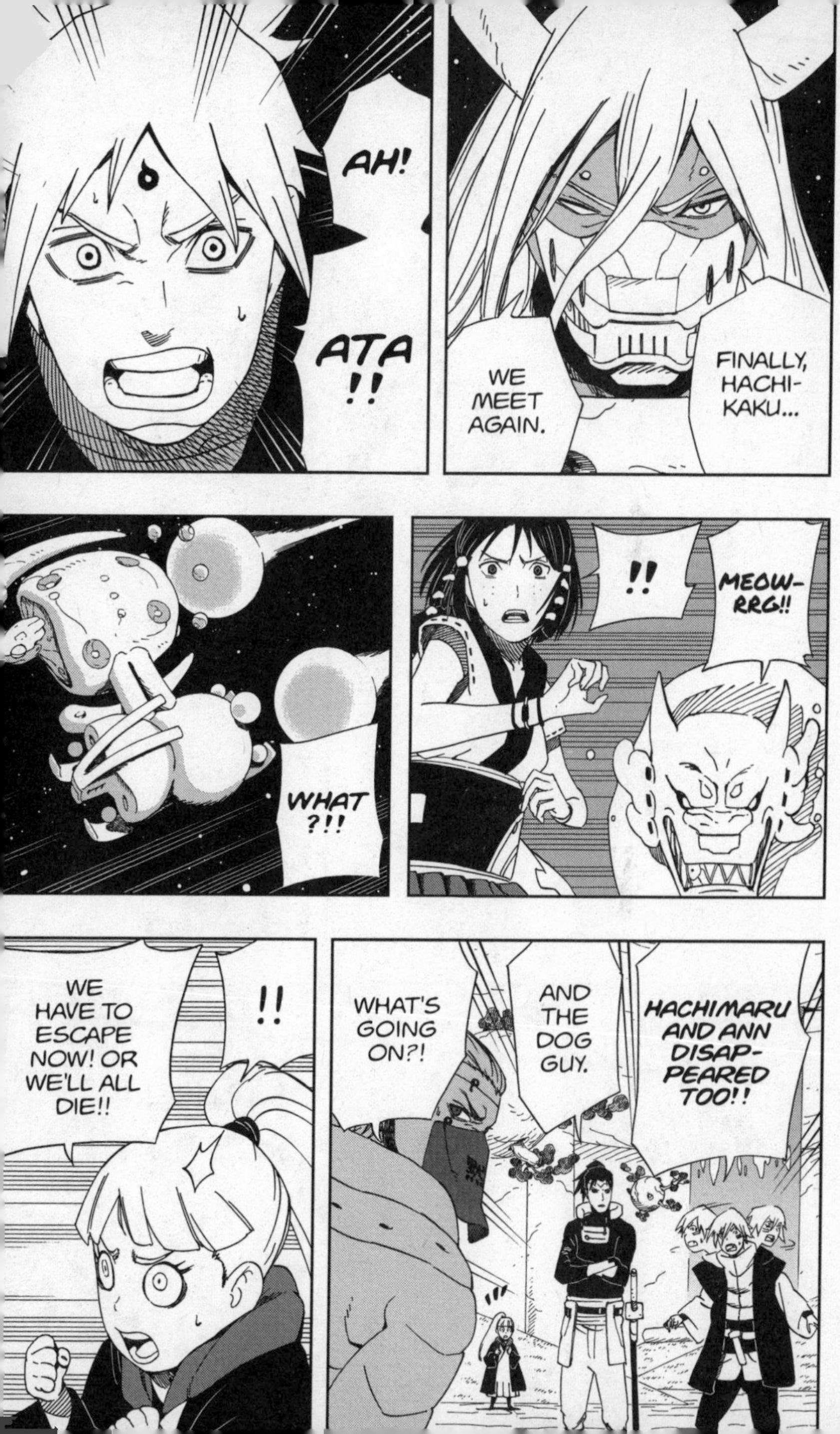
FINALLY, HACHI-KAKU...
WE MEET AGAIN.
AH!
ATA !!
MEOW-RRG!!
!!
WHAT ?!!
HACHIMARU AND ANN DISAP-PEARED TOO!!
AND THE DOG GUY.
WHAT'S GOING ON?!
!!
WE HAVE TO ESCAPE NOW! OR WE'LL ALL DIE!!

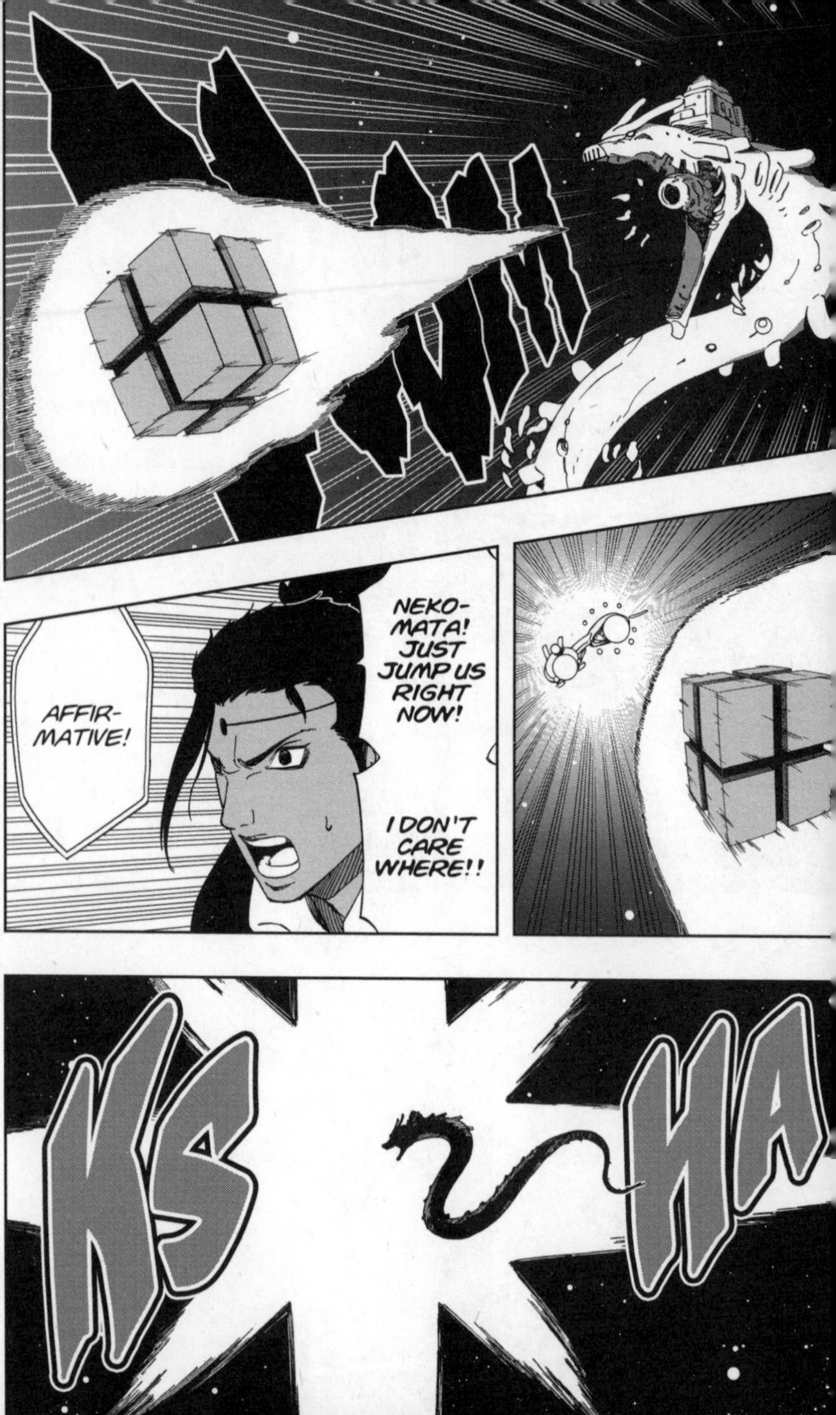
NEKO-MATA! JUST JUMP US RIGHT NOW!
I DON'T CARE WHERE!!
AFFIR-MATIVE!
KS HA

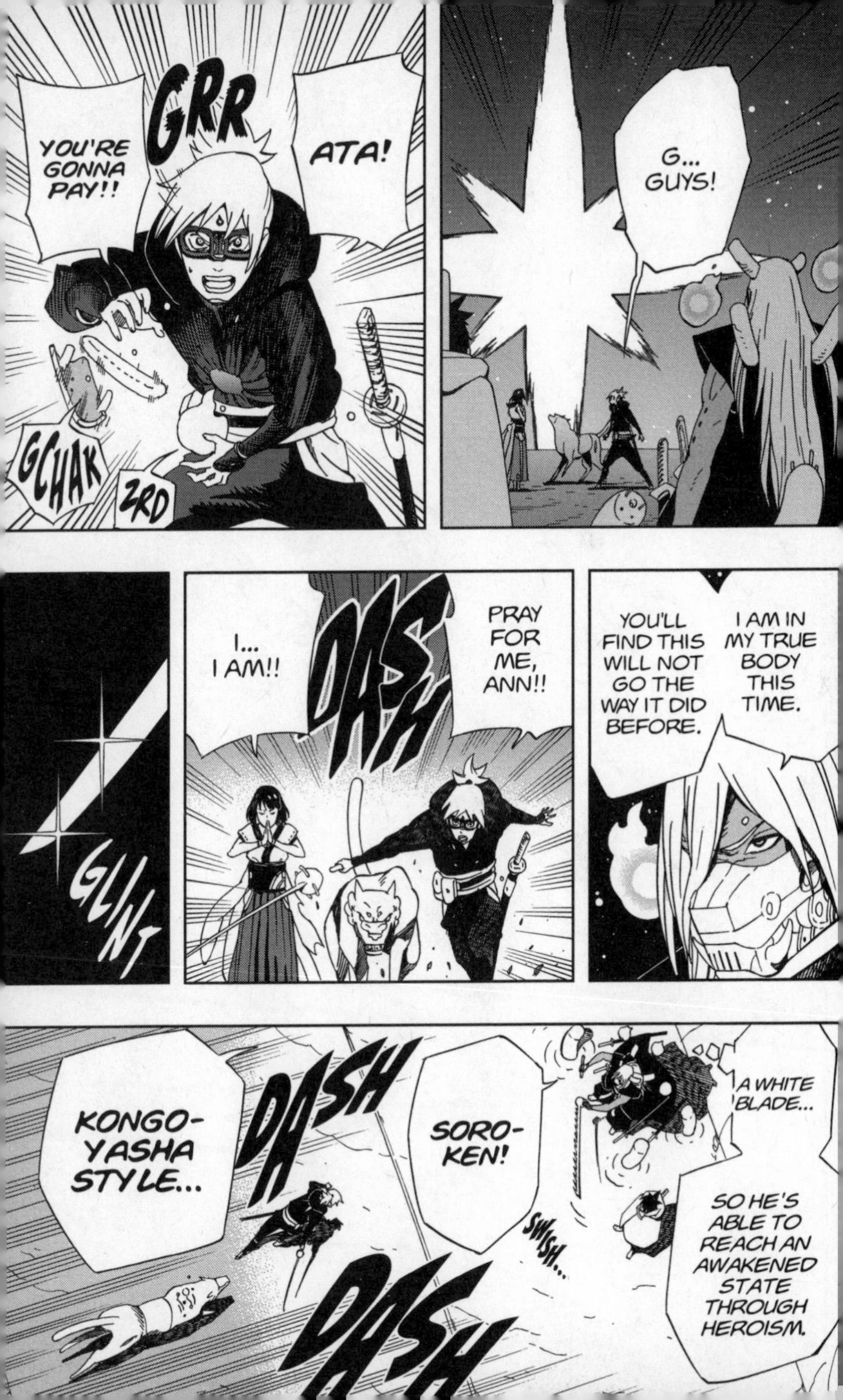
G... GUYS!
ATA!
GRR
YOU'RE GONNA PAY!!
GCHAK
ZRD
I AM IN MY TRUE BODY THIS TIME.
YOU'LL FIND THIS WILL NOT GO THE WAY IT DID BEFORE.
PRAY FOR ME, ANN!!
DASH
I... I AM!!
GLINT
A WHITE BLADE...
SO HE'S ABLE TO REACH AN AWAKENED STATE THROUGH HEROISM.
SWISH...
SORO-KEN!
DASH
KONGO-YASHA STYLE...
DASH

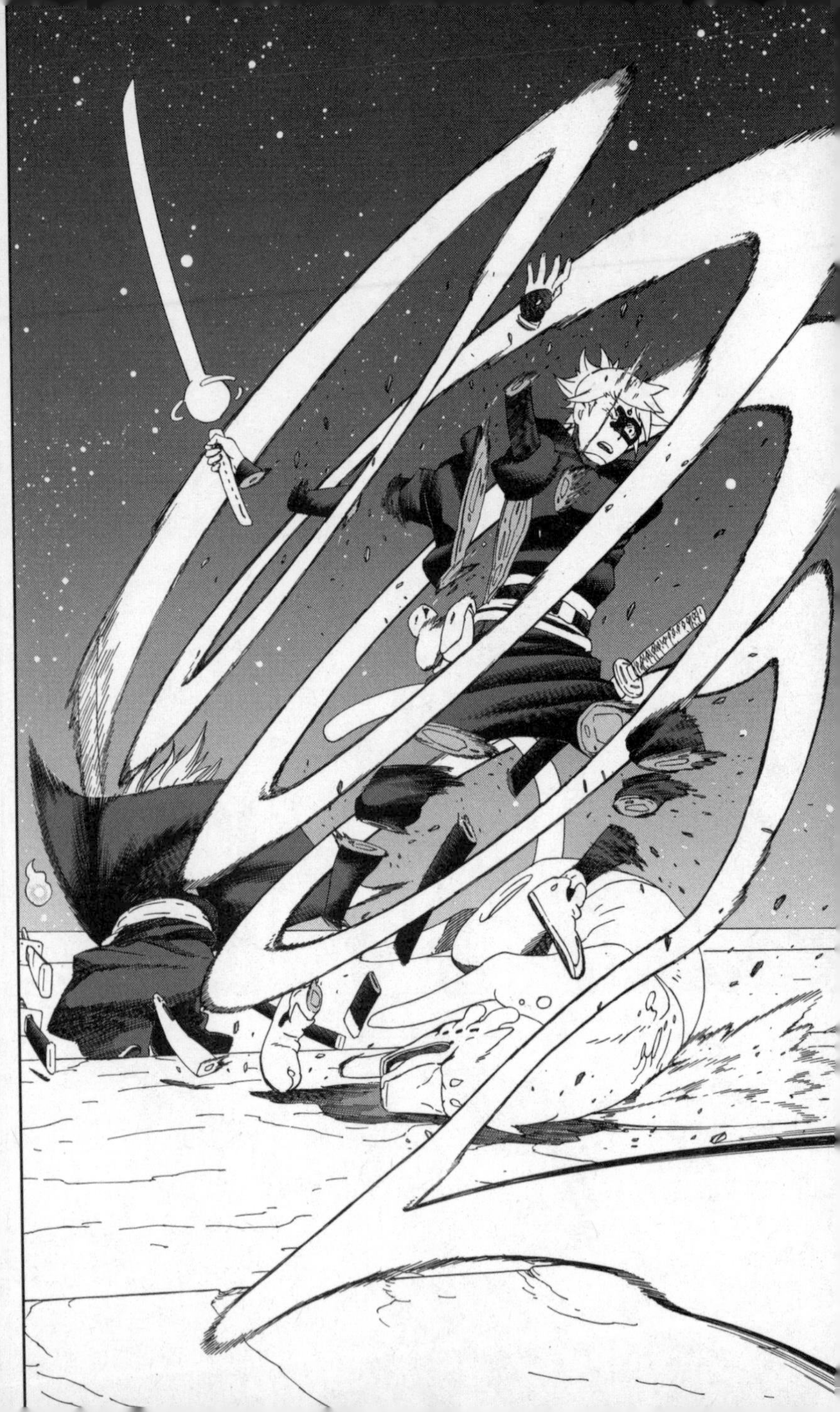

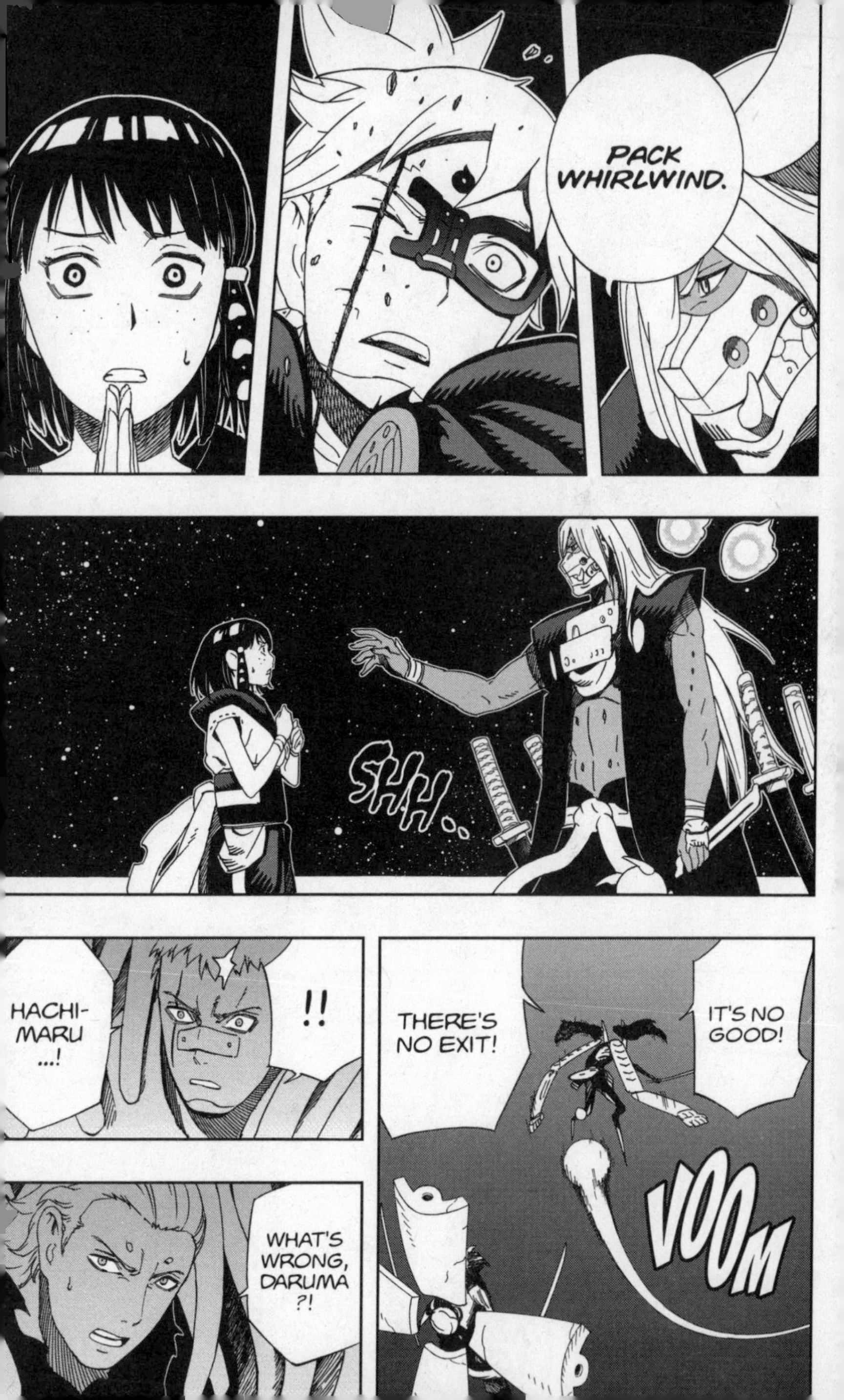
PACK WHIRLWIND.
SHH...
IT'S NO GOOD!
THERE'S NO EXIT!
VOOM
HACHI-MARU ...!
!!
WHAT'S WRONG, DARUMA ?!

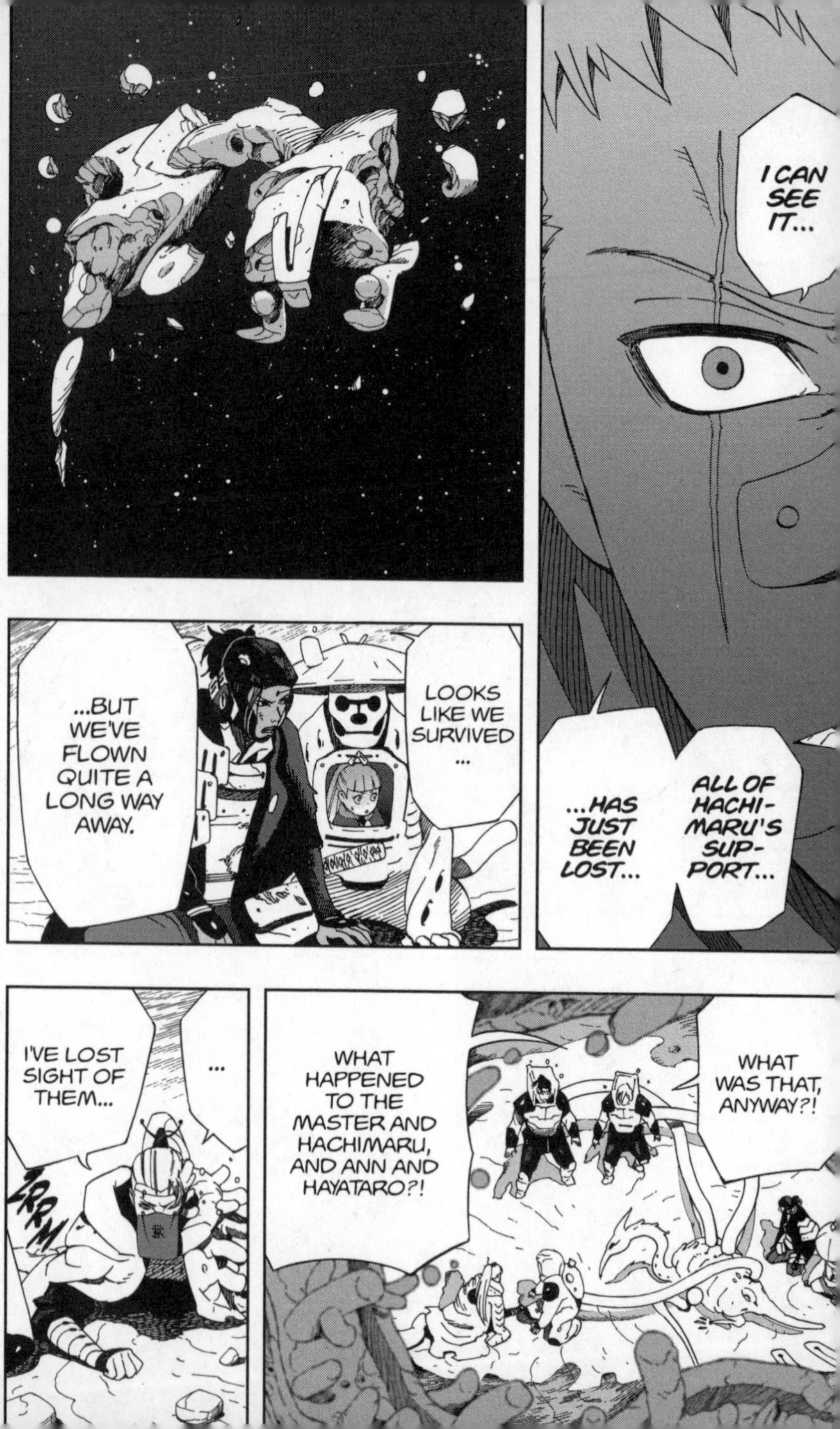
I CAN SEE IT...
ALL OF HACHIMARU'S SUPPORT...
...HAS JUST BEEN LOST...
LOOKS LIKE WE SURVIVED ...
...BUT WE'VE FLOWN QUITE A LONG WAY AWAY.
WHAT WAS THAT, ANYWAY?!
WHAT HAPPENED TO THE MASTER AND HACHIMARU, AND ANN AND HAYATARO?!
...
I'VE LOST SIGHT OF THEM...

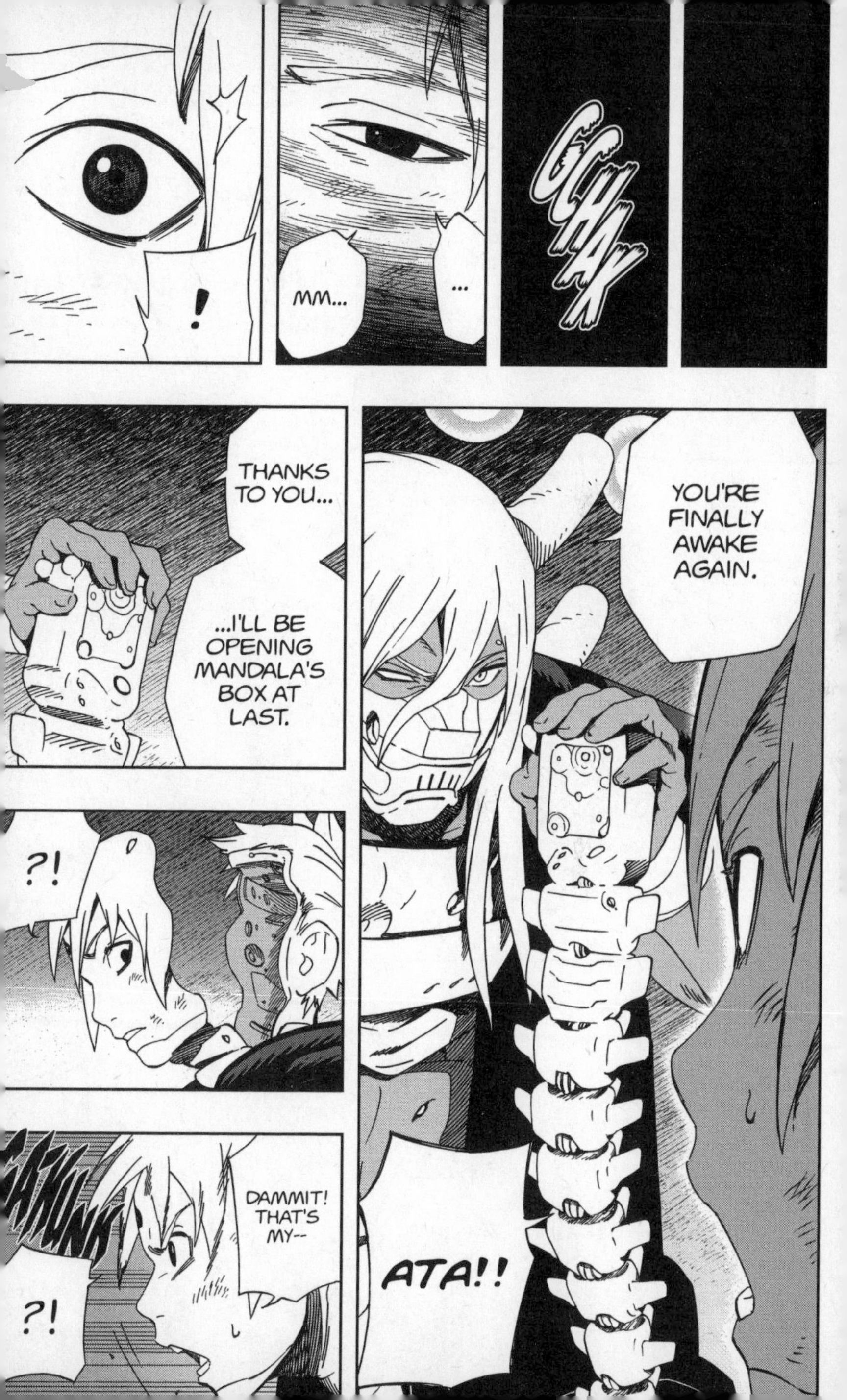
GCHAK
...
MM...
!
YOU'RE FINALLY AWAKE AGAIN.
ATA!!
THANKS TO YOU...
...I'LL BE OPENING MANDALA'S BOX AT LAST.
?!
DAMMIT! THAT'S MY--
?!

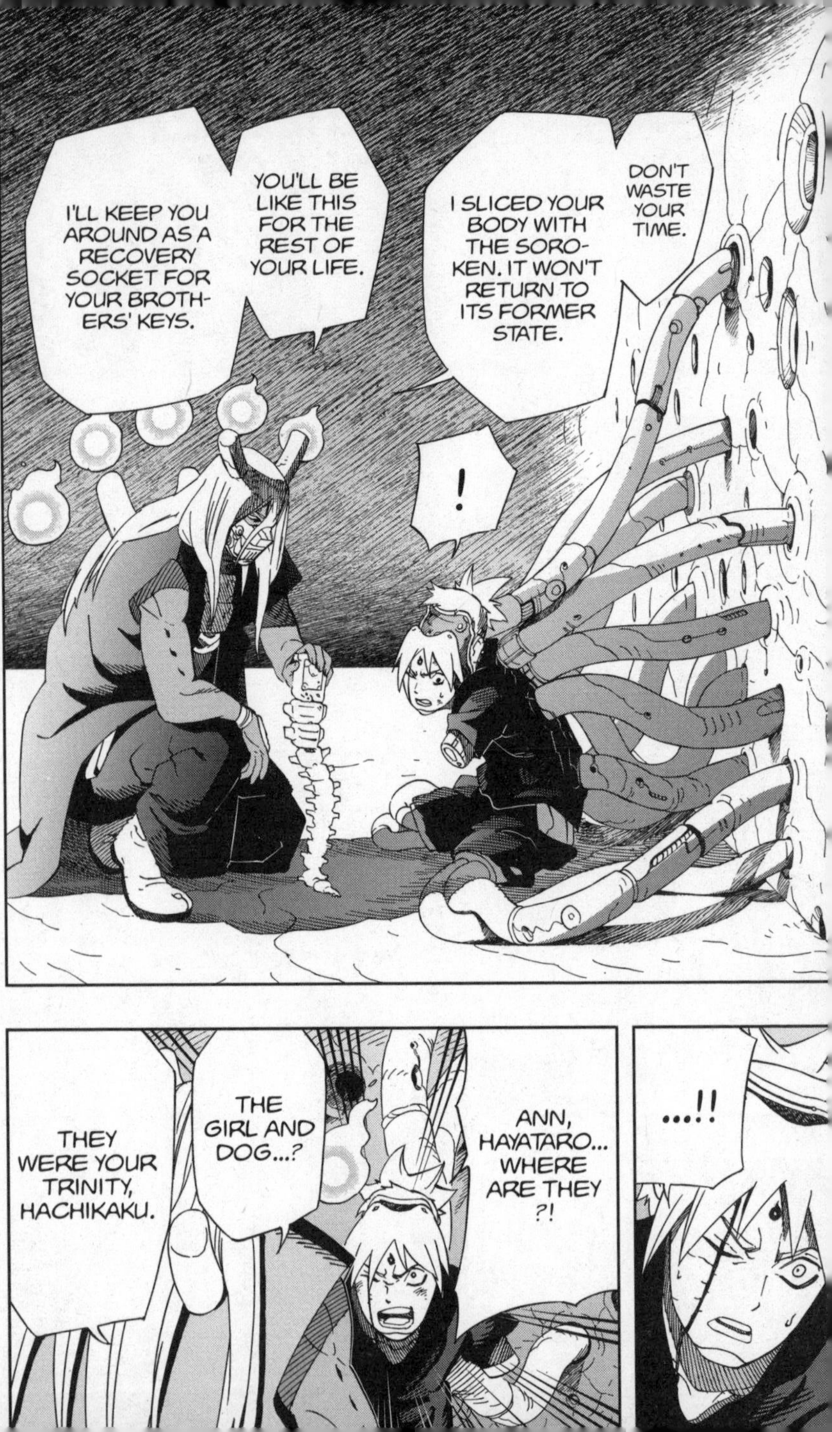
DON'T WASTE YOUR TIME.
I SLICED YOUR BODY WITH THE SORO-KEN. IT WON'T RETURN TO ITS FORMER STATE.
!
YOU'LL BE LIKE THIS FOR THE REST OF YOUR LIFE.
I'LL KEEP YOU AROUND AS A RECOVERY SOCKET FOR YOUR BROTHERS' KEYS.
...!!
ANN, HAYATARO... WHERE ARE THEY ?!
THE GIRL AND DOG...?
THEY WERE YOUR TRINITY, HACHIKAKU.

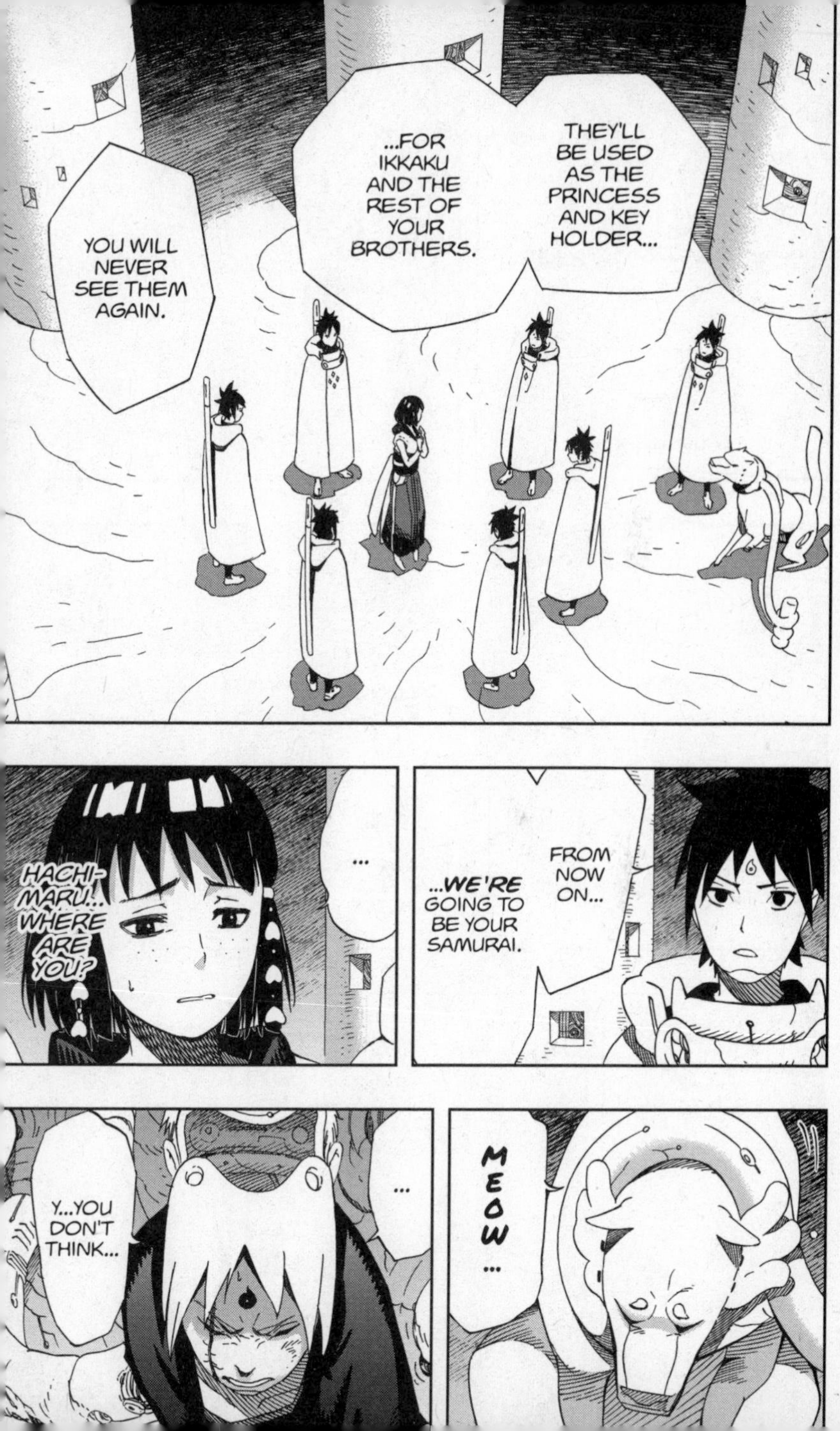
THEY'LL BE USED AS THE PRINCESS AND KEY HOLDER...
...FOR IKKAKU AND THE REST OF YOUR BROTHERS.
YOU WILL NEVER SEE THEM AGAIN.
FROM NOW ON...
...WE'RE GOING TO BE YOUR SAMURAI.
...
HACHIMARU... WHERE ARE YOU?
MEOW...
...
Y...YOU DON'T THINK...

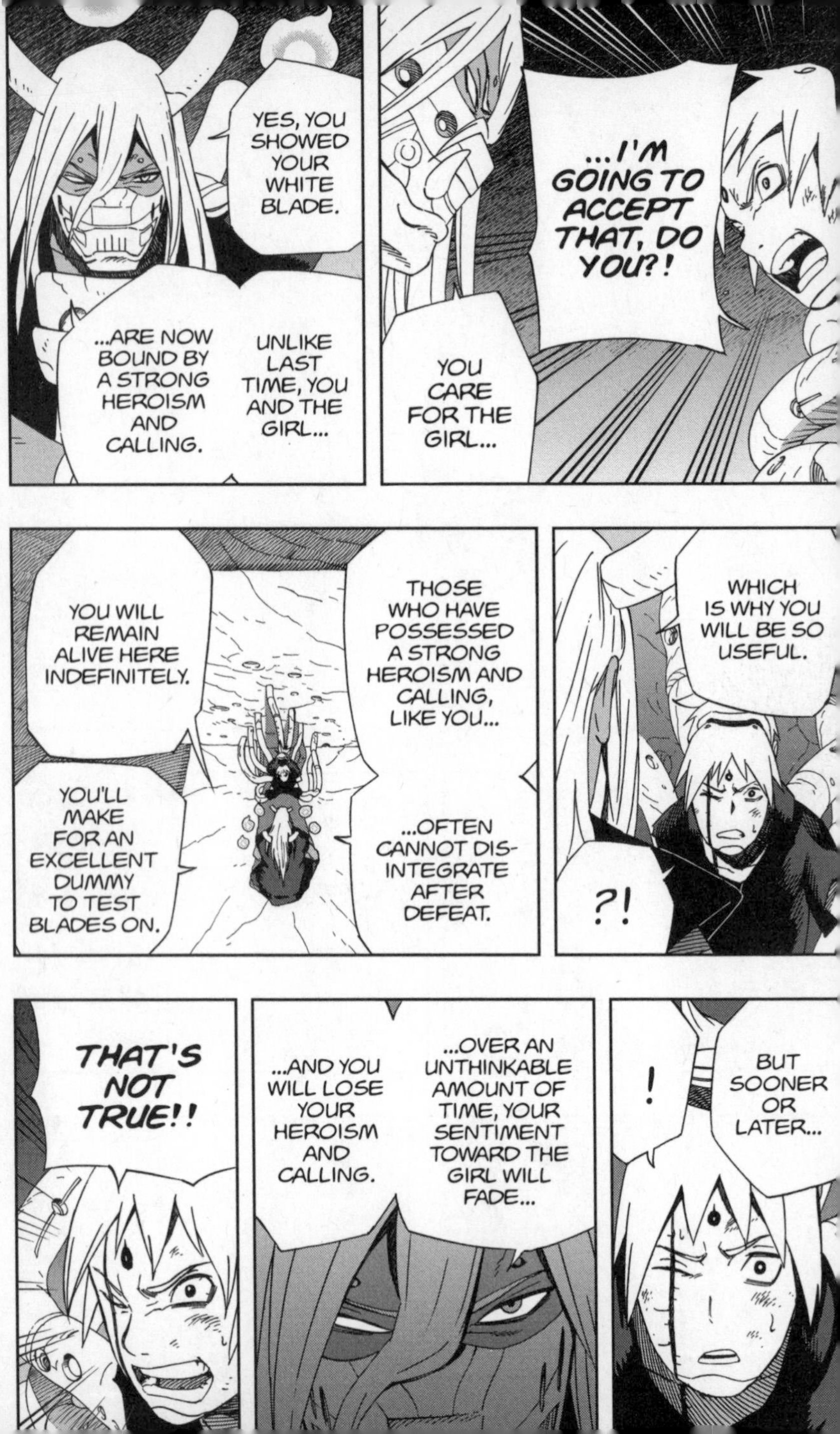
...I'M GOING TO ACCEPT THAT, DO YOU?!
YOU CARE FOR THE GIRL...
YES, YOU SHOWED YOUR WHITE BLADE.
UNLIKE LAST TIME, YOU AND THE GIRL...
...ARE NOW BOUND BY A STRONG HEROISM AND CALLING.
WHICH IS WHY YOU WILL BE SO USEFUL.
?!
THOSE WHO HAVE POSSESSED A STRONG HEROISM AND CALLING, LIKE YOU...
...OFTEN CANNOT DIS-INTEGRATE AFTER DEFEAT.
YOU WILL REMAIN ALIVE HERE INDEFINITELY.
YOU'LL MAKE FOR AN EXCELLENT DUMMY TO TEST BLADES ON.
BUT SOONER OR LATER...
!
...OVER AN UNTHINKABLE AMOUNT OF TIME, YOUR SENTIMENT TOWARD THE GIRL WILL FADE...
...AND YOU WILL LOSE YOUR HEROISM AND CALLING.
THAT'S NOT TRUE!!

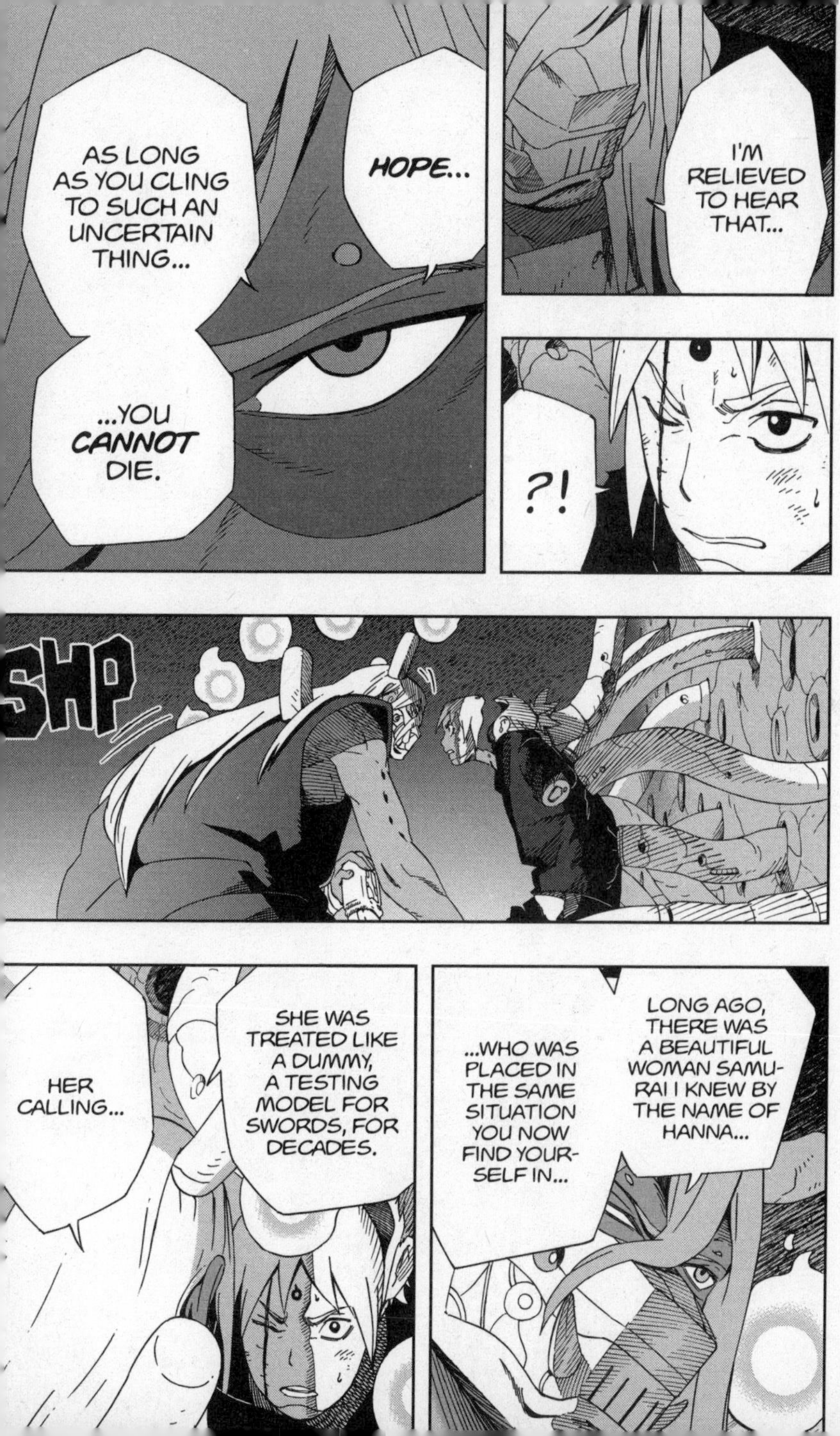
I'M RELIEVED TO HEAR THAT...
?!
HOPE...
AS LONG AS YOU CLING TO SUCH AN UNCERTAIN THING...
...YOU CANNOT DIE.
SHP
LONG AGO, THERE WAS A BEAUTIFUL WOMAN SAMU-RAI I KNEW BY THE NAME OF HANNA...
...WHO WAS PLACED IN THE SAME SITUATION YOU NOW FIND YOUR-SELF IN...
SHE WAS TREATED LIKE A DUMMY, A TESTING MODEL FOR SWORDS, FOR DECADES.
HER CALLING...

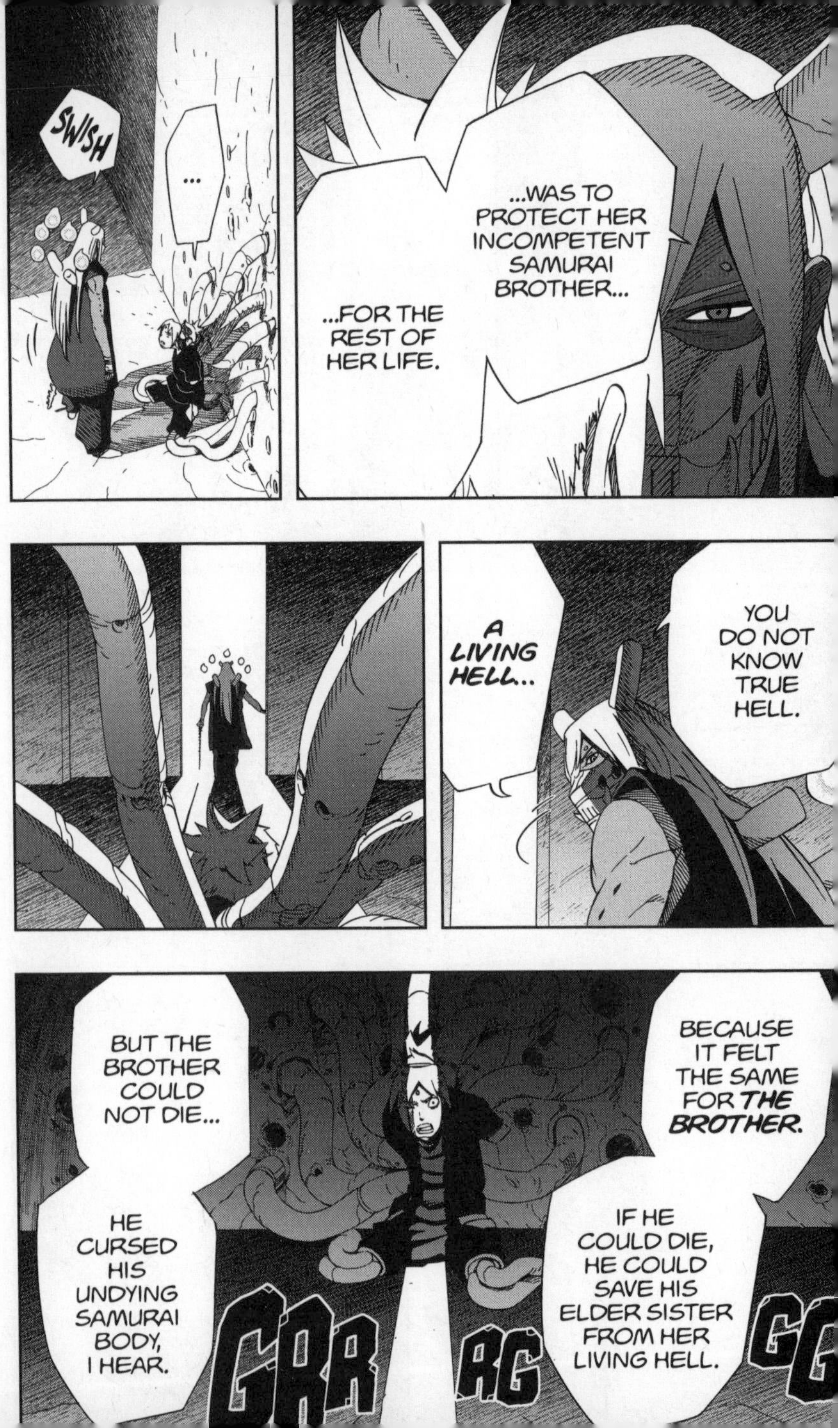
...WAS TO PROTECT HER INCOMPETENT SAMURAI BROTHER...
...FOR THE REST OF HER LIFE.
SWISH
...
YOU DO NOT KNOW TRUE HELL.
A LIVING HELL...
BECAUSE IT FELT THE SAME FOR THE BROTHER.
BUT THE BROTHER COULD NOT DIE...
IF HE COULD DIE, HE COULD SAVE HIS ELDER SISTER FROM HER LIVING HELL.
HE CURSED HIS UNDYING SAMURAI BODY, I HEAR.
GG
RG
GRR

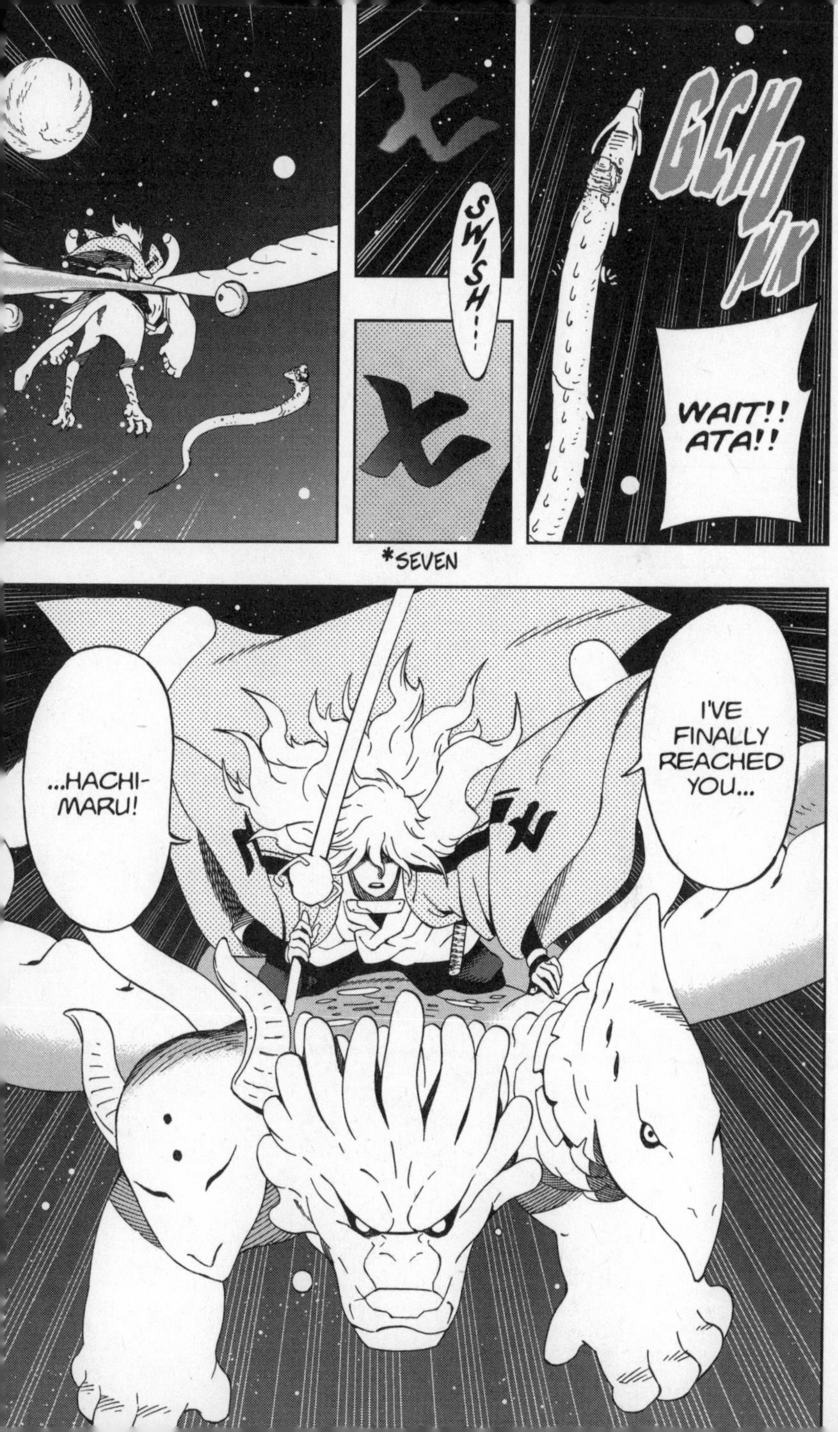
GCHUNK
WAIT!! ATA!!
SWISH!!
*SEVEN
I'VE FINALLY REACHED YOU...
...HACHI-MARU!

Storyboard Reveal!
Chapter 40 (Vol. 5, pg. 127)

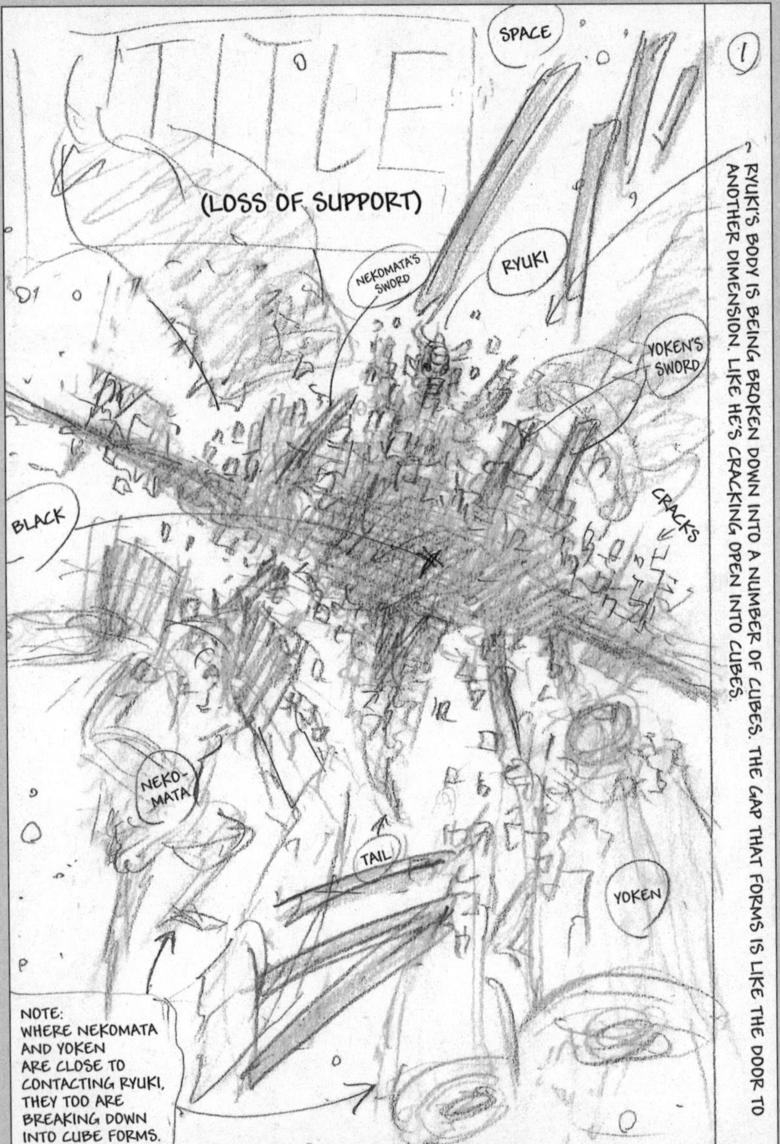

1
RYUKI'S BODY IS BEING BROKEN DOWN INTO A NUMBER OF CUBES. THE GAP THAT FORMS IS LIKE THE DOOR TO ANOTHER DIMENSION. LIKE HE'S CRACKING OPEN INTO CUBES.
SPACE
(LOSS OF SUPPORT)
RYUKI
NEKOMATA'S SWORD
YOKEN'S SWORD
CRACKS
BLACK
NEKO-MATA
TAIL
YOKEN
NOTE:
WHERE NEKOMATA AND YOKEN ARE CLOSE TO CONTACTING RYUKI, THEY TOO ARE BREAKING DOWN INTO CUBE FORMS.

CHAPTER 41: NANASHI THE SAMURAI

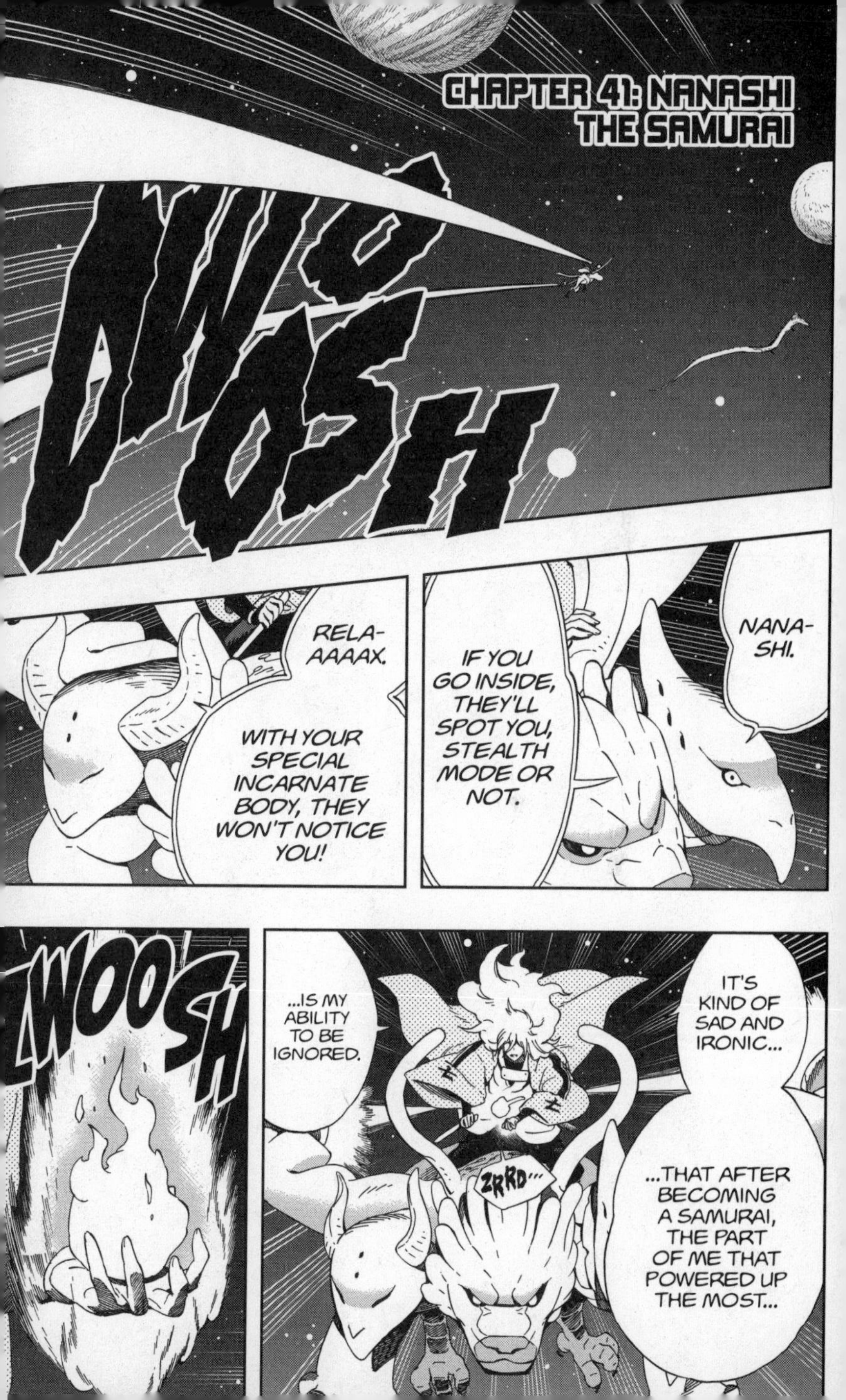
DWOOSH
NANA-SHI.
IF YOU GO INSIDE, THEY'LL SPOT YOU, STEALTH MODE OR NOT.
RELA-AAAAX.
WITH YOUR SPECIAL INCARNATE BODY, THEY WON'T NOTICE YOU!
IT'S KIND OF SAD AND IRONIC...
...THAT AFTER BECOMING A SAMURAI, THE PART OF ME THAT POWERED UP THE MOST...
...IS MY ABILITY TO BE IGNORED.
ZRRD...
WOOSH

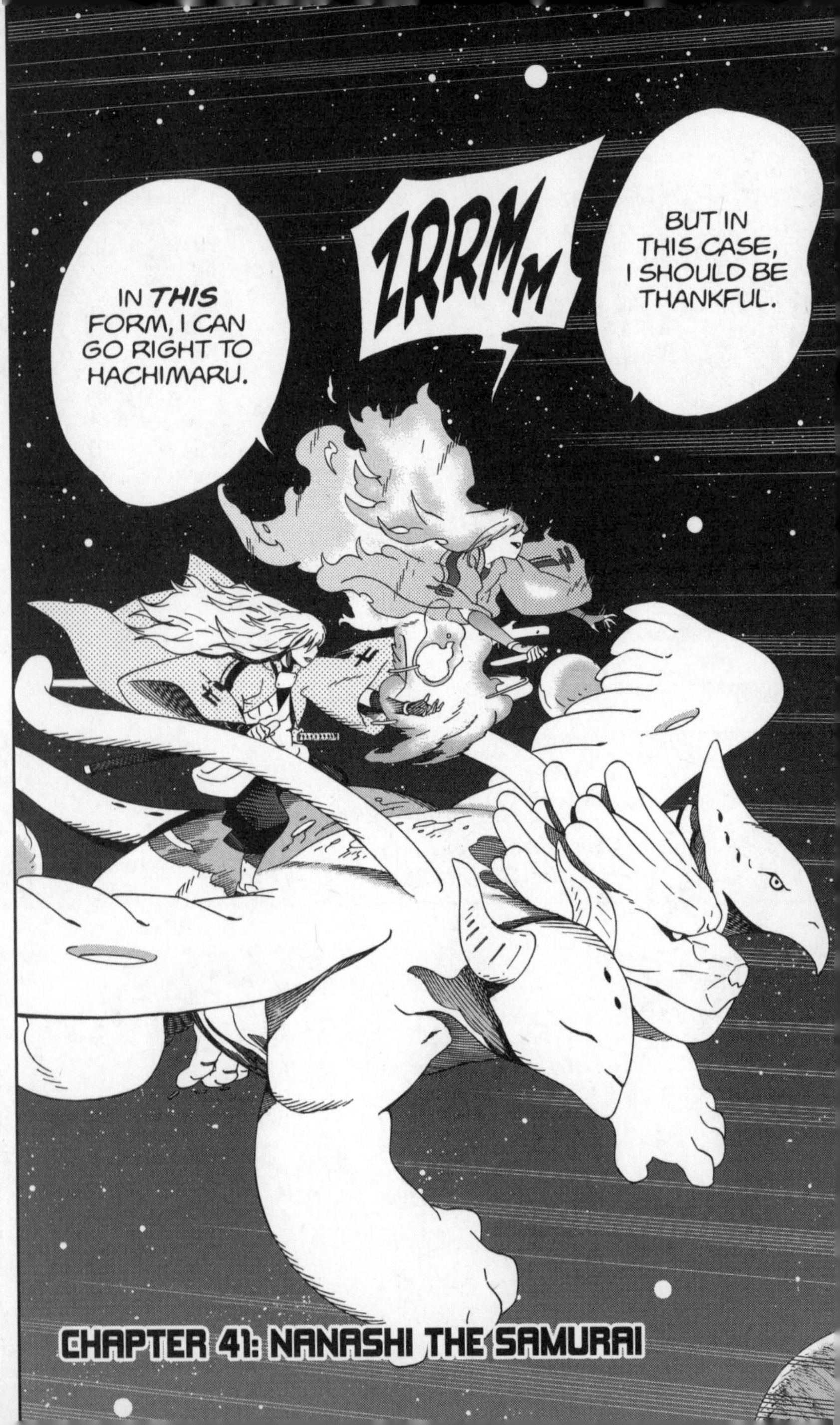
BUT IN THIS CASE, I SHOULD BE THANKFUL.
ZRRMM
IN THIS FORM, I CAN GO RIGHT TO HACHIMARU.

CHAPTER 41: NANASHI THE SAMURAI

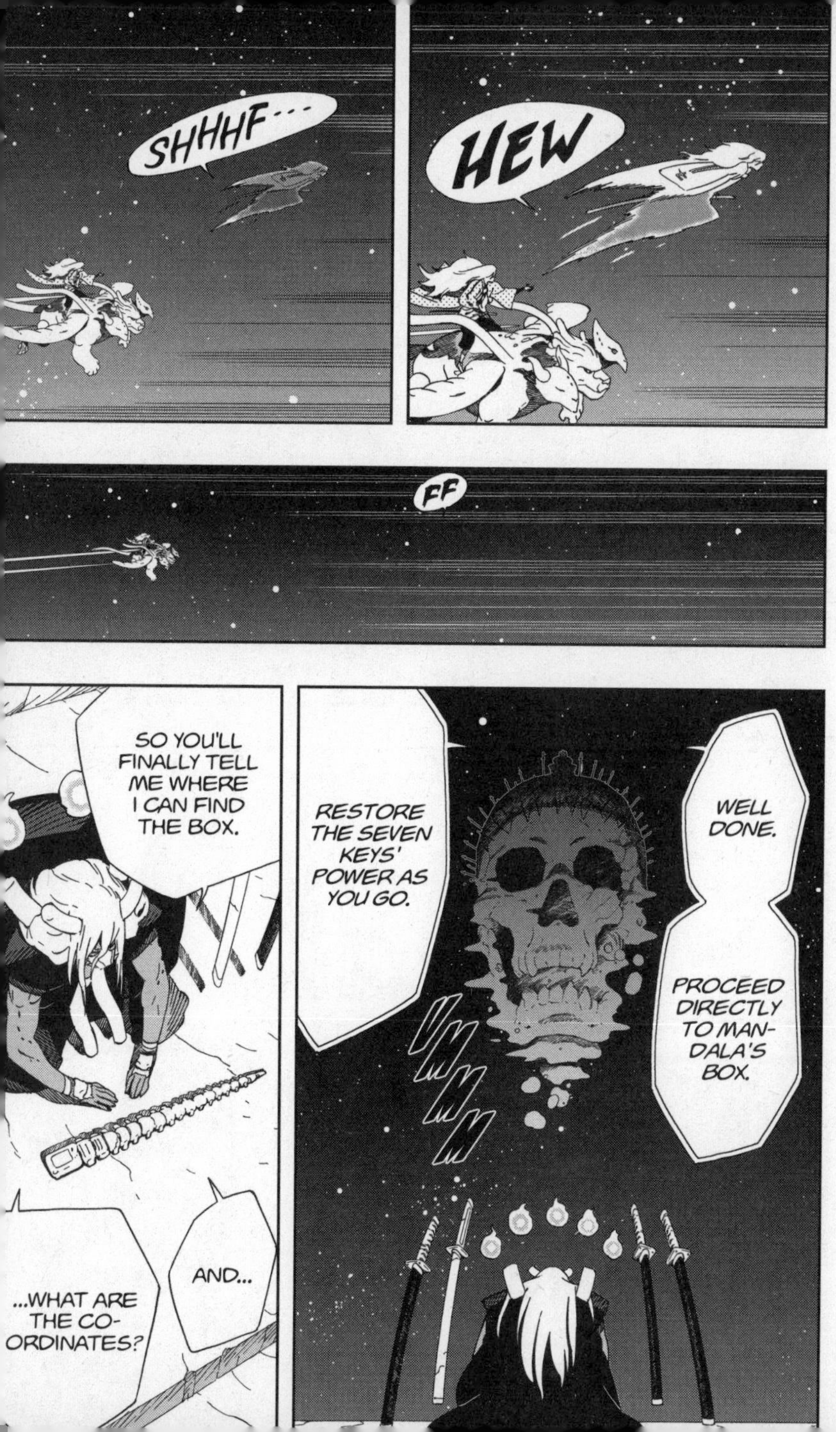
HEW
SHHHF...
FF
WELL DONE.
PROCEED DIRECTLY TO MAN-DALA'S BOX.
RESTORE THE SEVEN KEYS' POWER AS YOU GO.
SO YOU'LL FINALLY TELL ME WHERE I CAN FIND THE BOX.
AND...
...WHAT ARE THE CO-ORDINATES?

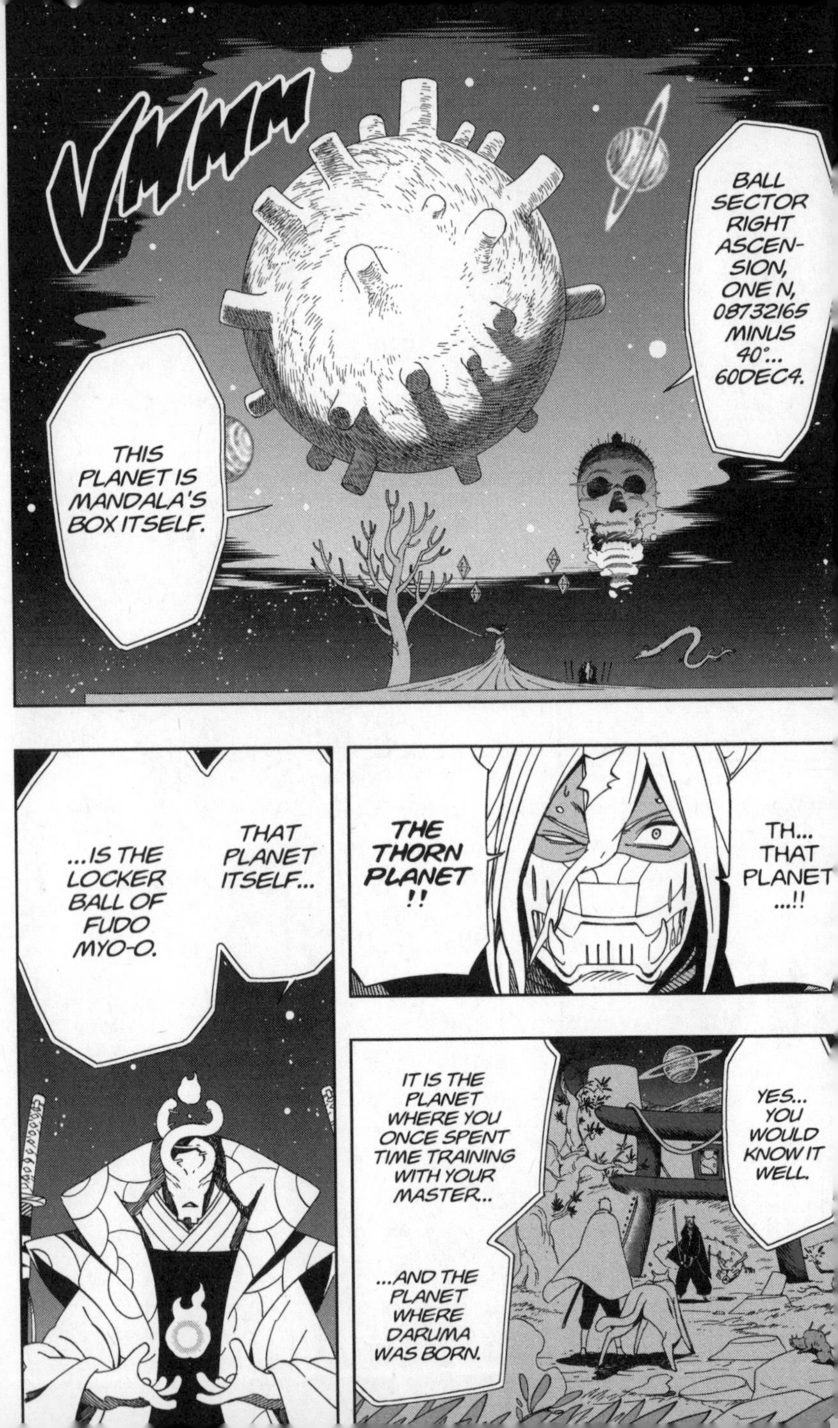
BALL SECTOR RIGHT ASCEN-SION, ONE N, 08732165 MINUS 40°... 60DEC4.
VMMM
THIS PLANET IS MANDALA'S BOX ITSELF.
TH... THAT PLANET ...!!
THE THORN PLANET !!
YES... YOU WOULD KNOW IT WELL.
IT IS THE PLANET WHERE YOU ONCE SPENT TIME TRAINING WITH YOUR MASTER...
...AND THE PLANET WHERE DARUMA WAS BORN.
THAT PLANET ITSELF...
...IS THE LOCKER BALL OF FUDO MYO-O.

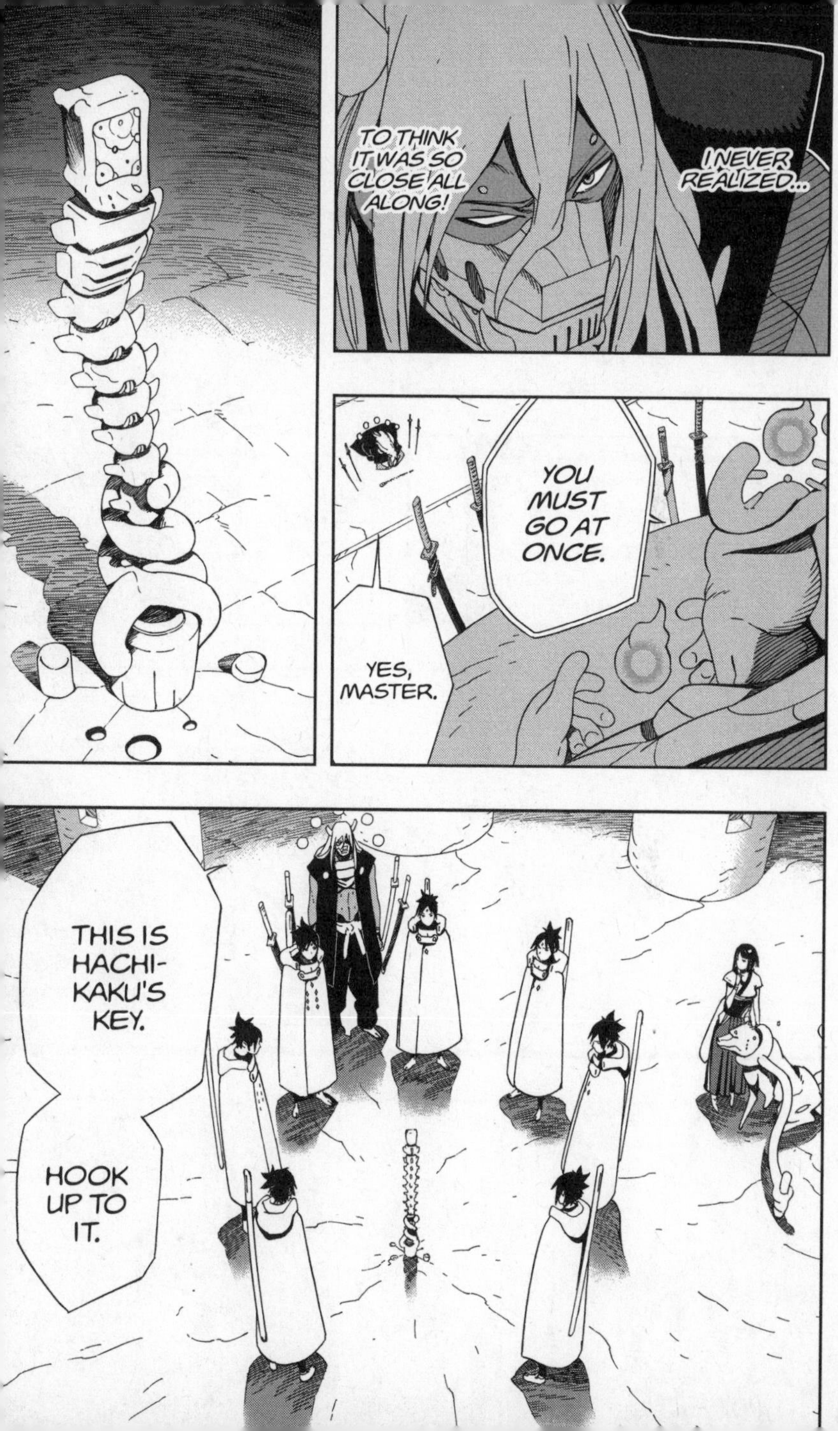
I NEVER REALIZED...
TO THINK IT WAS SO CLOSE ALL ALONG!
YOU MUST GO AT ONCE.
YES, MASTER.
THIS IS HACHI-KAKU'S KEY.
HOOK UP TO IT.

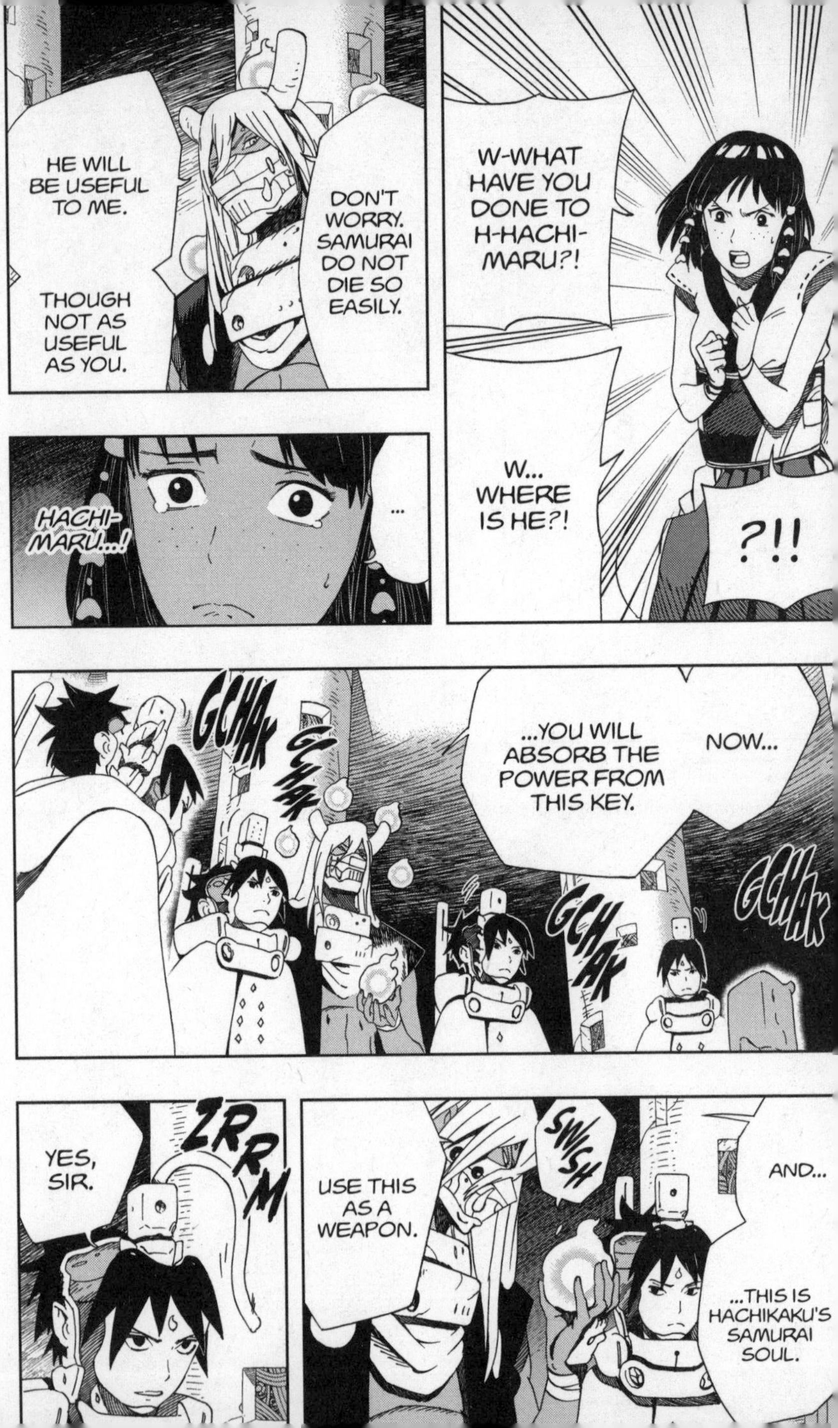
W-WHAT HAVE YOU DONE TO H-HACHI-MARU?!
W... WHERE IS HE?!
?!!
DON'T WORRY. SAMURAI DO NOT DIE SO EASILY.
HE WILL BE USEFUL TO ME.
THOUGH NOT AS USEFUL AS YOU.
...
HACHI-MARU...!
NOW...
...YOU WILL ABSORB THE POWER FROM THIS KEY.
GCHAK
GCHAK
GCHAK
GCHAK
AND...
...THIS IS HACHIKAKU'S SAMURAI SOUL.
SWISH
USE THIS AS A WEAPON.
ZRRM
YES, SIR.

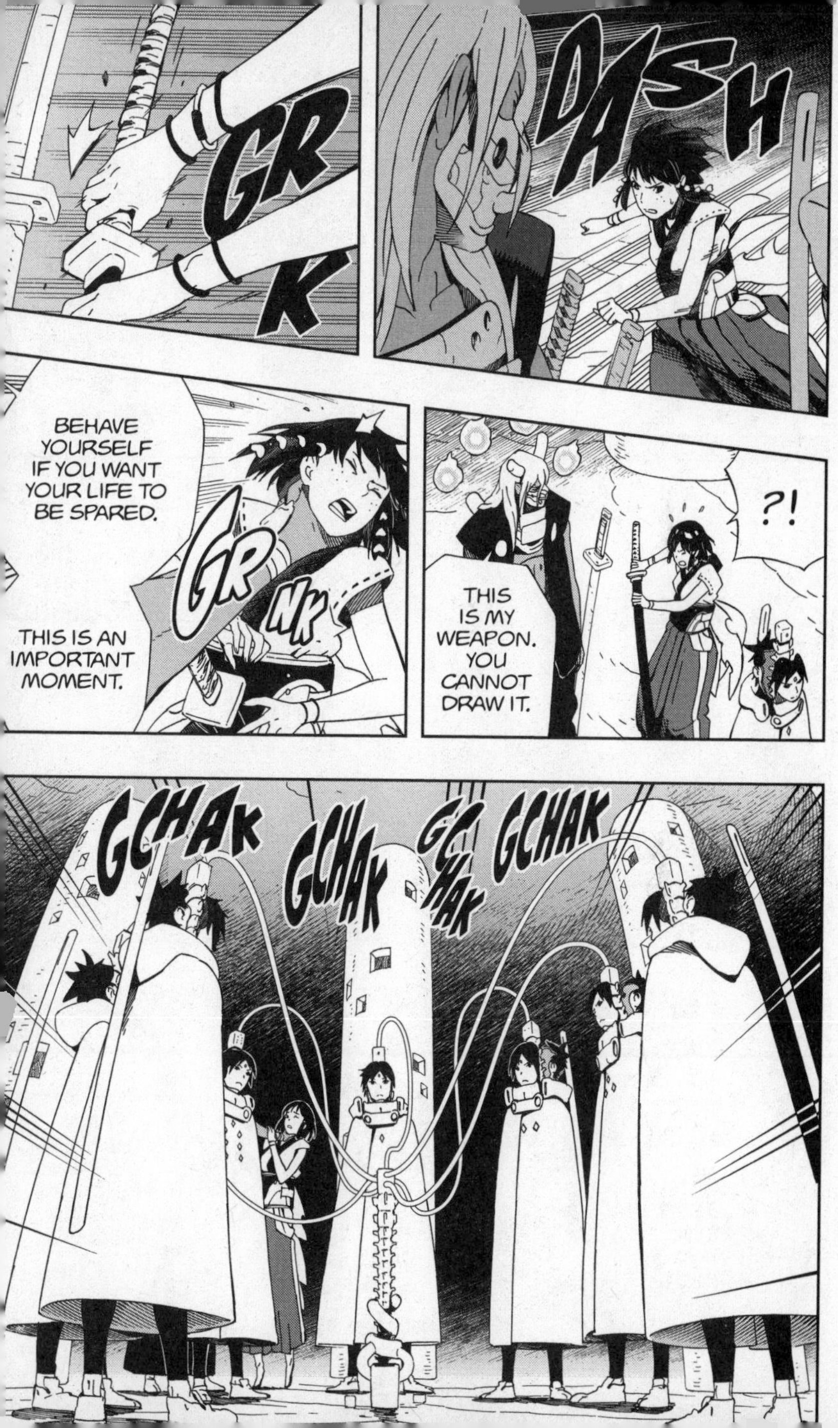

DASH
GRK
?!
THIS IS MY WEAPON. YOU CANNOT DRAW IT.
BEHAVE YOURSELF IF YOU WANT YOUR LIFE TO BE SPARED.
GRNK
THIS IS AN IMPORTANT MOMENT.
GCHAK
GCHAK
GCHAK
GCHAK

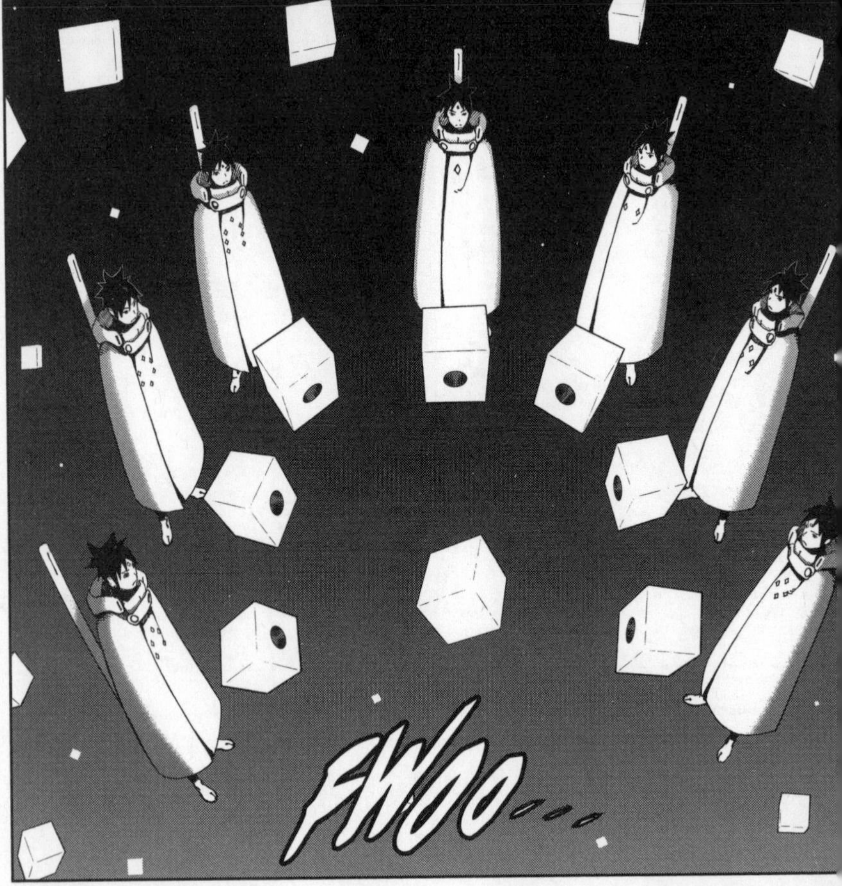
FWOO...

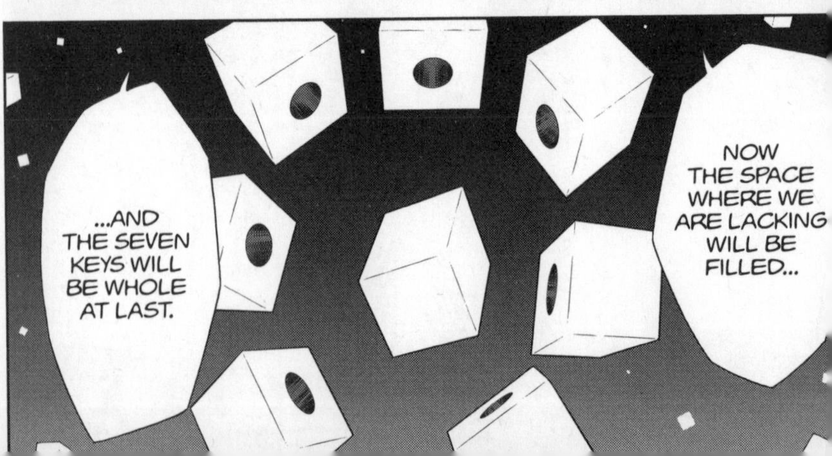
NOW THE SPACE WHERE WE ARE LACKING WILL BE FILLED...
...AND THE SEVEN KEYS WILL BE WHOLE AT LAST.

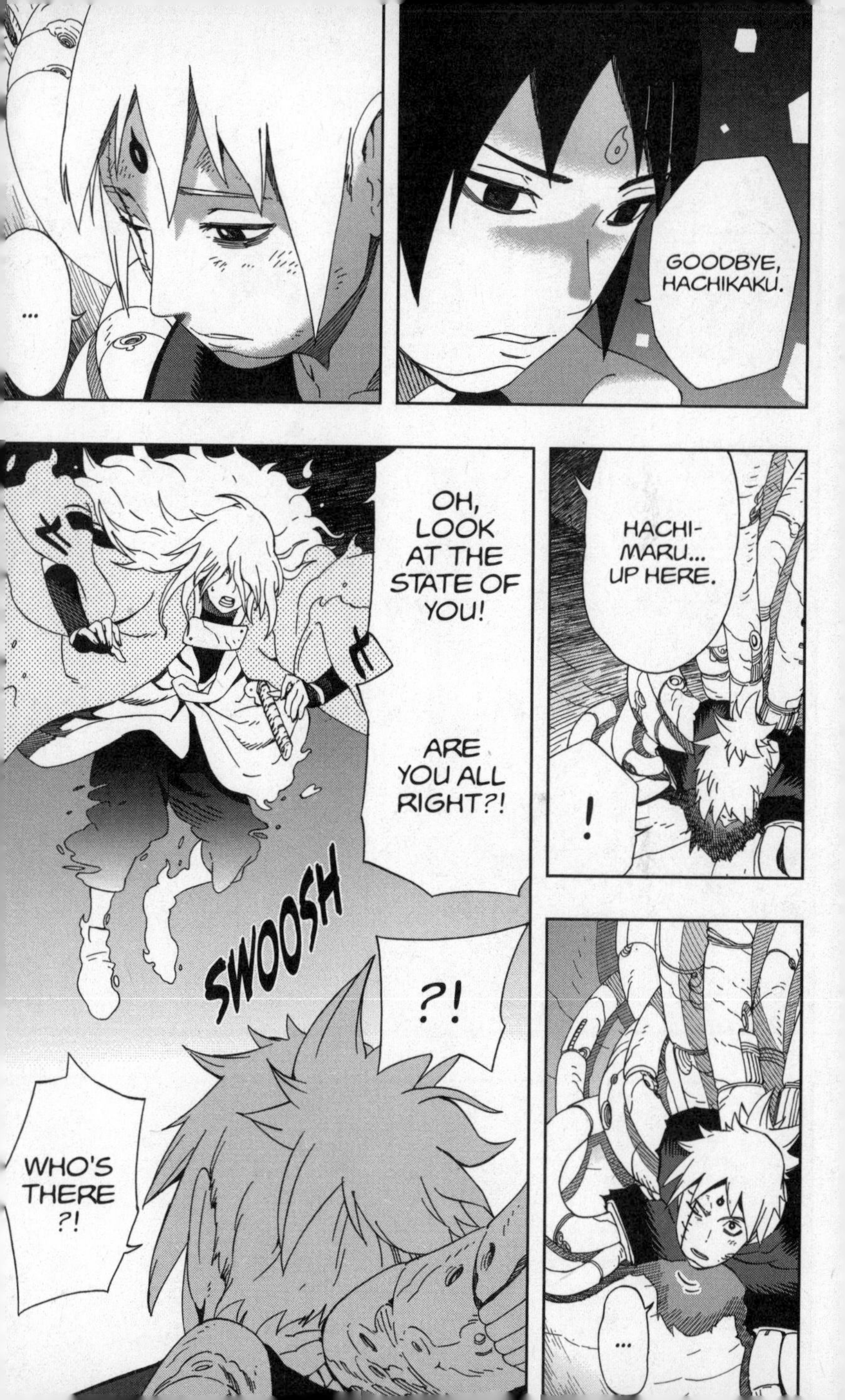
GOODBYE, HACHIKAKU.
...
HACHI-MARU... UP HERE.
!
...
OH, LOOK AT THE STATE OF YOU!
ARE YOU ALL RIGHT?!
SWOOSH
?!
WHO'S THERE ?!

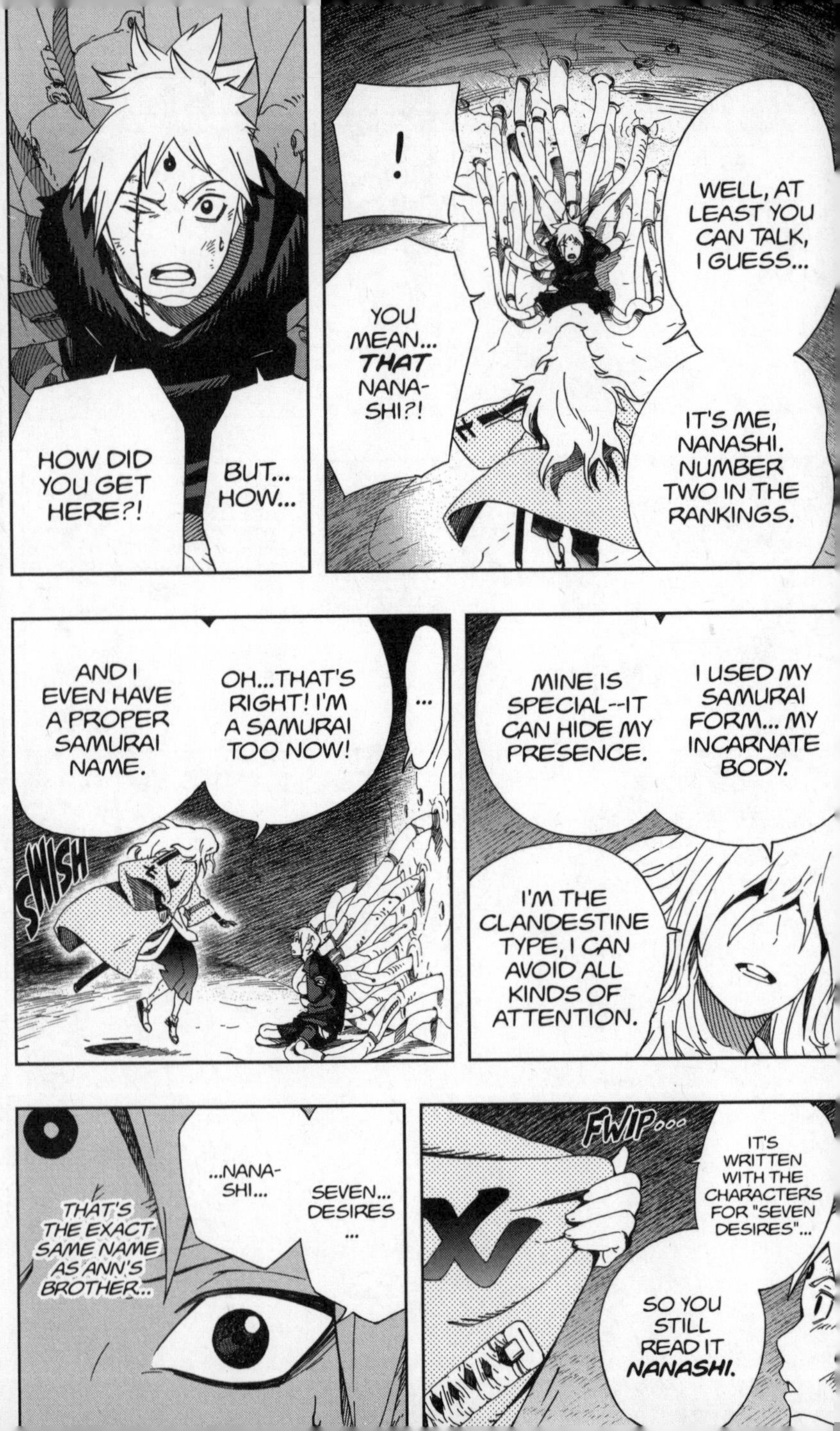
WELL, AT LEAST YOU CAN TALK, I GUESS...
!
IT'S ME, NANASHI. NUMBER TWO IN THE RANKINGS.
YOU MEAN... ***THAT*** NANASHI?!
BUT... HOW...
HOW DID YOU GET HERE?!
I USED MY SAMURAI FORM... MY INCARNATE BODY.
MINE IS SPECIAL--IT CAN HIDE MY PRESENCE.
I'M THE CLANDESTINE TYPE, I CAN AVOID ALL KINDS OF ATTENTION.
...
OH...THAT'S RIGHT! I'M A SAMURAI TOO NOW!
AND I EVEN HAVE A PROPER SAMURAI NAME.
SWISH
FWIP...
IT'S WRITTEN WITH THE CHARACTERS FOR "SEVEN DESIRES"...
SO YOU STILL READ IT ***NANASHI.***
SEVEN... DESIRES...
...NANASHI...
THAT'S THE EXACT SAME NAME AS ANN'S BROTHER...

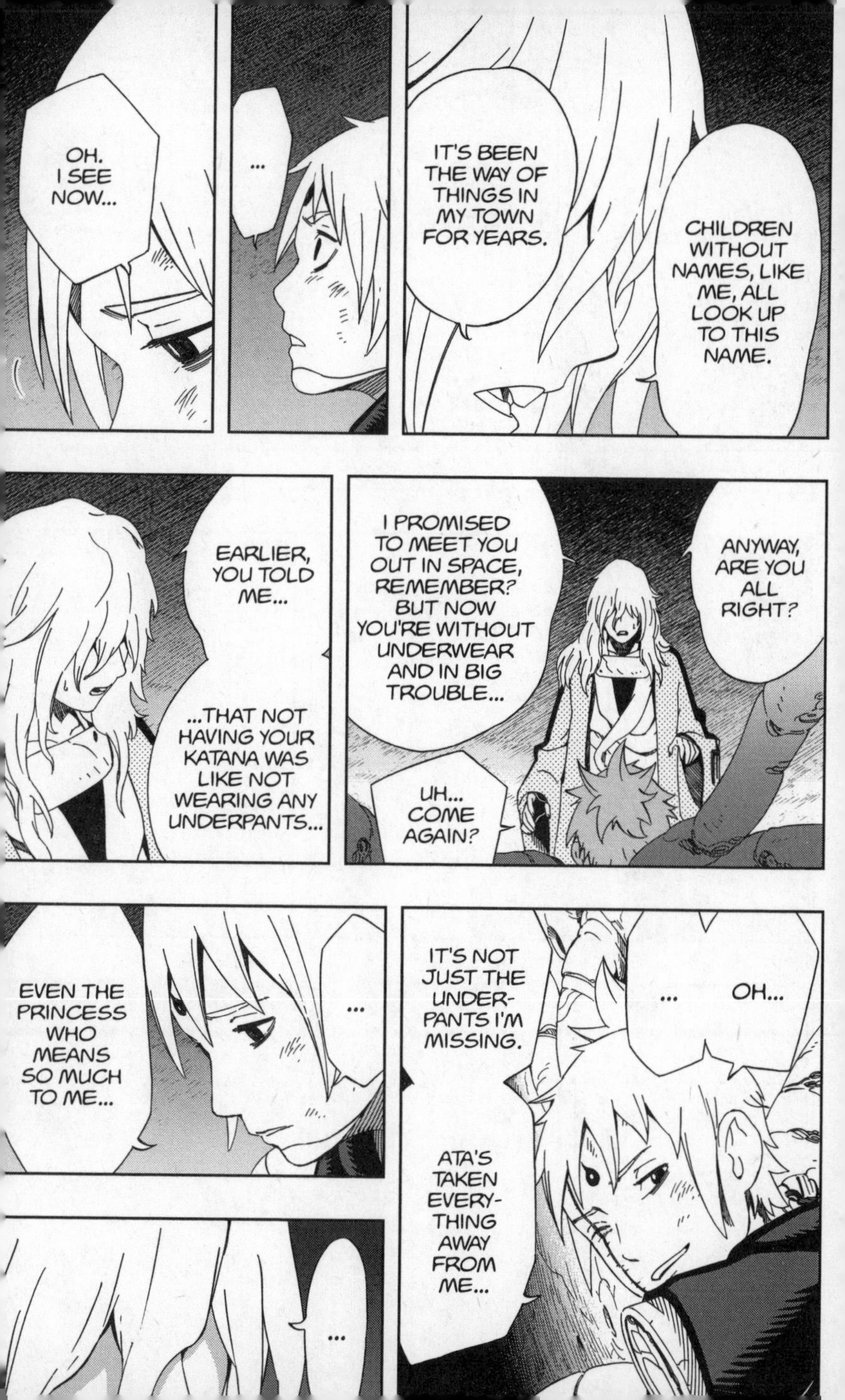
CHILDREN WITHOUT NAMES, LIKE ME, ALL LOOK UP TO THIS NAME.
IT'S BEEN THE WAY OF THINGS IN MY TOWN FOR YEARS.
...
OH. I SEE NOW...
ANYWAY, ARE YOU ALL RIGHT?
I PROMISED TO MEET YOU OUT IN SPACE, REMEMBER? BUT NOW YOU'RE WITHOUT UNDERWEAR AND IN BIG TROUBLE...
UH... COME AGAIN?
EARLIER, YOU TOLD ME...
...THAT NOT HAVING YOUR KATANA WAS LIKE NOT WEARING ANY UNDERPANTS...
OH...
...
IT'S NOT JUST THE UNDER-PANTS I'M MISSING.
ATA'S TAKEN EVERY-THING AWAY FROM ME...
...
EVEN THE PRINCESS WHO MEANS SO MUCH TO ME...
...

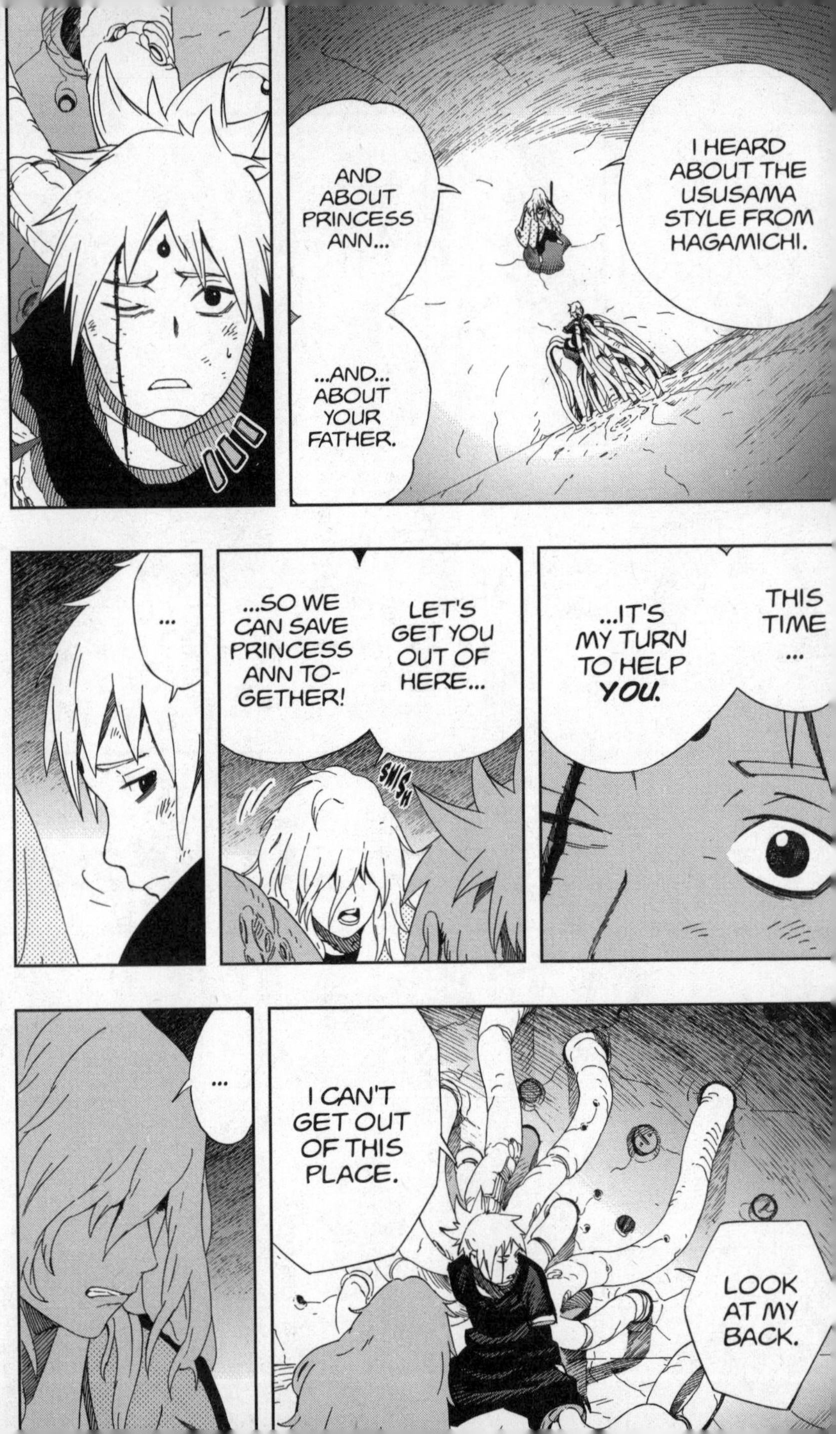
I HEARD ABOUT THE USUSAMA STYLE FROM HAGAMICHI.
AND ABOUT PRINCESS ANN...
...AND... ABOUT YOUR FATHER.
THIS TIME...
...IT'S MY TURN TO HELP *YOU*.
LET'S GET YOU OUT OF HERE...
...SO WE CAN SAVE PRINCESS ANN TOGETHER!
SWISH
...
I CAN'T GET OUT OF THIS PLACE.
LOOK AT MY BACK.
...

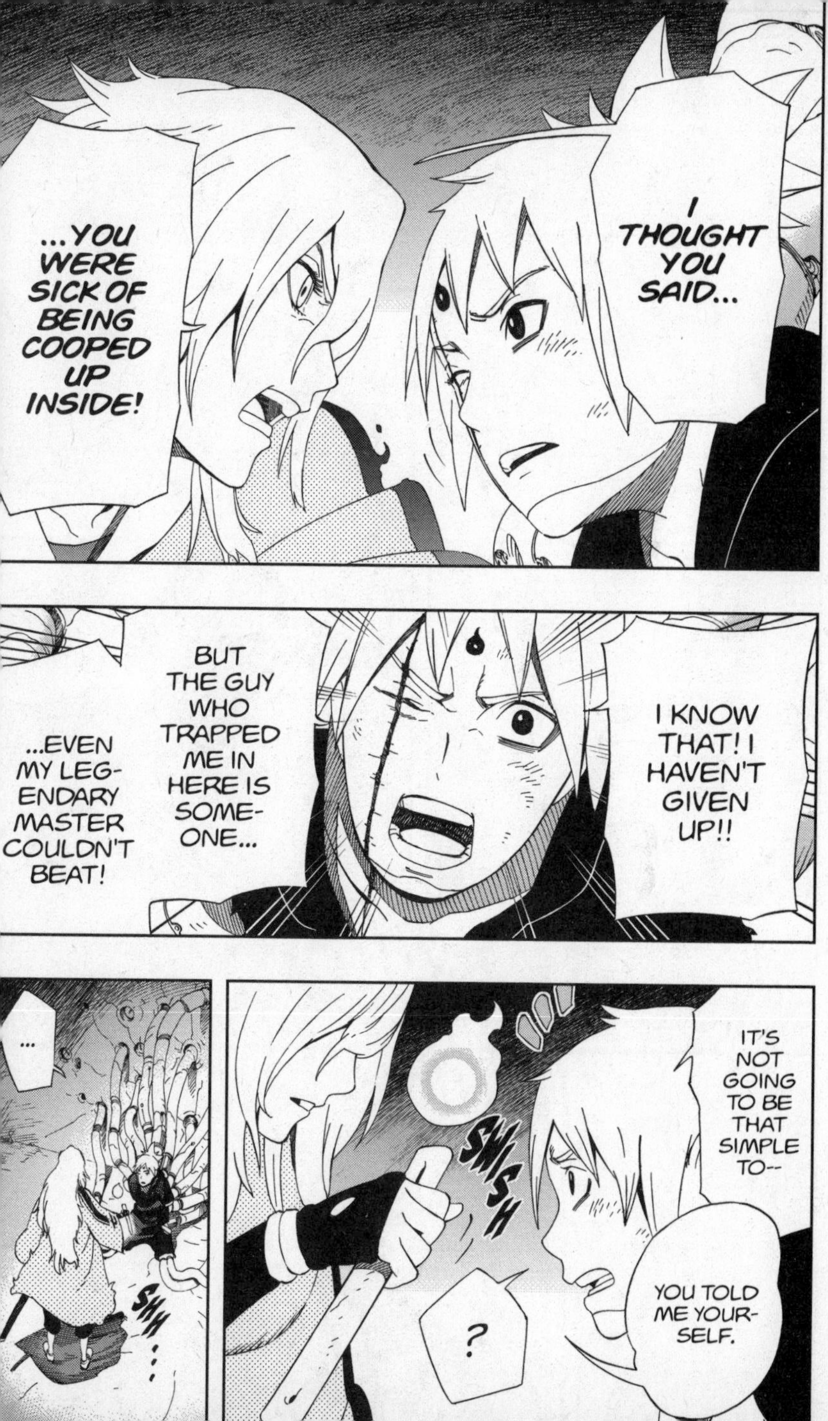
I THOUGHT YOU SAID...
...YOU WERE SICK OF BEING COOPED UP INSIDE!
I KNOW THAT! I HAVEN'T GIVEN UP!!
BUT THE GUY WHO TRAPPED ME IN HERE IS SOMEONE...
...EVEN MY LEGENDARY MASTER COULDN'T BEAT!
IT'S NOT GOING TO BE THAT SIMPLE TO--
SWISH
YOU TOLD ME YOURSELF.
?
...
SHH...

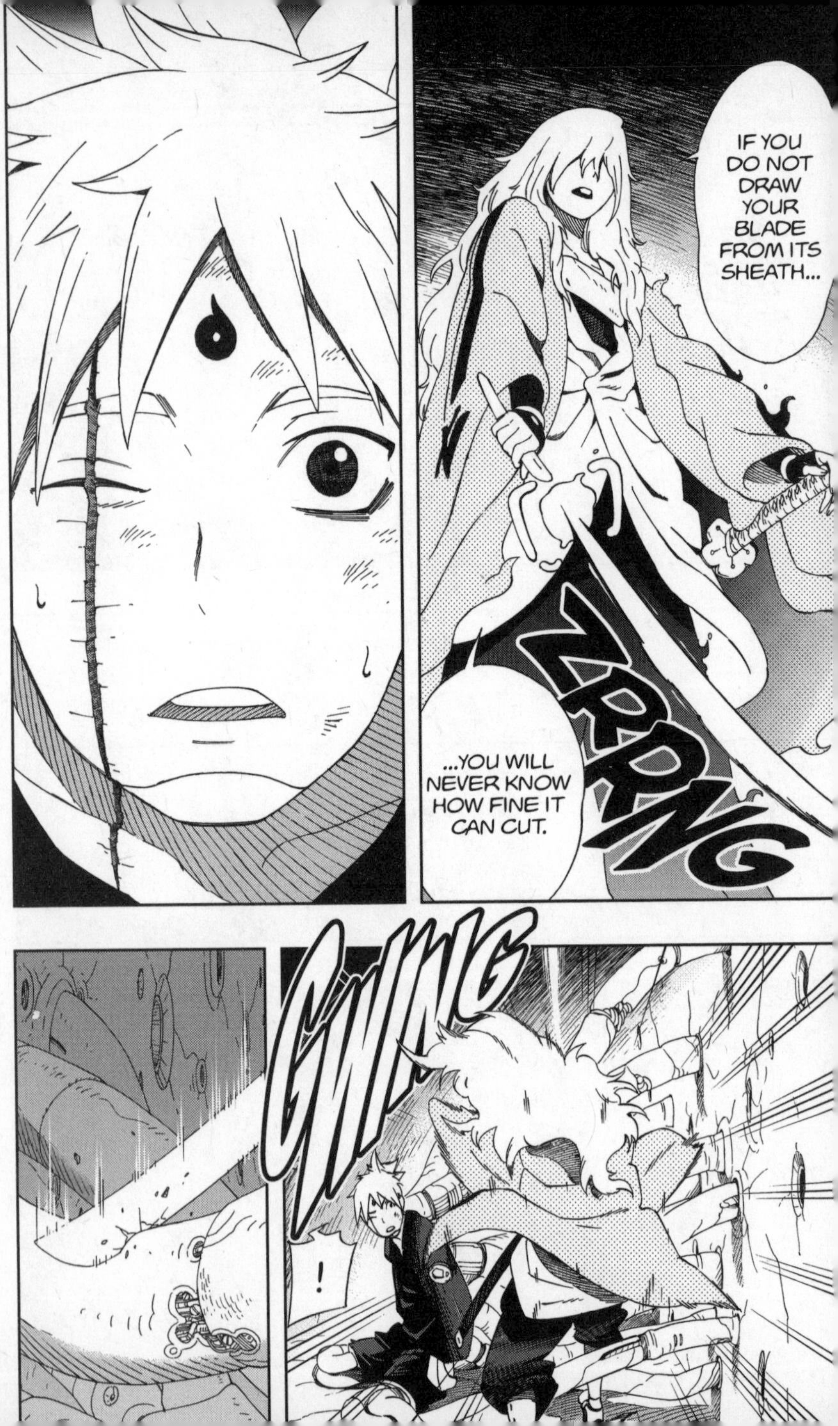
IF YOU DO NOT DRAW YOUR BLADE FROM ITS SHEATH...
ZRRNG
...YOU WILL NEVER KNOW HOW FINE IT CAN CUT.
CHING
!

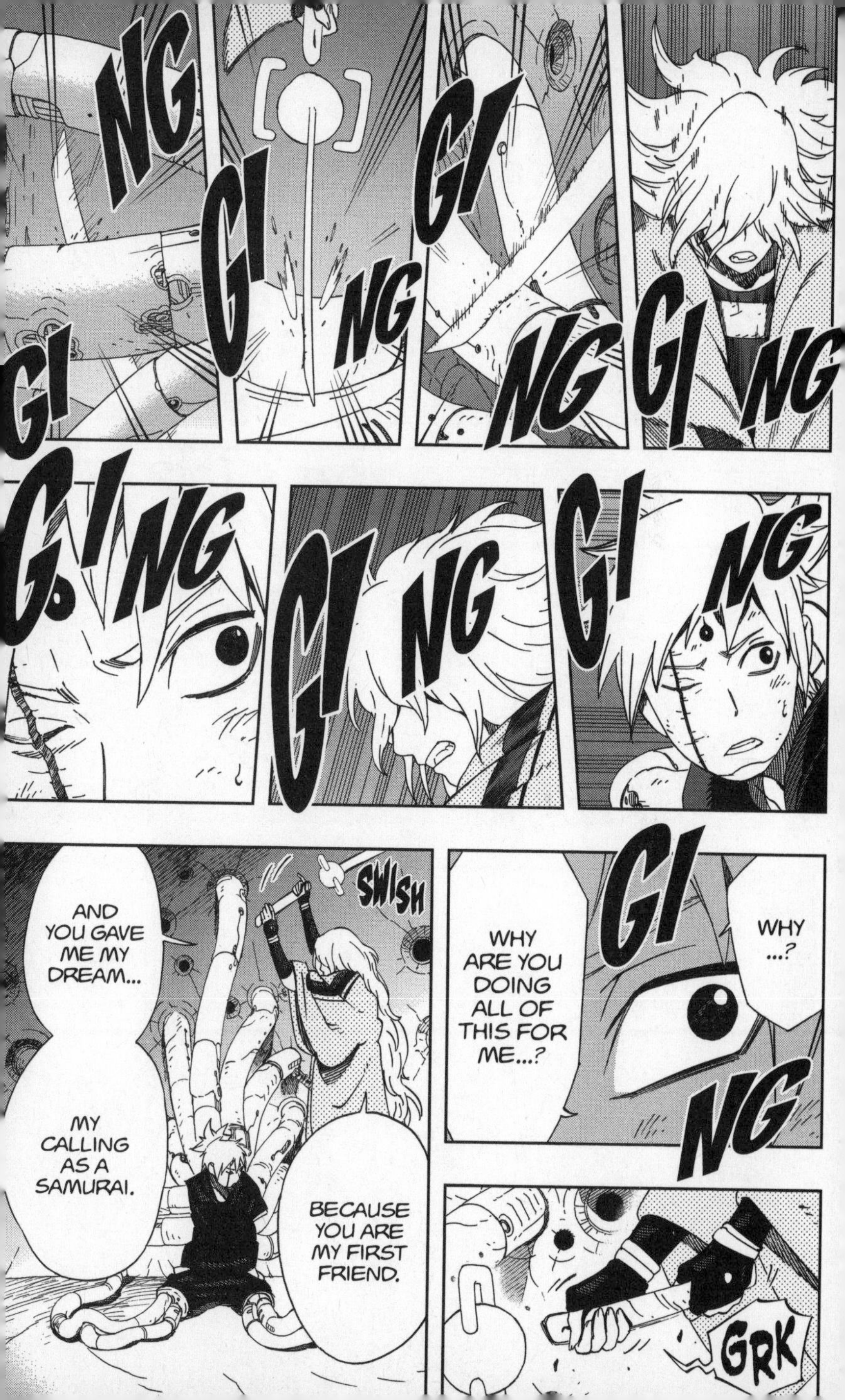
GI NG
GI NG
GI NG
NG GI
GI NG
GI NG
GI NG
WHY ...?
WHY ARE YOU DOING ALL OF THIS FOR ME...?
GI NG
GRK
SWISH
BECAUSE YOU ARE MY FIRST FRIEND.
AND YOU GAVE ME MY DREAM...
MY CALLING AS A SAMURAI.

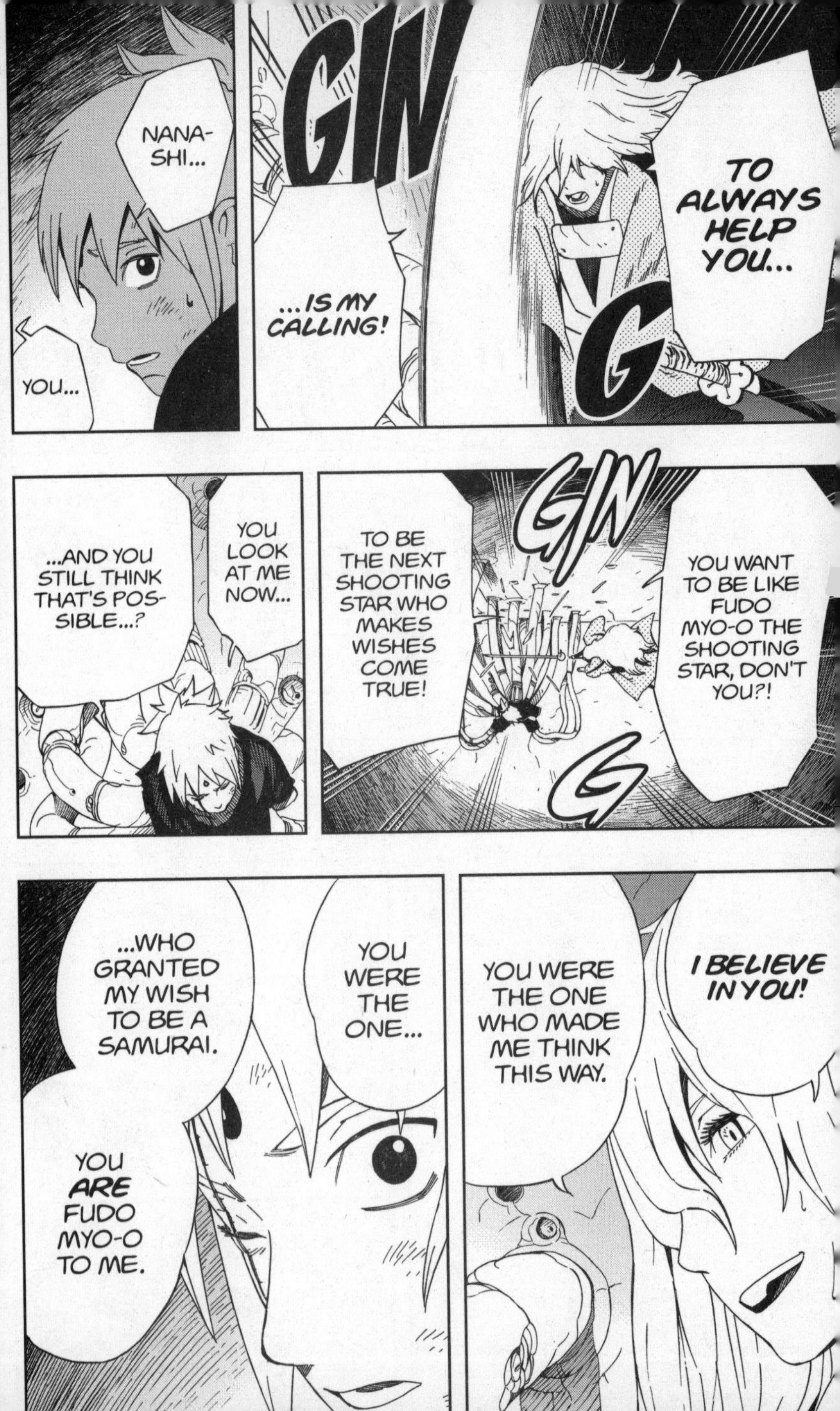

TO ALWAYS HELP YOU...
GIN
G
...IS MY CALLING!
NANA-SHI...
YOU...
GIN
G
YOU WANT TO BE LIKE FUDO MYO-O THE SHOOTING STAR, DON'T YOU?!
TO BE THE NEXT SHOOTING STAR WHO MAKES WISHES COME TRUE!
YOU LOOK AT ME NOW...
...AND YOU STILL THINK THAT'S POS-SIBLE...?
I BELIEVE IN YOU!
YOU WERE THE ONE WHO MADE ME THINK THIS WAY.
YOU WERE THE ONE...
...WHO GRANTED MY WISH TO BE A SAMURAI.
YOU ARE FUDO MYO-O TO ME.

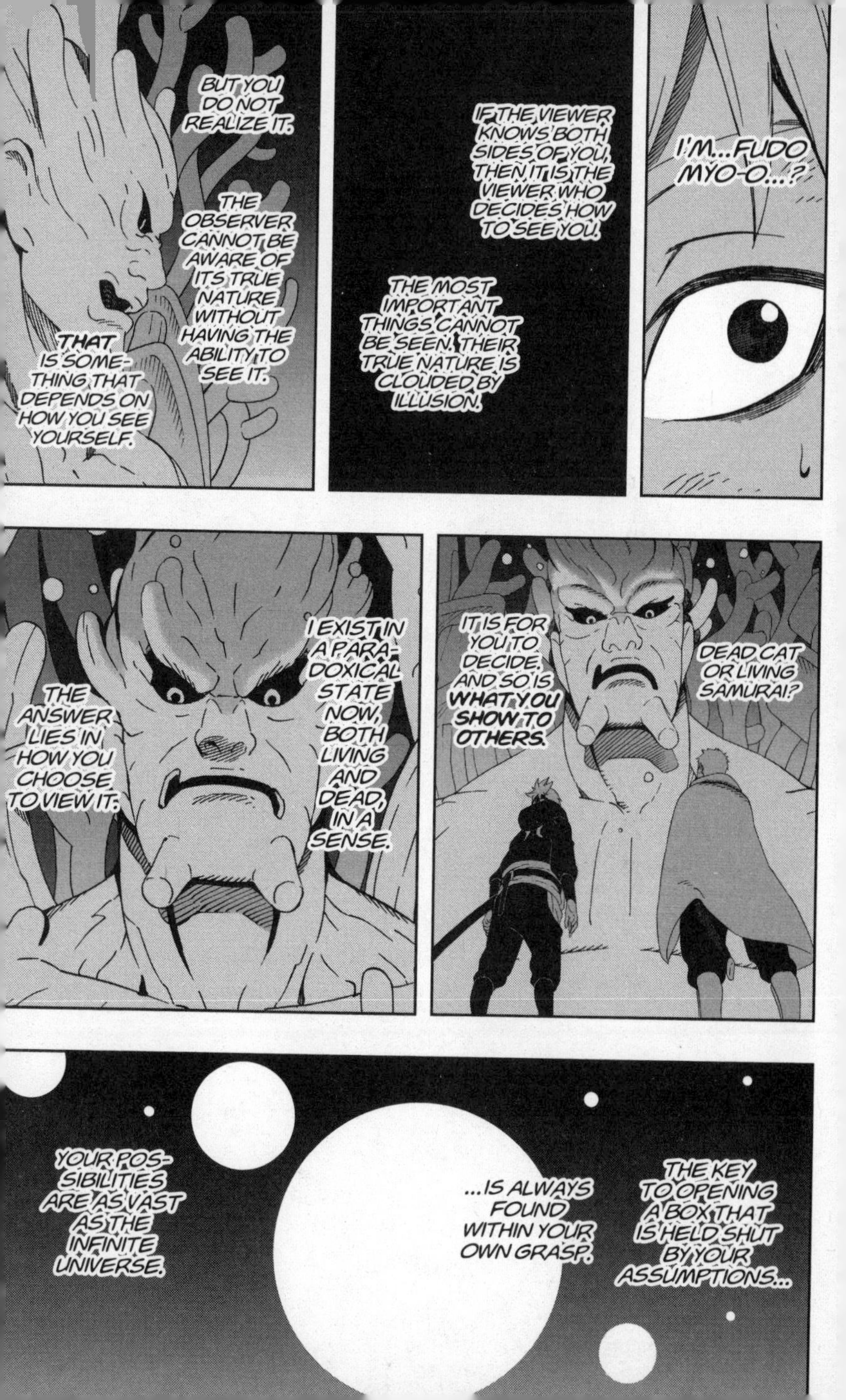
I'M...FUDO MYO-O...?
IF THE VIEWER KNOWS BOTH SIDES OF YOU, THEN IT IS THE VIEWER WHO DECIDES HOW TO SEE YOU.
THE MOST IMPORTANT THINGS CANNOT BE SEEN. THEIR TRUE NATURE IS CLOUDED BY ILLUSION.
BUT YOU DO NOT REALIZE IT.
THE OBSERVER CANNOT BE AWARE OF ITS TRUE NATURE WITHOUT HAVING THE ABILITY TO SEE IT.
THAT IS SOMETHING THAT DEPENDS ON HOW YOU SEE YOURSELF.
DEAD CAT OR LIVING SAMURAI?
IT IS FOR YOU TO DECIDE. AND SO IS **WHAT YOU SHOW TO OTHERS.**
I EXIST IN A PARADOXICAL STATE NOW, BOTH LIVING AND DEAD, IN A SENSE.
THE ANSWER LIES IN HOW YOU CHOOSE TO VIEW IT.
THE KEY TO OPENING A BOX THAT IS HELD SHUT BY YOUR ASSUMPTIONS...
...IS ALWAYS FOUND WITHIN YOUR OWN GRASP.
YOUR POSSIBILITIES ARE AS VAST AS THE INFINITE UNIVERSE.

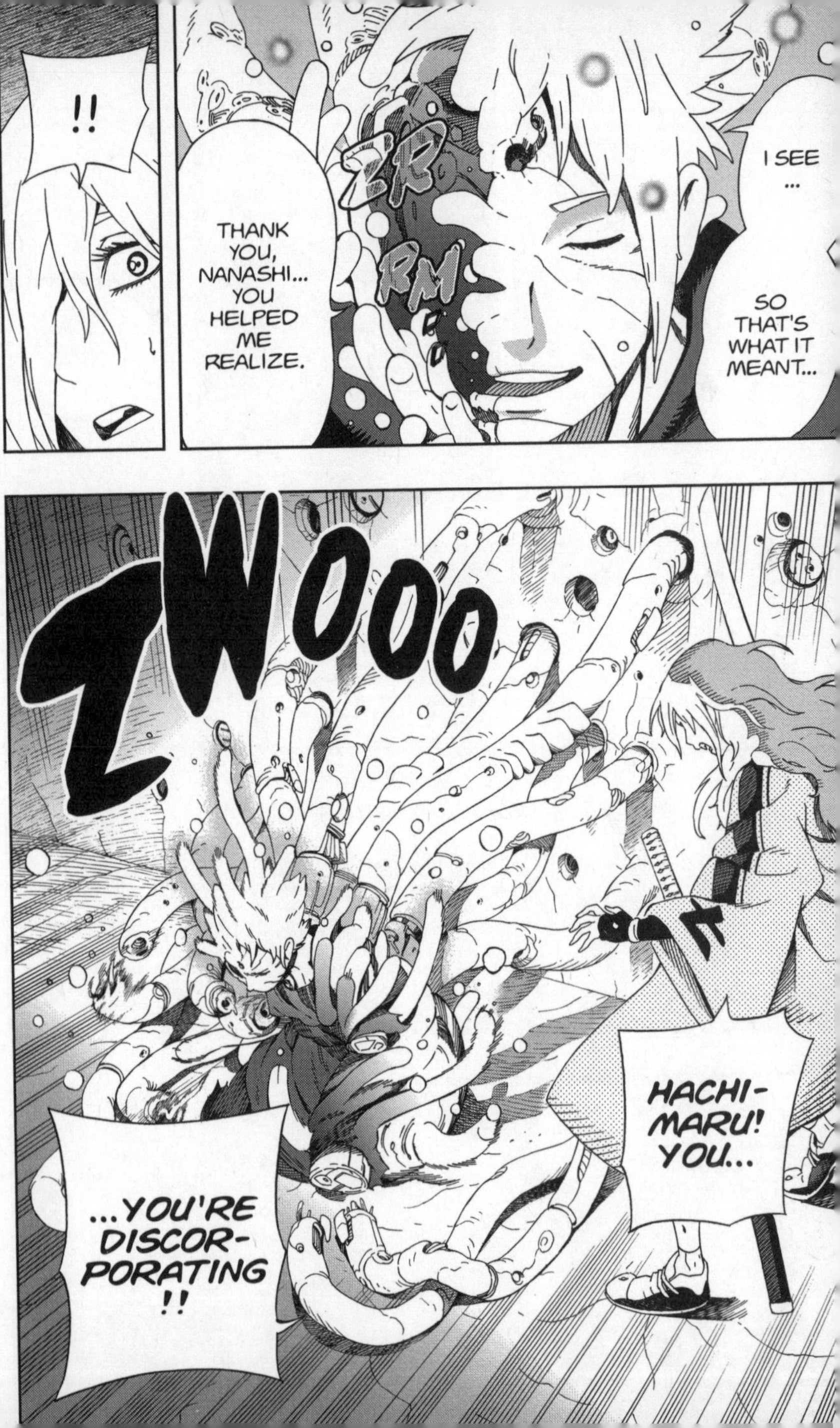
I SEE ...
SO THAT'S WHAT IT MEANT...
ZRRM
THANK YOU, NANASHI... YOU HELPED ME REALIZE.
!!
ZWOOO
HACHI-MARU! YOU...
...YOU'RE DISCOR-PORATING !!

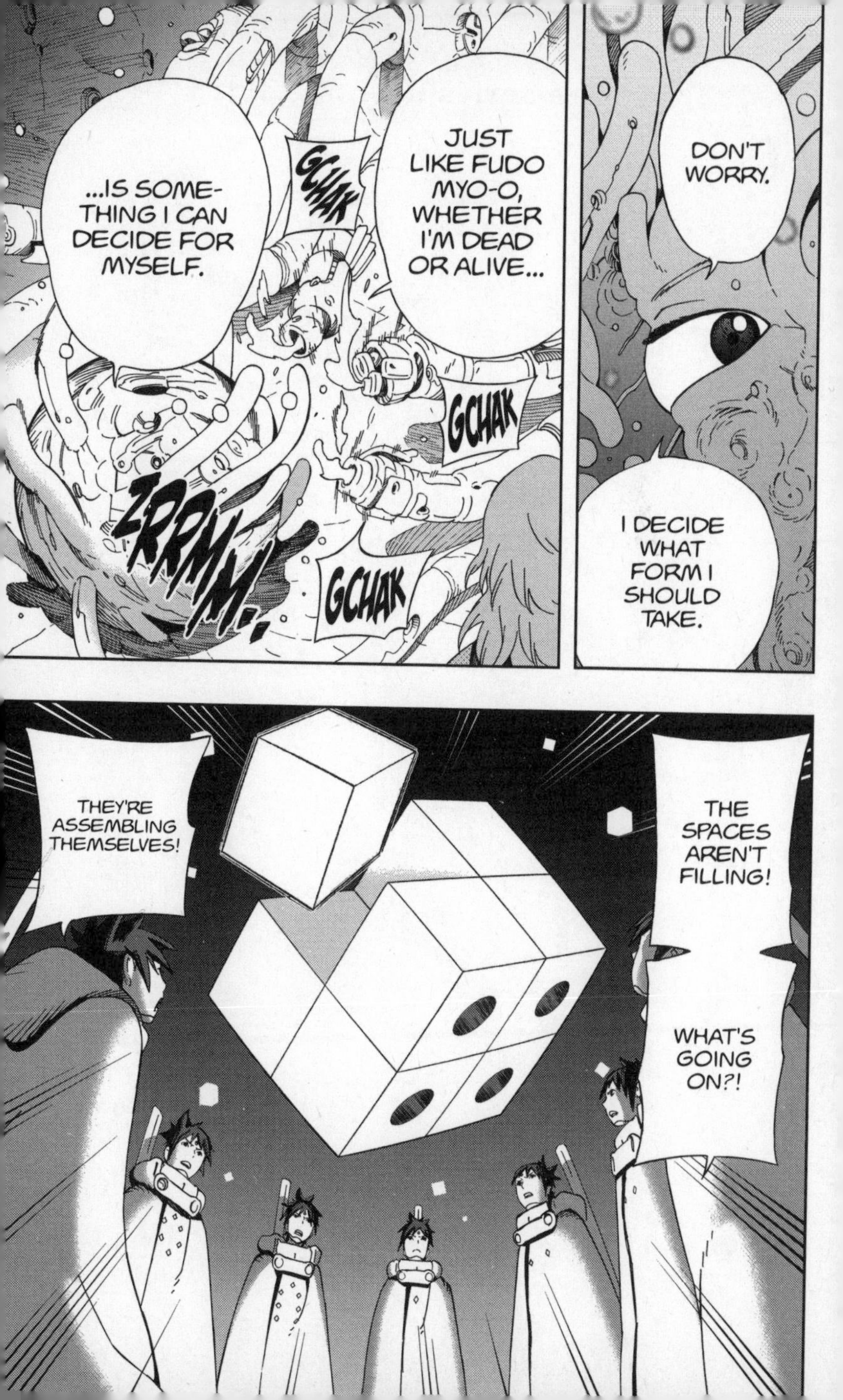
DON'T WORRY.
I DECIDE WHAT FORM I SHOULD TAKE.
JUST LIKE FUDO MYO-O, WHETHER I'M DEAD OR ALIVE...
GCHAK
...IS SOME-THING I CAN DECIDE FOR MYSELF.
GCHAK
ZRRMM
GCHAK
THE SPACES AREN'T FILLING!
WHAT'S GOING ON?!
THEY'RE ASSEMBLING THEMSELVES!

Pre-Series Rough Designs (Okubo)

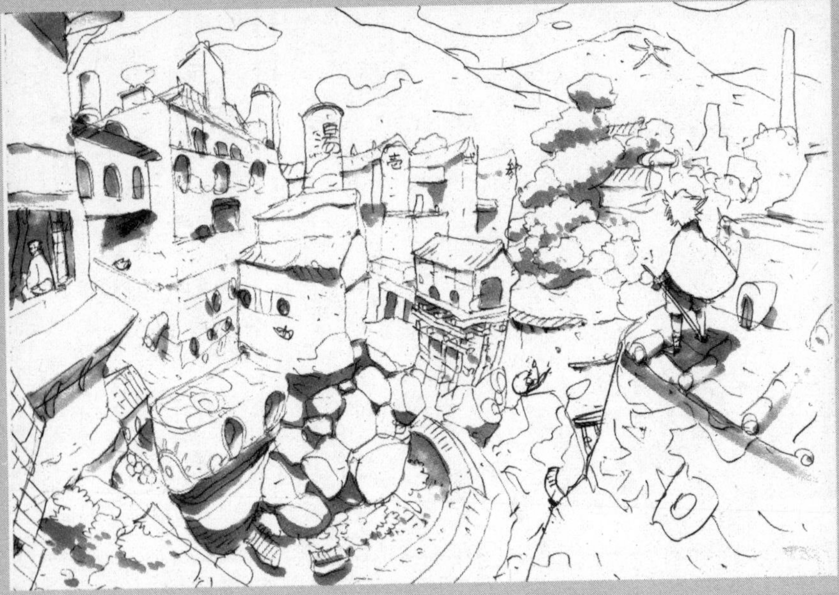

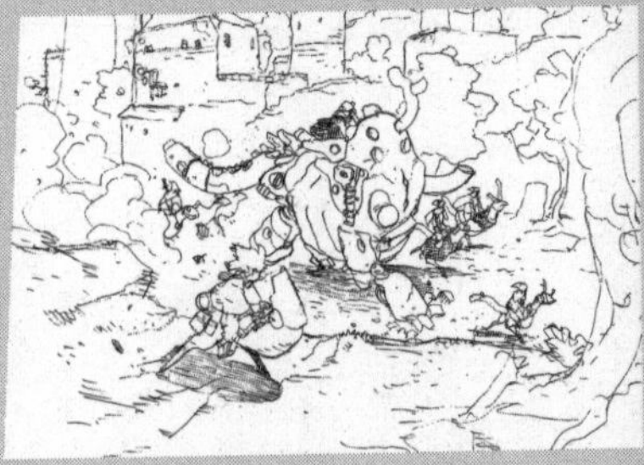

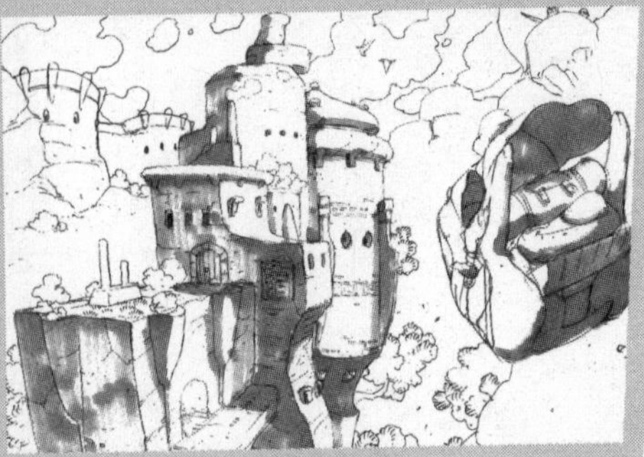

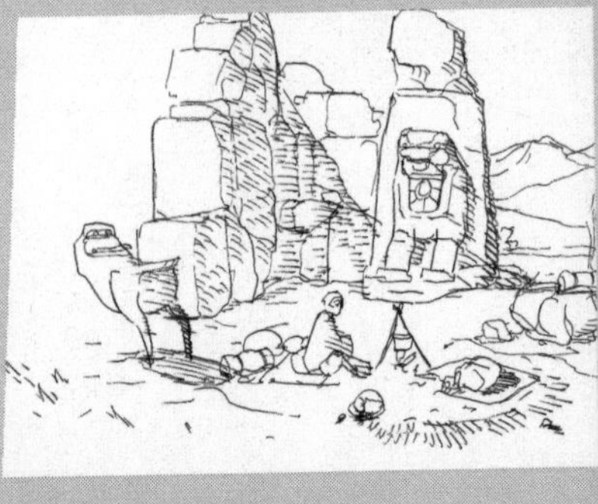

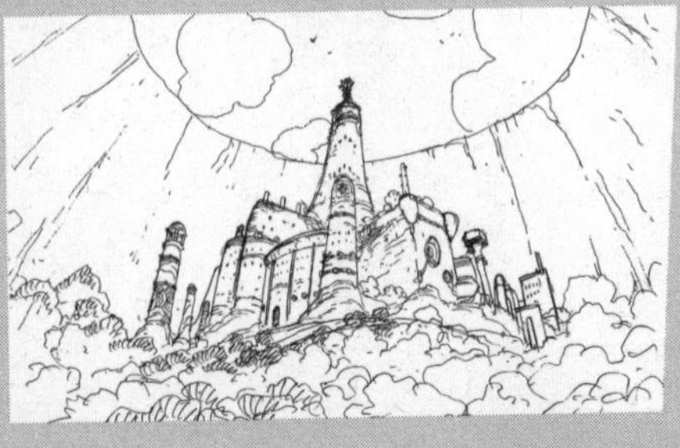

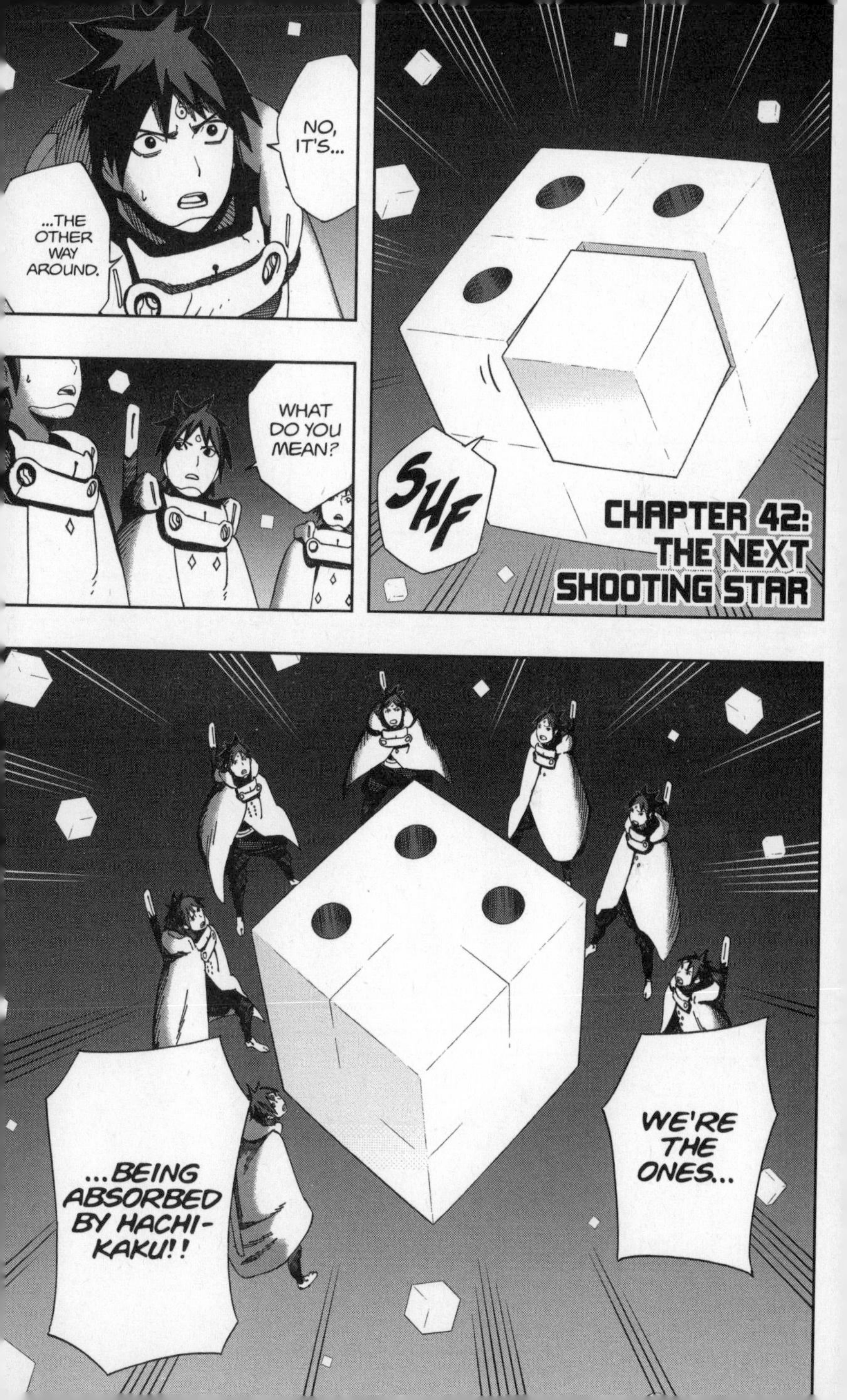
SHF
CHAPTER 42: THE NEXT SHOOTING STAR
NO, IT'S...
...THE OTHER WAY AROUND.
WHAT DO YOU MEAN?
WE'RE THE ONES...
...BEING ABSORBED BY HACHI-KAKU!!

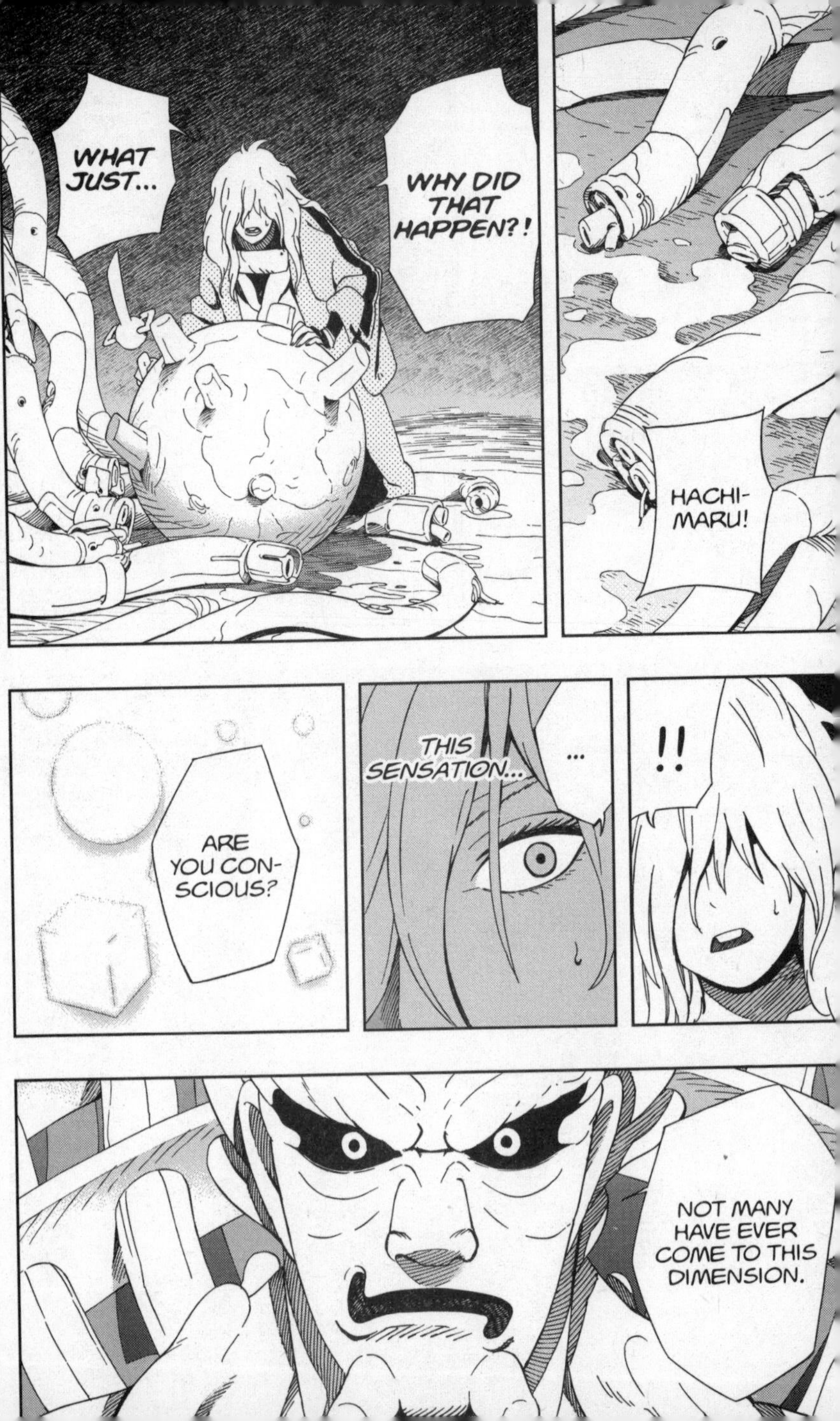
HACHI-MARU!
WHY DID THAT HAPPEN?!
WHAT JUST...
!!
...
THIS SENSATION...
ARE YOU CON-SCIOUS?
NOT MANY HAVE EVER COME TO THIS DIMENSION.

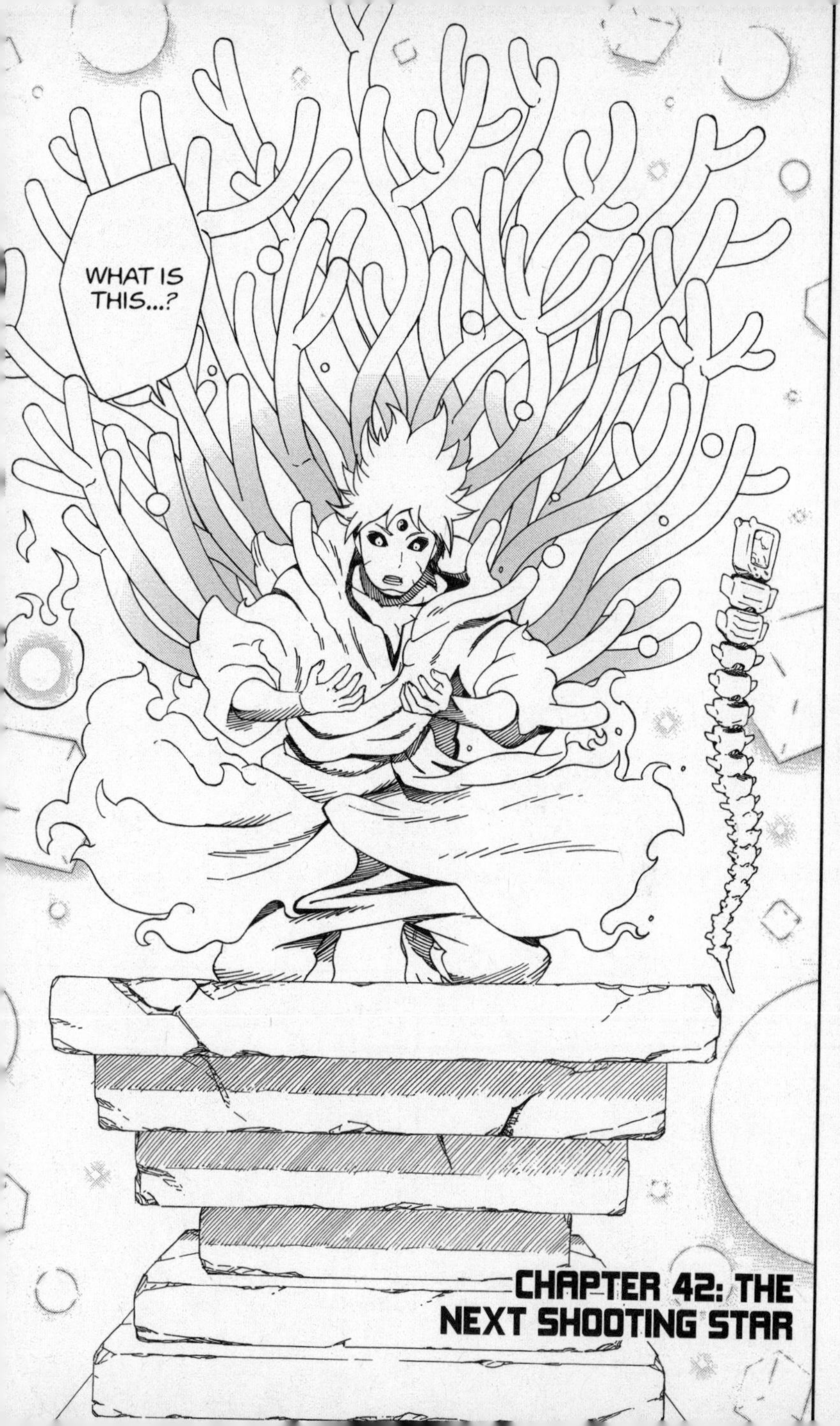
WHAT IS THIS...?
CHAPTER 42: THE NEXT SHOOTING STAR

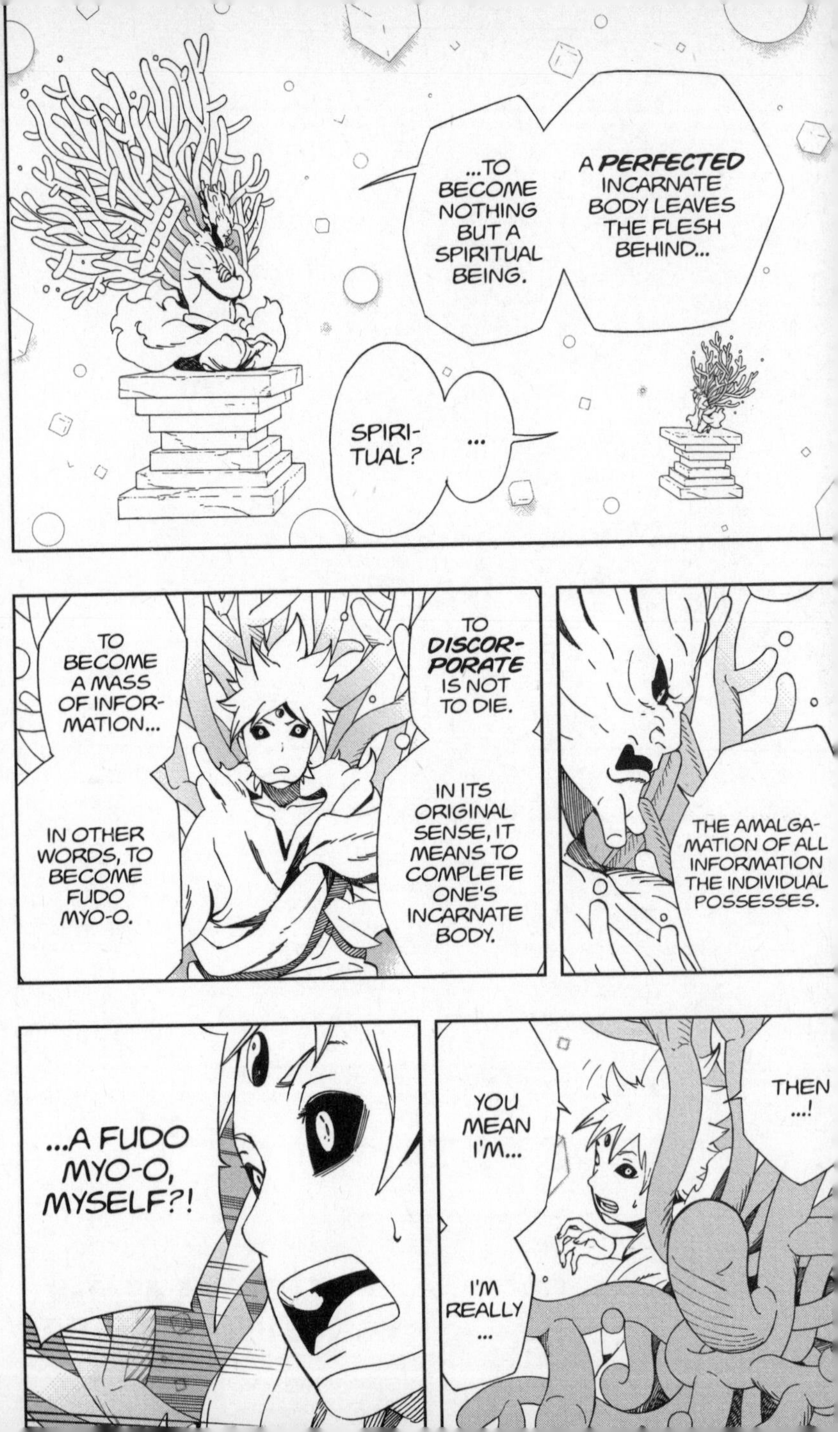
A PERFECTED INCARNATE BODY LEAVES THE FLESH BEHIND...
...TO BECOME NOTHING BUT A SPIRITUAL BEING.
...
SPIRI-TUAL?
THE AMALGA-MATION OF ALL INFORMATION THE INDIVIDUAL POSSESSES.
TO DISCOR-PORATE IS NOT TO DIE.
IN ITS ORIGINAL SENSE, IT MEANS TO COMPLETE ONE'S INCARNATE BODY.
TO BECOME A MASS OF INFOR-MATION...
IN OTHER WORDS, TO BECOME FUDO MYO-O.
THEN ...!
YOU MEAN I'M...
I'M REALLY ...
...A FUDO MYO-O, MYSELF?!

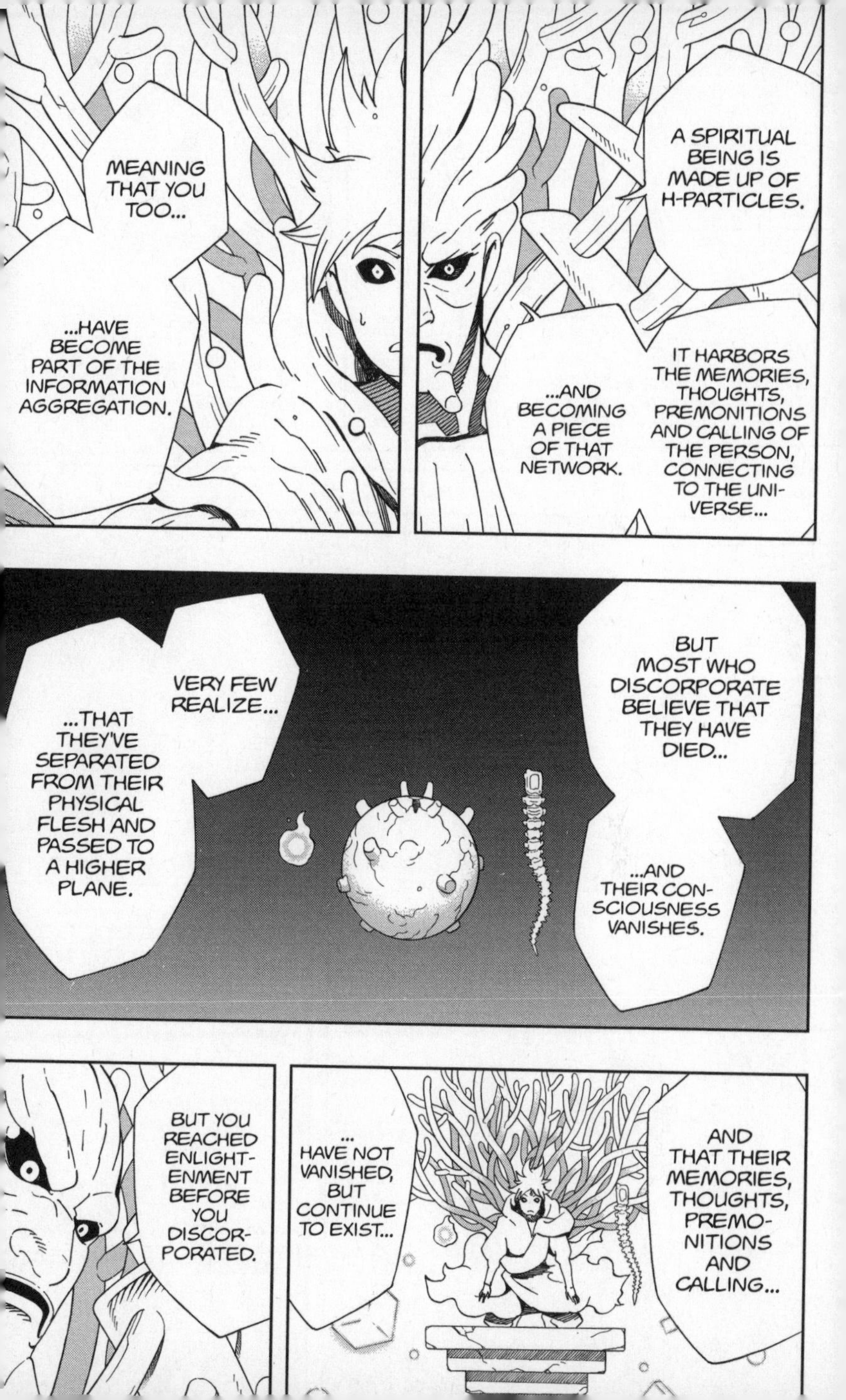
A SPIRITUAL BEING IS MADE UP OF H-PARTICLES.
IT HARBORS THE MEMORIES, THOUGHTS, PREMONITIONS AND CALLING OF THE PERSON, CONNECTING TO THE UNI-VERSE...
...AND BECOMING A PIECE OF THAT NETWORK.
MEANING THAT YOU TOO...
...HAVE BECOME PART OF THE INFORMATION AGGREGATION.
BUT MOST WHO DISCORPORATE BELIEVE THAT THEY HAVE DIED...
...AND THEIR CON-SCIOUSNESS VANISHES.
VERY FEW REALIZE...
...THAT THEY'VE SEPARATED FROM THEIR PHYSICAL FLESH AND PASSED TO A HIGHER PLANE.
AND THAT THEIR MEMORIES, THOUGHTS, PREMO-NITIONS AND CALLING...
...HAVE NOT VANISHED, BUT CONTINUE TO EXIST...
BUT YOU REACHED ENLIGHT-ENMENT BEFORE YOU DISCOR-PORATED.

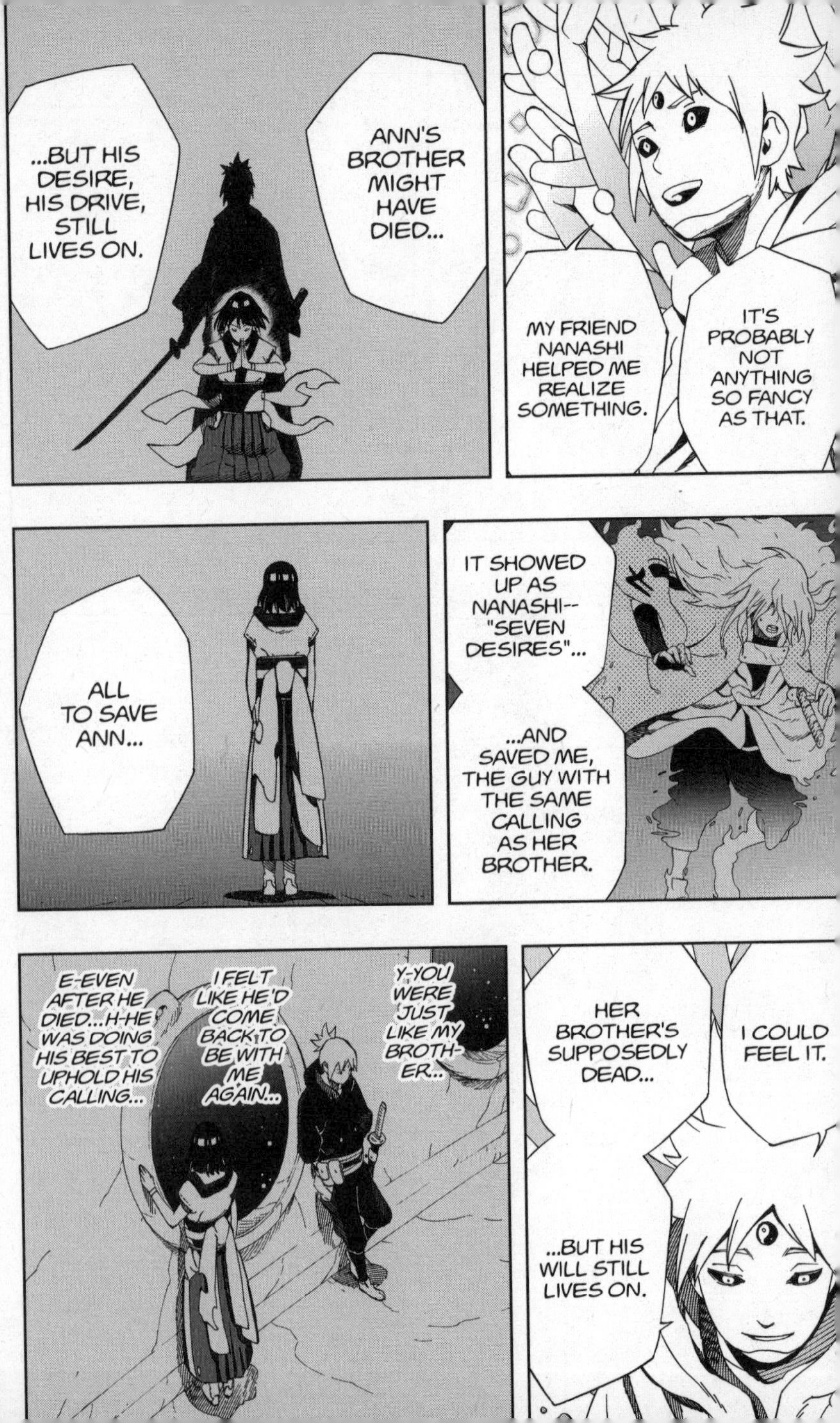
IT'S PROBABLY NOT ANYTHING SO FANCY AS THAT.
MY FRIEND NANASHI HELPED ME REALIZE SOMETHING.
ANN'S BROTHER MIGHT HAVE DIED...
...BUT HIS DESIRE, HIS DRIVE, STILL LIVES ON.
IT SHOWED UP AS NANASHI--"SEVEN DESIRES"...
...AND SAVED ME, THE GUY WITH THE SAME CALLING AS HER BROTHER.
ALL TO SAVE ANN...
I COULD FEEL IT.
HER BROTHER'S SUPPOSEDLY DEAD...
...BUT HIS WILL STILL LIVES ON.
Y-YOU WERE JUST LIKE MY BROTH-ER...
I FELT LIKE HE'D COME BACK TO BE WITH ME AGAIN...
E-EVEN AFTER HE DIED...H-HE WAS DOING HIS BEST TO UPHOLD HIS CALLING...

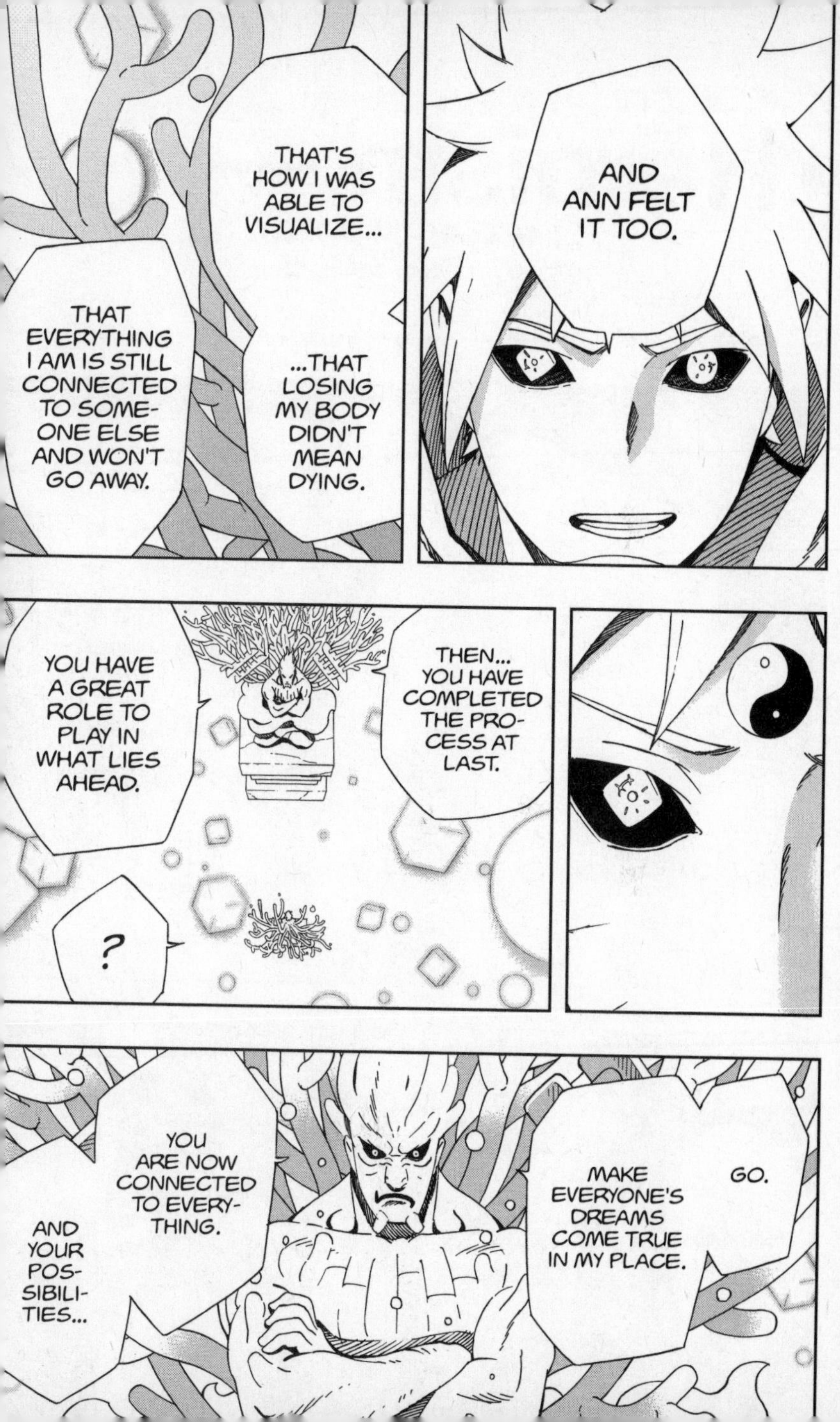
AND ANN FELT IT TOO.
THAT'S HOW I WAS ABLE TO VISUALIZE...
...THAT LOSING MY BODY DIDN'T MEAN DYING.
THAT EVERYTHING I AM IS STILL CONNECTED TO SOMEONE ELSE AND WON'T GO AWAY.
THEN... YOU HAVE COMPLETED THE PROCESS AT LAST.
YOU HAVE A GREAT ROLE TO PLAY IN WHAT LIES AHEAD.
?
GO.
MAKE EVERYONE'S DREAMS COME TRUE IN MY PLACE.
YOU ARE NOW CONNECTED TO EVERYTHING.
AND YOUR POSSIBILITIES...

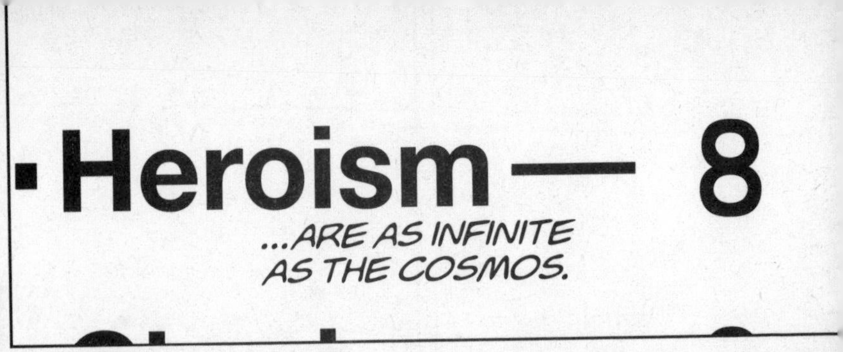

·Heroism — 8
...ARE AS INFINITE AS THE COSMOS.

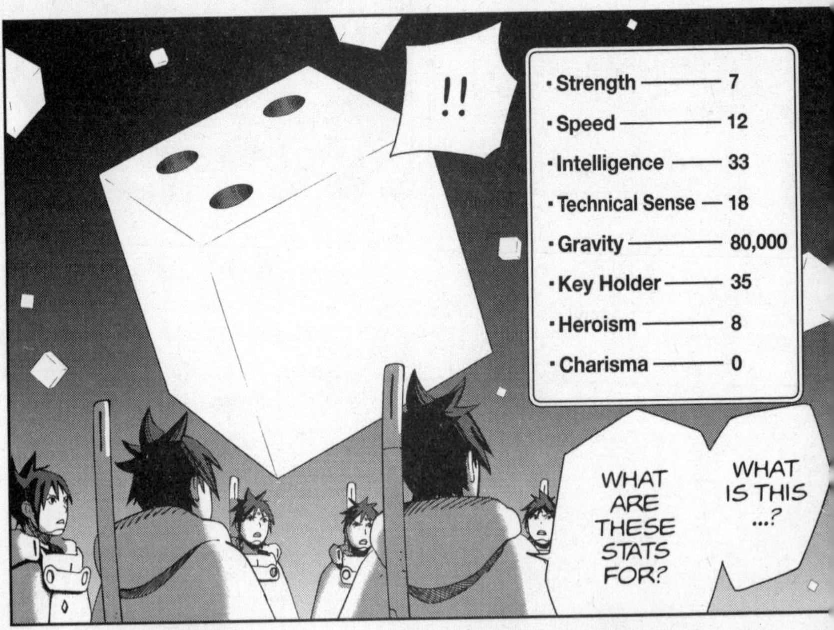

· Strength — 7
· Speed — 12
· Intelligence — 33
· Technical Sense — 18
· Gravity — 80,000
· Key Holder — 35
· Heroism — 8
· Charisma — 0
!!
WHAT IS THIS ...?
WHAT ARE THESE STATS FOR?

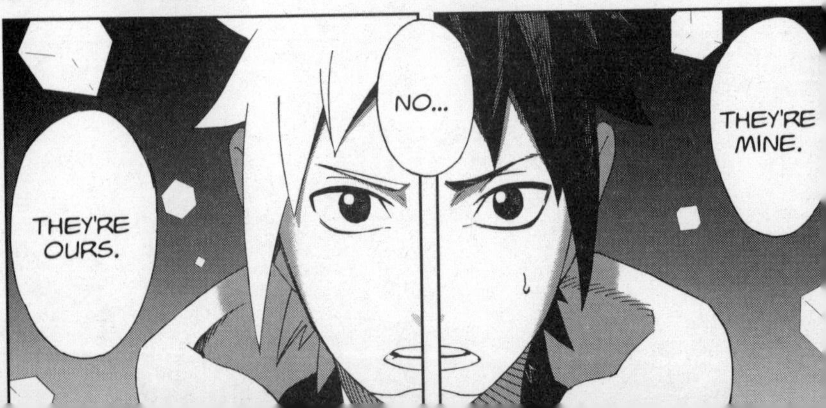

THEY'RE MINE.
NO...
THEY'RE OURS.

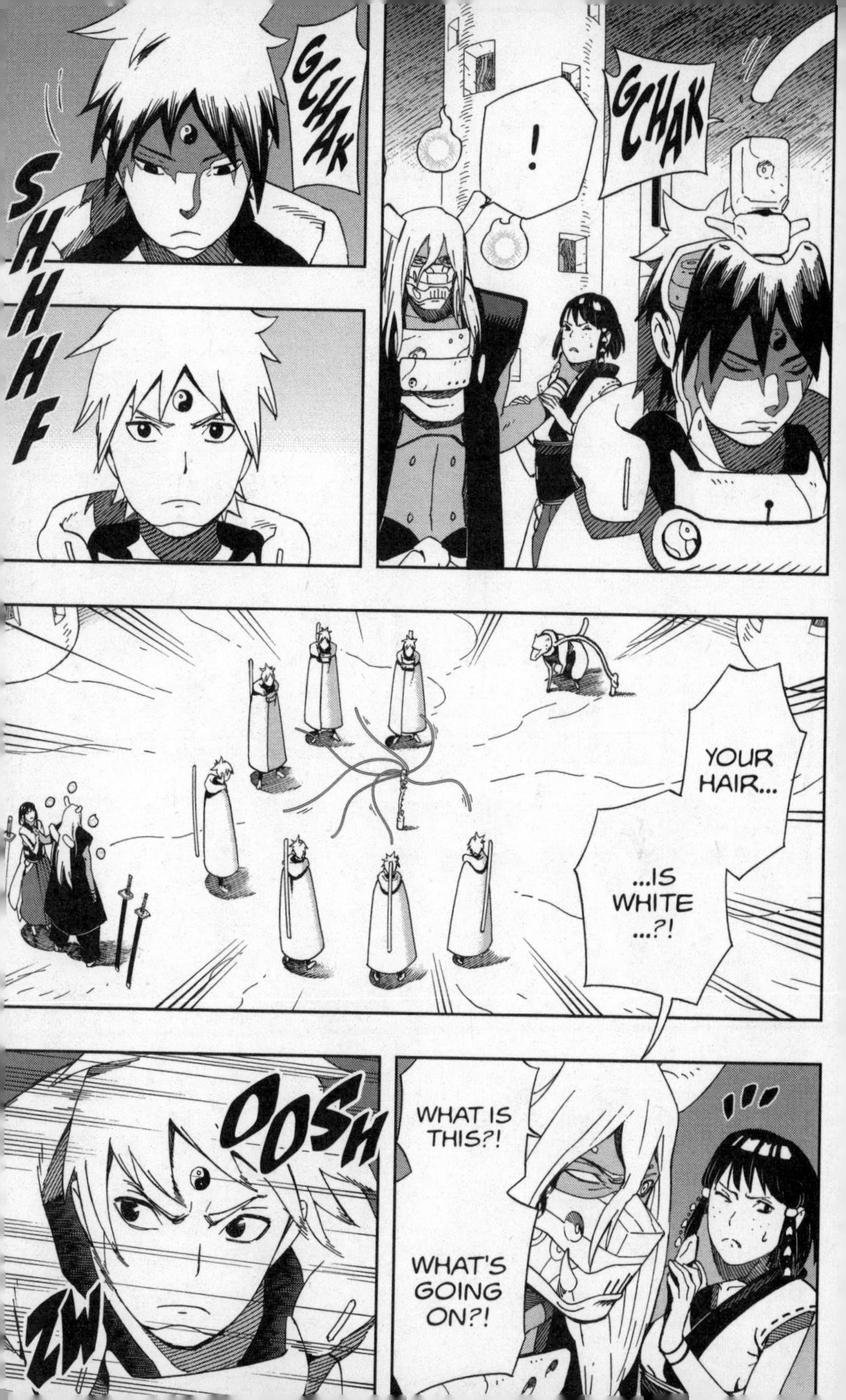

GCHAK
!
GCHAK
SHHHF
YOUR HAIR...
...IS WHITE ...?!
WHAT IS THIS?!
WHAT'S GOING ON?!
OOSH
ZW

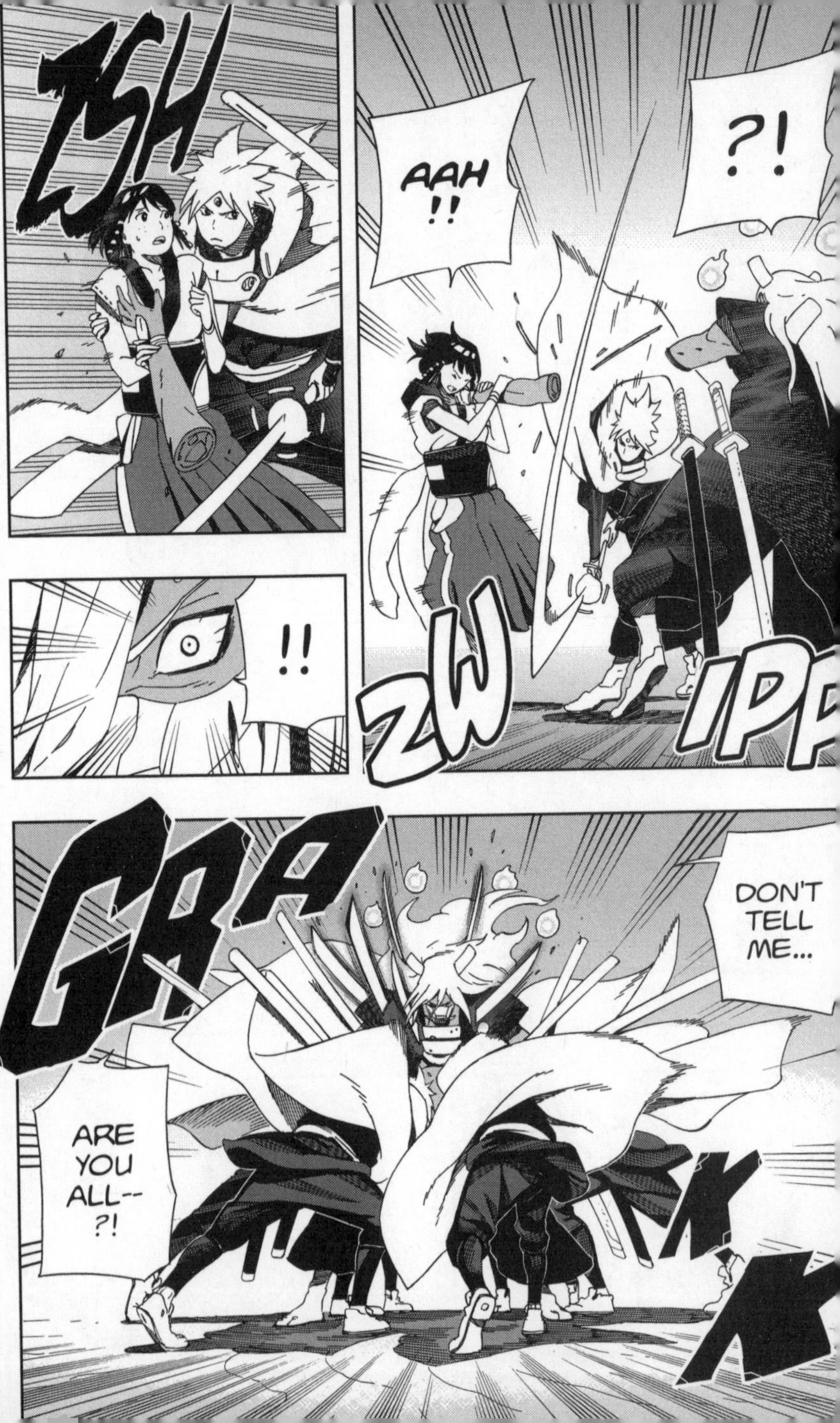
?!
AAH !!
ZW
IPP
TSH
!!
DON'T TELL ME...
GRA
ARE YOU ALL-- ?!
KK

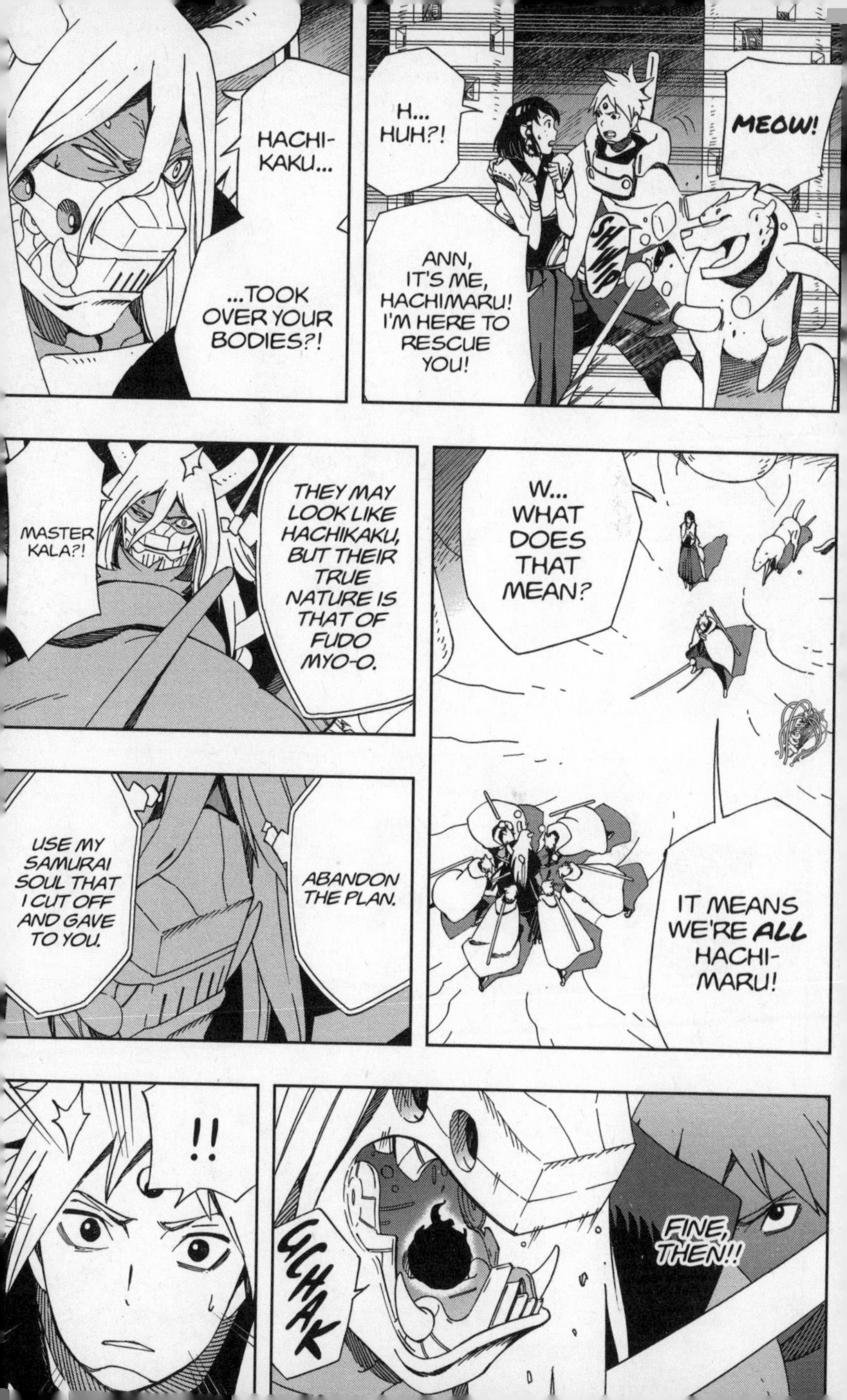
MEOW!
H... HUH?!
ANN, IT'S ME, HACHIMARU! I'M HERE TO RESCUE YOU!
SHWIP
HACHI-KAKU...
...TOOK OVER YOUR BODIES?!
W... WHAT DOES THAT MEAN?
IT MEANS WE'RE **ALL** HACHI-MARU!
THEY MAY LOOK LIKE HACHIKAKU, BUT THEIR TRUE NATURE IS THAT OF FUDO MYO-O.
MASTER KALA?!
ABANDON THE PLAN.
USE MY SAMURAI SOUL THAT I CUT OFF AND GAVE TO YOU.
FINE, THEN!!
UCHAK
!!

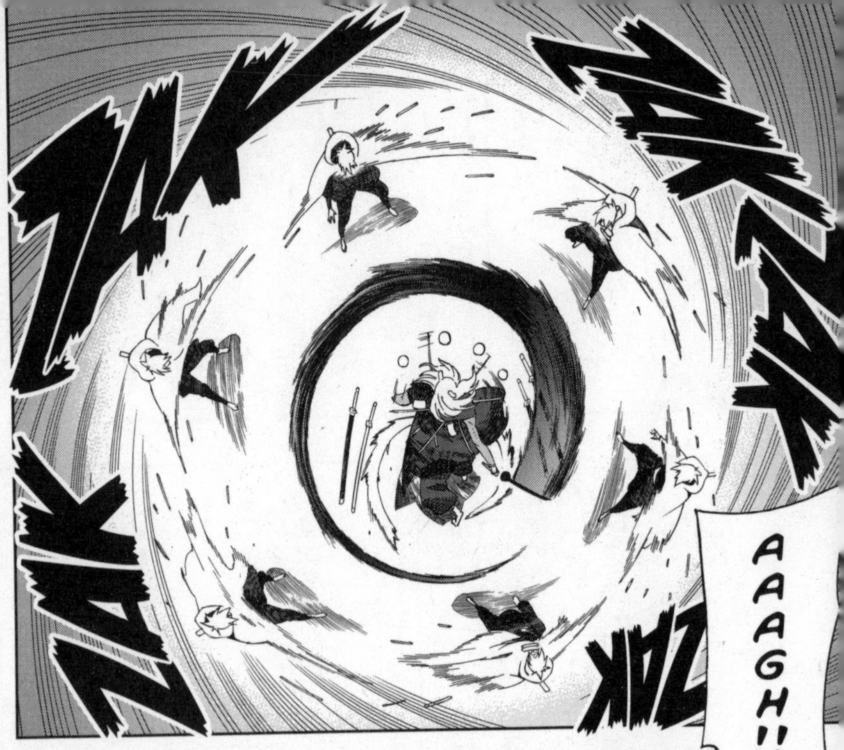
ZAK
ZAK
AAAGH!!
ZAK
ZAK

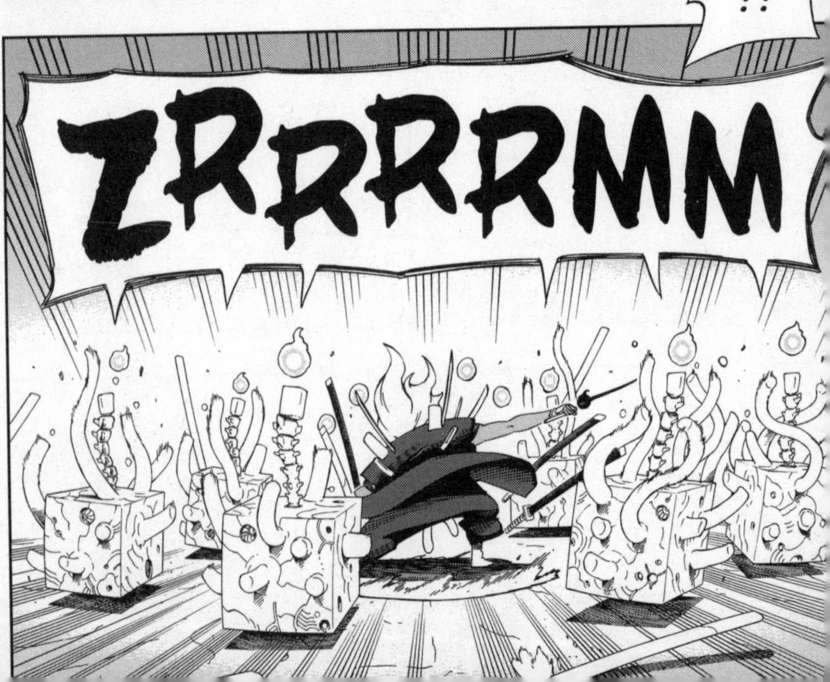
ZRRRRMM

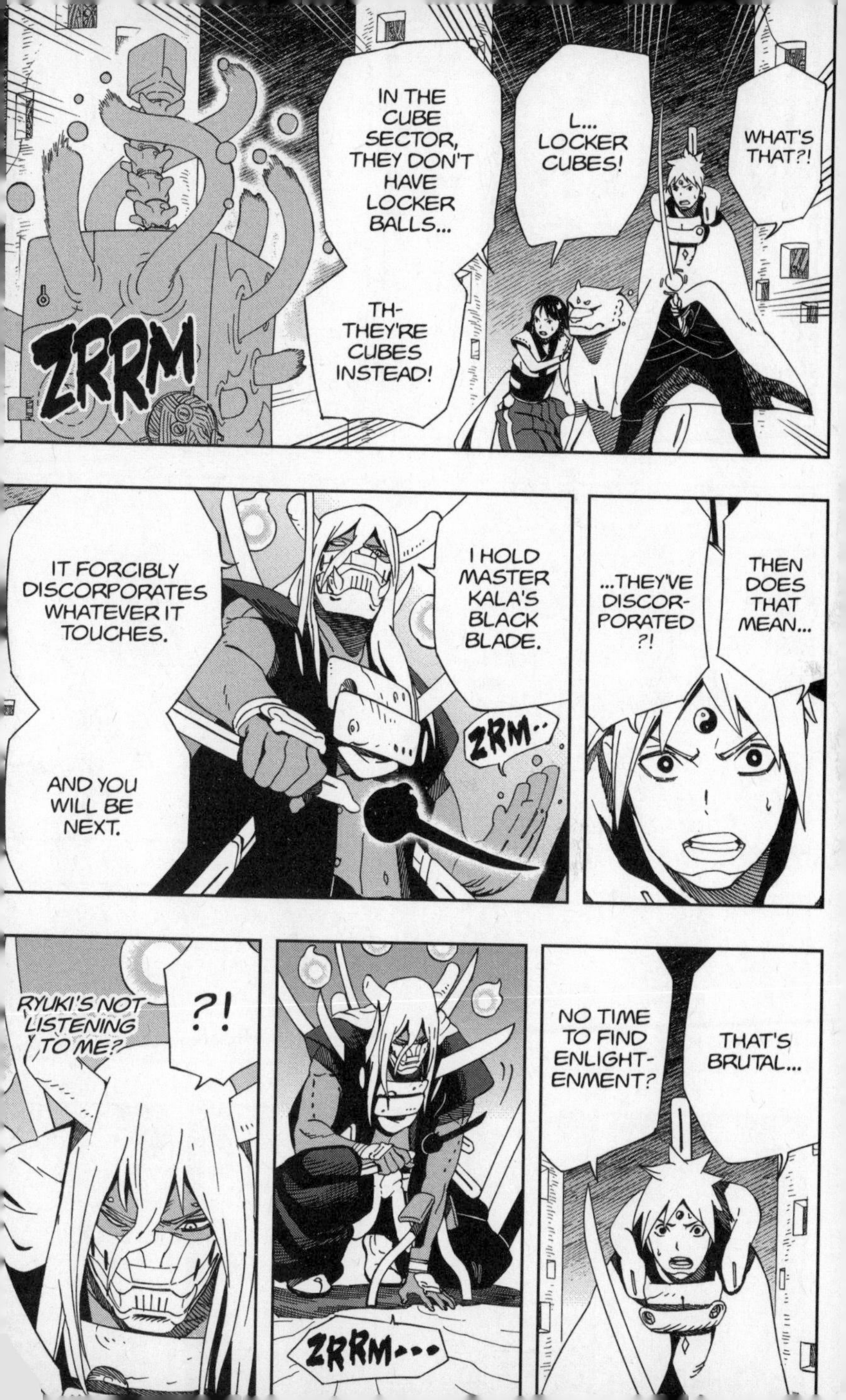
WHAT'S THAT?!
L... LOCKER CUBES!
IN THE CUBE SECTOR, THEY DON'T HAVE LOCKER BALLS...
TH- THEY'RE CUBES INSTEAD!
ZRRM
THEN DOES THAT MEAN...
...THEY'VE DISCORPORATED?!
I HOLD MASTER KALA'S BLACK BLADE.
ZRM..
IT FORCIBLY DISCORPORATES WHATEVER IT TOUCHES.
AND YOU WILL BE NEXT.
THAT'S BRUTAL...
NO TIME TO FIND ENLIGHTENMENT?
ZRRM...
?!
RYUKI'S NOT LISTENING TO ME?

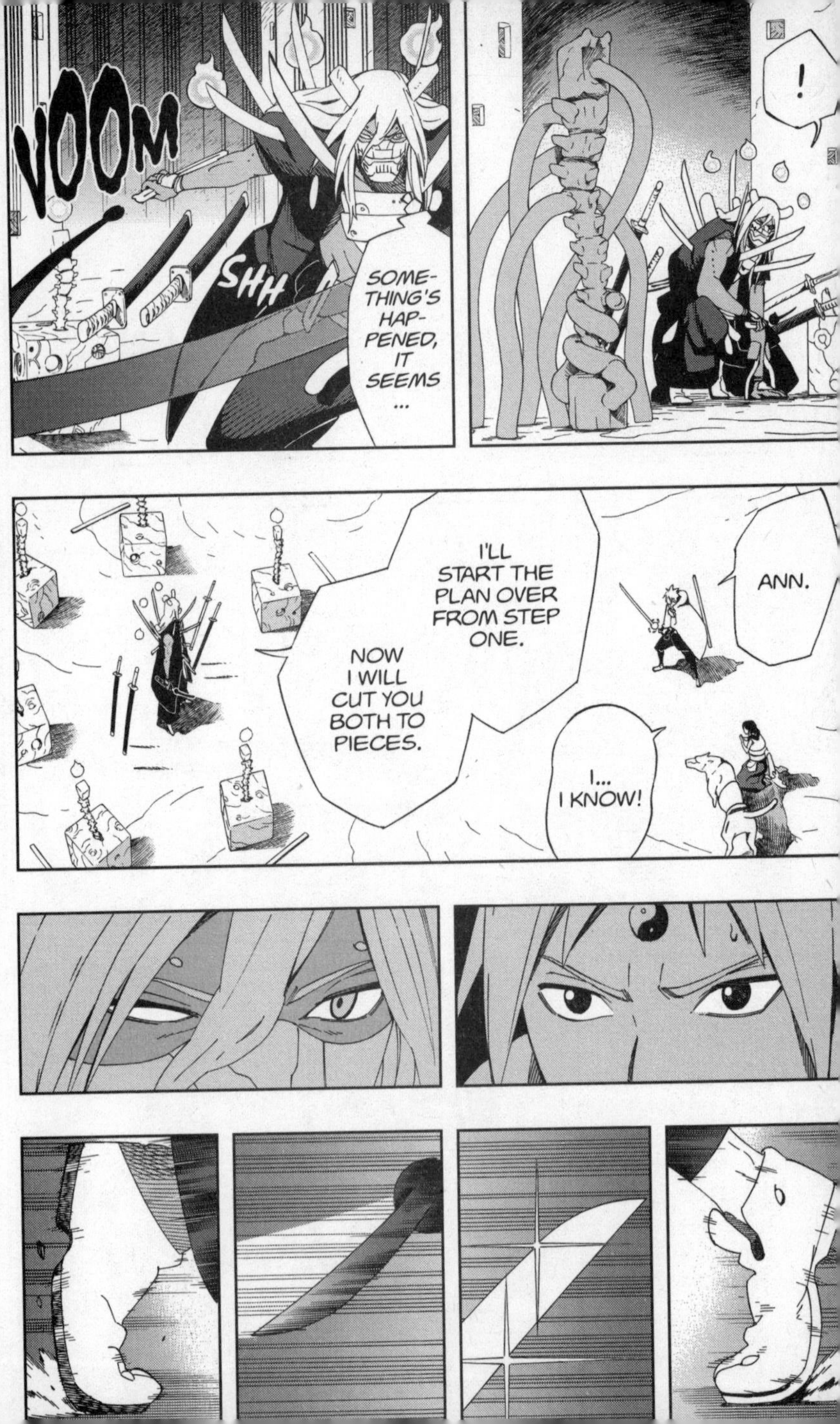
!
VOOM
SHH
SOMETHING'S HAPPENED, IT SEEMS...
ANN.
I... I KNOW!
I'LL START THE PLAN OVER FROM STEP ONE.
NOW I WILL CUT YOU BOTH TO PIECES.

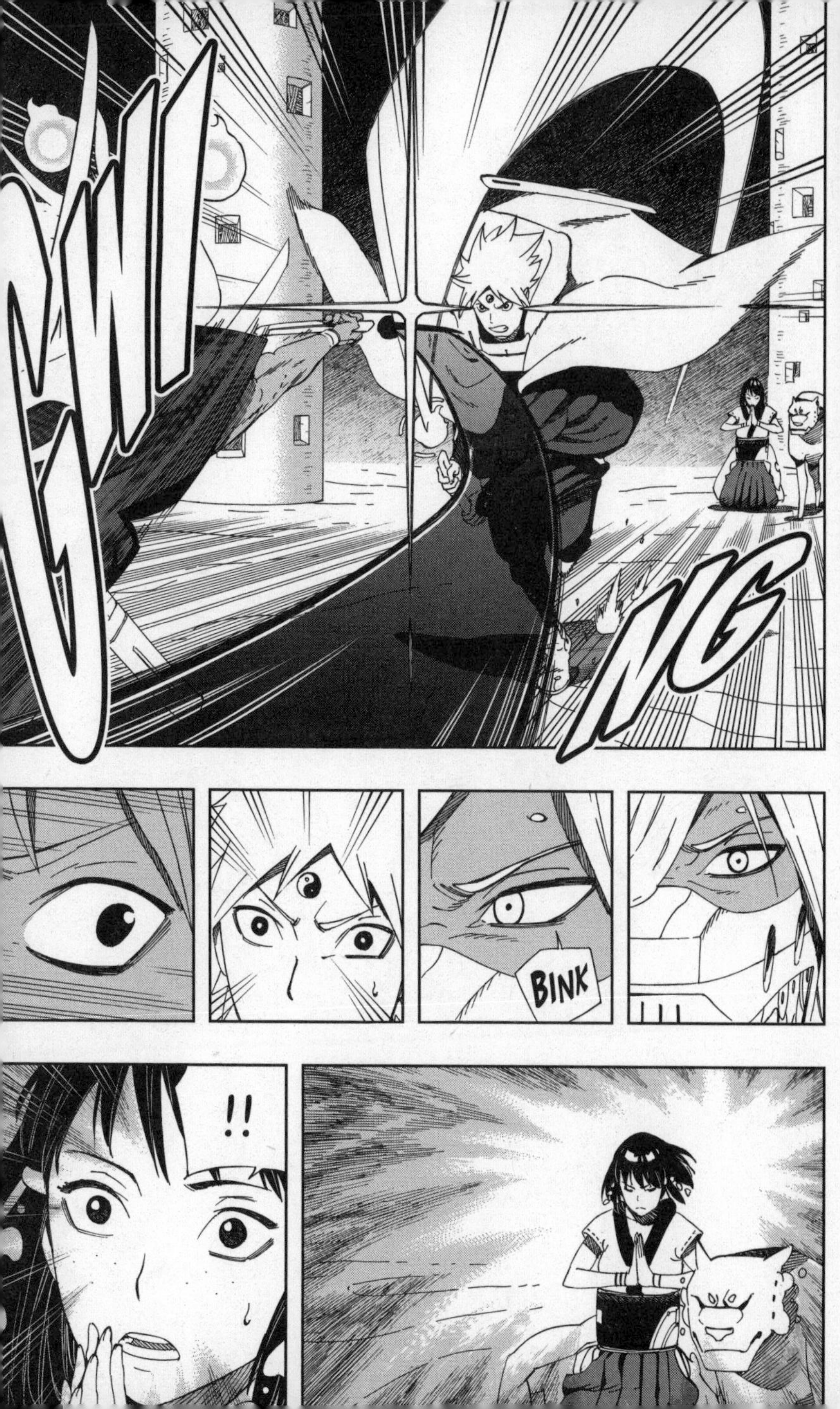
SHING
BINK
!!

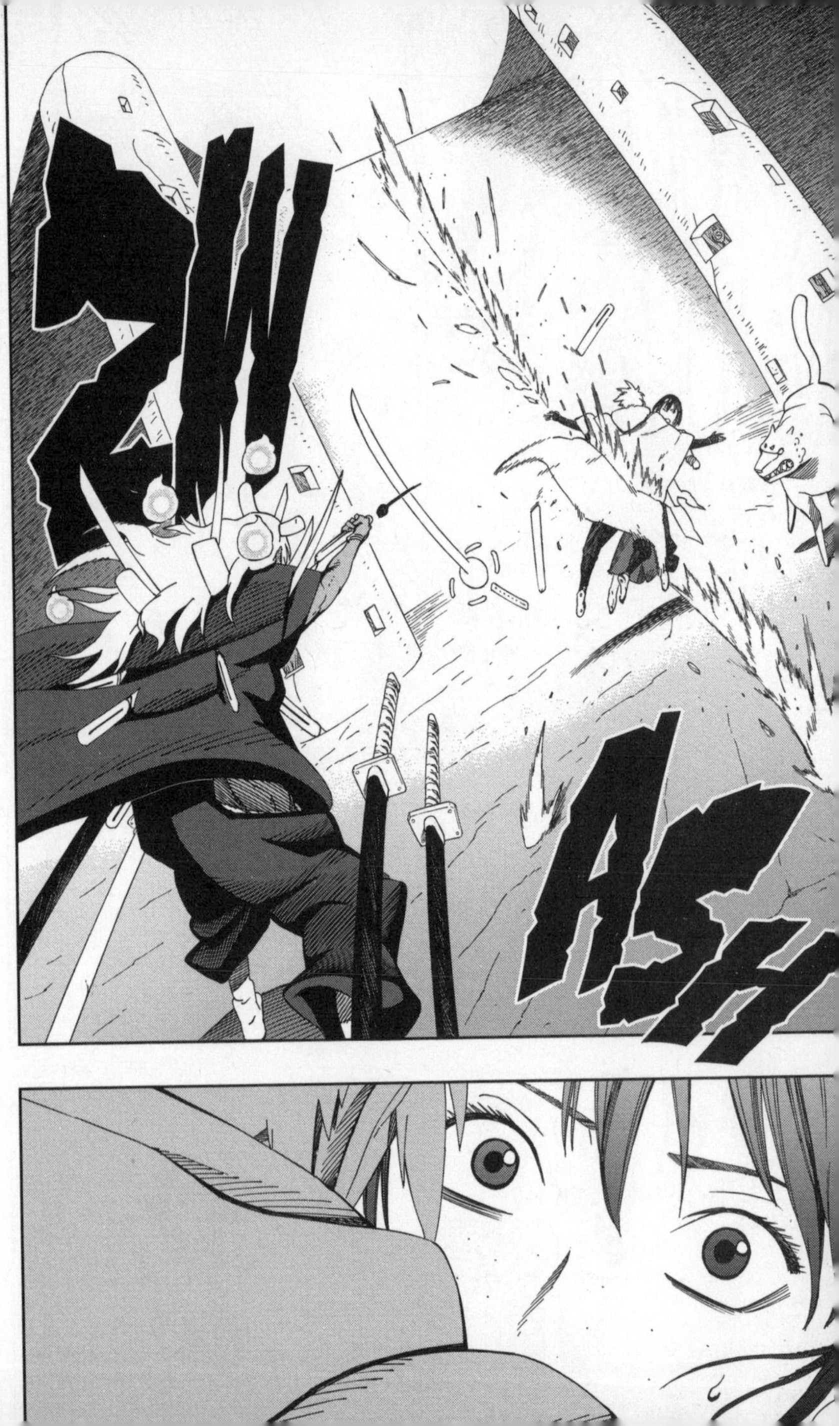
ZW
ASH

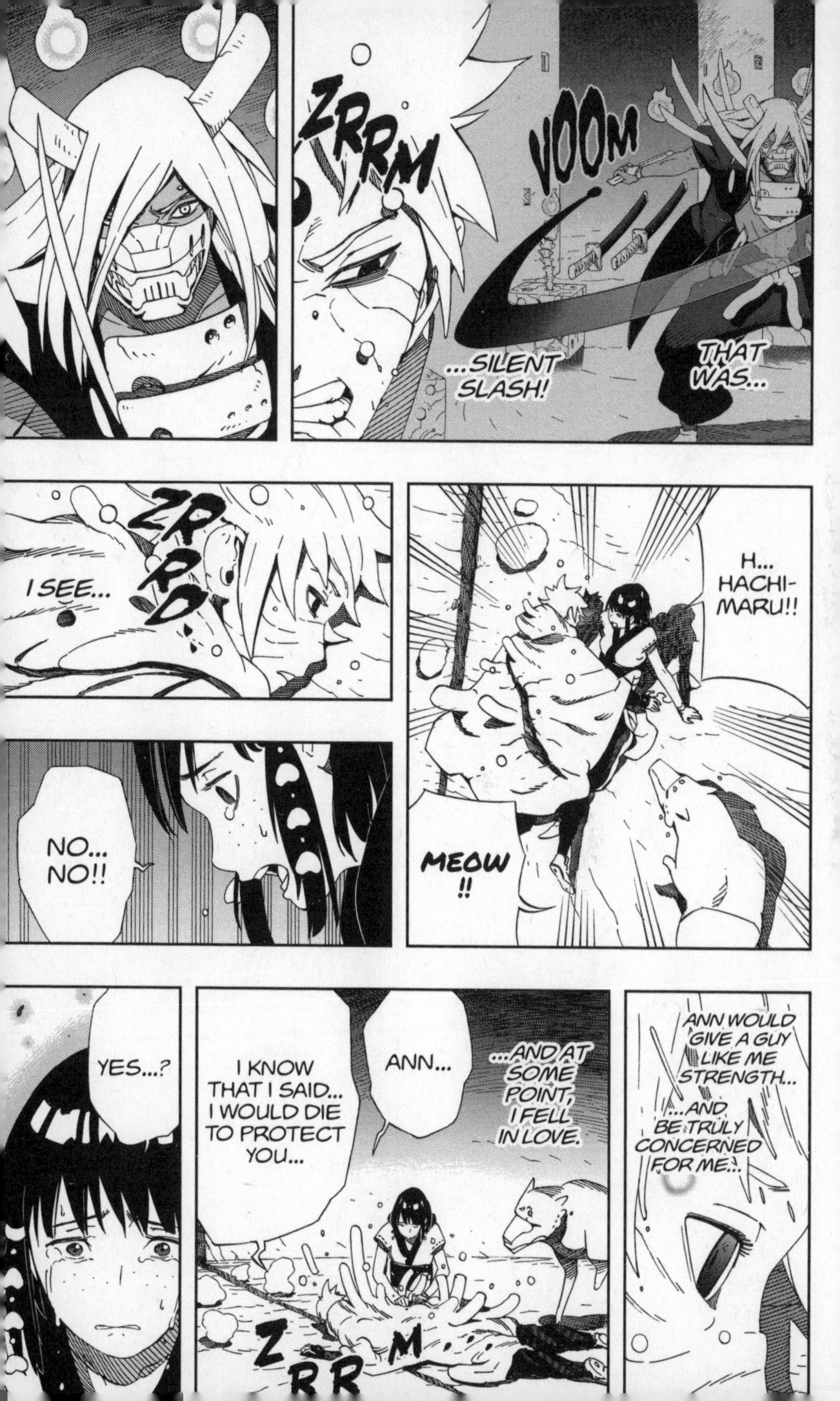
VOOM
THAT WAS...
...SILENT SLASH!
ZRRM
H... HACHI-MARU!!
MEOW!!
I SEE...
ZRRD
NO... NO!!
ANN WOULD GIVE A GUY LIKE ME STRENGTH...
...AND BE TRULY CONCERNED FOR ME...
...AND AT SOME POINT, I FELL IN LOVE.
ANN...
I KNOW THAT I SAID... I WOULD DIE TO PROTECT YOU...
ZRRM
YES...?

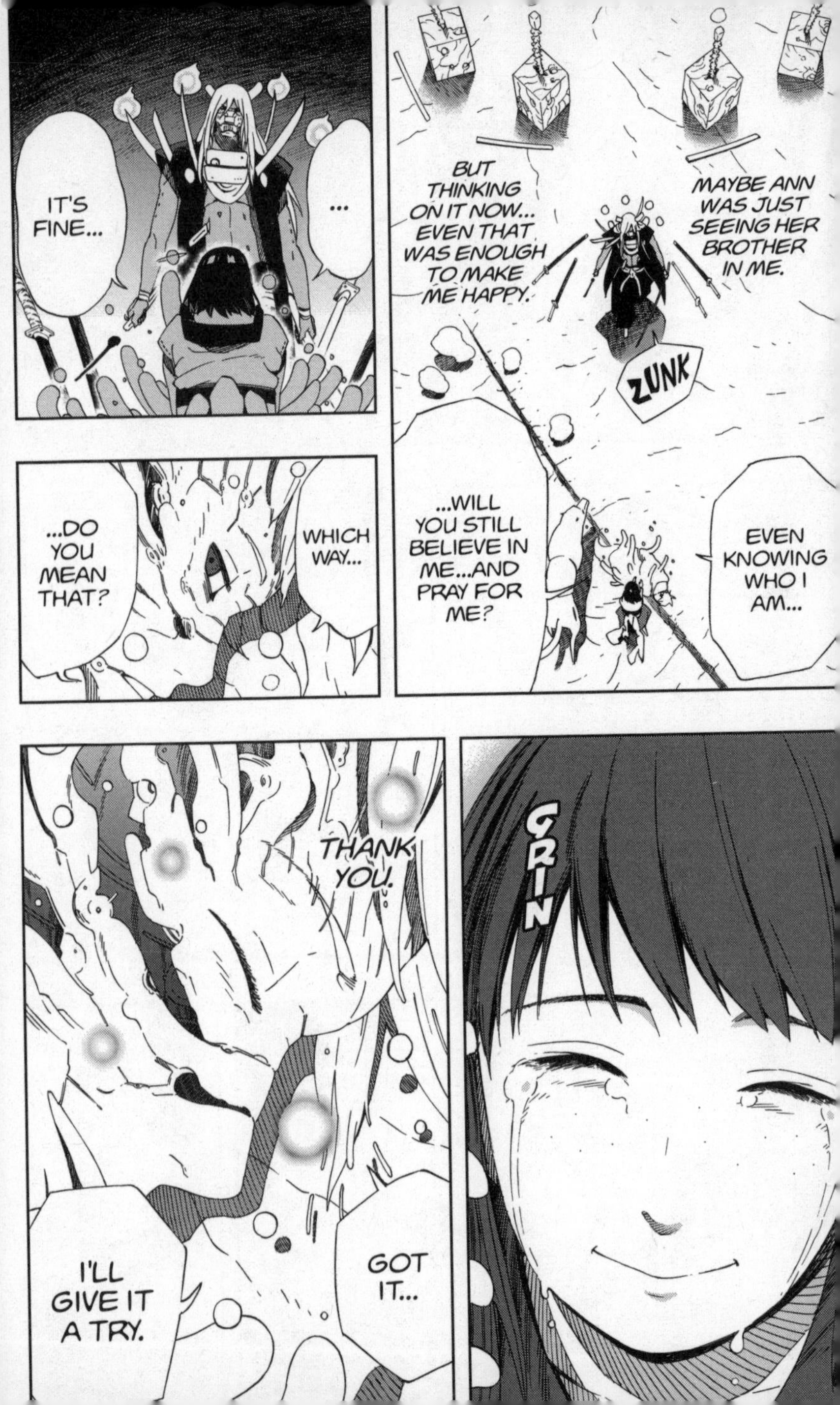
MAYBE ANN WAS JUST SEEING HER BROTHER IN ME.
BUT THINKING ON IT NOW... EVEN THAT WAS ENOUGH TO MAKE ME HAPPY.
ZUNK
EVEN KNOWING WHO I AM...
...WILL YOU STILL BELIEVE IN ME...AND PRAY FOR ME?
...
IT'S FINE...
WHICH WAY...
...DO YOU MEAN THAT?
GRIN
THANK YOU.
GOT IT...
I'LL GIVE IT A TRY.

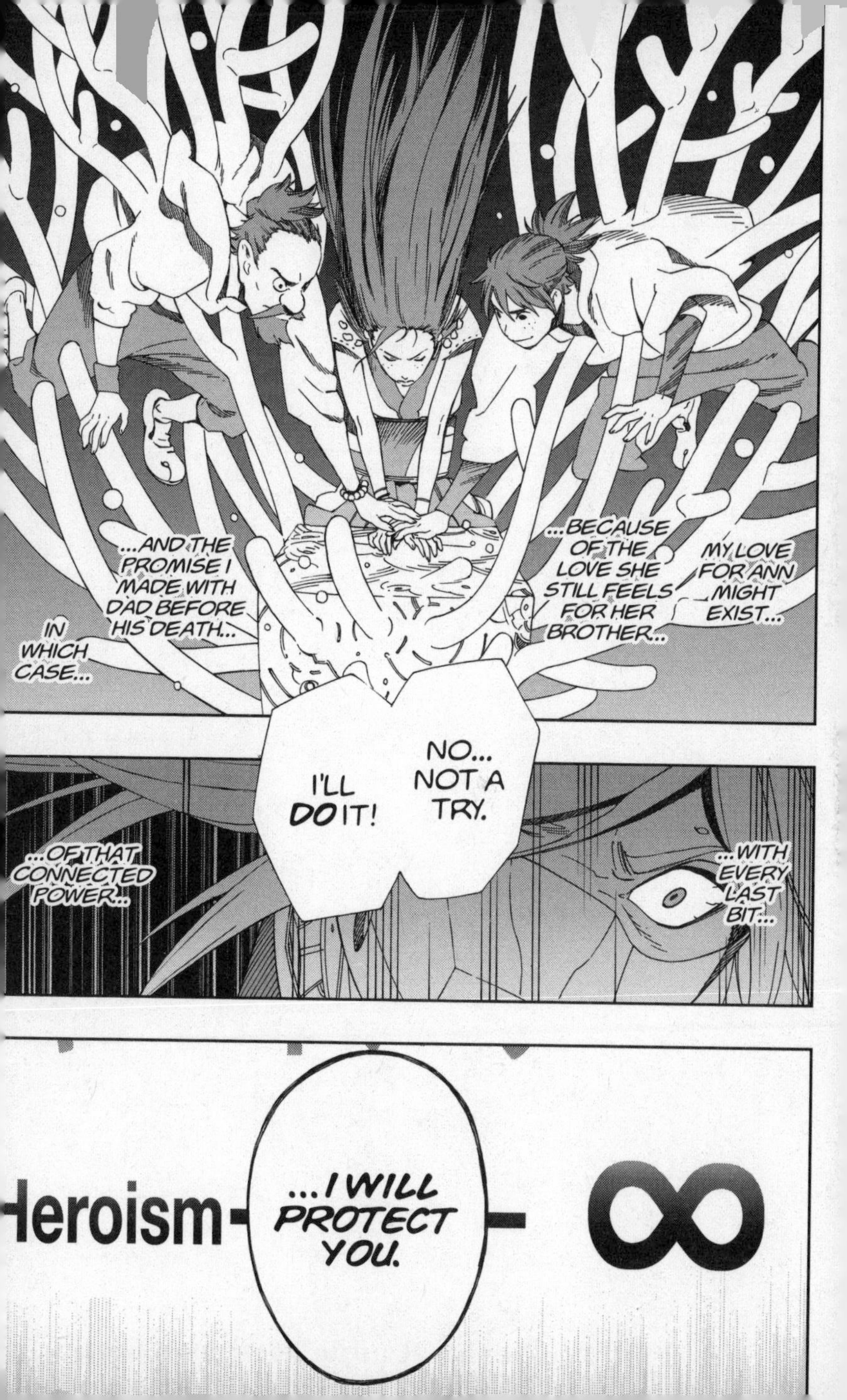
MY LOVE FOR ANN MIGHT EXIST...
...BECAUSE OF THE LOVE SHE STILL FEELS FOR HER BROTHER...
...AND THE PROMISE I MADE WITH DAD BEFORE HIS DEATH...
IN WHICH CASE...
NO... NOT A TRY.
I'LL DO IT!
...WITH EVERY LAST BIT...
...OF THAT CONNECTED POWER...
Heroism-
...I WILL PROTECT YOU.
-∞

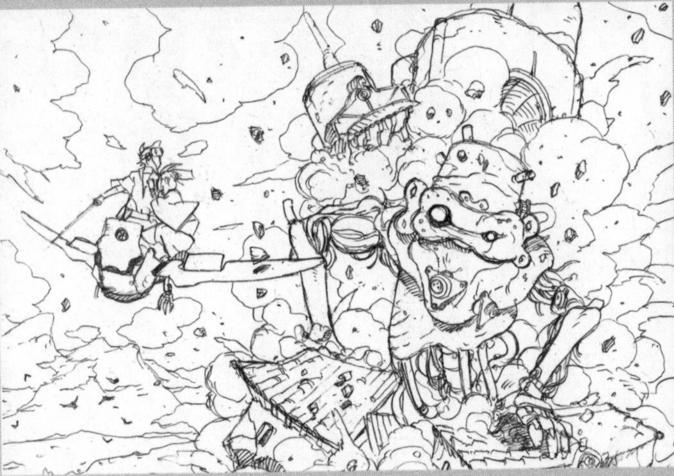

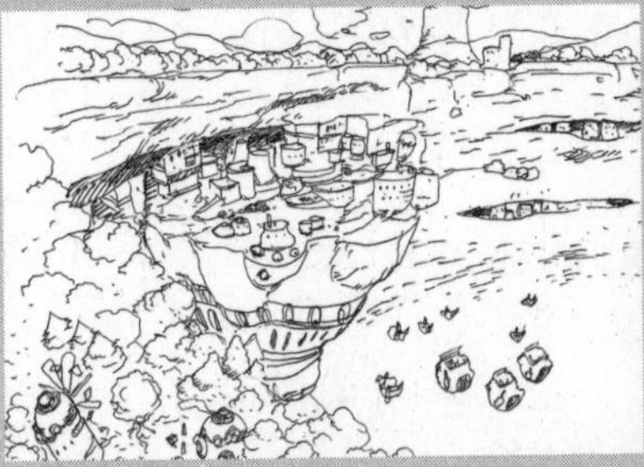

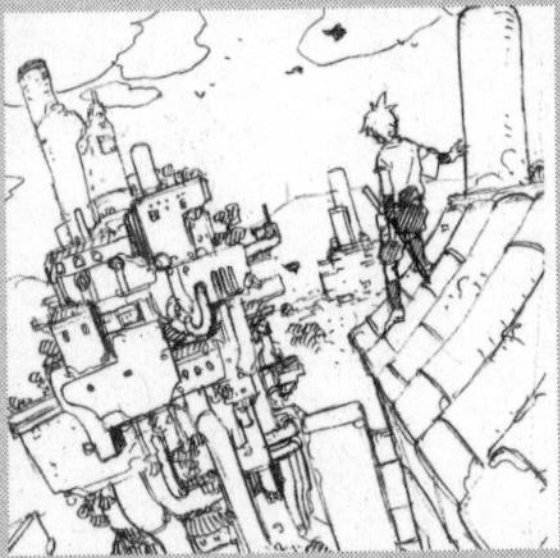

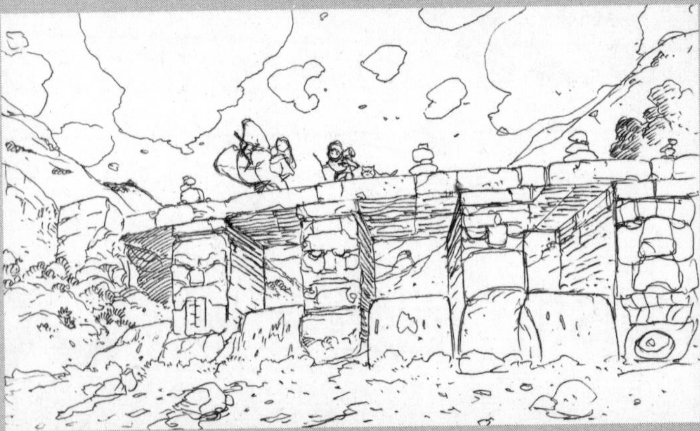

Pre-Series Rough Designs (Okubo)

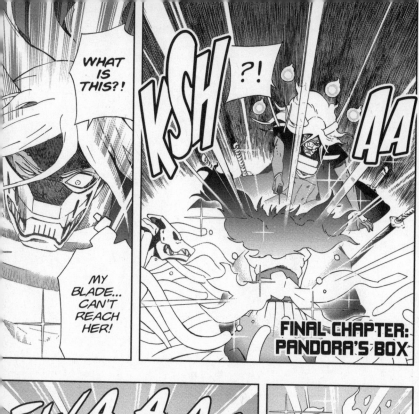

KSH
?!
AA
FINAL CHAPTER: PANDORA'S BOX
WHAT IS THIS?!
MY BLADE... CAN'T REACH HER!
FWAAAAA
GCHAK

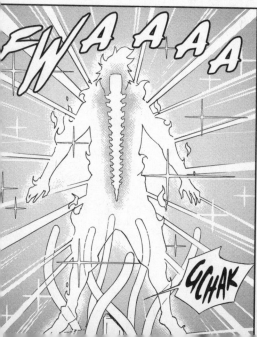

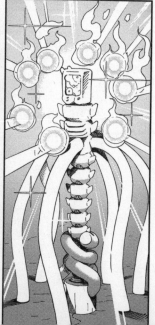

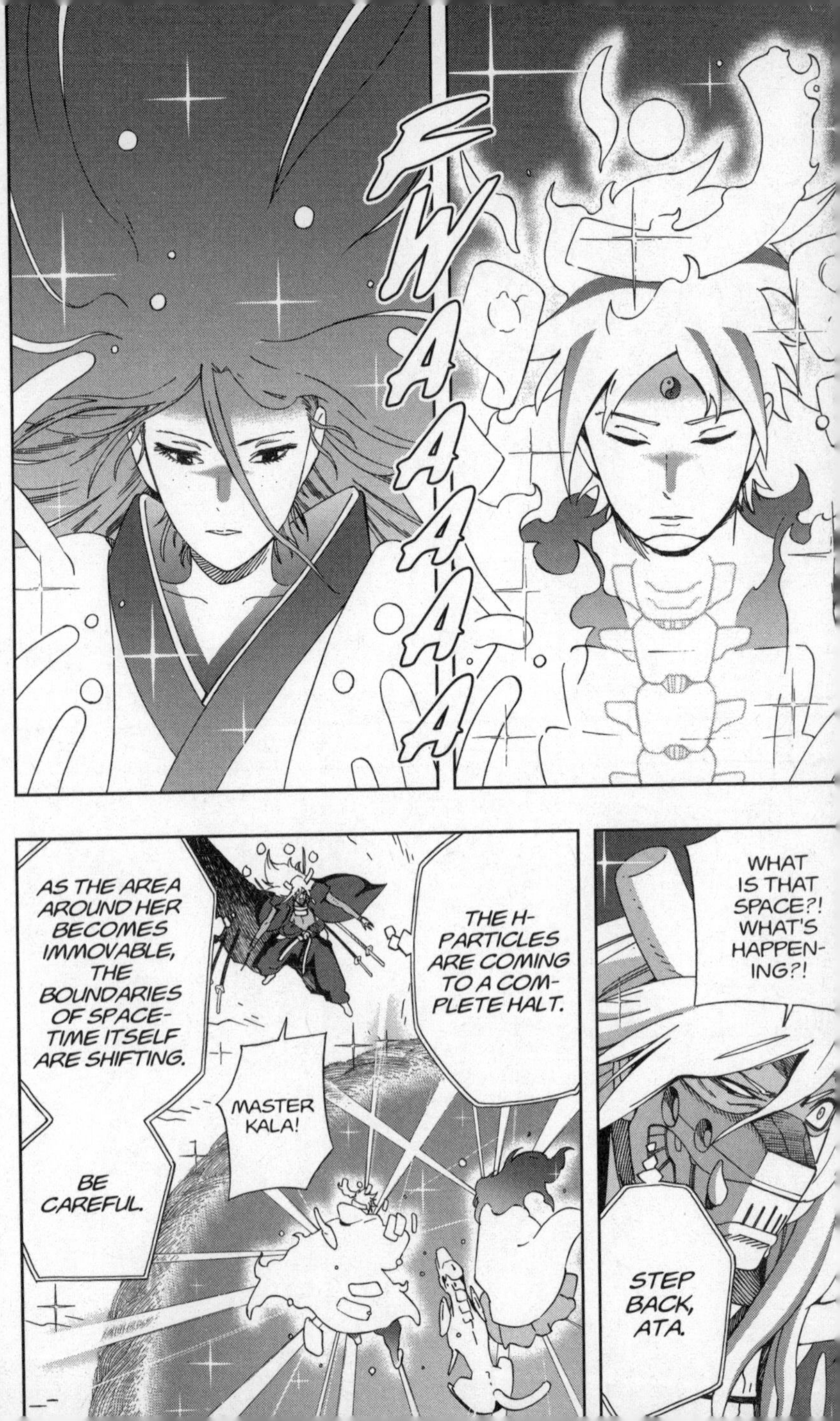
FWAAAAAAA
WHAT IS THAT SPACE?! WHAT'S HAPPEN-ING?!
STEP BACK, ATA.
THE H-PARTICLES ARE COMING TO A COM-PLETE HALT.
AS THE AREA AROUND HER BECOMES IMMOVABLE, THE BOUNDARIES OF SPACE-TIME ITSELF ARE SHIFTING.
MASTER KALA!
BE CAREFUL.

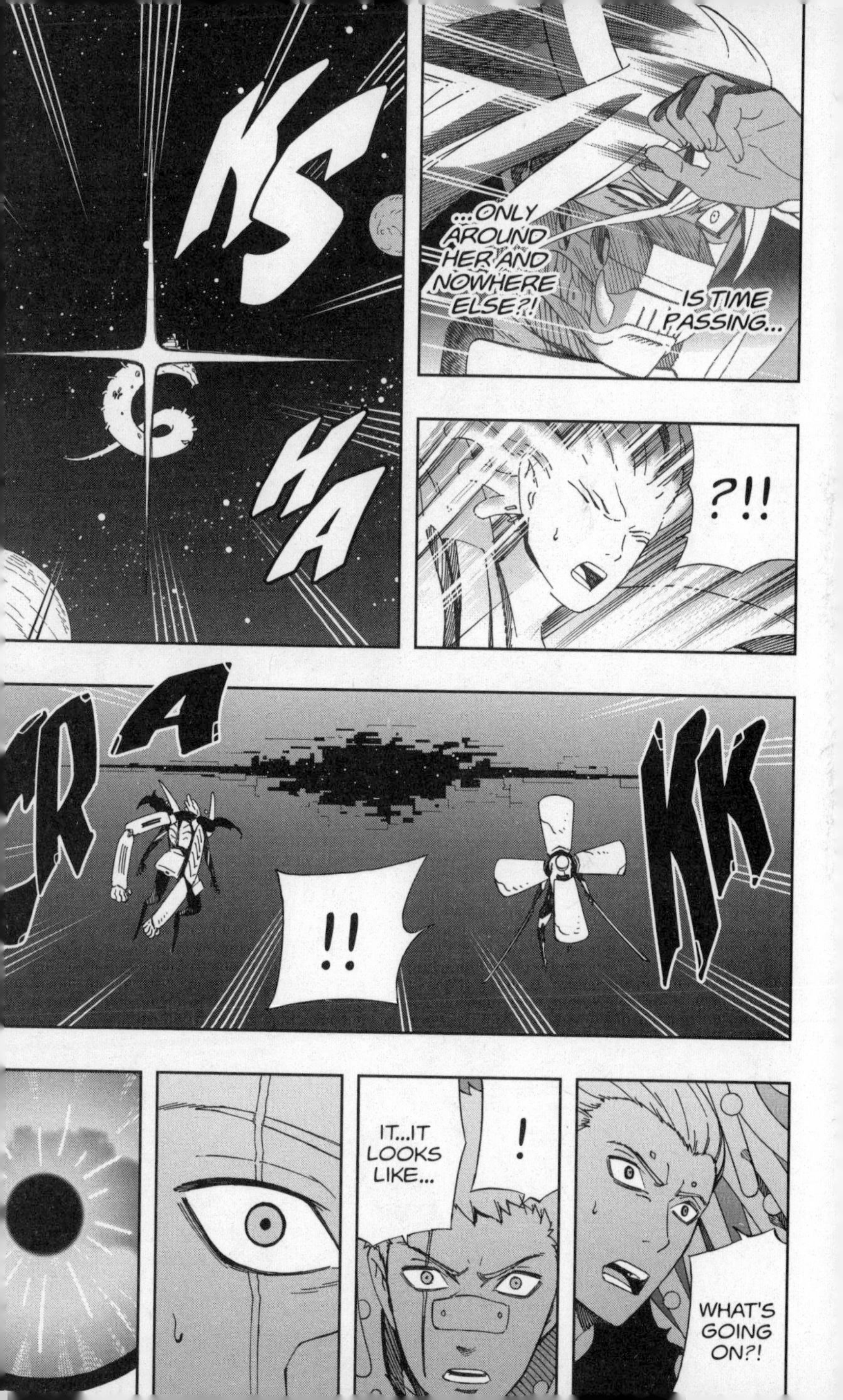
IS TIME PASSING...
...ONLY AROUND HER AND NOWHERE ELSE?!
?!!
KS
HA
KK
!!
CR
A
WHAT'S GOING ON?!
!
IT...IT LOOKS LIKE...

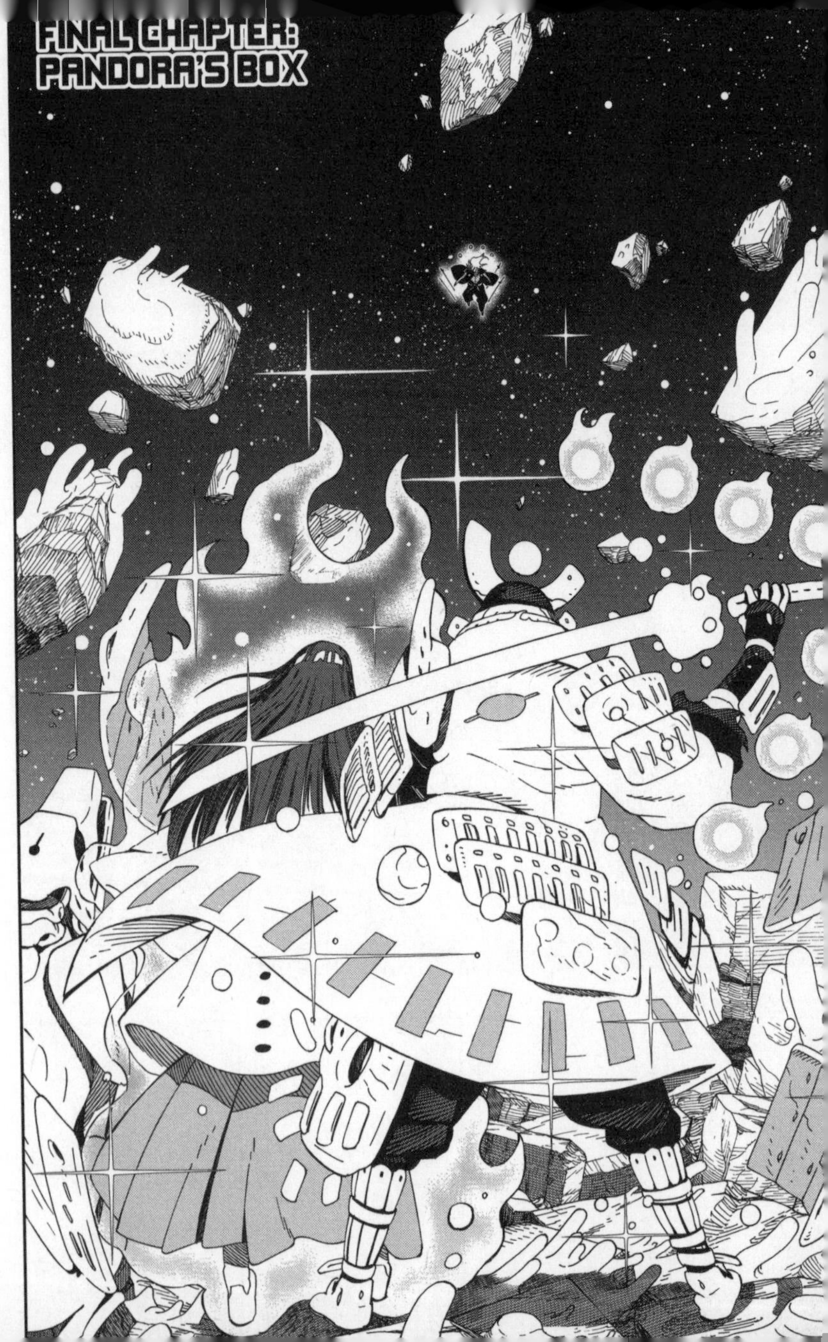
FINAL CHAPTER:
PANDORA'S BOX

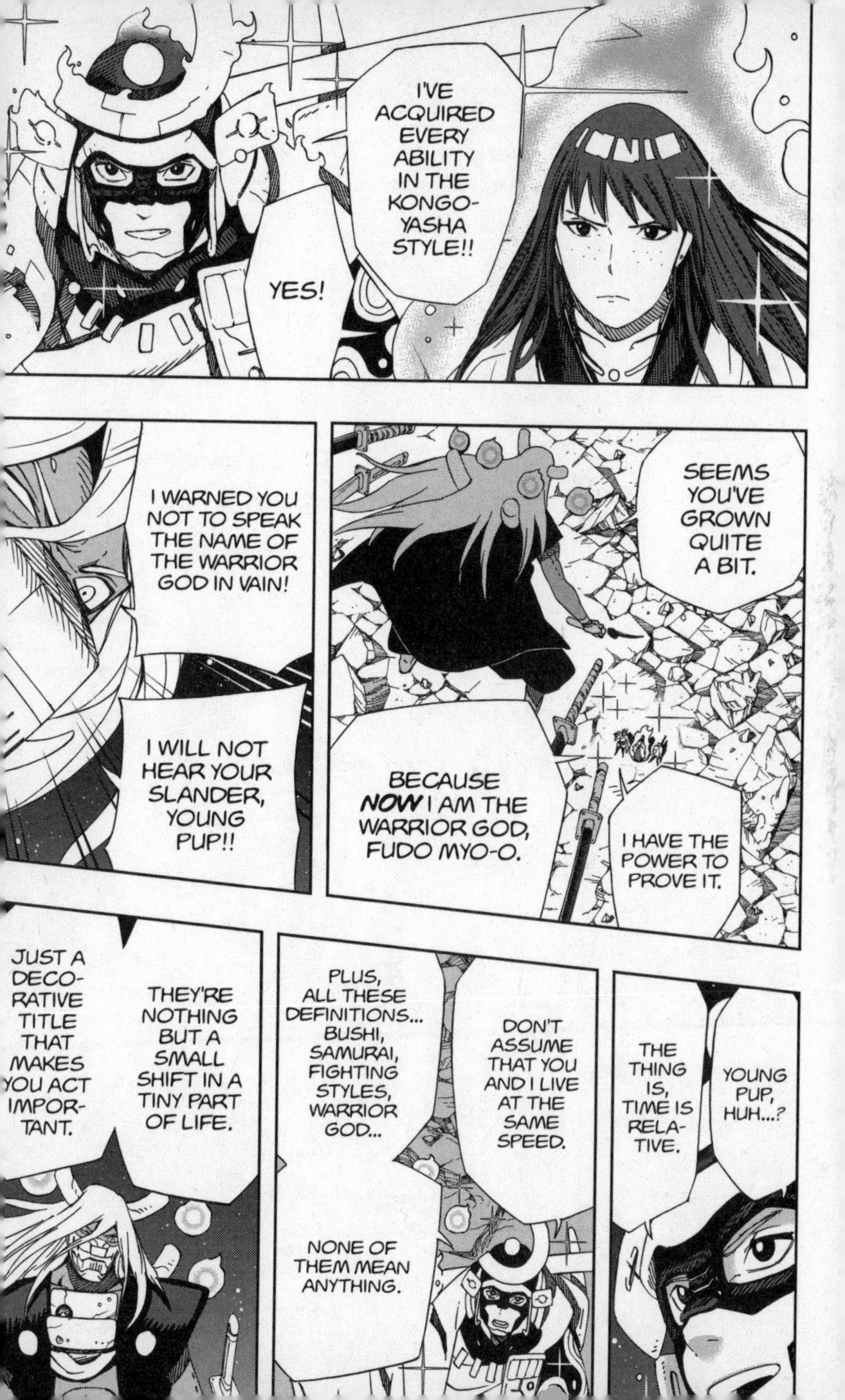
I'VE ACQUIRED EVERY ABILITY IN THE KONGO-YASHA STYLE!!
YES!
SEEMS YOU'VE GROWN QUITE A BIT.
BECAUSE ***NOW*** I AM THE WARRIOR GOD, FUDO MYO-O.
I HAVE THE POWER TO PROVE IT.
I WARNED YOU NOT TO SPEAK THE NAME OF THE WARRIOR GOD IN VAIN!
I WILL NOT HEAR YOUR SLANDER, YOUNG PUP!!
YOUNG PUP, HUH...?
THE THING IS, TIME IS RELATIVE.
DON'T ASSUME THAT YOU AND I LIVE AT THE SAME SPEED.
PLUS, ALL THESE DEFINITIONS... BUSHI, SAMURAI, FIGHTING STYLES, WARRIOR GOD...
NONE OF THEM MEAN ANYTHING.
THEY'RE NOTHING BUT A SMALL SHIFT IN A TINY PART OF LIFE.
JUST A DECORATIVE TITLE THAT MAKES YOU ACT IMPORTANT.

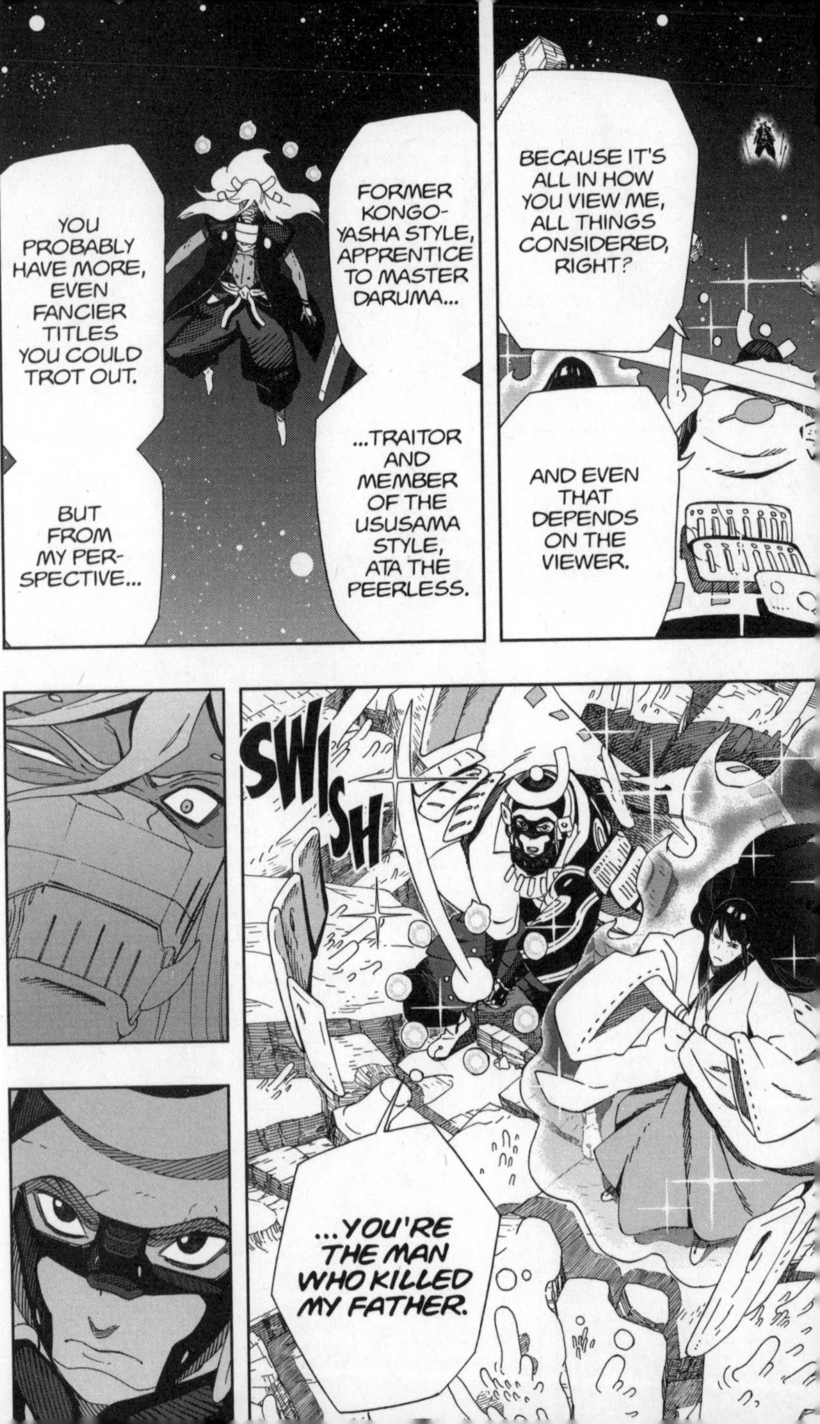
BECAUSE IT'S ALL IN HOW YOU VIEW ME, ALL THINGS CONSIDERED, RIGHT?
AND EVEN THAT DEPENDS ON THE VIEWER.
FORMER KONGO-YASHA STYLE, APPRENTICE TO MASTER DARUMA...
...TRAITOR AND MEMBER OF THE USUSAMA STYLE, ATA THE PEERLESS.
YOU PROBABLY HAVE MORE, EVEN FANCIER TITLES YOU COULD TROT OUT.
BUT FROM MY PER-SPECTIVE...
SWISH
...YOU'RE THE MAN WHO KILLED MY FATHER.

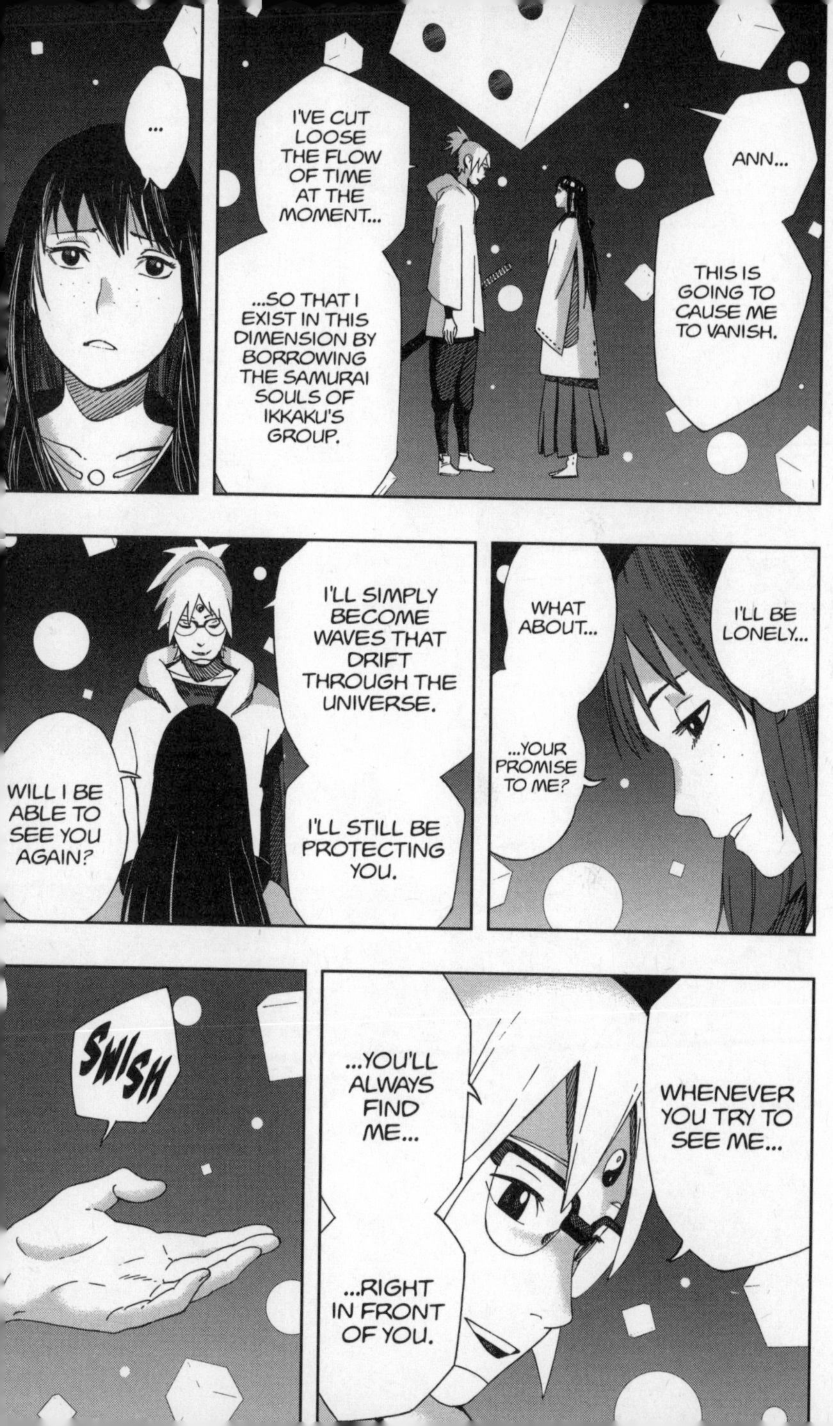
ANN...
THIS IS GOING TO CAUSE ME TO VANISH.
I'VE CUT LOOSE THE FLOW OF TIME AT THE MOMENT...
...SO THAT I EXIST IN THIS DIMENSION BY BORROWING THE SAMURAI SOULS OF IKKAKU'S GROUP.
...
I'LL BE LONELY...
WHAT ABOUT...
...YOUR PROMISE TO ME?
I'LL SIMPLY BECOME WAVES THAT DRIFT THROUGH THE UNIVERSE.
I'LL STILL BE PROTECTING YOU.
WILL I BE ABLE TO SEE YOU AGAIN?
WHENEVER YOU TRY TO SEE ME...
...YOU'LL ALWAYS FIND ME...
...RIGHT IN FRONT OF YOU.
SWISH

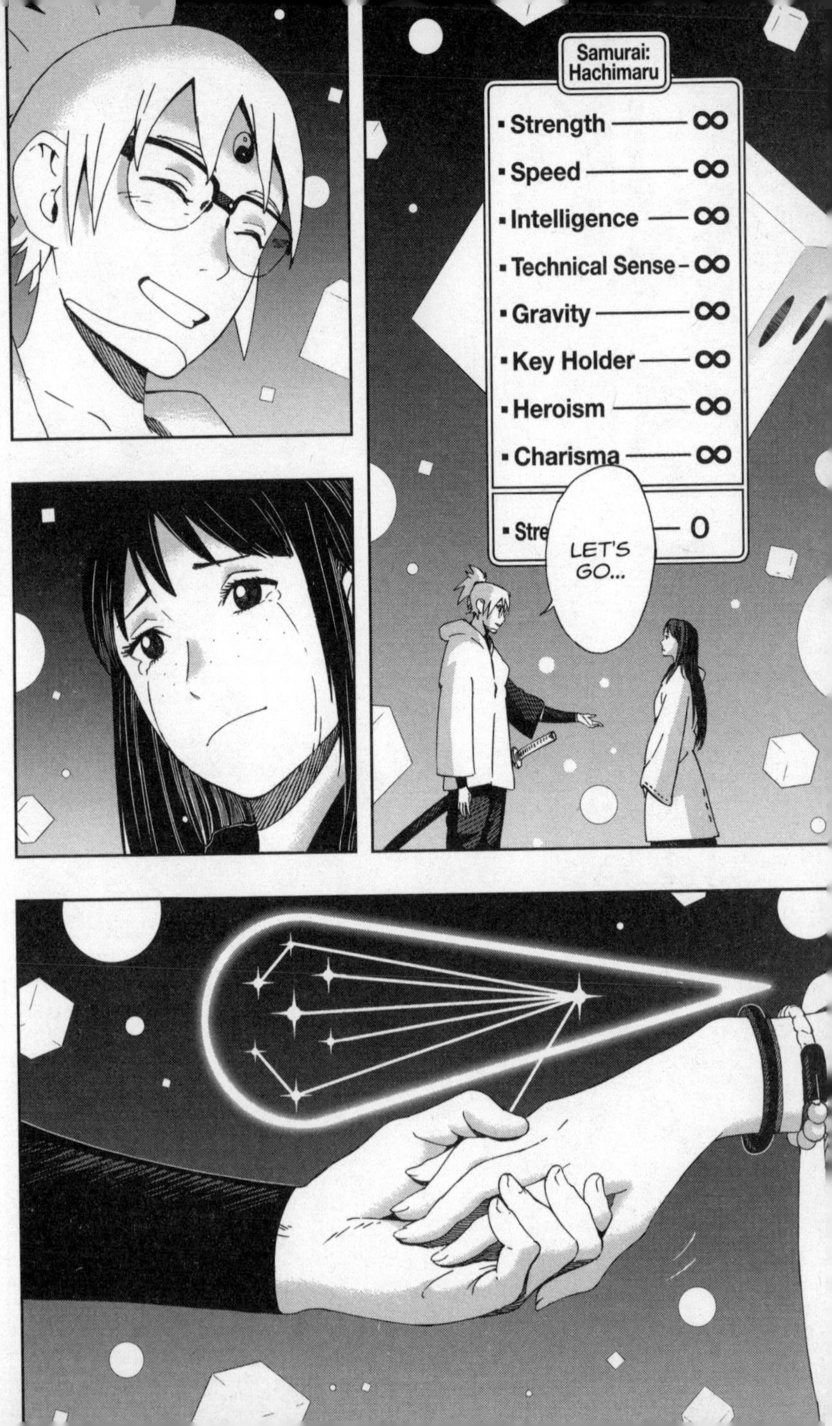
Samurai: Hachimaru
▪ Strength ——— ∞
▪ Speed ——— ∞
▪ Intelligence ——— ∞
▪ Technical Sense - ∞
▪ Gravity ——— ∞
▪ Key Holder ——— ∞
▪ Heroism ——— ∞
▪ Charisma ——— ∞
▪ Stre ——— 0
LET'S GO...

HE'S GOING TO CALL FORTH A SHOOTING STAR?!!

N...NO! IT CAN'T BE!

...YASHA STYLE...

KONGO...

SHOOTING STAR SWORD

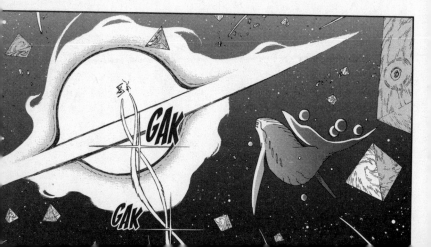

GAK

GAK

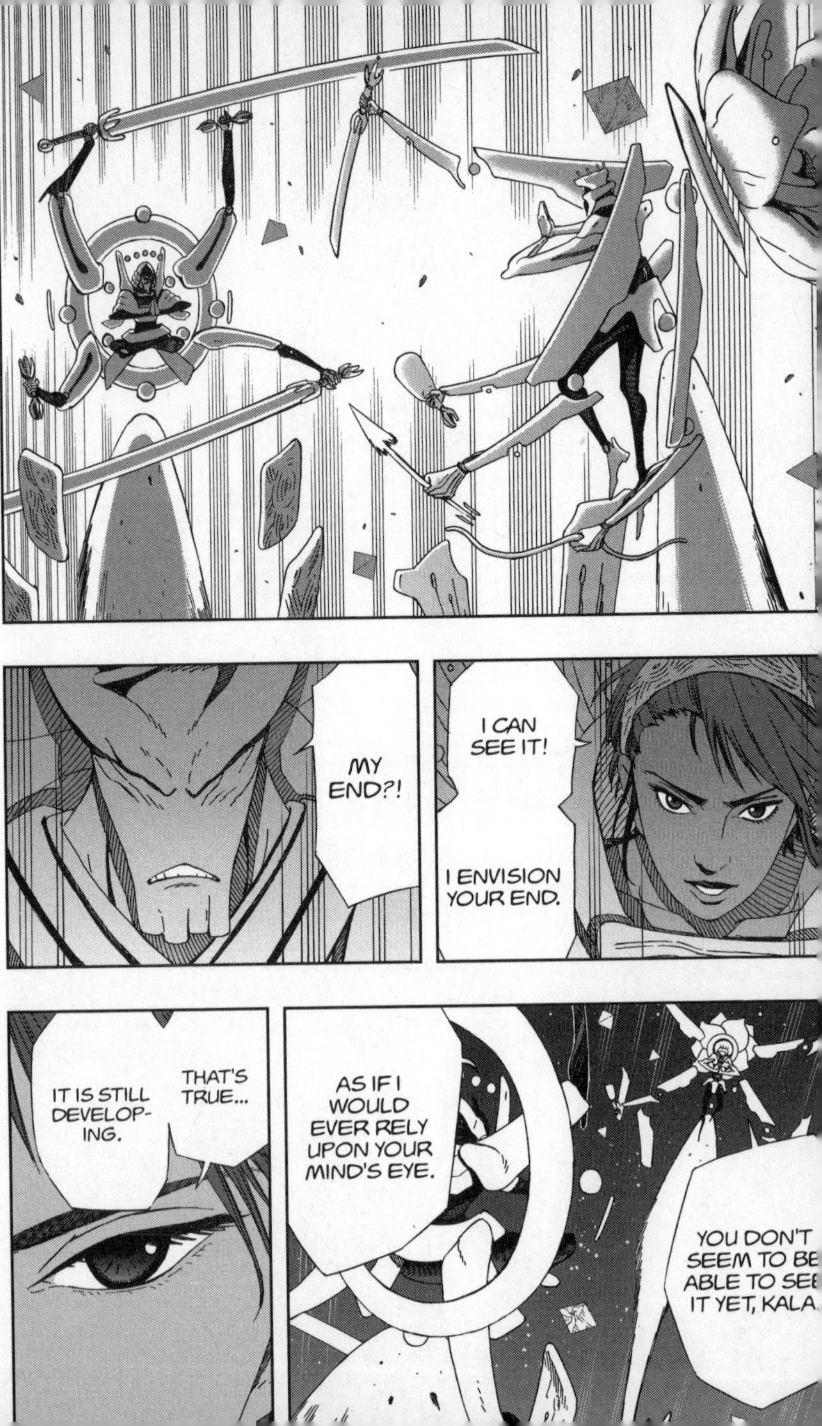
I CAN SEE IT!
I ENVISION YOUR END.
MY END?!
YOU DON'T SEEM TO BE ABLE TO SEE IT YET, KALA
AS IF I WOULD EVER RELY UPON YOUR MIND'S EYE.
THAT'S TRUE...
IT IS STILL DEVELOP-ING.

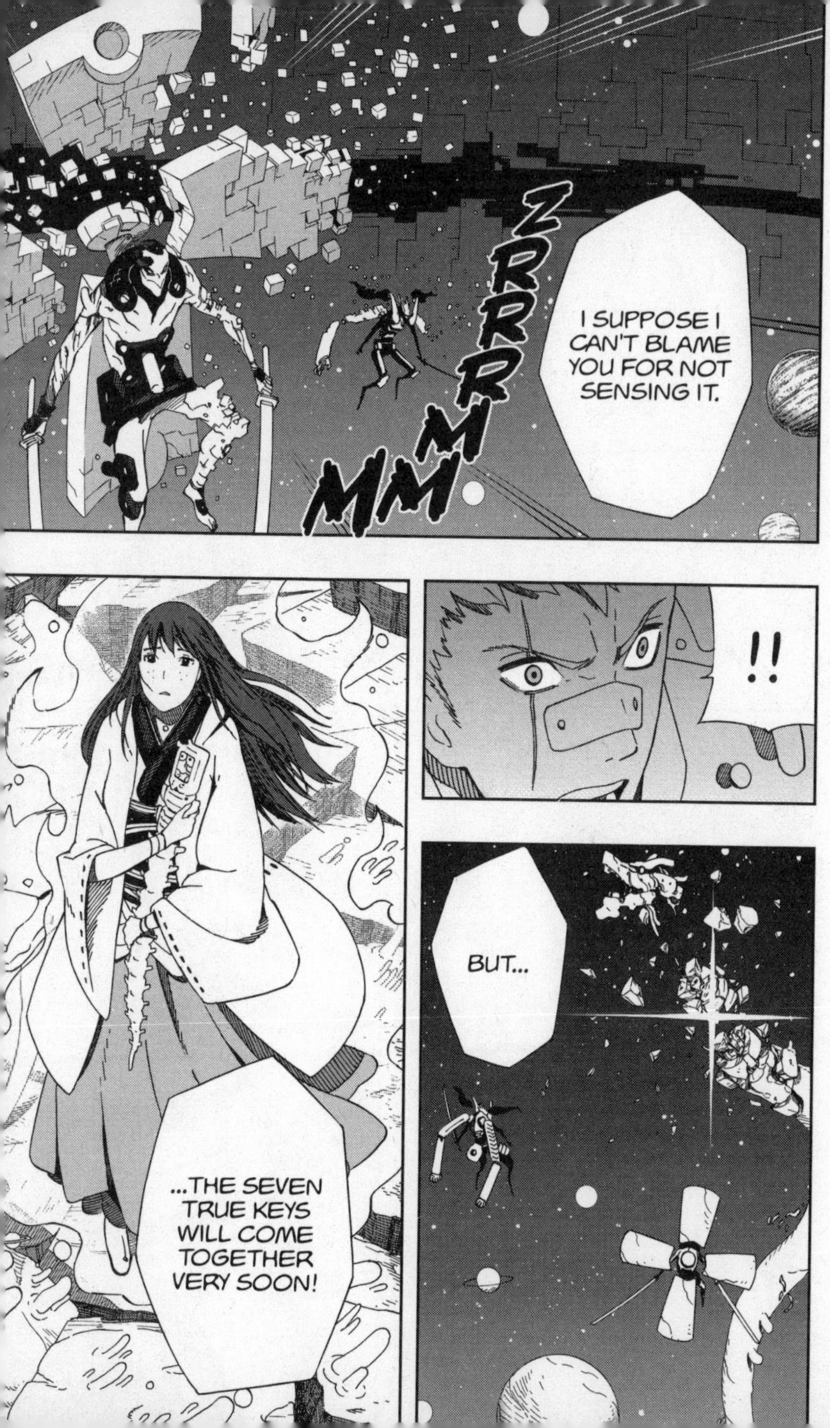
I SUPPOSE I CAN'T BLAME YOU FOR NOT SENSING IT.
ZRRRMMM
!!
BUT...
...THE SEVEN TRUE KEYS WILL COME TOGETHER VERY SOON!

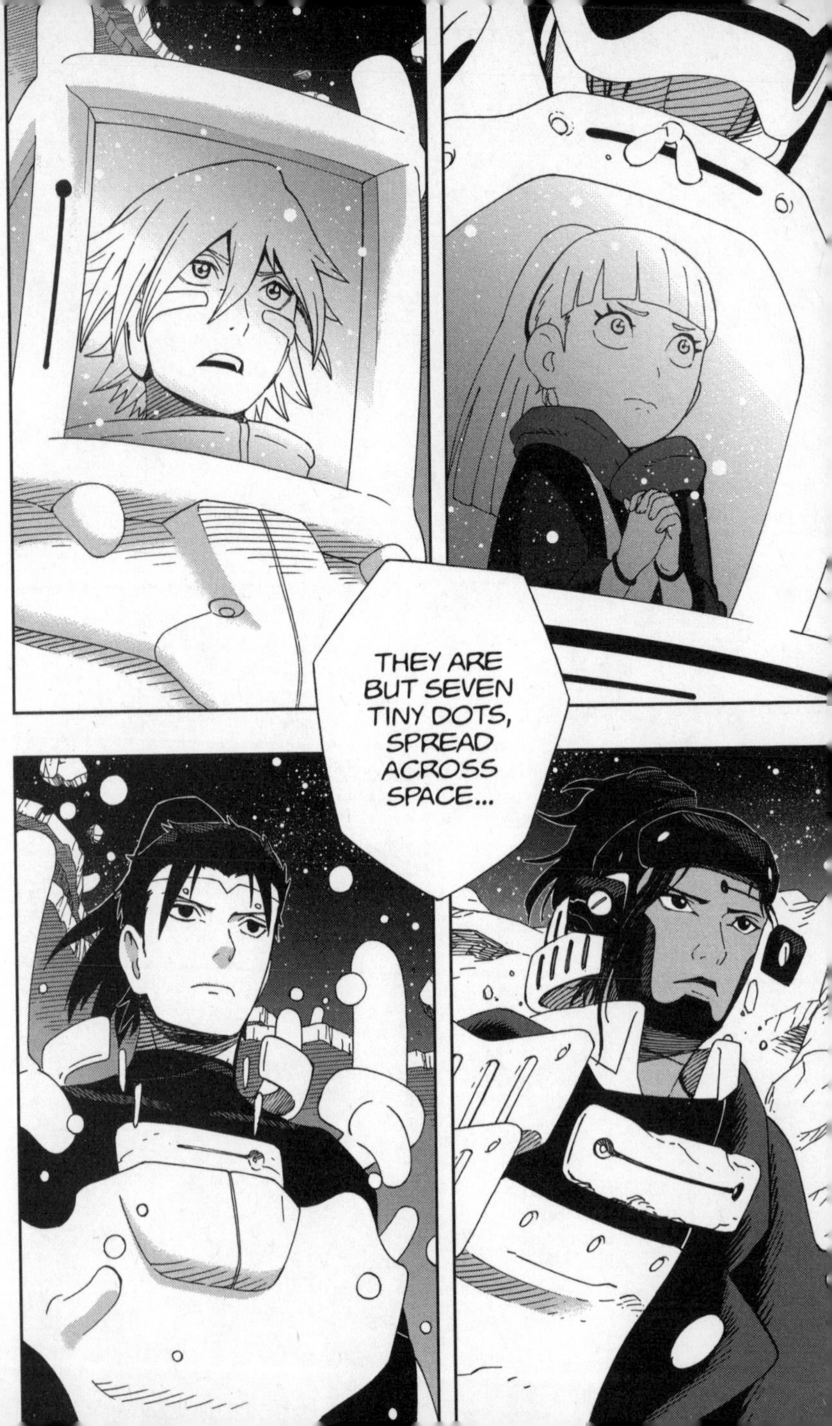
THEY ARE BUT SEVEN TINY DOTS, SPREAD ACROSS SPACE...

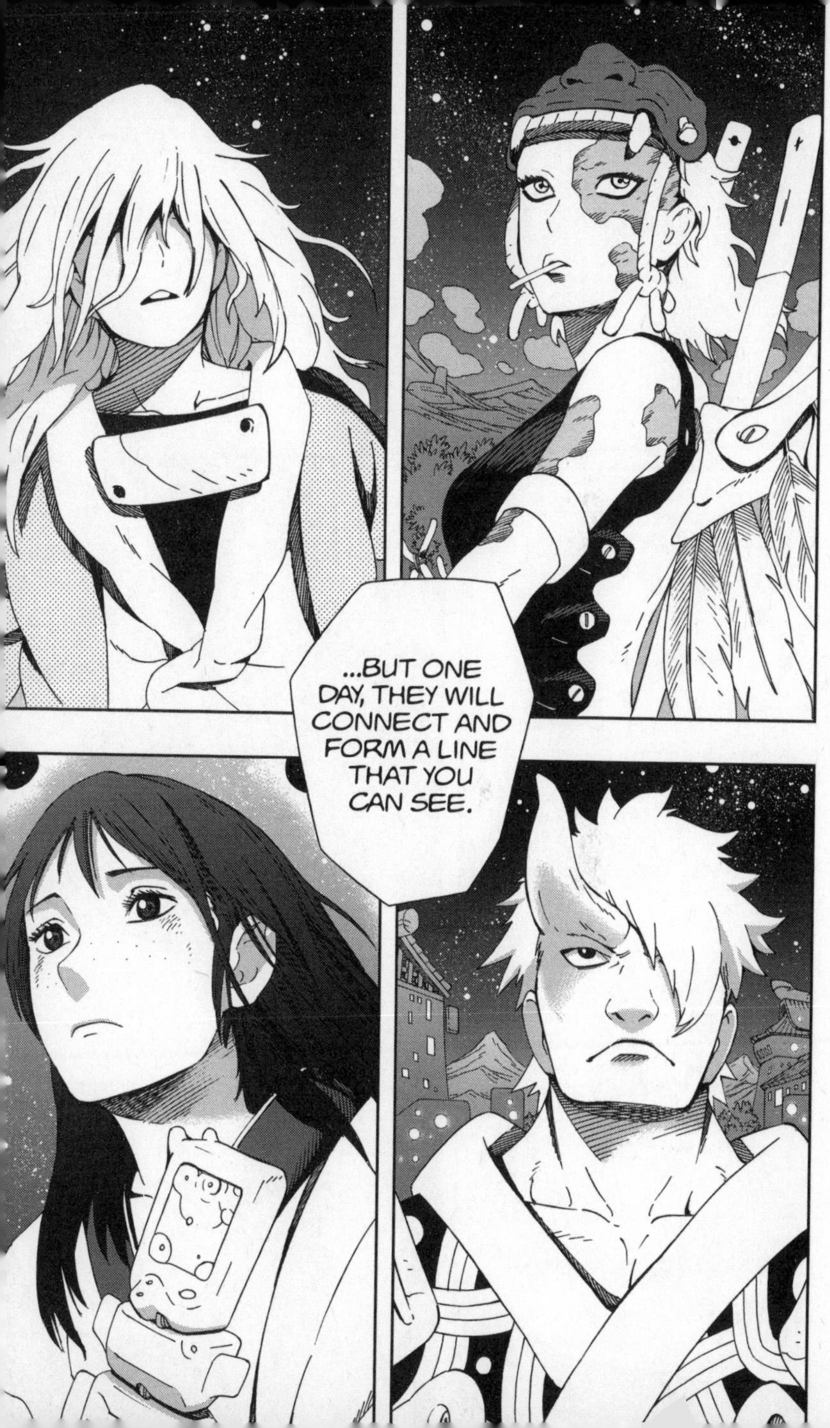
...BUT ONE DAY, THEY WILL CONNECT AND FORM A LINE THAT YOU CAN SEE.

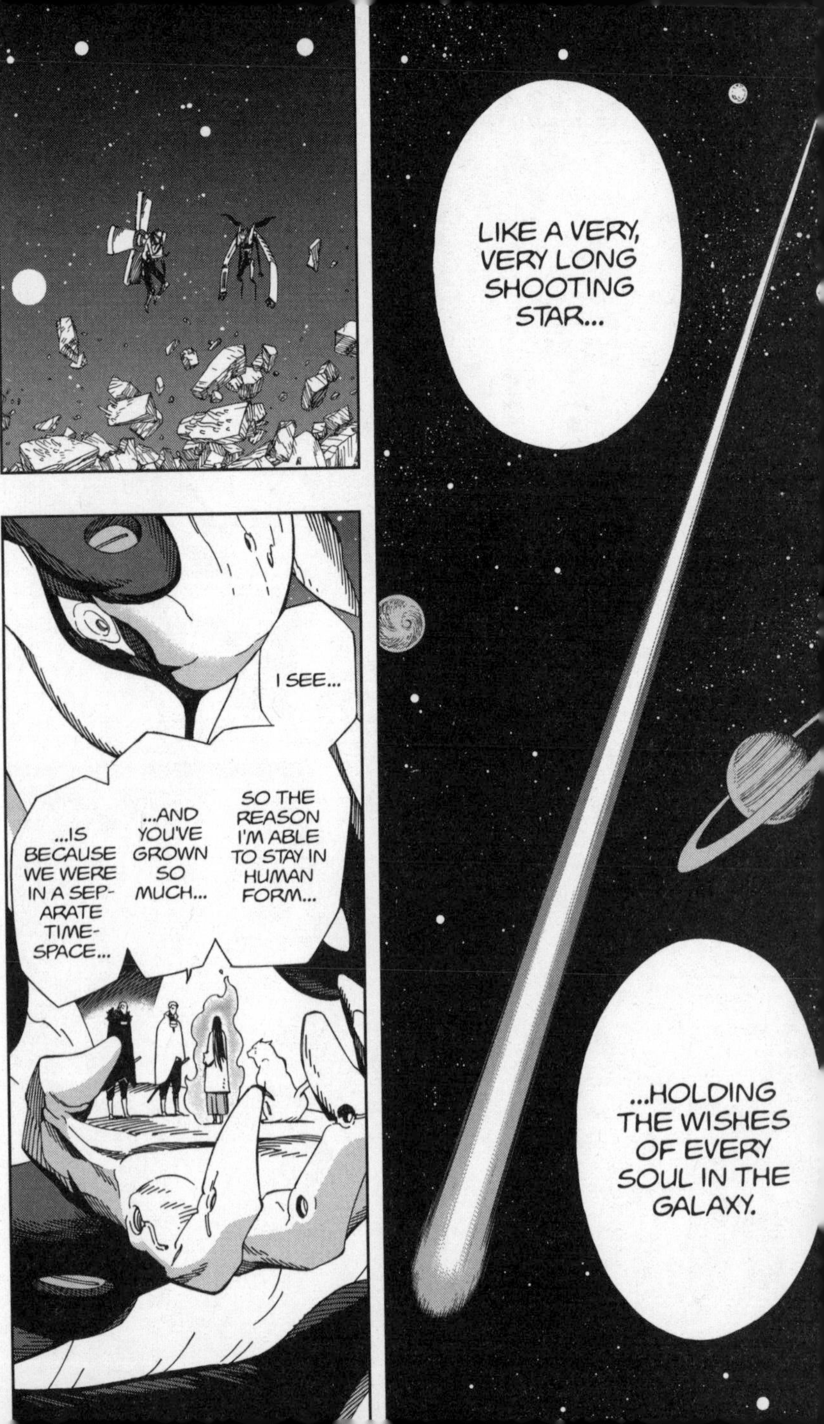
LIKE A VERY, VERY LONG SHOOTING STAR...
...HOLDING THE WISHES OF EVERY SOUL IN THE GALAXY.
I SEE...
SO THE REASON I'M ABLE TO STAY IN HUMAN FORM...
...AND YOU'VE GROWN SO MUCH...
...IS BECAUSE WE WERE IN A SEPARATE TIME-SPACE...

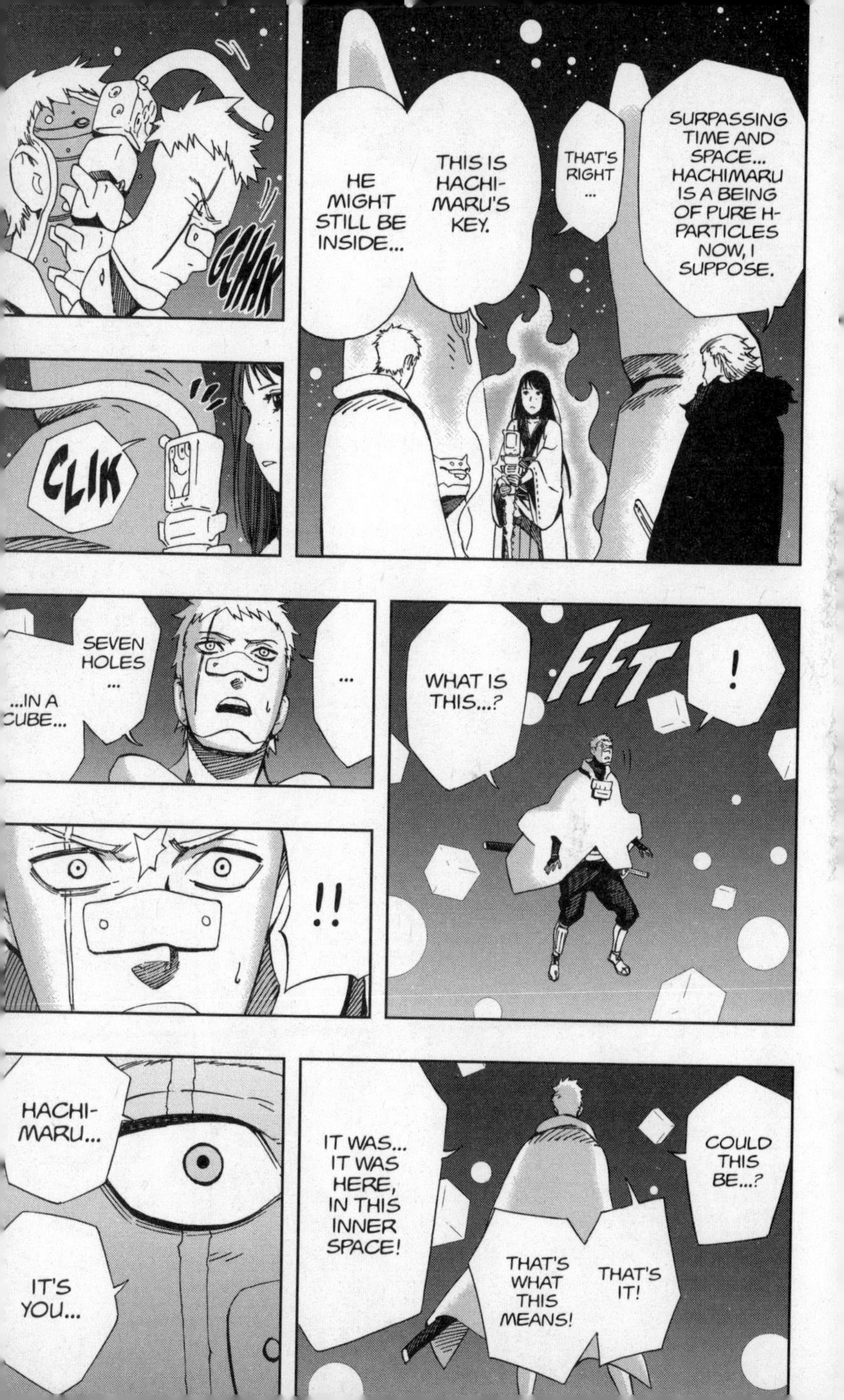
SURPASSING TIME AND SPACE... HACHIMARU IS A BEING OF PURE H-PARTICLES NOW, I SUPPOSE.
THAT'S RIGHT ...
THIS IS HACHIMARU'S KEY.
HE MIGHT STILL BE INSIDE...
GCHAK
CLIK
!
FFT
WHAT IS THIS...?
...
SEVEN HOLES ...
...IN A CUBE...
!!
COULD THIS BE...?
THAT'S IT!
THAT'S WHAT THIS MEANS!
IT WAS... IT WAS HERE, IN THIS INNER SPACE!
HACHIMARU...
IT'S YOU...

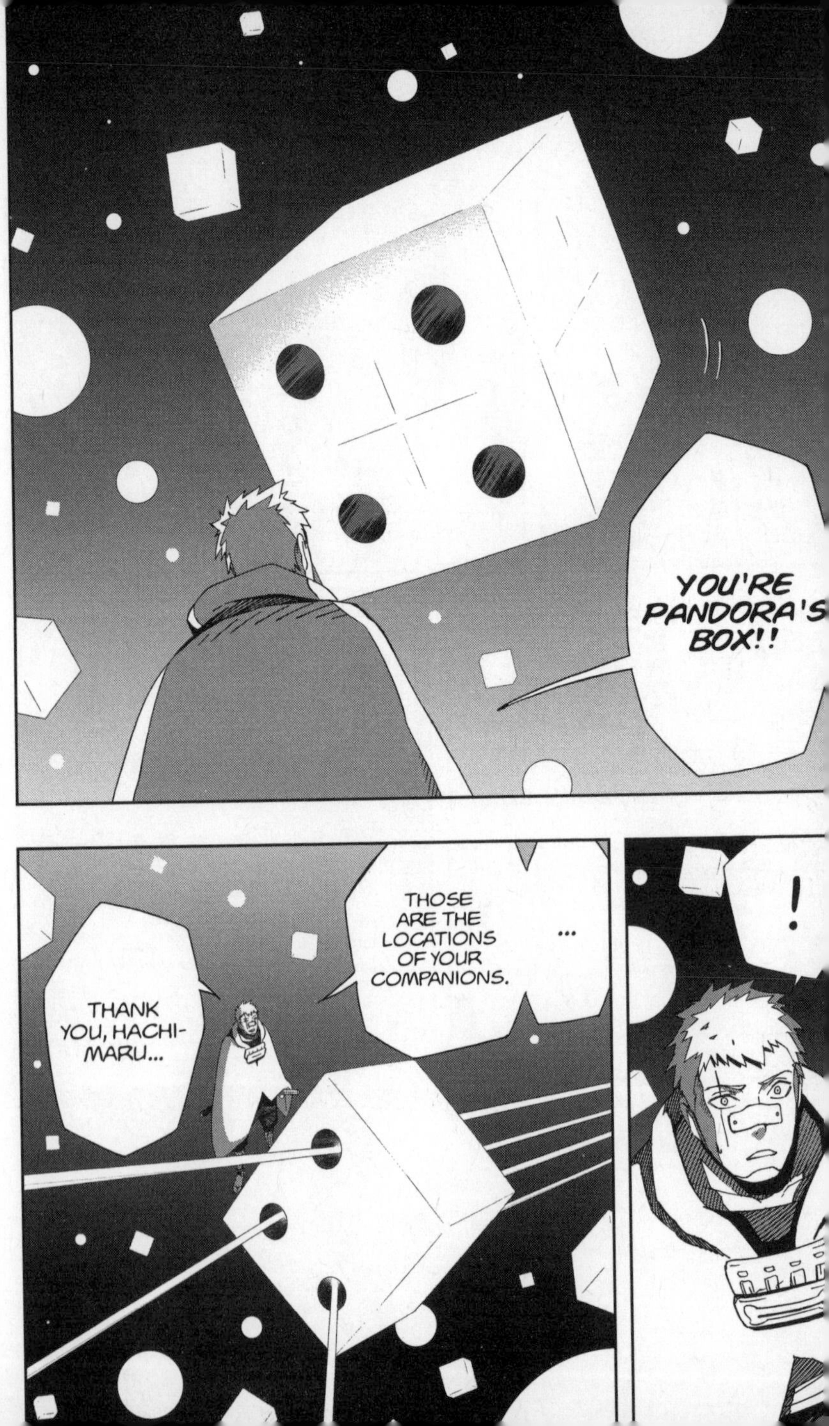
YOU'RE PANDORA'S BOX!!
!
...
THOSE ARE THE LOCATIONS OF YOUR COMPANIONS.
THANK YOU, HACHI-MARU...

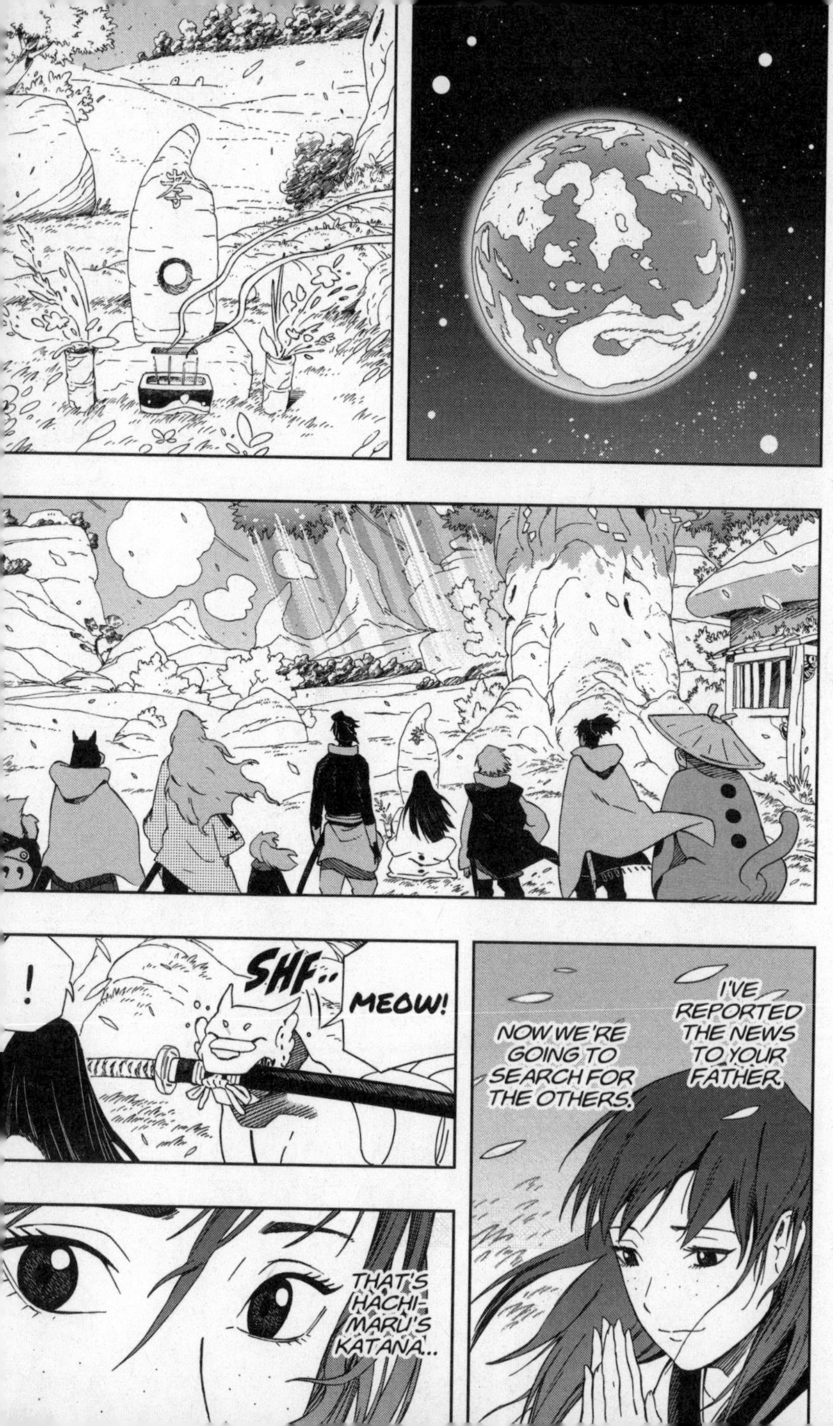
I'VE REPORTED THE NEWS TO YOUR FATHER.
NOW WE'RE GOING TO SEARCH FOR THE OTHERS.
MEOW!
SHF..
!
THAT'S HACHI-MARU'S KATANA...

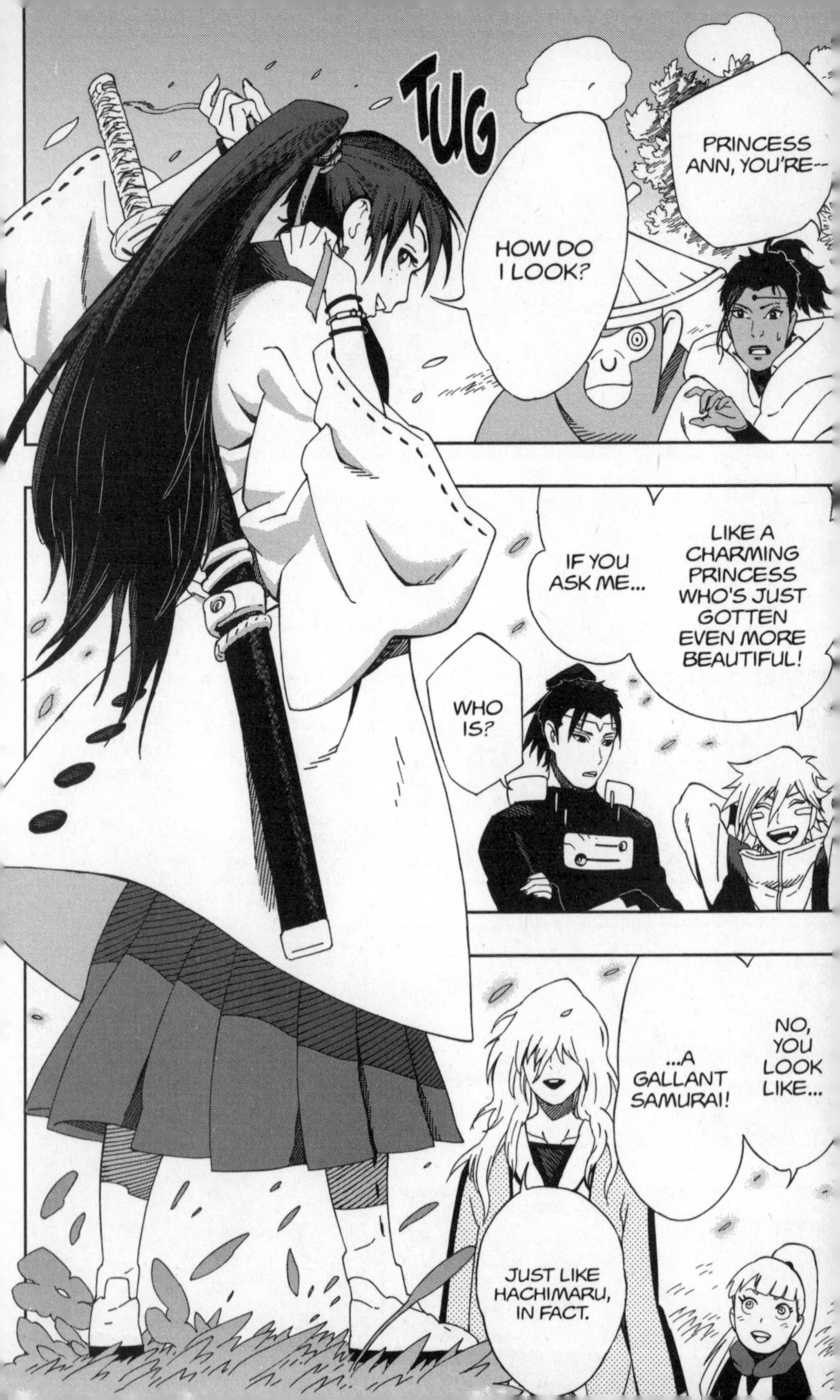
PRINCESS ANN, YOU'RE--
TUG
HOW DO I LOOK?
LIKE A CHARMING PRINCESS WHO'S JUST GOTTEN EVEN MORE BEAUTIFUL!
IF YOU ASK ME...
WHO IS?
NO, YOU LOOK LIKE...
...A GALLANT SAMURAI!
JUST LIKE HACHIMARU, IN FACT.

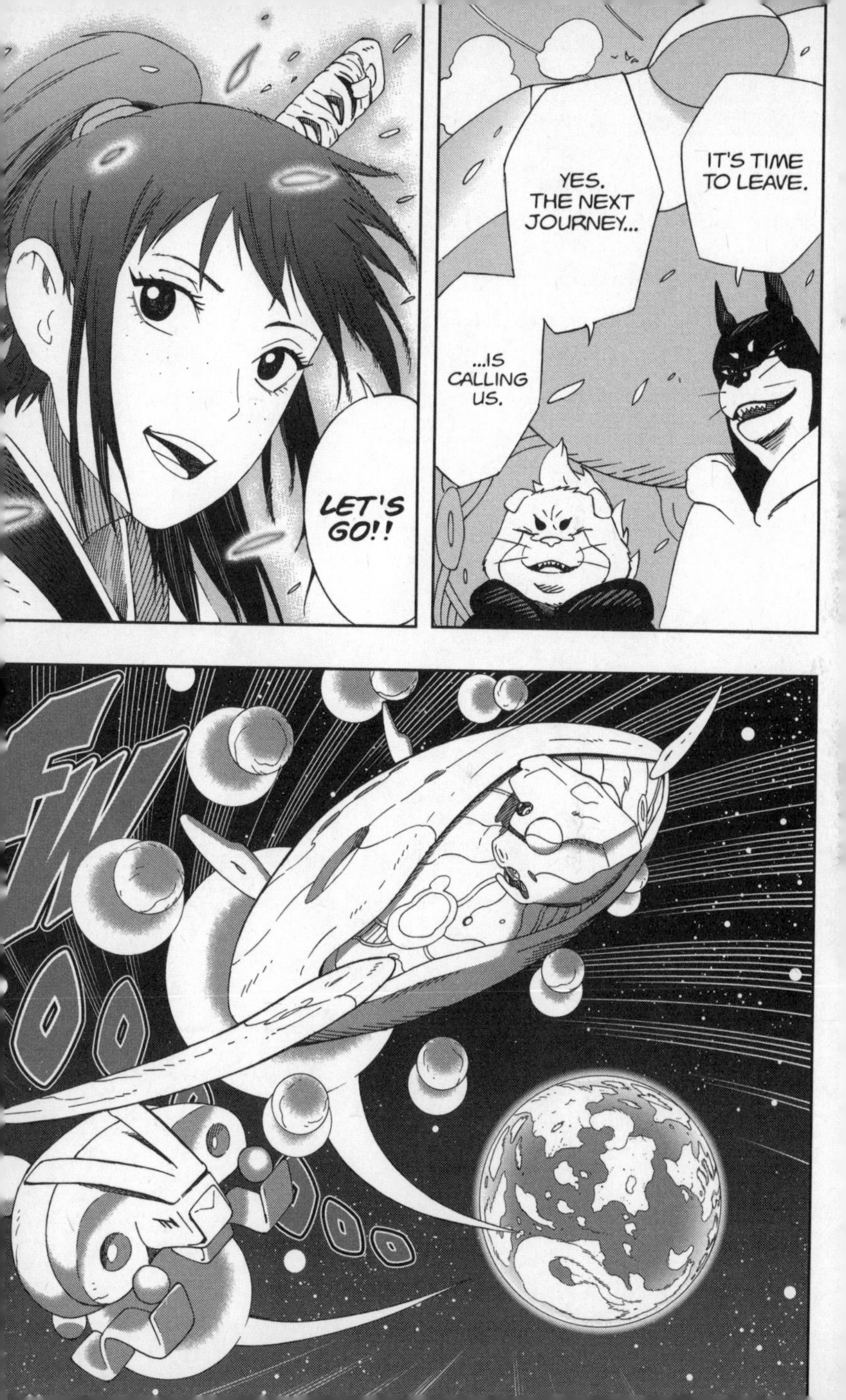
IT'S TIME TO LEAVE.
YES. THE NEXT JOURNEY...
...IS CALLING US.
LET'S GO!!

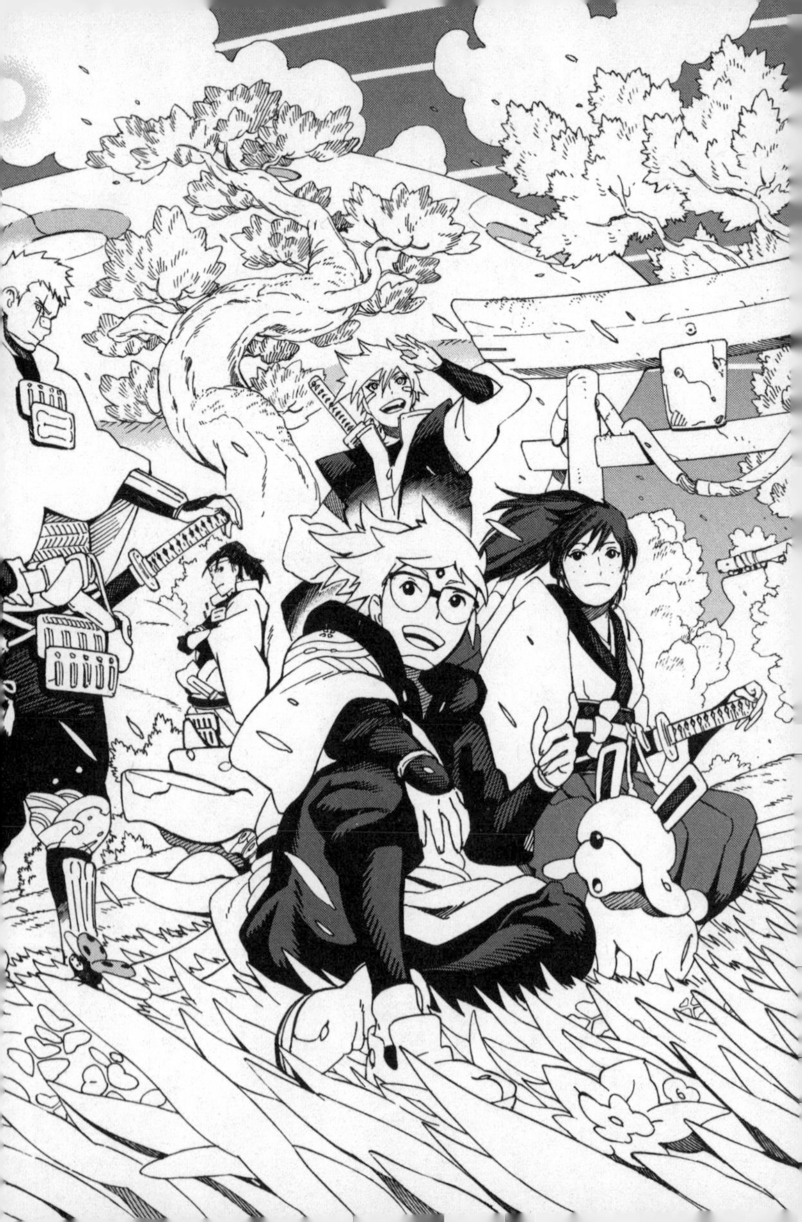

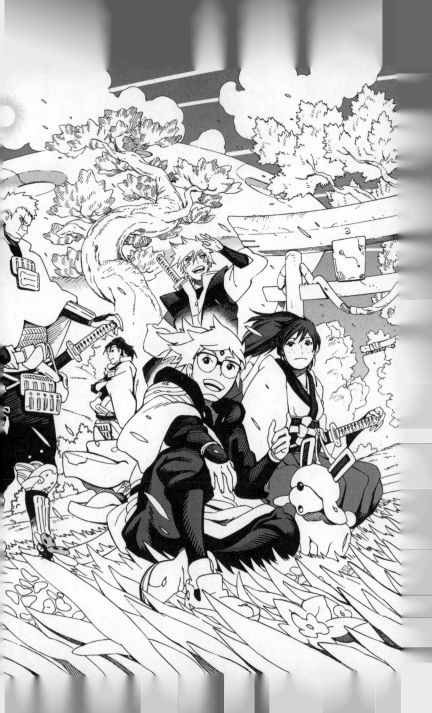

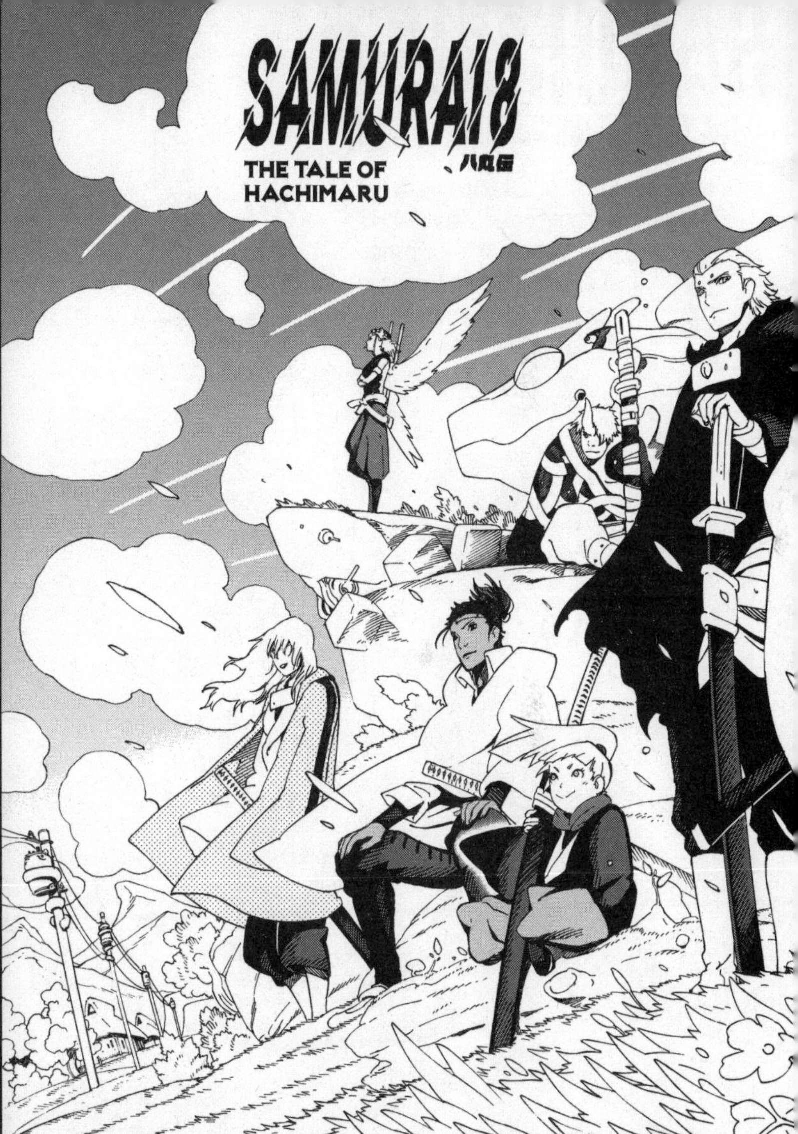
SAMURAI8
THE TALE OF
HACHIMARU
八丸伝

YOU'RE READING THE WRONG WAY!

SAMURAI 8
THE TALE OF HACHIMARU

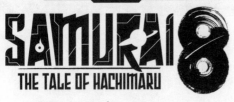

reads from right to left, starting in the upper-right corner. Japanese is read from right to left, meaning that action, sound effects and word-balloon order are completely reversed from English order.

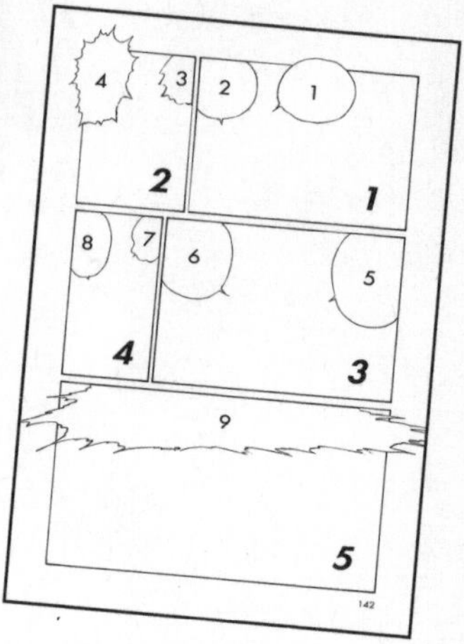
1
2
3
4
5
6
7
8
9
1
2
3
4
5
142

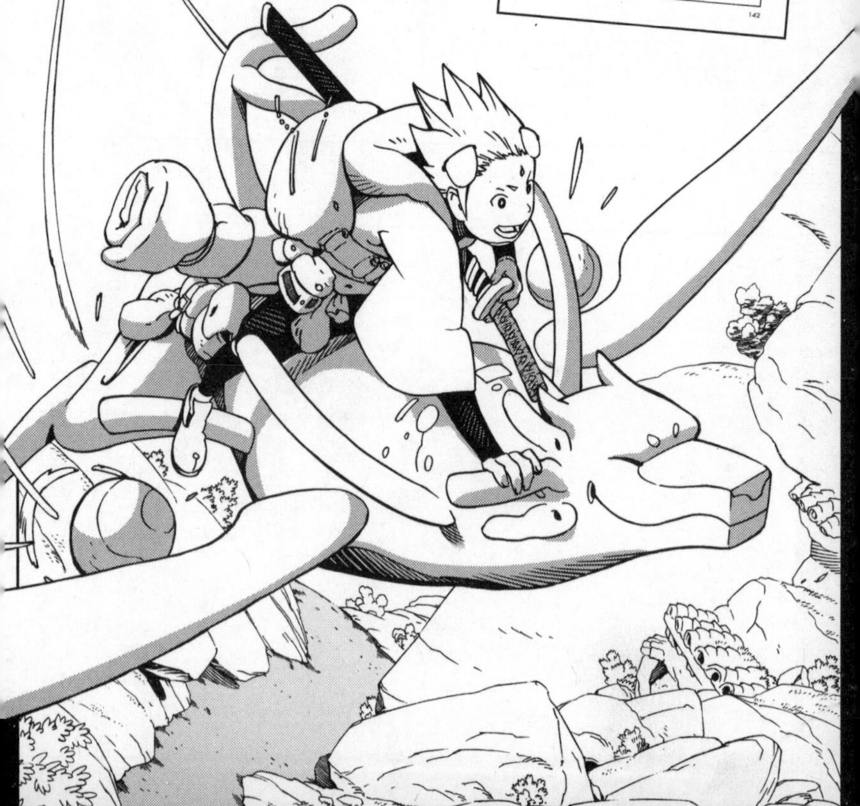